Cavan: Essays on the History of an Irish County

Cavan

Essays on the History of an Irish County

EDITED BY

Raymond Gillespie

IRISH ACADEMIC PRESS

This book was set in 10.5 on 12 point Ehrhardt for
IRISH ACADEMIC PRESS
Kill Lane, Blackrock, Co. Dublin, Ireland
and in North America for
IRISH ACADEMIC PRESS
5804 NE Hassalo St, Portland, Oregon 97213.

A catalogue record for this title
is available from the British Library.

ISBN 0-7165-2553-4 cased
0-7165-2554-2 pbk

Printed in Ireland
by ßetaprint Ltd, Dublin.

Contents

Notes on Contributors

MARGARET CRAWFORD is Research Officer in the Department of Economic and Social History, Queen's University Belfast. She has written extensively on social conditions in early-nineteenth century Ireland and particularly on the impact of the Famine on Irish society.

BERNADETTE CUNNINGHAM is a librarian in the Dublin Diocesan Library and an occasional lecturer in modern history at St Patrick's College, Maynooth. She has written widely on Gaelic society in the sixteenth and seventeenth centuries.

PATRICK J. DUFFY is associate professor of Geography at St Patrick's College, Maynooth. He has recently completed a historical atlas of the diocese of Clogher, *Landscapes of south Ulster* (Belfast, 1993)

ALAN FORD lectures in church history at the Department of Theology in the University of Durham. His works on the reformation in Ireland include *The Protestant reformation in Ireland, 1590–1641* (Frankfurt, 1987)

RAYMOND GILLESPIE teaches modern history and local history at St Patrick's College, Maynooth. He had edited a number of county studies and has written extensively on early modern Ireland. He is currently preparing a study of popular religion in seventeenth century Ireland.

JAMES KELLY lectures in history at St Patrick's College, Drumcondra. Specialising in the eighteenth century his most recent book is *'That damn'd thing called honour'; duelling in Ireland, 1570–1860* (Cork, 1995).

GERARD MORAN is the author of *A Radical Priest in Mayo: Fr Patrick Lavelle, the Rise and Fall of an Irish Nationalist, 1825–86*. He has also co-edited volumes on the history of county Longford and county Mayo.

CIARAN PARKER is the author of a Ph.D. thesis at Trinity College, Dublin on medieval Cavan and some of his findings have been published in *Breifne*. He is currently research editor at the Cavan County Museum.

EILEEN REILLY is a graduate of St Patrick's College, Maynooth and is currently completing a doctoral thesis at Oxford University on popular fiction in late nineteenth-century Ireland.

Preface

The origins of this book lie not with its editor but with Cumann Seanchais Bhreifne who for almost forty years have been engaged in exploring the history of county Cavan and the surrounding areas and publishing their results in a scholarly form in their journal *Breifne*. Most of the essays which make up this volume began life as a series of lectures to the society in the winter of 1993–4. During that time the authors were able to share not only of the hospitality of the Society but also the wealth of local knowledge on the history of the county which exists there and without which this volume would have been much poorer. The constant interest and enthusiasm of Most Revd Dr Francis McKiernan, bishop of Kilmore, ensured that the project went more smoothly than it otherwise might. The practical support of Tom Sullivan, then chairman of the Society, made the visits of the speakers to Cavan pleasurable and the task of the editor a relatively simple one. Without the financial assistance of Cavan County Council and the Bank of Ireland in Cavan town this volume would not have been possible at all. Bernadette Cunningham compiled the index. The staff of Irish Academic Press have, with their usual good humour and efficiency, transformed the text into a handsome volume which if it succeeds only in arousing the curiosity of its readers about the complexity of the evolution of one of the regions of Ireland will have achieved its aim.

RAYMOND GILLESPIE

Introduction: People, Place, and Time

RAYMOND GILLESPIE

The study of local history in Ireland since the seventeenth century has proceeded sporadically. Until the middle of the nineteenth century the Anglo-Irish county gentry led the way either by their own efforts, such as E.P. Shirley's *History of Monaghan*, published in 1879, or by establishing local historical societies, such as those in counties Kildare or Kilkenny. Nineteenth-century Cavan lacked such a gentry grouping. Many of the most prominent Cavan gentry were absentees and others, such as the Farnhams, were more concerned with the economic and moral improvement of their tenantry rather than in understanding the past. The emergence of local history in Cavan was therefore a feature of the twentieth century, and under the influence of another group. Those who pioneered the study of local history did so as part of a wider interest in many aspects of the Irish past under the influence of the movement of cultural nationalism. They included teachers and parish clergy interested in understanding the evolution of their own regions. Thus the *Journal of the Breifne Antiquarian and Historical Society* was born in 1920. As enthusiasm for the new pastime spread the diocese of Ardagh founded its journal in the 1930s and Down and Connor about the same time. The importance of the ecclesiastical link in the forging of the study of local history in south Ulster is clear in the diocesan basis of the three major journals in the region, *Clogher Record*, founded in 1953, *Seanchas Ardmhacha*, established in the following year, and *Breifne*, in 1958.

The origins of the study of local history in south Ulster helps to explain why Cavan as a county has received relatively little attention from historians. When *Breifne* was established its focus was on the native Irish lordship of that name rather than the modern county. Arguably the most important of the modern historians of the region, Philip O'Connell, was insistent that 'county histories, as such, lack the necessary historical background and the principle must be regarded as scientifically unsound' since they represented recent creations and not 'historical principalities'.[1] Even after sixty years O'Connell's views command respect. Today's local historian is conscious that the county, in some parts of Ireland at least, is a relatively recent creation and the awareness of a county identity at a popular level is a creation of the nineteenth century. Newspapers, the G.A.A. and popular politicisation at the county level following the widening of the franchise in 1884 all contributed to this

process.[2] Moreover in the case of Cavan there are peculiar problems in trying
to use the county to study the local past. The dramatic landscape and economic differences between the north-west of the county, which has much in
common with Ulster, and the south-east which had more in common with
Leinster make it almost impossible to generalise about the county as a whole.

Despite these strictures this is primarily a book about a county: Cavan.
There are a number of reasons why many of the contributors to this volume
have chosen to use the county as the unit of study. The first is convenience.
On a practical level the county was, and still remains, the unit used by central
government for gathering material which means that evidence, especially for
the nineteenth century, is most easily accessible at county level. However, not
all the essays focus directly on the county. Those dealing with the period
before 1600 focus on the lordship of east Breifne since it was that institution
which gave coherence to the region and those exploring religious change have
used the unit most conveneient for such studies, the diocese of Kilmore,
which formed the basic unit of ecclesiastical administration and record keeping.

On a theoretical plane there are reasons for considering the region which
now forms county Cavan as something more than merely an administrative
convenience. In short the region, whether measured by lordship, county or
diocese, has a 'personality' of its own. The origins of that 'personality' are
clearly complex but one theme recurs in many of the essays and seems to
account for at least part of the elusive distinctiveness of Cavan: its position as
a cultural frontier within south Ulster and north Leinster.[3] Traditionally part
of the province of Connacht, that part of the lordship of Breifne which
became county Cavan in the late sixteenth century had, since at least the
twelfth century, been the meeting ground of a number of cultures. To the
north lay the lordships of O'Neill, O'Donnell and Maguire and to the south
the Anglo-Norman region of the pale. The O'Reillys of Cavan drew on
aspects of each culture; sharing the political ideas of lordship with the north
and west and an understanding of the importance of markets, money and the
common law with the Anglo-Normans of the pale. Contacts with adjoining
regions intensified in the early modern period, particularly when palesmen
acquired lands in the south eastern part of Cavan, and the entire county
subsequently became part of the scheme for the plantation of Ulster. The
county continued to be a frontier area, being affected by developments in
neighbouring regions although such influences were not always without tension or always from one direction. In the nineteenth century its ambivalent
position created a political paranoia in which a county supposedly part of
Ulster, and containing such Unionist stalwarts as Edward Saunderson, be-
haved rather as one might expect a county in Leinster to do. Again in the
early nineteenth-century world of religion, Ulster ideologies made an impact
as evangelical protestantism tried to extend its hold beyond the heartland of
the province into its more peripheral areas. The result was the 'second refor-

mation' linking economic, religious and political change, which began on the Farnham estate in the 1830s.[4] The creation of such a fluid situation of often competing pressures operating in one area was not always welcome. While early eighteenth-century government was prepared to tolerate presbyterian-ism in the heartland of Ulster, where it was powerless to stop its spread, an attempt to set up a presbyterian congregation at Belturbet in 1712 was quickly stopped by the prosecution of the Monaghan presbytery.[5]

This brief consideration of one of the factors which gave rise to the 'personality' of Cavan suggests that in studying a region there are factors other than purely topographical or administrative concerns to be examined in determining a unit for study. All historians are concerned with three variables, people, place and time. Of the three, local historians have seen place as the most importance variable, emphasising the 'particularity' of the place being studied. Boundaries such as those of parish or county are assigned paramount importance and the local evidence of topography becomes central to an understanding of a region. Thus Philip O'Connell in the 1930s claimed that 'for the satisfactory interpretation of the successive phases of our history an intimate knowledge of local topography is essential'.[6] Indeed O'Connell's first ventures into the history of the diocese of Kilmore produced a series of fine studies of the topography and evolution of a number of parishes in the diocese published in the *Journal of the Breifne Antiquarian and Historical Society*. Yet, as Patrick Duffy's essay reminds us, the landscape of Cavan was above all a 'humanised landscape'. It was created by people who shaped the landscape for their own ends and it was they who mapped out the network of townlands which appear on the first edition of the Ordnance Survey maps of the 1830s. However the apparent immutability of that network is deceptive. The fully formed townland structure conceals another complex of subdivisions of pottles, pints and even fields all of which were named by people. These disappeared because people no longer found them useful whereas the townland lasted because it became part of an administrative system of taxation and data collection set up by central government. In this way the landscape became structured and tamed by people. Moreover as Duffy's essay also indicates there was not just one set of boundaries created by people. Townlands were part of a structure of baronies, parishes (both medieval and, in the case of the Catholic church, nineteenth-century), the county and the diocese. Each of these units reflects a different experience and to select only one is to limit the scope of any local study, both chronologically and thematically.

What these essays suggest is that place is not the crucial variable for the local historian, and therefore the varied use of the lordship, the diocese and the county for studies within one volume matters little. Rather it reflects the diverse nature of human experience within one region. It is the people who occupied that place, whether townland, county or diocese, which should be our main concern. Ciaran Parker and Bernadette Cunningham's essays both stress the importance of family networks in understanding how medieval and sixteenth-century Cavan evolved. The lordship of the O'Reilly's of east Breifne provided a coherence for those who lived in this region before the formation of the county. From the late sixteenth century a new element in the identity of those who lived in the region, that of confessional allegiance, came to have an importance which became enduring. How that allegiance was shaped, often over a considerable period of time, is described by Alan Ford and James Kelly who deal with the reformation and the counter reformation in the diocese of Kilmore. In the course of the nineteenth century such religious denominations were solidified and came to have a particular political significance. Thus the political history of the nineteenth and early twentieth century, as revealed in Gerard Moran and Eileen Reilly's essays, becomes the story of how groups of people contending for power in the region went about organising themselves to achieve their own ends.

Familial and party politics and ecclesiastical change require the discussion of particular groups of people within the region, prominent figures such as great lords, parish priests and bishops, and MPs form the centre of this story. In some ways this is a traditional focus. The introduction to Philip O'Connell's *Diocese of Kilmore* is replete with the names of those who later became prominent in various spheres of life 'to show that Breiffne ranks very high as the birth place of Irish genius'.[7] However many of the people who lie at the root of the local historian's reconstruction of past worlds are not those who might appear important at first glance. The fabric of local society was often not created by the prominent but the ordinary. For this reason the essays by Raymond Gillespie and Margaret Crawford aim to reconstruct the fabric of life at two rather different points in the past. Using two crises, the plantations of the seventeenth century and the Great Famine of the nineteenth, these essays try to show how ordinary people responded to dramatic change.

To understand the evolution of local societies as the changes taking place among groups of people living in a particular place over time must shift the focus of the local historian away from a rather myopic view of the practice of local history. The people of Ireland have always been mobile. Colonisation in the seventeenth century and emigration in the nineteenth are only dramatic illustrations of this truism. Some 121,291 people emigrated from Cavan between 1851 and 1911.[8] However, in addition to these dramatic events there was a continual movement in and out of the county. Merchants and farmers sold their produce on a national market, priests came and went from the Irish colleges in Europe and later Maynooth, absentee landlords visited the county and MPs came from and went to Dublin and later London. Cavan men also experienced a wider world as the result of war.

All of these developments drew the people of Cavan into a wider social network and exposed them to a range of ideas beyond the local experience and hence helped to shape their world. Such 'brokers' acted as channels of new ideas into the locality. Oxford, Cambridge and Trinity College, Dublin graduates all feature in Alan Ford's description of the reformation in Kilmore and James Kelly's essay shows by the early ninteeenth century the priest trained in the ideals of the counter reformation at Maynooth or another major seminary was beginning to become a prominent feature of everyday life in Cavan. Later in the same century Gerard Moran's essay shows how the ideas of national politics came to be imported into the county through a network of clubs and societies. Perhaps most dramatically the failure of the potato crop at a national level in 1847 left its distinctive local mark on Cavan as described in Margaret Crawford's analysis of the Famine. That interchange between the national and local experiences is also at the heart of the essays by Ciaran Parker, Bernadette Cunningham and Raymond Gillespie. Even wider contexts need to be employed in the case of Eileen Reilly's examination the First World War, when international developments had an impact on the county. There were also other influences which conspired to ensure that Cavan shared in the experiences of the wider world. The growth of literacy in the nineteenth century and the rise of local newspapers, such as the *Anglo-Celt*, both ensured that issues broader than those of the county came to be considered important.

The study of local history is, therefore, moving away from a preoccupation with a sense of a particular place and towards an understanding of the complex social networks which the people who lived in those places created to manage their everyday existence. The task is a complex one for it embraces not only the traditional preoccupations of historians: politics, religion and great men, but a much wider world which includes economics, culture, society, landscape and the fabric of everyday life.[9] The result will be a description of the Cavan past rather different to that already achieved. This book does not present all the detail of such a description. It is rather an attempt to open up new perspectives on the past of the region now known as county Cavan. It can, perhaps, be seen as a series of bore holes through the complicated social fabric of the past which provides a series of glimpses of that world. The focus and breadth of vision of those glimpses can be much improved by local historians studying both the themes examined in this book and others, such as the workings of the linen industry and the great landed estates, which have been omitted here, in their own areas. Cavan, as a watershed between Connacht, Ulster and Leinster, is a region of particular importance in understanding the evolution of these areas and in the interaction between them. The elusive 'personality' of Cavan remains to be captured.

Perspectives on the Making of the Cavan Landscape

P. J. DUFFY

'The Irish landscape is a tangled series of inscriptions, signs and symbols which reflect the complicated prehistory and history of settlement and culture in this relatively small but diverse island'.

W. J. Smyth[1]

The aim of this essay is to provide a geographical overview of the Cavan region refracted, as it were, through the lenses of a variety of sources. In this way we can throw light on some of the problems in studying the evolution of the Cavan landscape. The concept of landscape evolution forms a convenient frame of reference. 'Landscape' can be defined as the territorial expression of the imprint of society in material and non-material forms through past time. The 'making' of that landscape, a term used especially by geographers, emphasises the centrality of society's role in the emerging morphology of the landscape.

To most Irish people, Cavan conveys images of a borderland lying to the north of the midlands and forming part of south Ulster—a hilly region of drumlins, abundant surface water, small farms and farmhouses girdling the hillsides with a tangle of by-roads connecting distinctively-named towns and villages. Its geographical location is clearly one of its most important defining characteristics. The provincial, diocesan and county boundaries which delimit this region, for instance, are of great endurance and antiquity, reflecting a borderland and frontier region for many centuries. Ultimately, any understanding of the modern landscape assumes some knowledge of its historical evolution, and in the Cavan region, its past experiences have been influenced in no small measure by its location in the broad belt of drumlins bordering the south of Ulster.

It has been said of England, and it is equally true of Ireland, that 'there are few blanks on the map ... almost everywhere is a place with a meaning and a character of its own'.[2] Places evolve over time; they are the stages on which our predecessors, the people who have passed through these places, played out their parts, modifying, moulding, building and shaping the landscape, putting their stamp on it so that each place represents each generation's contribution to its making. The apparent randomness of much of the visible landscape reflects these incremental contributions to the organisation of that landscape at different times in the past. What is sometimes called the 'human-ised' landscape, therefore, is the end result of our ancestors' efforts at organ-ising their lives, economies, communities and landscapes according to the circumstances and conditions of their times. Until the mass-production of concrete blocks, garden nurseries and universal tastes in everything from house to hedge design, 'local-ness' prevailed, and local places retained their vernacular characters in plants, crops, houses, dress, language, song and cus-toms.

Seamus Heaney, in writing about our consciousness of the past, has elo-quently illustrated the primacy of landscape and place in human understand-ing. He has spoken of how inherited objects transmit the climate of a lost world which should not be undervalued: 'The rooms where we come to consciousness, the cupboards we open as toddlers, the shelves we climb up to ... the secret spots we come upon in our earliest solitudes out of doors, the haunts of our first explorations in outbuildings and fields at the verge of our security...at such moments we have our first inklings of pastness and find our physical surroundings invested with a wider and deeper dimension ...'.[3] Our landscape, especially our childhood landscape—our first place—must have such a significance. It is our contact with our pasts and the people who have occupied and put their mark on this space before our time: they have touched the stones, the fields, the hedges, the furniture of the landscape. And because of this we value it.

Apart from this instinctive feeling about the depth of meaning in land-scape, today's world has led to a new awareness of the value of the inherited artifacts and landscapes which surround us. The tourism industry has in-vested many of our countrysides and towns with opportunities which were not available to our ancestors in these places. The postmodern world has afforded many people from near and far the leisure to contemplate the land-scape. This 'tourist gaze' has encouraged us to dissagregate the landscape into its component parts, for better presentation and marketing perhaps, but also for better understanding and appreciation generally.[4]

The principal ingredients of any Irish landscape may be broadly catego-rised into three elements, hinted at in Estyn Evans' trinity of habitat, heritage and history. There are the topographical features of, for instance, mountains, valleys, bogs, lakes and streams, the ecological elements of plant cover, trees and heath and the human impact of settlement—the built environment and cultural iconographies of placenames, religion and tradition. The cultural impact is the consequence of processes acting slowly on the landscape over long periods of time resulting, for example, in English landscapes so 'tamed, trimmed and humanised as to give the impression of a vast ornamental farm', or American landscapes 'of uncontrollable chaos inhabited by happy acci-dents'.[5] In Ireland one can reasonably see the intimate reflections of the cultural diversity of four hundred years in the contrast between the sabbath

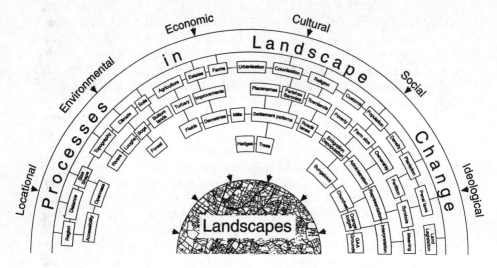

Figure 1   Processes in Landscape Change

staidness, punk hedgestyles and tidy farmscapes of north Down and the dishevilled and untidy landscapes of south Ulster.

This landscape perspective can be conveniently illustrated in a diagram (figure 1) which shows the interaction of the processes of change. These express themselves territorially in the shape and spatial patterning of the landscape. Thus, for example, underdeveloped and marginal regions, urban industrial districts, the location and morphology of settlement as well as other manifestations of territorial organisation are all the consequences of historical processes operating over generations. These proceses can be grouped into those which are the consequences of locational, environmental, economic, cultural, social, political and other factors. The territorial expression of these processes in varying ways and in different circumstances has resulted in the landscape order which we have inherited today.

The simplicity of such a classification must be qualified by taking account of the way in which human behaviour—in the past just as today—in its relations with the landscape, results from variations and changes in ideology, attitudes and prejudices. Economic, social or political responses by society to change, for instance, are often based on partial or biassed information. Again perceptions or interpretations of these processes in the past, or their landscape expressions today, can frequently vary from person to person, community to community: there are almost as few 'irrefutable facts' relating to the landscape's history as relate to its community's past. The 'storied' landscapes of Henry Glassie's Ballymenone, Seamus Heaney's Bann valley, or W.B. Yeats' Sligo, are cases in point.[6] 'Places are made by narrative accretion, they are communicated to us in stories'.[7] This chapter is designed to illustrate in a

general way how the Cavan landscape has been the consequence of the impact
and interaction of these processes of change in the past.

I

As suggested above, and as reinforced in Ciaran Parker's essay below, understanding Cavan's past necessitates consideration of the significance of its regional location. Much of the behaviour of the lowly or lordly occupiers of east
Breifne or Cavan over the past millennium, as they developed and 'organised'
their landscape, was influenced by the relationship of the area to areas and
communities around it.

In the late medieval and early modern period, east Breifne was one of a
belt of small, minor lordships running across the southern extremity of Ulster, bordering on the northern and north western edge of the Pale. Indeed
until the fourteenth century, Breifne was a kingdom or territory which had
strong political associations with the O'Rourkes and Connacht. In the sixteenth century the O'Reillys, like the Mac Mahons of Airghialla and Maguires
of Fermanagh, were wedged between the Gaelic strongholds to the north in
Ulster and the strenghtening English bridgehead to the south in the Pale.
Lord Deputy Sussex in 1562, while acknowledging that Breifne was considered part of Connacht, assigned it to Ulster for strategic reasons because 'it
bordereth upon the English Pale'. To late sixteenth century Tudor strategists,
the earl of Tyrone 'was held to be the chief hinge on which the doors of peace
or trouble did hang in those parts'[8] and O'Reilly's Cavan was vulnerably
positioned on the threshold.

Loyalty to the crown among the south Ulster lordships correlated closely
with proximity to Dublin and on this basis, the O'Reillys were among the
most consistenty loyal for much of the sixteenth century.[9] Punitive expeditions could be mounted into the Breifne fairly rapidly: 'six rebels' heads were
brought to Dublin by one Mr Plunkett, who took them in the rescue of a prey
upon the borders of Louth, being some of the O'Reillys'.[10] Indeed the southern districts of Breifne which were closest to the Pale had for long come
under the influence of its community. By the late sixteenth century, they
contained a fair sprinkling of Palesmen such as Plunketts, Flemings and
Nugents, among their landowners.[11] In addition to political and military acu-
men, the O'Reillys also practised astute marriage alliances which mirrored
their borderland role—at various times in the sixteenth century marrying into
Old English families from Meath, or Gaelic O'Donnells, O'Connors or
O'Farrells. However, O'Reilly also fell within the orbit of the O'Neills of
Tyrone and, in consequence of the earl's political dominance, became engulfed in the nine years war. As a result, and in spite of many years allegiance
to the crown, the lands of Cavan were ultimately included in the Ulster

plantation scheme with all that this implied for the subsequent development of the region and its landscapes of country and town.

Inclusion in the Ulster plantation was undoubtedly significant in the shaping of the Cavan landscape but, like south Armagh for example, its experience continued to a great extent to reflect its marginal location—on the southern borders of Ulster and on the edge of the plantation scheme. The cultural and economic impacts on the landscape reflected this marginality. The settler community, for instance, tended to be patchier and more exposed than its counterpart in the north and east of the province. The shape and extent of Cavan, elongated along the southern margins of Ulster, was also important. In many ways, the location of districts within the modern county *vis-á-vis* Ulster, on the one hand, and the midlands on the other, is relevant to the experience of the landscape. For example, the mountainous north-west was remote and poor. The central lakeland of Loughtee had close associations with Fermanagh, facilitated by the easier mode of water transportation. This influenced the initial development and experience of the plantation settlement in these districts in the early seventeenth century. By the 1620s, many poor and remote districts in Cavan had been abandoned by their settlers, like those who had fled from Clankee 'to Clandeboys from whence they came'.[12] The estate of Tonagh, south of the 'Denn mountains' also failed to attract settlers.[13]

II

The environmental legacy of Cavan with its myriad hills and its impeded drainage and lakelands had an important influence on the shaping of the landscape by its occupiers. While, by the Soil Survey's definitions of the late twentieth century, it contains relatively little marginal land, its drumlin gley soils need considerable management to make them efficient. In the midlands to the south, by contrast, both grass and cows grow more easily. In south Ulster, the poorly-drained gleys are plastered in the form of drumlins around substructures of hummocky shale, resulting in the wet landscape of Patrick Kavanagh's stoney grey soil. Until the seventeenth century, the Breifne together with Airghialla and the Fews of Armagh represented a region which was difficult of access, and almost as great a barrier as any mountain range. Indeed the high hills of Cavan and Monaghan have not infrequently been characterised as mountains in the past; the hills of east Cavan, for example, are clearly represented as 'mountains' in the Down Survey maps of 1657 (figure 2). Bishop William Bedell, who was appointed to the diocese of Kilmore in 1629, was reported to have his house 'situate in the county of Cavan in the province of Ulster in Ireland, in a country consisting altogether of hills very steep and high, the valleys between being most commonly boggs and loughs ...'.[14] The political boundaries of the Gaelic territories of south Ulster with

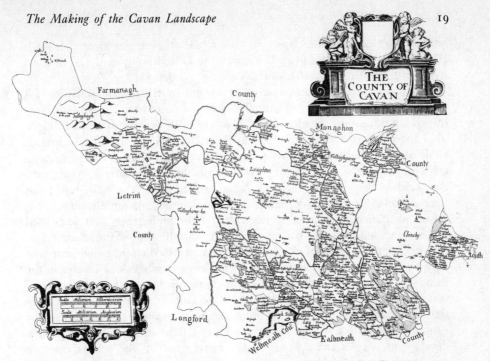

Figure 2   Cavan from Petty's *Hiberniae Delineatio* (1685), based on his Down
              Survey 1657.

the midland region of Ireland coincided remarkably with serried ranks of
drumlins, separated by scrubland and wet bottom lands, which made movement, especially by military groups, particularly fraught. This was a country
of 'rheums, fluxes and distempers' for which uisce beatha and sweat houses
were the traditional remedies. Through the middle ages, the borders of Breifne
were marked by castles, such as Ballaghanea, Mullagh, Muff and Finnea,
guarding the few passes into the region. This south Ulster region presented a
challenge not only to the Dublin government but also to its local lords attempting to consolidate their poorly-endowed territories. There, as Bernadette
Cunningham's essay shows, insubordinate minor branches of the ruling family, sheltered by the region's internal fragmentation into hills and sodden
lowlands, frequently threatened the internal peace of the lordship.

The geographical distribution of environmental resources had important
implications for the eventual working out of economic and cultural patterns
on the landscape. There are difficulties in assessing environmental conditions
in the early modern period because generations of husbandry and improvements have made the use of more recent sources somewhat questionable.
Philip Robinson, however, has made a sustainable case for regarding townland
size as a proxy for land quality in the sixteenth century.[15] Evidence from
Monaghan and Fermanagh would certainly suggest that under the Gaelic
system of land assessment, agricultural land units—such as tates or polls-

were smaller in the better lands. In Cavan, the areas in the lucht tigh lands
(Loughtee), held by the main branch of the O'Reillys, around Cavan town
had the greatest density of townlands (see p. 29 below).

Although the tenement valuation of Ireland by Sir Richard Griffith was
only undertaken in the post-Famine period, and so reflects the consequences
of agricultural improvements since the seventeenth century, it helps to highlight the range of land quality within the county (figure 3). The lucht tigh
lands of the O'Reillys around the lakes in north central Cavan were strategi-
cally located at the centre of the Gaelic lordship and contained some of the
best land in the area. As in many other planted areas, the lucht tigh lands
were especially selected for the favoured and important undertakers in the
Ulster plantation. Successful settlement by these undertakers had significant
positive repercussions for this landscape in the following centuries, in terms
of both farm management and landscape design. By the mid nineteenth century, for instance, a large proportion of the most highly valued houses in the
county had been built in this region which also had a significant number of
resident landowners. In contrast, lack of seventeenth-century settlement in
the least valuable land lying in the mountainy panhandle to the west of the
county had negative repercussions in terms of farm size and later landscape
development. Thus the uplands in the eastern part of the county between
Bailieborough and Monaghan were described by the travelling artist Gabriel

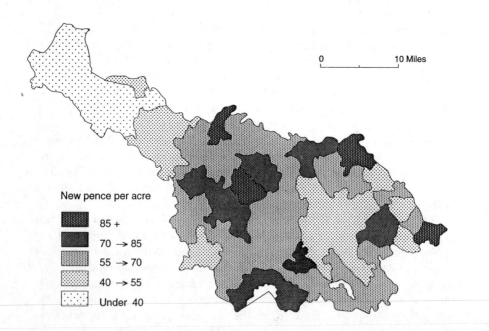

Figure 3   Land Quality: Griffith's Valuation of Cavan

Berenger in 1779 as looking 'poor, the land coarse, the cabins as if going to ruin, half-thatched, several bogs close to the road ...'.[16]

The environmental legacy has been subjected to considerable changes and modification, particularly as a result of agricultural improvement from the seventeenth century. Most importantly this was represented by such developments as drainage of the bottomlands. Thomas Raven's 1634 survey of Farney in south Monaghan, for example, showed a number of 'wet' boundaries, which subsequently became firmed up as the wetlands and marshy intervening lands were drained and reclaimed.[17] As late as the 1830s, the Ordnance Survey could refer to the effects of drainage and flood control on lowering water levels in lakes. On a larger scale, one can distinguish between the differing types and scale of agricultural improvements in varying regions across the county, positively around the Mullagh and Cootehill areas and more negatively in the uplands to the west. These obviously interrelate with the social and cultural processes resulting from plantations and settler in-migrations during the seventeenth century. The lists of grand jury presentments throughout the eighteenth century contain copious detail on the small incremental improvements made to the environmental legacy. Apart from drainage, there was the continuous improvement of the road network—straightenings, fillings-in, bridge-building, culverts, piecemeal modifications which have led to the rich, if scarred, heritage of roads in the county today.

There was a piecemeal, day-by-day, year-by-year, decade-by-decade modification of the physical endowment—drains and ditches, enclosures and hedges, reclamation and abandonment, cabins and housing—as the fabric of settlement wove its mesh across the skeleton of hills and valleys. Much of this settlement pattern was born out of social and cultural distinctions in the rural and urban population, whether of class (landowner, big farm, cottier, long lease, tenant-at-will), ethnicity or religion.

III

The processes of economic change clearly connect with social and cultural dimensions of land and its ownership. Estates, big and small, for example, fragmented, extensive, resident or non-resident all had varying impacts on the evolution of the landscape. In terms of understanding the modern landscape undoubtedly the establishment of a framework of landed estates as part of the Ulster plantation is a significant milestone. Within this frame, the broad canvas of landscape changes was mediated through the agency of leases and other mechanisms of the estate system. It seems logical, and most nationalist historiography has confirmed, that for the settlement plans to work in a colonial situation the best land should go to the planter. Robinson, however, suggests that in the case of the Ulster settlement this was not always the case,[18] due largely to the inadequacies of the plantation's preparatory surveys

and maps which provided unreliable indications of the value of lands. However, good land could be assessed by observation and Sir John Davies was
well aware that Cavan's Loughtee barony was 'the best in the county' and
should be reserved for the crown. As it turned out, it was allocated to English
undertakers, regarded by the government as being critical to the success of
the settlement because of their perceived superior capital assets.

Figure 4 shows the allocation of lands in Cavan under the Ulster plantation scheme. The principal consequence of the implementation of the scheme
was the granting of consolidated blocks of land to undertakers. Apart from
the allocation of the O'Reilly lucht tigh lands to English undertakers, the
baronies of Clankee and Tullyhunco were designated for Scottish undertakers. Lands for the native Irish and the ex-soldiers and government officials
(grouped together as servitors) were allotted in a broad arc extending southwards from the modern Cootehill area and westwards to the Longford border.
Apart from the proportion granted to the head of the O'Reilly family, Mulmory,
most of the native Irish freeholders were small grantees of one or two polls.
The impression created by the geography of the distribution is that they were
given whatever lands remained after the servitors had been satisfied in
Clanmahon, Castlerahan and Tullygarvey baronies. Many of the servitors in
Cavan were Palesmen such as Sir Thomas Ashe, Sir John Elliot and Sir James
Dillon, part of a long-established tradition of holding land in the Breifne,

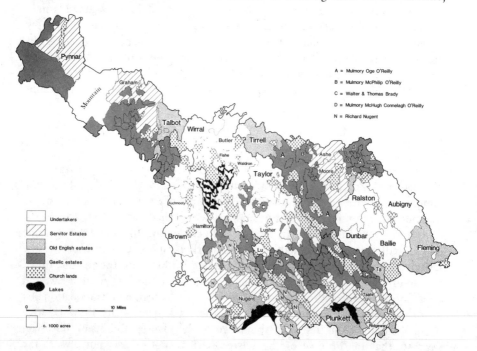

Figure 4   Ulster plantation allocation of lands in Cavan, 1610–20

which is well-reflected in the map showing extensive 'Old English' estates relatively untouched by the plantation. Edward Dowdall, a Castlerahan landlord, was described in the 1622 survey as being a recusant with several tenants from the Pale. In this sense, the servitor contribution to the Cavan settlement may have diverged somewhat from the original intentions of the planners of the scheme. Palesmen probably had less commitment to a radical change in society and settlement on their new estates than had British settlers. The beginnings of the substantial modification of some parts of the landscape appear in the early plantation surveys, however. In 1622, for example, Sir Richard Waldron's estate in Loughtee was described as having thirty houses with English families, 'a windmill and very good tillage, inclosures and stores of English cattle'.[19] In contrast, the native Irish estates—and some Palesmen's lands, such as Dowdall's—continued older patterns of landuse, including ploughing by the tail 'with their garrans'.

Though one should not assume that the geography of plantation estates shaped all subsequent landscape patterns—much land changed hands throughout the seventeenth century for example—it is not entirely a coincidence that the distribution of Protestants in the landscape of the county in 1861 (see figure 10, p. 33), shows especially low proportions in the districts allotted to Gaelic, Old English and servitor landowners in the early seventeenth century. In contrast, the largest Protestant communities, up to and exceeding one-third of the 1861 electoral division populations, were to be found mainly in the areas allotted to Scottish and English undertakers as part of the plantation scheme.

Though there were some changes in personnel, the undertaker estates continued and consolidated their position up to 1641 (figure 5). The native Irish estates, amounting to about twenty-two per cent of the profitable land of the county in 1610, fell to sixteen per cent in 1641. Evidence suggests that Gaelic landholders generally in Ireland at this time experienced contraction and decline in the face of superior land management and investment strategies by the new British settlers.[20] Although it is difficult to identify precisely the ethnic origin of some of the individuals concerned, it appears that the Old English further consolidated their grip on the lands of Cavan, especially in the southern part of the county, before 1641. The Cromwellian land settlement subsequently made a clean sweep of extensive parts of mid- and south-west Cavan (figure 6). Some of the Old English properties survived the change, but all the native Irish properties changed to settler hands. The essential difference between the Ulster plantation scheme, with its emphasis on colonial settlement and community development, and the Cromwellian confiscation, was that the latter placed little or no emphasis on settlement. Much of the Cromwellian settlement was characterised by the assembly of extensive estates by predatory land speculators. In the south of Cavan, for example, new owners such as the Massereenes, Beresfords, Lewises and Cootes appeared. In Tullyhaw in the north-west of the county, the Massereenes,

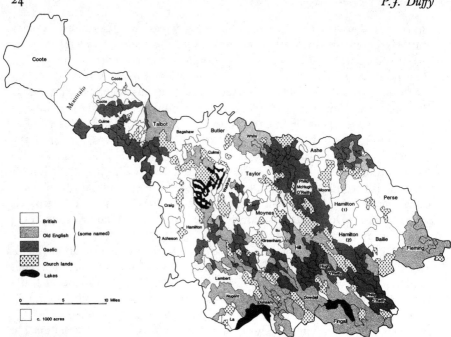

Figure 5 (above) 1641 ownership of lands in Cavan
Figure 6 (below) Cromwellian land grants in county Cavan

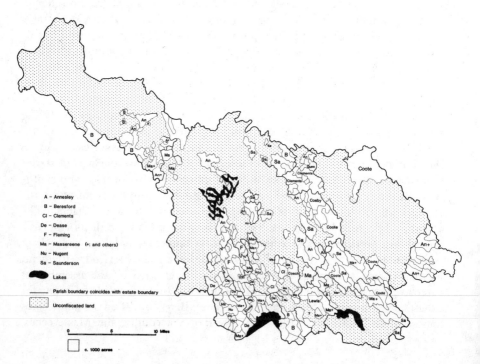

Beresfords and Cootes again appear. Families such as Annesley, Massereene, Saunderson, Coote and others were involved in many land deals, throughout south Ulster and further afield, often involving soldiers' land shares. Annesley, one of the commissioners for the Cromwellian settlement, was involved in over twenty shares in Cavan not counting deals in a dozen other Irish counties. Together with genuine small grantees who settled on their properties, the Cromwellian programme established a pattern of small estates, many of which were subsequently consolidated in a variety of speculative land deals.

The territorial and social structure of estates, which had emerged by the nineteenth century from the seventeenth century revolution in landownership, is the key to understanding much of the modern landscape of Cavan (figure 7). Towns and villages, farms, roads, railways and housing patterns can all be understood within a framework of estate management, the effectiveness of which varied greatly over a county containing, as Jones Hughes has pointed out, 'the tail end of Ireland's most complicated web of great landed properties' extending into south-east Ulster.[21] The largest and most consolidated estates were to be found in the baronies of Upper and Lower Loughtee, Clankee and Tullyhunco—which had been allocated to undertakers in the Ulster plantation—and Tullygarvey, where some notable Cromwellian estates had been assembled. The most valuable estate properties extended from the Coote lands on the Monaghan border to Lord Farnham's property around Cavan town. It is also clear that many of the estates in Cavan were highly fragmented. The Farnham, Saunderson, Annesley and Garvagh estates, for example, were scattered over an extensive area, a reflection of the speculative origins of many of these properties in the previous centuries. Figure 7 also identifies estates whose owners were absentee in 1876, as well as estates with houses and demesnes, both of which give a rough indication of levels of management, investment and interest in their properties by landowners. The map, however, takes no account of the problem of non-residence on estates in the preceding century and it probably understates the real effect of absenteeism in that many of the landowners may have lived only part of the year in Cavan. These details correlate strongly with Jones Hughes' map of the valuation of estates in 1870. Measured by these criteria the landscapes in Cavan in which the forces of modernisation were most extensive ran from Cootehill to Cavan and Belturbet, with another district adjoining the Longford–Meath border. In addition to houses and demesnes, these areas also supported a suite of towns and villages which originated in the conditions of the Ulster plantation. With the county town of Cavan on the Farnham estate, all of these towns were associated with strong estate cores. On the other hand, the poor barony of Tullyhaw, and comparatively poor lands of Clankee were characterised by a high level of absenteeism among landowners. In these poor areas, and also in districts running westwards from Shercock to the Leitrim border, non-resident fragments of property were accompanied by wide variations in leasing arrangements, rental valuations and general levels of estate management to

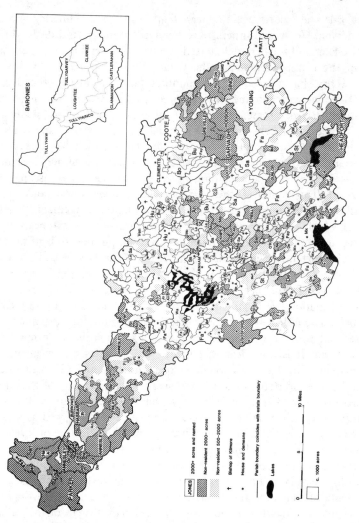

Index to Figure 7

Except where indicated in brackets below, the first two letters of the landowner's name are printed on the map where the property is too small to include the whole name.

Adams, Benjamin	Farnham, Lord	Knipe, John	Saunderson, Col. Alex (Sa)
Annesley, earl of	Fay, James	Lanesboro, earl of	Saunderson, Mrs Mary (Sa 2)
Beresford, Lord (Be)	Finlay	Marley, Louisa	Scott
Beresford, John (Be 1)	Fleming, Maj.-Gen.	Maxwell, Somerset	Smith, William
Beresford, J.D. (Be 2)	Garvagh, Lady	Moore, Samuel	Singleton, Henry
Boyle, Maxwell	Gosford, earl of	Nesbitt, C.T.	Storey, Jane
Burrowes	Greville, Col.	Nesbitt, A.	Venables, Revd E.B.
Clements, Theophilus	Hassard, Alexander	Nixon	Vernere, John
Coote, Richard	Hassard, Richard	O'Reilly, Anthony	Young, Sir John (Lord Lisgar)
Coote, Charles	Headfort, Marquis of	Parker	Wallace
Dease, Gerald	Hodson, Sir George	Pratt, Col.	
Dobbs, Leonard	Humphreys, William	Ruxton, William	
Dunlop, Mrs	Jones, John C.	Saunders, Richard (San)	

Figure 7   Cavan estates in the mid-nineteenth century

produce what has been called more 'haphazard, unregulated and protracted processes of colonisation and settlement'.[22]

IV

In the process of settling and developing the landscape for human use, societies invariably shape that landscape according to the norms, values and priorities of their particular culture. This produces what have been called 'humanised' or cultural landscapes which reflect many of their cultural characteristics. The territorial structure of the Cavan landscape, for example, is an important component in understanding its nature. The hierarchy of places such as townlands, parishes and baronies represents the process of 'territorialisation' of the landscape which can be viewed as both a by-product of and a pre-requisite for economic and cultural development. This territorial structure is the framework within which all the processes of landscape modification and change occur and within which they can be best understood. In the course of settling any region, one of the earliest processes was an ongoing division and subdivision of the landscape as part of its organisation for human use. In general, it might be said that this division into territories reflects the economic and social priorities of the culture group. In Ireland we have inherited a tangled web of territorial divisions which reflects this historical process. Most of these divisions represent the state at which society's territorialisation had arrived by the late sixteenth century, when new English colonial policies began to record, for confiscation or sale, land and property in Ireland. Some layers of territorial order were in the process of becoming defunct; others had long since disappeared. The early political territories of Gaelic Ireland—the tuatha—may have disappeared by the late middle ages, but their shadowy reflections can be seen in many of the barony boundaries. The counties, of course, represent in the main the crown's adaptation of existing Gaelic political lordships in the sixteenth and early seventeenth centuries. Ballybetaghs, which persisted throughout many Gaelic regions up to the early and mid-seventeenth century and which represented the variety of sept lands held under Gaelic landownership systems, became defunct following the seventeenth-century settlements. However, it is possible that their shape and extent influenced the geography of many of the estates which emerged in the seventeenth and eighteenth centuries.

A further unit, the parish, based on these secular landownership structures of ballybetagh and lordship and focussed on small country churches, was given official status following the twelfth-century church reforms. This was reinforced by their adoption by the Church of Ireland in the sixteenth century. These parishes survived as important units for various civil administrative functions up to the twentieth century. The territorial manifestation of the Catholic church parochial structure reflected the expression of an outlawed

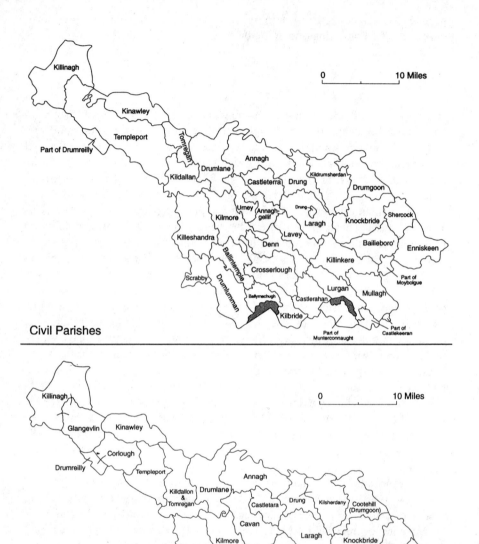

Figure 8   Civil and Catholic parishes of county Cavan

and impoverished institution in the seventeenth and eighteenth centuries. In many parts of the country, especially areas of manorial settlement with their tiny parish units, ad hoc arrangements which bore little resemblance to the obsolete medieval parishes emerged. The latter were maintained by the Established Church more for legal, property and income reasons than for any evangelical or congregational reason. In south Ulster, however, where a fairly substantial Protestant community gave a semblance of viability to the large Gaelic medieval parishes, the Catholic church found little difficulty in continuing to operate in these units.[23] For this reason, as in Monaghan and to a lesser extent parts of Fermanagh, the medieval and Catholic parishes in Cavan are largely identical, as figure 8 shows.

The smallest territorial unit to survive from the medieval period is the townland, which has become so close to the lives of rural dwellers now that it is often taken for granted. Though there are many conflicting views on the origins of these units, in general it seems that townlands are the fairly extensive remnants of a fundamental landholding layer in the middle ages. Reflecting the 'local-ness' of pre-modern society, these land units had a variety of local designations. These appear in the seventeenth century evidence as tates in Monaghan and Fermanagh, polls in Cavan, ballyboes, ploughlands, cartrons elsewhere.[24] The term 'townland' became universal with the standardisation which came with incorporation in a modern centralising state in the seventeenth century. The townlands, effectively a territorial expression of land assessments—areas which had an established customary stocking capacity, for cows usually—probably also operated as the equivalent of a family holding. Certainly following the revolution in landownership in the seventeenth century, this small territorial unit became the basic unit for tenurial purposes. With the parishes, this unit also became the basic unit for the collection of data by central and local government from the seventeenth to the twentieth centuries making it a useful unit for historical study.

In Cavan, using the coarse web of parishes as an averaging medium, it is possible to see hints of the territorial logic in these divisions. The baronies of Upper and Lower Loughtee, for example, which contain some of the best land in the county, have the smallest average townland size. In Kilmore parish, the townlands average 165 acres, in Urney 157, Annagelliff 183, Drumlane 157, Castleterra 133, Drung 164 and Annagh 191 acres. This contrasts with townlands in excess of 300 acres in the south eastern hills of Cavan, where the land is poorer—in Lavey 313 acres, Killinkere 326, Bailieborough 332 and Castlerahan with 330 acres. Predictably they are also extensive in the northwest parishes of Kinawley (290 acres), Killinagh (300 acres) and Templeport (250 acres). Here it is likely that many of these units emerged quite late, probably in the later eighteenth century, as population expanded into previously unsettled mountainous districts. There are noticeable variations between the average size of townlands in Monaghan and in Cavan, and it would seem safe to assume that this range of sizes in Cavan simply reflects the internal territorial organisation of the land resources in the south-Ulster lordships of Breifne and Airghialla.

The process of the territorialisation of the landscape did not stop at poll, tate or townland level. These units were subdivided, possibly in response to population pressure and landholding fragmentation, and this is reflected in Cavan's micro units of pints, pottles, and gallons, for example. In the eighteenth century subdivision as far down as field units continued as part of the day-to-day running of a farm. Enclosures began following the Ulster plantation. With reclamation and drainage, enclosures were encouraged through the aegis of the larger estates. Throughout the eighteenth century one would expect that agents and estate managers, such as those on the Headfort estate in the 1740s, would have tried to introduce some order into the progress of hedges and ditching by tenant farmers by, for example, including clauses for enclosure in leases. One popular device was to offer free quicksets to tenants to encourage planting. On smaller, more fragmented and often absentee properties, enclosure progressed largely through the initiative of the occupiers of the lands rather than through landlord intervention. Indeed subdivision and subletting of farms, one of the principal landscape media for pre-Famine population growth, was effectively a tenant initiative.[25] The farm was the community's workspace where changes were wrought in response to the exigencies of the market or the dictates of landowners or necessities of survival. As well as considering farm structure it might be possible at this level to discern differences in land and estate management in the layout of fields. On a broad regional or national scale there are certainly correlations between field and farm size, with small farm regions being characterised by small average fields. In maps the Cavan borderland emerges strikingly on the southern frontier of a small farm and small field region abutting on the larger farms and fields of the midlands (figure 9).

Naming the landscape was another fundamental aspect of the process of territorialisation. Topomyns are especially important as indicators of cultural landscapes. This south Ulster borderland strikingly reflects in its townland names the medieval frontier with the Pale. Southwards across this frontier there is a significant increase in the number of English placenames in the Pale, and Breifne's borders are marked by an overwhelmingly Gaelic named landscape which relates exclusively to the physical qualities of the environment, though those districts adjoining the midlands contain an above-average number of names with cultural connotations. As one would expect, hilliness is a quality which is repeatedly reflected in the names. There is a wide variety of Irish names for hills—for long hills, round hills, flat hills, towering hills— subtle expressions of the value of the land and its utility for farmers or cattlemen of the middle ages: lurgan, tulach, cabhán, cor, mullach, cnoc. The most common name elements in the whole south Ulster area are Druim, Cor, Coill, Doire and Mullach. The bottom lands and the lakeshores, which also feature largely in perceptions of this drumlin landscape, have names which refer to

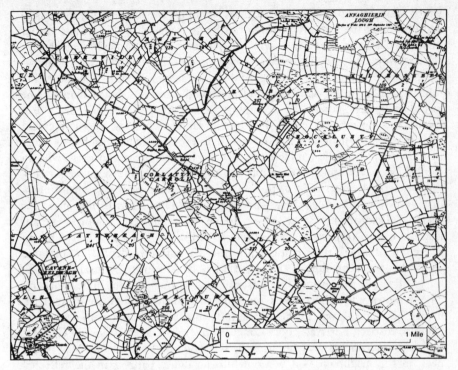

Figure 9 Field patterns. *Ordnance Survey*

botanical features particularly, such as doire and coill, as well as eanach and cluain.[26]

The townland names have been fortuitously recorded as part of seventeenth century land confiscations. However, there existed a plethora of other names for smaller divisions of land, which were not sytematically recorded. Many, like field names, were probably late in origin; many are in English and probably changed frequently as memories faded. Examples across south Ulster refer to the characteristics of fields in terms of shape, size, quality, or other distinctive features. These local names which are an intimate part of the cultural landscape have fallen out of use with decline in the numbers of farms and the intensity of farming. Many have been recorded in an unsystematic manner by the Folklore Department in University College Dublin or have been occasionally published in local historical journals.

It is interesting that in most Ulster counties there was no transformation in placenames by the immigrant settler communities to match the other changes they instigated in the morphology of the landscape. Clearly the land was already well named, and the secure transfer and maintenance of ownership of the land throughout the seventeenth century depended on the accurate retention of the existing Gaelic nomencalture. By contrast, the names of the towns, which were introduced as part of the plantation, are dramatically successful expressions of the new order which was being imposed in this remote corner of south Ulster. Names like Virginia, Kingscourt, Bailieborough, Cootehill or Butlersbridge, all vibrant country markets in this densely populated country-side, speak volumes of the colonial intent and achievement of the plantation scheme. Later, in the eighteenth and nineteenth centuries, house names came to reflect another passing fad in naming the landscape. Essentially an English import the custom was established by the landowning class to complement their newly built mansions and demenses. In the wider countryside it is likely that house naming was undertaken mainly by the bigger farmers, who in south Ulster were almost invariably the descendants of the seventeenth century settlers. A great many of the houses simply adopted the townland name in a gesture of superiority over the more lowly inhabitants of the place, for example, Lisdrum House or Arboy Lodge. Many however adopted fanciful English names (especially incorporating 'lodge' or 'cottage'), betraying an awareness of where their cultural priorities, if not antecedents, lay. In some ways, this preoccupation of the last century is akin in its cultural impact to today's fixation with names like Tuscany or Aylesbury Downs, The Cloisters, The Willows and other names for modern housing developments in Irish towns.[27] Around Cavan, in the last century, there were houses with names like Mount Prospect, Earlsvale, Fort Lodge, Groveview Lodge, Waterloo Cottage; near Virginia, there were Grousehall, Rockmount, Fortwilliam, New Prospect; in the neighbourhood of Cootehill, no doubt bathing in the reflected glory of Bellamount House, were Ashfield Lodge, Rockdell, Millvale, Faybrook View, Rockford Cottage. Though these names have been recorded in the Ordnance Survey's six-inch maps of the region, it is doubtful if many of them persist to this day and the class which introduced them has for the most part vanished from the countryside.

Religious belief is a fundamental cultural trait. Apart from obvious land-scape symbols such as churches, rectories, and perhaps Orange Halls, religion in Ireland has had an important formative role in the landscape generally. The immigrant settlers who came in the seventeenth century in response to English colonial policy were Protestant in the main and land acquisition and exploitation were their primary objectives. This meant that Protestant communities only fully developed in depth where land resources and prospects were viable and it was here that they attempted to achieve their objective of introducing English style 'civility' in tidy enclosed landscapes with arable predominating over pasture. There was a two-fold process throughout south Ulster of Protestant consolidation on the good lands and withdrawal from poorer lands, to which the Catholic population was gradually displaced. This process was also linked with the territorial expression of bigger estates, which in Cavan had developed most successfully on the older undertaker areas or where some post Cromwellian settlements, like that of the Coote family, were successful. In 1861, twenty per cent of the Cavan population was Protestant,

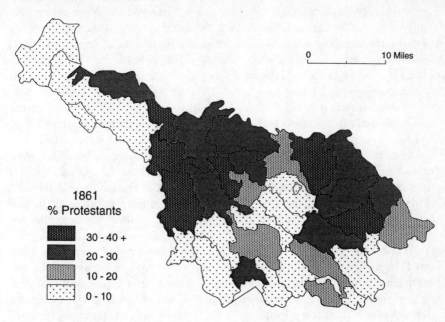

0   10 Miles

1861
% Protestants

30 - 40 +
20 - 30
10 - 20
0 - 10

Figure 10   Distribution of Protestants in county Cavan, 1861

overwhelmingly Church of Ireland (figure 10). The single variable of the Protestant population mapped for 1861, reflects a whole series of linked factors that impacted on the landscape. Districts where more than one-fifth of the population was Protestant are linked to the environmentally-favoured areas where undertaker settlement was significant, and to areas of large estates with highly valued cores and high levels of residency and management. In these regions, therefore, there was a substantial Protestant class living in a landscape which reflected a well-established and stable rural management structure of big farms, big well-hedged fields, good farmhouses and a sprinkling of country mansions and demesnes.

v

That there was an intimate link between the parcellation of the land among its occupiers and the shaping of the landscape is obvious. This is dramatically exemplified in almost any landscape on the western seaboard, the 'new west' whose fields were literally manufactured by its inhabitants. Whether or not they were controlled or ignored by the landowners, it was the small farmers of Cavan who girdled the hillsides with their houses, paths and lanes; their 'streets', farmyards and haggards; as well as barn lofts, byres and cart houses, they divided their hills into fields and planted the hedgescapes. Together with the mills and blacksmiths' shops, tea shops, chapels and churches, schoolhouses and public houses, they defined the social texture of the landscape up to the early twentieth century. The vernacular landscape of one-storied and, in the early twentieth century, two-storied farmhouses on the side of the hill linked by narrow lanes with the road was very characteristic of the small-farm landscape of south Ulster.

In the 1841 census, the Cavan and Leitrim drumlin belt represented the southernmost extremity of some of the most densely populated districts in Ireland. The parts of Cavan adjoining county Monaghan, for example, had settlement densities in excess of 400 persons per square mile, which they shared with much of Monaghan, south Armagh and the Lagan valley. This level of intensity of occupation and fragmentation of the land was a product of the opportunities offered tenants by the domestic linen industry in the late eighteenth century. By the mid nineteenth century, however, when the domestic stage of the industry was in rapid decline, these densities and the tiny farms and fields which accompanied them, were measures of great rural poverty.[28] In Cavan the smallest, poorest farms were found in parishes along the Monaghan border, across the middle of the county and in the north west, a pattern showing uncanny links with areas of Cromwellian land speculation in the seventeenth century, speculation that was based on an environmental legacy of poor land resources.

It was out of these landscapes of poverty that thousands of people emigrated continuously up to the 1950s, unable to cope with their deprivation or rejecting their limited opportunities. The pattern of rural decline in the twentieth century once again illuminates some well-worn structures—the north west, north east and mid-county districts losing half or more of their 1911 populations by the end of the 1950s. In contrast, the historic centre of the county, the old lucht tigh lands around Cavan town maintained their population levels, as did districts around some of the small country towns.

Demographic decline meant a slow contraction in the lineaments of the landscape of many areas, lanes overgrown and derelict, farmhouses and fields in the marginal edges abandoned. Much of the fieldscape of Cavan, however, has remained unchanged since the mid-nineteenth century. Since the 1960s, gradually one part, then another, of this characteristic Cavan landscape has had new houses added. The emergence of the bungalowed countrysides, which signified a new chapter in the making of the landscape, and the imposition of much more universal, standardised artifacts—verandahs with double garages, cypress hedges, lawns and rockeries—paralleled the disappearing small farms which are being replaced with bigger farms and large industrial farm buildings.

VI

Most of the cultural and economic processes which have been discussed here have obvious ideological and political ramifications. The relationship between Ireland and Britain, for many centuries, was unquestionably a political one and it has been argued that Ireland's regional economic structure and the spatial expression of its regional landscapes have been induced by the nature of the colonial relationship with England. Certainly the Ulster plantation had a political motivation and the fruits of this are clear in the ethno-political geography of south Ulster, where Breifne's ancient boundary with Fir Mánach was promoted to international frontier status in 1921.

As we began, so we return to the primacy of regional location as a factor of significance in understanding Cavan. The establishment of the political border redefined Cavan—and other south Ulster regions—as peripheral to two states and undoubtedly retarded their economic development potential. Fermanagh, with which Cavan and Leitrim had intimate links for centuries, became the 'west' in Northern Ireland. Cavan likewise became marginalised on the north-western edge of the Irish Free State. In political and economic terms it was later redefined as administratively part of the west, a return to its late medieval regional context: Connacht and the 'three counties of Ulster' became one region, as the Undeveloped and Disadvantaged Areas of the 1950s.

The political processes which led to particular definitions of landscape and regions, have also provided the context for a range of ideology-based interpretations of landscapes and events. Ultimately it may be conceded that the foregoing thoughts on influences in the making of the Cavan landscape may be revised or represented differently by different points of view. 'Competing interests—ecological, commercial and spiritual—produce opposing textual readings' of landscape.[29] Today when there are so many environmental pressures, numerous lobbies have emerged to present a variety of viewpoints on landscapes and environments. One can talk of 'constructions' of landscape heritage, for example, and with the expansion of the tourism industry and especially the tourism-driven growth of interest in heritage, there is increasing emphasis on different approaches to representing and interpreting our cultural heritage and cultural landscapes. Interpretations of the west of Ireland and the meaning of its landscapes, for instance, can result in 'varied versions of the West'.[30] The distinctive landscapes of the west of Ireland have been represented in the fiction of J.M. Synge and W.B. Yeats, in the paintings of Paul Henry and Sean Keating, in song and folklore and in the writings of scholars like Estyn Evans. Today the west has a vocal lobby to represent it as a region of depopulation and decline in need of state support. In south Ulster, a nationalist interpretation of the events which led to the creation of the Republic of Ireland and the separation of Cavan from its northern hinterland would contrast with that of a unionists. A Cavan Catholic's interpretation of the origins and achievement of the Ulster plantation might be quite different from that of a Protestant from Bailieborough. Brian Graham has tried to come to terms with the intricacies of cultural identity in Ireland and Ulster, and, among other things, its repercussions for understanding the landscape. He suggests that 'if the meaning of heritage icons is ideologically driven, then revisionism must lead to an academic re-evaluation or even redefinition of that iconography' and heritage's 'meaning must alter as the definition of that which it represents changes'.[31] The understanding of the Big House and demesne is a case in point.

One could also say (with Patrick Kavanagh) that the Cavan farmer's jaundiced view of his fields and hills will differ from those of the Dublin or foreign tourist's view of these same 'little lyrical fields'. Feminist ideologies can also see places in a different light: the landscape as the home of women. Some women writers have suggested that not enough attention has been paid to the work of Estyn Evans, for example, in examining the minutiae and intimate detail of domestic landscapes of vernacular houses and farmyards which undoubtedly reflect the influence of generations of womenfolk.[32] Ideological points of view or differing social or economic perspectives might bring different understandings to bear on a range of landscape artifacts—the development of enclosures, the backstreets of the town, the locations of Catholic or Protestant churches, the place of the landed estates, the Big House and rural settlement patterns. Just as the Great Famine as a towering event in the nineteenth century is being re-examined from a variety of perspectives, its landscape setting might also be reappraised in the light of different attitudes to the participants in this chapter of tragedy.

VII

There are a variety of approaches to understanding the making of the landscape of Cavan. Many such approaches use traditional sources, others demand innovative interrogation of traditional interpretations. All of them emphasise the importance of the past in explaining and understanding our landscape heritage, as well as the need to appreciate the significance of even our ordinary landscapes as points of contact with our past.

> And the newness that was in every stale thing
> When we looked at it as children: the spirit-shocking
> Wonder in a black slanting Ulster hill
> Or the prophetic astonishment in the tedious talking
> Of an old fool will awake for us and bring
> You and me to the yard gate to watch the whins
> And the bog-holes, cart-tracks, old stables where Time begins.
>
> Patrick Kavanagh, 'Advent'

Cavan: A Medieval Border Area

CIARAN PARKER

The theme of this essay is the extent to which geographical location played a part in shaping the fate of the Cavan region between the coming of the Anglo Normans and the end of the fifteenth century. Its marginal position imbued it with aspects of great interest to the historian for it is through an examination of such areas that the respective influences of separate cultural and social forms upon each other can be discerned. The geopolitical situation of medieval Cavan provides a further bonus for historians. The contacts between its rulers and the Anglo Normans mean that the surviving source material of the Anglo Norman lordship of Ireland can be used to considerably augment the evidence which can be gleaned from an examination of native Irish annalistic compilations.

Instead of describing medieval Cavan as a 'border area' it might perhaps be better to think, not in terms of one border but of several. Naturally, the most important of these lay between Cavan and the areas of Anglo-Norman settlement in Meath and Uriel to the south and east. Furthermore, this represented a cultural frontier, but it was a frontier which was permeable. There were other, less definite and intangible dividing-lines between the Irish of Connacht and Leinster, and then subsequently between Connacht and Ulster. These changed over time but only to a gradual extent, as they were dependent on the strength of certain families in the respective areas to attract and maintain sufficient following and support.

Medieval Cavan was dominated by the lordship of east Breifne, but it is important to realise that this was not a coherent political entity with identifiable limits, to which modern county Cavan is some form of a successor. East Breifne was identifiable with the area of control of its ruling family, the Uí Raghallaigh. It was, after all, due to their activities that the area had achieved and subsequently maintained its separate political identity. However, the extent and nature of their control varied, sometimes, from one ruler to the next. Much of the west of present-day county Cavan seldom came under their overlordship as its petty rulers, the MagShamhradháins of Teallach Eachach and the MagThíghernáins of Teallach Dhonnchadh, tried to utilise their medial position between the Uí Ruairc and Uí Raghallaigh to achieve some measure of autonomy.

The Uí Raghallaigh did not emerge onto the historical stage until the early twelfth century, and the earliest reference to them is in 1128 when Cathal O Raghallaigh was killed by Conchobhair Mac Lochlainn whilst fighting along-side Tíghernán O Ruairc, the overlord of the whole of Breifne at that time.[1] In this regard, they may be viewed as upstarts when compared to more well-established septs such as the Uí Chonchobhair or the Uí Bhríain, yet it must be said that up until this point east Breifne had been something of a political backwater where few events noteworthy of the annalists' attentions occurred. The Uí Raghallaigh, whose power was concentrated in the area of Machaire Gailenga, north of Lough Ramor, had enjoyed a position of autonomy untroubled by interference from their Uí Ruairc overlords. In the second quarter of the twelfth century, Tíghernán O Ruairc sought to exploit the political fragmentation of the kingdom of Meath for his own advantage, and the Uí Raghallaigh resented the upsurge of interest in their lands, especially when they were faced with the possibility of their replacement as rulers in Machaire Gailenga by Tíghernán's son.[2] In 1155, Goffraidh O Raghallaigh staged a revolt but it was not until after the violent deaths of Goffraidh and his son Cathal na gCaorach that the uprising was finally quelled.[3] While their strategy had been unsuccessful, it is noteworthy that the first significant stirrings of the Uí Raghallaigh can be placed within the context of the attempts by the Uí Ruairc to establish greater control in Meath. Just over a decade after the suppression of the Uí Raghallaigh rebellion the Uí Ruairc's control in east Breifne was in turn to be successfully challenged from Meath. The first result of the Anglo-Norman arrival was to inject a new and much more turbulent element into Irish provincial geopolitics. Hugh de Lacy, who received a grant of the kingdom of Meath from Henry II in 1172, was anxious to end Tíghernán O Ruairc's influence both in Meath itself and on its borders.[4] The Uí Raghallaigh were initially sympathetic and they were amongst the few Irish families to remain loyal during the siege of Dublin by O Ruairc and Ruaidhrí O Conchobhair in 1171, when the future of the Anglo-Norman intervention in Ireland appeared fragile.[5] Once the Anglo-Normans had consolidated their control in Meath, such friendship evaporated, although historical details, either relating to internal developments in east Breifne or to its rulers' relations with the Anglo Normans, are scarce for this period. Fighting occurred between the Uí Raghallaigh and their western neighbours, the Uí Ruairc and the MagThighernáins, but no reference has survived of conflict further to the east.[6] As a consequence of its proximity to Meath, Breifne came within the sphere of influence of Hugh de Lacy, and at the time of his assassination in 1186 he was described by one annalist as king of Meath, Breifne and Uriel.[7] Ten years later, his son Walter received a grant of unspecified lands 'beyond the lakes of Therebrun'.[8]

It is unclear when the first Anglo-Norman presence was established in Cavan. However, the remains of mottes, probably dating from the last decade of the twelfth century, survive at Knockatemple and Moybolgue.[9] Following

Walter de Lacy's disgrace and forfeiture by King John in 1210 his lands were taken into the king's hands, and this may have been the occasion for the construction of further fortified sites at Kilmore and Belturbet.[10] The reaction of the Uí Raghallaigh to this is unknown, although in 1212 their leader was a prisoner of the seneschal of Meath.[11] Military conquest was not accompanied by settlement or colonisation; the land itself was too poor and unsuitable for cereal production and the establishment of manors. Yet these considerations did not preclude a desire to exert as much control over the area as possible.

In 1220, Walter de Lacy, following his rehabilitation, gained the submission of the Uí Raghallaigh and subsequently built a castle on an island in Lough Oughter.[12] Walter's place in Breifne was soon taken by his half brother, William 'gorm' de Lacy, who seldom acted in consort with Walter's wishes. In 1224, William launched a revolt in an attempt to pressurise Henry III to restore the earldom of Ulster to Walter's brother, Hugh, but when this collapsed he retreated to the fort of Lough Oughter. The Uí Raghallaigh, eager to exploit this situation to their advantage, co-operated with the royal army led by William Marshal the younger which captured William de Lacy and two years later, following Marshal's withdrawal, Cathal O Raghallaigh destroyed the de Lacys' stronghold at Kilmore.[13] This did not engender any response from the Anglo-Normans until 1233 when William 'gorm' de Lacy, apparently acting on his own initiative, launched an ill-fated invasion of east Breifne in which he was mortally wounded.[14] The Uí Raghallaigh's lands were subsequently left free from attempts at military conquest for well over a century and a half.

Having regained control of east Breifne, as well as neutralizing the threat from the Anglo Normans of Meath, Cathal O Raghallaigh and his brother Cú Chonnacht sought to reverse the historical domination of east by west Breifne through a conquest of the Uí Ruairc, a policy which was aided by the inability of Tíghernán's descendants to exercise control, even at a local level. The Uí Raghallaigh enjoyed the approval of Feidhlim O Conchobhair, king of Connacht, who considered them to be a buffer against Anglo-Norman penetration of the north-west of Ireland. During the 1230s the Uí Chonchobhair had witnessed the gradual erosion of their own territories by the Anglo-Normans, so that support from any quarter was invaluable. Within less than a decade this cordiality was reversed, in part due to Feidhlim's gradual replacement at the apex of his family by his belligerent son Aedh, who considered the Uí Raghallaigh as rivals to his own plans for west Breifne. The Uí Raghallaigh's strategic importance had also been called into question in 1250 by their assistance of the Anglo-Norman justiciar, Maurice fitz Gerald, in an attack on the Uí Conchobhair's allies, the Uí Néill of Tír Eoghan.[15]

Aedh O Conchobhair sought to resuscitate Uí Ruairc power in west Breifne while simultaneously undermining the control of the Uí Raghallaigh. The latter's alliance with fitz Gerald had understandably angered Brian O Néill of Tyrone and in 1255 he launched a series of punitive raids against east Breifne.[16]

Although this must be seen in the context of the alliance between the Uí Néill and Aedh O Conchobhair, it was significant as the first, though inconclusive, intervention in the affairs of the area by a powerful Ulster family. In the same year, O Conchobhair set up a rival puppet regime in east Breifne under Cathal O Raghallaigh's son, Conn.[17] Matters came to a head in the following year when O Conchobhair, assisted by Conchobhair O Ruairc, led an army into the Uí Raghallaigh's territory. In an engagement at Magh Slécht, Cú Chonnacht and Cathal na Beithigh O Raghallaigh, along with many other members of the sept were slain, owning to the failure to effect a rendezvous with the Anglo-Normans of Connacht.[18]

In the immediate aftermath of the battle, the Uí Ruairc regained the overlordship of the whole of Breifne with Aedh O Conchobhair's backing. Yet such control could only be ephemeral as east Breifne was too far away from the theatre of conflict in central Connacht, and Aedh O Conchobhair was satisfied to have eliminated the rivalry of the Uí Raghallaigh in order to turn his attention to his Anglo-Norman rivals. The battle of Magh Slécht, whilst delivering a cruel blow to the Uí Raghallaigh, had a much more important long-term result as it ended the latter's expansionism into west Breifne. Henceforth, the family's control was confined to eastern Breifne and the later medieval history of Breifne Uí Raghallaigh can be said to date from 1256. Breifne itself was to remain partitioned for the rest of the middle ages but at a theoretical level many chiefs of the Uí Raghallaigh and Uí Ruairc claimed to be lords of the whole of Breifne, but this had no practical significance.[19]

The late thirteenth century offered some hope for a revival of Uí Raghallaigh fortunes. On Aedh O Conchobhair's death in 1274 his family descended into internecine feuding from which they hardly ever emerged in the medieval period and consequently the position of their allies, the Uí Ruairc, was much weaker. Yet the renaissance of east Breifne was largely due to one personality; Giolla Iosa Ruadh O Raghallaigh, a grandson of Cathal na Beithigh and the son, though possibly illegitimate, of Domhnall ruadh who had died alongside his father at Magh Slécht.[20] On attaining the chieftainship in 1293 the most serious threat to his position came once again from Connacht in the form of the Clann Muircheataigh Uí Chonchobhair, the descendants of Muircheatach Muimhneach (died 1210), a brother of Ruaidhrí the 'last ard Rí'. They considered themselves to be the rightful rulers of Connacht, and the descendants of Cathal crobhdhearg, including Feidhlim and Aedh, as usurpers. After leaving the Uí Chonchobhair's territory in the mid thirteenth century they led an itinerant existence, receiving asylum from one ruler, only to be expelled when they had outstayed their welcome. Their political aspirations placed them perpetually at odds with the main sept of the Uí Chonchobhair, as well as making them an embarrassment to their erstwhile hosts.

In the 1280s they had found shelter amongst the Uí Ruairc who did not object to their presence for as long as their activities were directed against external targets. They also formed an alliance with the MagThíghernáins of

Teallach Dhonnchadh who lived immediately to the west of the Uí Raghallaigh. As a consequence Giolla Iosa ruadh's predecessor, Fearghal O Raghallaigh, had been compelled to move his residence from the vicinity of Drumlane to Tullac Mongain, although not even this was far enough away from the Clann Muircheataigh to escape attack.[21] In 1293, Fearghal was killed by one Mac an Mháighistir, a member of a cadet branch of the MagThíghernáins who was probably acting with the connivance of the Clann Muircheataigh, while five years later the Clann Muircheataigh slew Brian MagShamhradháin, chief of the Teallach Eachach.[22] For the next two decades their incursions preoccupied Giolla Iosa until in 1317 they were decisively beaten in a battle at Kilmore.[23] Having been expelled by the Uí Ruairc in 1340, they invaded east Breifne again in 1370 and 1391, but on both occasions they were defeated and expelled by the Uí Raghallaigh.[24]

Giolla Iosa's ability to withstand attacks on his western flank was partly due to the minimalization of hostilities along Breifne's eastern borders. This was achieved through the cultivation of links with one of the most powerful Anglo-Norman barons of the day, Sir Richard de Burgh, earl of Ulster who possessed a vague suzerainty over the Irish rulers of the north of the island. De Burgh did not attempt to conquer east Breifne and was content instead with recognition of his superior position from its chief, who was bound to maintain, at his own expense and on his own lands, a contingent of de Burgh's buanacht or household mercenaries.[25] In return, de Burgh prevented attacks on the Uí Raghallaigh and intervened on Giolla Iosa's behalf with the government of the Anglo-Norman lordship. When some of the Uí Raghallaigh were arrested for raids on Nobber in county Meath, de Burgh prevented their trial by the king's justices in Ireland, by stating that they were his men and should be tried before his palatine court of the earldom of Ulster.[26] This paternalistic relationship ended with de Burgh's death in 1326 as his heir, the so-called 'Brown Earl', was unable to maintain his grandfather's network of influence. Nevertheless Richard de Burgh's involvement with Breifne established a precedent which was to become a feature of the area's history in the fifteenth century whereby prominent Anglo-Norman noblemen utilised their influence within Breifne (and other Gaelic lordships) in order to consolidate their broader political prestige.

Contacts between Giolla Iosa and the Anglo Normans of Meath and Uriel occasionally assumed a more personal nature. Of his thirteen sons, one was named Risteard, no doubt in honour of Earl Richard de Burgh; another son, Roolbh, was probably named after Ralph Pettit, the Uriel landholder; a third son, Sefraidh, after Sir Geoffrey de Geneville, who had inherited half of the de Lacys' lands in Meath; while a fourth was called Teaboid, perhaps after Sir Theobald de Verdon, whose father John had inherited a portion of the remainder of the de Lacys' lands.[27]

In 1315, Giolla Iosa retired into the Franciscan friary in Cavan in whose foundation he had been instrumental fifteen years before and the chieftainship was then held successively by four of his sons.[28] Relationships between them became progressively more tense throughout the fourteenth century, as each of Giolla Iosa's sons were loath to see any of their brothers and their progeny establishing too tight a control over the chieftainship. In 1369, Pilib was deposed and imprisoned by his nephew Maghnus.[29] Pilib had antagonised a considerable number of his relatives through his involvement in the suspension of bishop Risteard O Raghallaigh, another nephew, who had earned the censure of the archbishop of Armagh for his complete disregard for the church's rules regarding clerical celibacy.[30] After a short time, he was restored to power through the military intervention of Pilib MagUídhir of Fermanagh who liberated him from his incarceration in Clogh Oughter castle.

East Breifne had traditionally belonged to the political sphere of Connacht, yet the assistance that Pilib's had received from Pilib MagUídhir signified a greater identification of the area with the Gaelic lordships of Ulster. The late seventeenth century text *The genealogical history of the O'Reillys* contains an apocryphal and inaccurate anecdote relating to the events of 1369–70 which reflects this movement, although it confuses MagUídhir with the leader of the Uí Néill. Pilib's son Seán, it claimed, was married to a daughter of O Ruairc and at the time of Pilib's deposition she advised her husband to seek assistance from her father. If O Ruairc was uncooperative he was then to turn to O Néill and if he proved more forthcoming Seán was to be free to take a new wife from that family.[31]

The internal dissensions amongst the Uí Raghallaigh were but one feature of the area's history in the mid fourteenth century and Giolla Iosa's sons, in defiance of the *détente* between their father and the Anglo Normans, took advantage of the latter's greater vulnerability to pursue a more belligerent course. Giolla Iosa's immediate successor, Maelsheachlainn, died of wounds received on a raiding expedition against the Anglo Normans of Meath.[32] In the mid fourteenth century north Leinster was suffering from the lack of a strong baronial presence. The de Lacys had died out in the male line in 1241. Their lands passed to the husbands of two heiresses, namely Geoffrey de Geneville and John de Verdon. In time their families also died out and the lands devolved to absentees who preferred the relative comfort of their English manors to the risks of defending their Irish lands and their tenants from attack.

Inhabitants of areas lying near to the lands of the Irish were occasionally kidnapped pending the payment of ransoms which their friends and relatives were becoming increasingly unable to pay. In 1393, the exchequer of the lordship itself had to make financial contributions towards these ransoms.[33] Apart from contributing on such occasions from their own depleted resources, the government could do little to help. When the Uí Raghallaigh's raids were accompanied by similar hostile activity by other Irish septs of the area, such as the Uí Fearghail and Uí Chonchobhair Failghi, the justiciar of the lordship led a small military contingent to the zone of conflict, as in 1350 when Sir Thomas de Rokeby succeeded in bringing Cú Chonnacht O Raghallaigh to the king's peace.[34] Yet once these forces were withdrawn there was nothing to prevent the resumption of hostilities.

The most concerted drive against the Anglo-Normans was led by the descendants of Mathghamhain, another son of Giolla Iosa, who had been killed in 1336.[35] These were not territorial re-conquests since they had not formed a part of the twelfth century kingdom of Breifne but lay instead within the territory of Conmhaicne and as such were included in the medieval diocese of that name. The *Genealogical history* claimed that Mathghamhain's son, Tomás, had been responsible for destroying no less than eighteen castles that had been built by the Tuites, but this was an exaggeration.[36] Conflict was but one aspect of the relationship between the Irish and Anglo-Normans. A seventeenth century manuscript written by the antiquarian, Dr Thomas Fitzsimons, outlines his descent from Richard fitz Symon, a scion of an Anglo-Norman family of Meath, who, following a domestic dispute settled in east Breifne where he became the *secretan* to the aforementioned Tomás.[37] Furthermore, the *Genealogical history* asserts that it was at the time of the deposition of Pilip O Raghallaigh that the fitz Symons first entered Breifne.[38] However, there is no contemporary corroboration for either of these accounts.

The Uí Raghallaigh were also assisted by the arrival of members of the Hiberno-Norse family of the Mac Cába. The first reference to them in Ireland is comparatively late, dating from 1358, when their leader was killed fighting for the MagUídhirs of Fermanagh.[39] Their move to east Breifne occurred in the following decades, probably as a direct result of Pilip MagUídhir's assistance in Pilib O Raghallaigh's restoration. They became staunch allies of the Clann Mathghamhain, whose raiding activities provided them with adequate wages. In 1413, their leader, Lochlann Mac Cába, was killed in an attack on Kells in which Tomás Og O Raghallaigh of the Clann Mathghamhain, brother of the then ruler of east Breifne, was badly wounded.[40] They did not fight exclusively for the rulers of east Breifne and in 1453 their leader was described as the constable of Breifne, Airghialla and Fermanagh.[41] However, after Enrí Mac Cába's death in Longford in 1460, he was buried in Cavan, and the annalists record that two hundred and eighty axe-carrying relatives attended the obsequies.[42]

The extent to which the Irish were able to recover lands from the Anglo-Normans, not only in north Leinster but throughout Ireland, precipitated a number of large-scale English expeditions in the later fourteenth century. The largest of these, led by no less a figure than the English king, Richard II, landed in Ireland in the autumn of 1394. While the two previous military interventions had attempted to physically chastise the Irish (as well as compel absentee landholders to return and defend their lands), Richard possessed a plan which, he hoped, would lead to a resolution of the tensions between the Irish and Anglo-Normans. English kings of the later middle ages held the title of lord of Ireland, and while their authority had never been accepted by all Irish chiefs, the king remained in theory the ruler of all

Ireland. Richard thus sought to make this title a reality and become lord of both the Anglo Normans and the Irish. The first step in this policy was the traditional utilisation of coercion against the Irish. Once they had been sub-dued they were required to swear their loyalty to the English king as their liege lord and refrain from further hostilities. Richard, for his part, undertook to protect them from unwarranted molestations by the Anglo Normans. Amongst those who submitted to Richard were Seán son of Pilib O Raghallaigh, chieftain of east Breifne and one Giolla Iosa, probably the head of the Clann Mathghamhain.[43]

Richard's plan did not succeed for a variety of reasons but in Ulster at least, its failure was due to a conflict of motives between the king and the earl of March, the man whom he had entrusted to govern Ireland when he re-turned to England in May, 1395. Sir Roger Mortimer, earl of March was one of the absentees landholders whom Richard had compelled to join him on his campaign. Through his grandmother he had inherited the title of earl of Ulster while he had also inherited the lands of the de Verdons in Meath and Uriel.[44] He was determined to recreate the power of his ancestors and to reassert control over those lands that had been conquered by the Irish since the death of Richard de Burgh in 1326. This policy placed him on a collision course with the Irish of Ulster, but more importantly they were also in clear opposition to the attempts by Richard II to create personal ties with the Irish chiefs.

In his dealings with east Breifne, Mortimer demonstrated a commitment to protecting the lands of the Anglo Normans in Meath and Westmeath, as well as the potential to exert military pressure upon the Uí Raghallaigh. In 1396, he caused a pass to be cut through the wooded areas on the borders between Meath and Breifne.[45] This was to facilitate the pursuit of raiders as well as to provide the means to execute military intervention in Uí Raghallaigh territory. He also rebuilt the castle at Finnea on the southern border of the lands of the Clann Mathghamhain which had been destroyed during the invasion of Edward Bruce in 1315.[46] These moves seemed to be precursors for an attack upon east Breifne in order to compel its rulers to make personal submissions to Mortimer. However, the Uí Raghallaigh were relatively unim-portant to Mortimer whose greatest quarrel lay with the Uí Néill of Tír Eoghain, who had benefited most in territorial and political terms from the extinction of the de Burghs in Ulster. In any event, the threat posed by Mortimer to Breifne disappeared when, in 1398, he was killed by the Irish of the Wicklow mountains, leaving a minor as his heir.

While Mortimer's plans did not come to fruition the events of the 1390s heralded a more interventionist policy by the government of the Irish lord-ship in the internal affairs of east Breifne. In 1400, a succession dispute broke out when Giolla Iosa O Raghallaigh died after having ruled for less than a month. One segment of the family favoured Maolmhórdha, brother of Maghnus O Raghallaigh who had overthrown Pilib in 1369, while others supported

Eoghan, Pilib's grandson, who was later nicknamed 'na féasóige'. As internal support was not forthcoming he sought military assistance from the Anglo Normans, but this was insufficient to overcome his rival, and he was forced into exile for seventeen years.[47] Maelmhórdha's successor was Risteard of the Clann Mathghamhain and it was not surprising that he pursued the traditionally belligerent attitude of his relatives to the Anglo Normans of Meath. This eventually forced the king's lieutenant in Ireland, Sir John Talbot, to launch an invasion of Breifne in 1418. A truce was established but on returning from the meeting Risteard was drowned in Lough Sheelin, thus providing the opportunity for Eoghan na féasóige to make a comeback, possibly with Talbot's support.[48]

Whilst the Clann Mathghamhain had demonstrated a historical antipathy towards the Anglo Normans, this was to change in the 1420s, for while Eoghan na féasóige had received assistance from the government of the lordship of Ireland he proved, on attaining power, that he was not bound by this earlier alliance. He launched raids on Kells and its environs while at the same time ignoring complaints from the archbishop of Armagh about an attack made by his relatives on the priory of Fore.[49] In 1428, Talhot again invaded east Breifne but on this occasion he was supported by the Clann Mathghamhain and the Mac Cába family. Eoghan's castle at Cavan was burned and he once again found that he was unable to muster enough support from within Breifne to guarantee his position, yet he was in no position to turn, as he had in the past, to the Anglo Normans for help. He therefore approached Eoghan O Néill, lord of Tír Eoghan, for assistance to defeat Talbot and retain control.[50] In the early fifteenth century the Uí Néill were busily extending their hegemony throughout southern Ulster and naturally such military assistance was provided on the understanding that Eoghan na féasóige would give support to the Uí Néill in the future.[51]

Eoghan na féasóige was an interesting figure amongst Irish rulers of the later middle ages. The ideal of chieftainship, as enunciated by the poets of the age, was that of a brave, reckless but generous warrior. Eoghan, by contrast, earned plaudits for his contribution to peaceful pursuits. Both the Breifne annals and the *Genealogical history* credit him with the enactment of statutes. Unfortunately, the content and nature of Eoghan's laws are not known and they may never have been committed to paper at all, but a late seventeenth century description of agricultural practices in county Westmeath mentions a custom used by the country people concerning the sharing of crops, which they called the law of 'Owen with the beard.'[52]

Eoghan may also have been instrumental in the establishment of a market at Cavan. The economy of much of Gaelic Ireland was pastoral and self-sufficient. However, trade links had always existed between the Gaelic and Anglo-Norman areas based on primary products such as timber and fish. In 1433, the parliament of the lordship of Ireland complained that the towns of Meath were losing trade to markets at Granard and Cavan, and the merchants of Meath and Uriel were subsequently forbidden from attending them and trading with these areas.[53] The products most likely sought by these merchants were hides and wool-fells and they may well have been cheaper than those on sale at markets closer to home. It is frustrating that we know so little about this market, its frequency, the nature of the vendors, and its relationship with the rulers of east Breifne, for it is very unlikely that it could have taken place without their permission, if not active support. Eoghan and his successors were probably the greatest beneficiaries of the market. Some Gaelic chiefs enjoyed a right of purveyance over products like hides, and these no doubt found their way onto the market earning the lord a handsome windfall.[54] Although we know nothing about the identities of the merchants attending, they no doubt included both Anglo Normans and Irishmen. In 1390, for example, Mathghamhain and Maelsheachlainn O Raghallaigh received a licence from the government of the lordship to trade within county Meath.[55] There is no evidence, however, that at this time the market was accompanied by a permanent urban settlement.

A related development was the appearance of 'O'Reillie's money'. These were counterfeited English groats produced in response to a shortage of coin affecting the whole of Ireland in the mid-fifteenth century. It is not unlikely that they were in circulation at the market of Cavan as they were in general currency throughout Ireland and in 1456 the parliament of the lordship prohibited their receipt.[56] Furthermore, it is unclear where they were 'minted' as the techniques employed to produce them were relatively simple, if not crude, involving the plating of copies of authentic groats or the soldering together of impressions made on silver foil of the obverse and reverse of genuine coins.[57] Although contemporaries were quick to associate these tokens with the Uí Raghallaigh, there is no proof that they were produced by them or indeed in their territory.

In spite of the more progressive elements in Eoghan na féasóige's activities, he was still faced with the traditional internal and external threats to his rule. In 1447, Eoghan's brother Feidhlim, who had remained loyal up until then, decided to make a bid for the chieftainship, prompted possibly by illness on Eoghan's part. He arranged to meet Sir John Talbot at Trim, no doubt to discuss future support, but on his arrival he was cast into prison. Trim was one of the most important centres of pilgrimage in later medieval Ireland as its Marian shrine attracted the faithful from both Anglo-Norman and Irish areas. It was also a very unhealthy place, for any epidemic caused an upsurge in the numbers of those seeking divine assistance, thus spreading the disease. Not surprisingly, Feidhlim died shortly after his arrest.[58]

Eoghan na féasóige died in 1449 and his death was followed by the almost predictable succession dispute.[59] Both parties turned to external allies to maximise their internal opportunities, thus emphasising the extent to which east Breifne had attained strategic importance. Domhnall O Néill supported Eoghan's son, Seán an Einigh while Fearghal O Raghallaigh of the Clann Mathghamhain once again gained the assistance of Talbot and the earl of Ormond. Although Fearghal and his allies were initially defeated he soon received the backing of a potentially more influential patron: Richard, duke of York. Richard had been appointed king's lieutenant in Ireland in an attempt to remove him from the English political arena where there were many who considered him to have a far better right to the English throne than the imbecilic Henry VI. Richard's claims to the English throne were based on his descent in the female line from Edward III but far more relevant to his involvement in Meath and east Breifne was the fact that he was also the heir to the Mortimers, earls of March and Ulster.[60]

Fearghal O Raghallaigh was amongst the many Irish chieftains of Ulster and Leinster who submitted to Richard soon after his arrival in August, 1449, presenting him with a gift of three hundred and sixty cows.[61] Such a local affair as a disputed succession was too insignificant to warrant large-scale intervention, and the duke of York, having established his power-base amongst a considerable section of the nobility of the Irish lordship, returned to England in August 1450 in order to pursue his struggle against the Lancastrians. Fearghal O Raghallaigh, having lost the support of Eoghan na féasóige's brother who had earlier supported him, was forced to submit to his rival Seán an Einigh, who sealed the humiliation by the payment of a symbolic gift or tuarastál.[62]

The late fifteenth and early sixteenth century again saw east Breifne caught between the more powerful families of Gaelic Ulster and the government of the Irish lordship. In 1452, James Butler, the fourth earl of Ormond, during a campaign in north Leinster, forced the submission of the Uí Raghallaigh and extracted an agreement from them to refrain from raids on the king's subjects.[63] As this was one of the last acts of the earl before his death, Seán O Raghallaigh was able to ignore the terms of his submission and resume his hostilities. These led eventually to his death in 1460 following an attack on Drogheda when he was overtaken and slain by its citizens.[64] The Breifne area itself was not immune from counterattacks and Seán's son Toirdhealbhach was the recipient of a raid launched by Deputy Lieutenant Tiptoft in 1468 which led to the burning both of the Uí Raghallaigh castle at Tullac Mongan and of the nearby friary.[65]

The Uí Néill had enjoyed preeminence amongst the Irish of Ulster for over a century and a half, but in the 1470s their position was challenged by Aedh ruadh O Domhnaill of Tír Conaill. In 1470 he led a sizeable army that included contingents led by Domhnall O Ruairc and Tomás MagUídhir into east Breifne where he planned to have his O Ruairc ally inaugurated as ruler of all Breifne at the site of Corann Crúachan. He was also able to count on the backing of Brian O Raghallaigh, a son of Feidhlimidh who had launched the ill-fated coup against his brother Eoghan na féasóige. In the event, Aedh ruadh's designs for O Ruairc floundered due to the opposition of the MagThíghernáins whose lands lay near to the inauguration site. Toirdhealbhach

O Raghallaigh also received support from an unspecified group of Anglo Normans.[66] Although the ceremonial aspects of Aedh O Domhnaill's scheme came to nothing his second intervention in Breifne five years later had a more practical result when Toirdhealbhach O Raghallaigh was 'reconciled with O Ruairc', a phrase which implied a forced submission not only to O Ruairc but to O Domhnaill, to whom he was forced to hand over a kinsman as a hostage.[67]

The squabbles within the Uí Raghallaigh were accompanied in the late fifteenth century by a growing assertiveness towards the cadet branches of the family. We have already mentioned the role played by the Clann Mathghamhain against the Anglo-Normans of Westmeath. Yet in the fourteenth and early fifteenth century they were still entitled to hold the chieftainship of east Breifne, but after the death of Risteard in Lough Sheelin in 1418 they were unable to regain it, although Risteard's son, Risteard Óg, held the largely symbolic title of tánaiste before his death in 1469.[68] Their exclusion was in no small part due to internal dissensions within the family which included the murder of Seán mac Thomáis O Raghallaigh by his brother Fearghal in 1427.[69]

The Clann an Chaoich, by contrast, had always been denied an opportunity to rule. They were, it will be remembered, the descendants of Niall an Chaoch who had been killed at the battle of Magh Slécht. Their lands lay along the border of Breifne with Meath and their geographical location had led to both fraternisation and conflict with the Anglo Normans. In the third quarter of the fifteenth century, the family of Conchobhair, a son of Seán an Einigh, settled on lands in the area. They refused, however, to pay any rent or tribute to the Clann an Chaoich and in the ensuing attempts by the latter to force the issue Conchobhair was killed. The Clann an Chaoich agreed to pay an eric or blood fine of 1800 cows to Toirdhealbhach O Raghallaigh and pledged the lands in the lower part of their territory for its payment. The fine was probably set at an impossibly high level, and the Clann an Chaoich lost half of their lands to the main branch of the Uí Raghallaigh on defaulting on the fine's payment.[70]

In the 1490s, another disputed succession allowed the intervention of external forces into east Breifne's internal affairs. Toirdhealbhach's successor, his son Seán, had died after only four years as lord.[71] His brother Cathal, not having enough backing within Breifne, sought assistance from Gerald fitz Gerald, earl of Kildare who was eager to extend his influence in Ulster. The earl had already demonstrated his interests in the area five years earlier when he gave military support to the descendants of Cú Chonnacht O Raghallaigh in their attempts to hold onto their lands.[72] No side was able to win a convincing victory and the hostilities dragged on for over three years, during which crops and livestock were destroyed with the attendant misery for the area's inhabitants. Finally, in 1494, Kildare and his local ally were decisively beaten by Cathal O Raghallaigh, Eoghan na féasóige's grandson.[73] Because of its strategic position between Ulster and north Leinster, control of east Breifne remained on the Geraldine agenda and in 1514, the ninth earl of Kildare, in a violent assault on Cavan killed Cathal's son and successor Aodh, his brother and the constable of the Mac Cába gallowglasses.[74] For well over a decade, the area was rent by factionalism and ephemeral alliances. In 1524, the sons of Seán mac Cathail whose brother had been killed by Kildare rebelled against Eoghan ruadh, his successor and imprisoned him.[75] When Con Bacach O Néill of Tír Eoghain sent an army to Cavan to avenge this the aforementioned Sliocht Sheáin mac Cathail received assistance from Kildare. In 1526, one of them, Fearghal, was imposed by Kildare as chief but internal opposition only took the form of complaints reported by the annalists that there were elder and better men who could have been chosen.[76]

The 1530s were dramatic for the history of Ireland, not least because the decade witnessed a successful strategy by the English crown which resulted in the destruction of the Geraldine nexus of influence. The Uí Raghallaigh for their part assisted these developments by establishing direct contact with the crown in the early 1530s in an attempt to free them from dependence on either O Néill or Kildare.[77] Fearghal's brother, Maolmhórdha who succeeded him on his death in 1536 thus initiated a policy of cooperation with the English government in Ireland, to the extent that they became one of the crown's most steadfast allies in Ulster in the mid sixteenth century.[78]

East Breifne can thus be viewed as a border area in a number of different contexts. Its position on the periphery of the Anglo-Norman lordship, while giving its rulers and their cadet branches the opportunities for hostile incursions and territorial aggrandisement, also left it vulnerable to counterattacks and military intervention, often in a deliberate attempt to interfere in its internal affairs. Its trading links with Meath, Louth and Dublin involved it, albeit tentatively, in a commercial network that spread throughout western Europe, so that whilst many parts of Connacht and Ulster were remote, east Breifne could be said to be amongst the least marginalised and isolated of the Gaelic Irish lordships.

The border between Breifne and the Anglo-Norman lordship was not impenetrable. We have seen how, in 1390, two members of the Uí Raghallaigh were granted a licence to trade in county Meath, while in September 1410 Cathair and his brother Cormac O Raghallaigh had been allowed to reside, free from harassment, 'in marchiis de Kenlys' with their families and goods.[79] Some Irishmen from east Breifne were able to pursue careers in the ecclesiastical world. In 1422, John O'Reilly was the prior of the Augustinian house of Kells while in 1503 the annals recorded the death of Pilib O Raghallaigh, described as 'abbot of Kells'.[80]

Instances of marriage between the Irish of Breifne and the Anglo-Normans were very rare in the fourteenth and fifteenth centuries. In 1405, the daughter of William Betagh of Moynalty married one Aedh O Raghallaigh.[81] Contacts between the Irish and Anglo-Normans could have their negative side, in that the Cavan area suffered from outbreaks of plague and disease which had originated further afield. Risteard O Raghallaigh may have died as a result of the Black Death.[82] In 1485, Feidhlim mac Glaisne O Raghallaigh died of an unidentified plague as did two members of the Clann Mathghamhain four years later.[83]

East Breifne's geopolitical situation also left it open to more subtle influences as embodied by the activity of Eoghan na féasóige, as well as by the possession of English and Norman French Christian names by members of the ruling élite. Much has been written about the 'Gaelicisation' of the Anglo Normans in Ireland, through the use of Irish as a vernacular, the adoption of Irish customs and costume and the employment of members of the Gaelic professional classes such as poets and brehons. However the experience of east Breifne hints that this cultural traffic was not always one-way.

Markets were not common in Gaelic areas, although this reflected a situation where most goods were produced domestically. Few other Irish rulers made laws, but even fewer lived by the archaic and pedantic strictures of the brehon law. Furthermore, even a tentative association with the production or circulation of currency was a novelty. The background to the establishment of the market at Cavan is unknown, but it no doubt sprang from an attempt by the local rulers to exploit an opportunity that had presented itself. The Uí Raghallaigh were good at grasping such opportunities, as the rulers of such an area had to be. Indeed, their very emergence onto the stage of history as rulers of a semi-independent lordship was conditioned by their willingness to use the Anglo-Norman newcomers to throw off the yoke of domination by the Uí Ruairc of west Breifne.

While pointing to the unique features of the lordship of east Breifne it is important to remember that the area and its rulers possessed similarities with other Gaelic lordships. The Uí Raghallaigh were not unique in having to deal with the Anglo-Norman newcomers, yet the Mac Murchadha of Leinster and the Uí Bhriain of Thomond, to name but two, were far more successful in the long-term, in redrawing the boundaries of their spheres of influence to their own advantage. The Uí Raghallaigh were also afflicted, in common with most other Gaelic lordships of the latter middle ages, by a chronic instability of political power which was a result of the lack of clear precedents of dynastic succession. We have seen how the activities of as far-seeing a personage as Eoghan na féasóige were put in jeopardy at his death by the almost routine succession dispute. In this respect the geographical proximity of Cavan to Dublin and the lands of the Anglo Normans facilitated intervention on such occasions.

Examinations of border areas such as medieval Cavan can help to elucidate elements in the relationship between the Irish and Anglo Normans which are too easily ignored in studies which take as their subject a broader geographical area.

The Anglicisation of East Breifne: The O'Reillys and the Emergence of County Cavan

BERNADETTE CUNNINGHAM

The 'new made county of Cavan', formed in 1579 out of the territory traditionally known as east Breifne, was symbolic of the changing nature of political power and social organisation in this south Ulster region during the sixteenth century. From before the middle of the sixteenth century, the Dublin government had taken a significant interest in the affairs of Ulster as it attempted to establish political and social stability in the area. The main strands of administrative reform included promoting the common law as a means of resolving disputes, encouraging native lords to hold their lands by English tenure and to adopt primogeniture inheritance as the principle of political succession, and seeking to fund the administration of the region through taxation paid to the crown.[1] The impact of official government-sponsored intervention on the politics of east Breifne was largely determined by the nature of the pre-existing political and social relationships there. A complex web of alliances linking the lordship of the O'Reillys of east Breifne with their near neighbours the O'Rourkes, O'Farrells, and Mac Mahons and also with the influential O'Neill and O'Donnell overlordships,[2] formed the framework within which the policies of the Dublin government necessarily operated.

As P.J. Duffy and Ciaran Parker have already indicated, the unique location of the territory of the O'Reillys, bounded by the three provinces of Ulster, Leinster and Connacht, gave its inhabitants a wide choice of potential allies who could be called upon in support of particular political objectives. Because of the ease with which disaffected individuals from among the O'Reillys could call on outside assistance in support of their cause, internal rivalries could be particularly disruptive in east Breifne. The consequence of such disputes was that a range of external political groupings came to have an interest in the internal politics of the O'Reillys. Simultaneously, the strategic position of east Breifne in the buffer zone between the English of the Pale and the Gaelic lordships of the north and north west, meant that the O'Reillys and other families in east Breifne were drawn in as participants in political disputes between the Pale and the provinces, over issues which were not necessarily of direct concern to themselves. Indeed it could be argued that

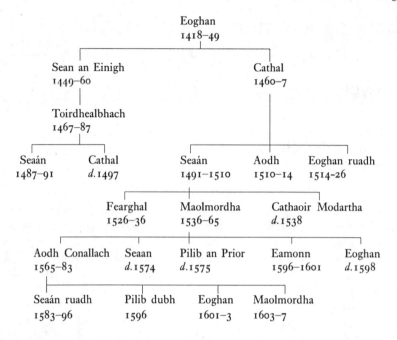

O'Reillys of East Breifne, 1418–1607

much of the eagerness of the Dublin government to control affairs in east
Breifne were motivated by Dublin's desire to establish effective jurisdiction in
parts of the province of Ulster to the north of the O'Reilly territory.

Developments within the Gaelic lordship of east Breifne in the course of
the sixteenth century influenced the formation of county Cavan, as factions
within the O'Reilly lordship allied themselves with the Dublin government in
opposition to local political rivals. The story of the emergence of the county
is the story of rivalries within the O'Reilly lordship over political control of
the territory; it is also the story of the involvement of outside powers, whether
O'Donnells, Maguires, Mac Mahons, O'Neills, the Anglo Irish of the Pale, or
the Dublin government. The concerns of more powerful Ulster lordships,
especially those of the O'Neills and O'Donnells had particular significance for
the fate of the O'Reillys, constraining their choices of potential allies, setting
boundaries on their political objectives, even influencing the type of warfare
to which the O'Reillys could resort. At the close of the sixteenth century, the
nine years war proved catastrophic for the leading families of the O'Reillys,
and in the early seventeenth century the gradual process of anglicization
which had been underway gave way to a more traumatic process of plantation,
which left the O'Reillys of east Breifne with little control over the direction of
political change.

I

In the early sixteenth century, the way the O'Reilly lordship functioned was in many ways typical of Gaelic society. The term lordship was not merely a geographical expression, but denoted a particular concept of government, involving quasi independent territories over which a lord exercised jurisdiction in military, legal, economic and even, to an extent, in religious matters. A small hereditary elite, drawn from a core kin group, exercised control over the remainder of the inhabitants of the lordship. The chief of a Gaelic lordship was lord of a people rather than of a given extent of land, for land without people to work it was of little value.[3] Any economic surplus generated was normally channelled into the chief's household. A lord's followers were important because they were the source of his political strength. In 1553 the chief of the O'Reillys was described as being able to muster 400 horsemen, 1000 kerne and 200 gallowglas; a significant local force.[4] In return for military service, a lord's followers could expect to be defended in time of war, and to be provided with arbitration in case of disputes. If such were not forthcoming, people could readily defect to another lord.

Given that the lordship was organised so that political and economic benefits accrued to the dominant lord, the selection of a lord was almost inevitably a contentious issue.[5] In the absence of a system of primogeniture inheritance, the man chosen as lord from within a particular kin group was usually selected on the basis of his military prowess and his ability to attract and sustain followers. On the death of a chief, the man's brothers uncles and sons could all legitimately contend for the position of chief. In some lordships there was little controversy, a clear leader emerging without much contest. East Breifne in the early sixteenth century, however, is a good example of the kind of repeated contentious disputes over political succession which could occur within the Gaelic political system. Such disputes undermined the political stability of the lordship and left it particularly vulnerable to outside interference.

The controversies recorded in the early sixteenth century annals which involved the O'Reillys were sometimes centred in neighbouring lordships such as the territory of the Mac Mahons,[6] Maguires,[7] and O'Donnells.[8] The participants were sometimes closer to home, involving the Magaurans,[9] whose territory lay within east Breifne in the region which became known as the barony of Tullyhaw. Frequently, however, the issues in dispute were internal to the O'Reilly kin group, as in the succession controversies recorded by the annals of the Four Masters in 1492, 1512, 1524, and 1526. In such circumstances it was usual for other lordships to become drawn into the dispute.

Following the death, in 1491, of Seaán son of Toirdhealbhach, the chief of the O'Reillys, his successor, Seaán son of Cathal was challenged by another Cathal, brother of the dead chief. In this dispute Cathal enlisted the aid of the Mac Mahons in support of his challenge to the principal claimant to the position of chief of the O'Reillys.[10] Further controversies involving Mac Mahons and O'Reillys on opposing sides were recorded by the annalists in 1506 and 1510. In 1506, when Hugh Roe, son of Glasny Mac Mahon was slain by O'Reilly (Seaán son of Cathal), and his sons, it is likely that O'Reilly was the aggressor.[11] A corresponding incident in 1510 resulted in the killing of Brian, son of Philip O'Reilly, by the sons of Redmond son of Glasny Mac Mahon. The annalist noted that Brian O'Reilly was killed 'while in pursuit of a prey', indicating that the Mac Mahons were not the aggressors.[12]

A more serious incursion into O'Reilly territory was recorded in 1514 when Gerald Fitzgerald, the new ninth earl of Kildare, led an expedition into east Breifne during which fourteen of the principal men of the O'Reillys were killed, including Aodh, son of Cathal, chief of the O'Reillys (1510–14), his brother Pilib, and his son also named Pilib. The Mac Cabe clan also suffered at Kildare's hand on that occasion with the capture of Maine, son of Mahon Mac Cabe. This onslaught, the resumption of an offensive by the previous earl of Kildare in Ulster, must have seriously weakened the principal sept of the O'Reillys.[13] However, it was an internal dispute ten years later which the annalist recorded as causing the desolation of all Breifne.

In 1524, two years before Eoghan ruadh, chief of the O'Reillys died, his son Cathal crubach was taken prisoner by his cousins, the sons of Eoghan ruadh's eldest brother Seaan. It is evident that despite the intervention of Con O'Neill, Seaán's sons had the strength to enforce their ambition to regain the chiefdom of east Breifne, and in 1526, the eldest of them, Fearghal succeeded his uncle, Eoghan ruadh, as chief of the O'Reillys. Fearghal achieved this position with outside assistance in opposition to senior contenders from among the O'Reillys.[14] Although the Annals of the Four Masters seemed to disapprove of his success against his seniors in 1526, Fearghal's obituary ten years later described him as a generous, potent, upright and truly hospitable man. This characterisation by the early seventeenth-century Franciscan compilers of the Annals of the Four Masters, along with the statement that he died after receiving the sacraments may have been influenced by O'Reilly support for the Observantine friars in Cavan.[15] The Four Masters' further description of him as Lord of Hy-Briuin and Conmaicne implying that his jurisdiction extended over the territories of west Breifne, and over the Mac Rannells of Conmaicne, was aspirational rather than a reflection of the political realities of the 1530s, by which time O'Reilly power had permanently retracted from Connacht.

Fearghal O'Reilly's four legitimate sons were not serious contenders for the position of chief in 1536 and he was succeeded by his own brother, Maol Mordha, who remained as chief of the O'Reillys for almost thirty years, allowing a generation of respite from the destructive succession disputes which had bedeviled east Breifne over the previous fifty years.[16]

This did not mean that Maol Mordha O'Reilly's years as chief of the O'Reillys were an era of peace. In 1537 the annalists recorded the death of

Brian son of Fearghal O'Reilly, at the hands of the English lord justice's men, who were described as aggressors in the Clan Mahon territory in the south west of the lordship. In a separate incident in the same year, Cathair Modartha, younger brother of the O'Reilly chief, was killed by the English.[17] A more serious escalation of the conflict between the O'Reillys and the English authorities occurred in 1552 as part of a broader offensive in Ulster by the Dublin government. On this occasion the O'Reillys were judged by the annalists to have offered effective military resistance to the aggressors, although the English administrators considered that they had imposed unprecedented order on the O'Reilly territory by 1553.[18]

The politics of the Clan Mahon region, in the southern part of east Breifne, as they developed over time, were more complex than the headlines of the annals reveal. The rivalries between the O'Reillys of Clan Mahon and their kinsmen further north, have been investigated by K.W. Nicholls. He has shown that this sept, descended from Mathghamhain O'Reilly (*d.*1327), after a period of political influence, found themselves excluded from having a serious claim to the lordship of east Breifne by the late fifteenth century. Their position declined further in the course of the sixteenth century as the sons of the ruling chief, Fearghal O'Reilly, and the sons of his brother and successor, Maol Mordha, began to exert influence in Clan Mahon. The decline in the political influence of the decendants of Mathghamhain O'Reilly illustrates a trend frequently discernible in the Gaelic political system where loss of eligibility for the position of chief of the lordship was followed by further political decline, as the sons of reigning chiefs sought to exert control in peripheral areas.[19]

The turbulent political history of the contenders to the position of O'Reilly in the first half of the sixteenth century and the declining fortunes of the Clan Mahon sept, was not unusual as a brief examination of the experience of the Magaurans, another of the smaller Gaelic septs within the east Breifne lordship, reveals. In the late fifteenth century, the Magauran territory in Tullyhaw was the target of attack by Toirdhealbhach, son of Seaán who was chief of the O'Reillys. An attack on Ballymagauran in 1485 was avenged immediately by Magauran and his followers who claimed to have killed or imprisoned sixteen of the O'Reillys and captured 200 horses.[20] Subsequent hostilities involving both Magaurans and O'Reillys which are recorded in the annals, the killing of Cathal son of Melaghlin Dubh Magauran in 1502 for instance, were in the context of internal rivalries among the Magaurans, where the O'Reillys were called upon in support of one faction. More localised internal disputes among the Magaurans were recorded in 1494, 1496 and 1512.[21] On occasion, the Maguires rather than the O'Reillys were drawn into the affairs of the Magaurans. The long term result of these disputes within the Magauran kin group was a decline in their political status. By the middle of the sixteenth century they had ceased to be politically significant in Breifne, and their traditional territory in the barony of Tullyhaw was among the lands deemed to be under the direct jurisdiction of Seaán [Sir John] O'Reilly by 1584.[22] The changing nature of the relationship between the Magaurans and the O'Reillys conforms to a pattern frequently discernible in Gaelic society where weaker political groups were effectively absorbed by stronger powers.[23]

II

In the wider political world, the interests of the O'Neills and O'Donnells formed an important aspect of the increasingly complex network of alliances affecting east Breifne by the middle of the sixteenth century. The O'Reillys had long tried to balance the claims of these two rivals who sought to claim rights of overlordship in Breifne. Resisting the advances of one overlord frequently necessitated becoming reliant on another, and the O'Reillys sometimes resorted to accepting the support of the earls of Kildare in resisting their powerful northern neighbours. After the decline of Kildare influence, some factions of the O'Reillys tried to use the influence of English lords deputy of Ireland to undermine the recurrent claims of the O'Neills to overlordship in east Breifne. The Dublin government's determination to curb the power of O'Neill meant that bolstering the ability of O'Reilly to withstand O'Neill's aggressions was seen as politically expedient by Elizabethan administrators. Thus, for strategic reasons, contacts between the O'Reillys of east Breifne and the Dublin government increased as the sixteenth century progressed, with significant implications for the east Breifne lordship.[24]

Within Gaelic society it was normal for alliances to be forged with external groups in support of local ambitions. There was always the risk, however, that those external powers might be the ultimate beneficiaries in what had originated as an internal power struggle. The Dublin government was one of those external agencies who was in a position which allowed it to be drawn into the politics of east Breifne in the course of the second half of the sixteenth century. The long term consequence of that development was that the political power of the O'Reillys was ultimately absorbed by the greater power of the Dublin government. One of the intriguing questions about the history of Gaelic societies in the sixteenth century is whether interventions by Elizabethan administrators in local affairs were perceived to be qualitatively different from interventions by other overlords. To what extent was support received from the Dublin administration perceived to be different from support received from O'Neill or O'Donnell? To what extent was involvement by representatives of the crown in the affairs of the O'Reillys seen to be different from the involvement of the O'Reillys in the political concerns of smaller septs? Each political transaction had its price as well as its reward, and the evidence of interaction between individual groups of the O'Reillys and the Dublin government, whether in surrender and regrant, composition deals, requests for land grants, or requests for pardons, suggests that the O'Reillys were well aware of the nature of the transactions they negotiated. It was not often possible, however, to predict the longer term consequences of such arrangements.

In seeking to enhance their local political and economic power, the O'Reillys forged alliances with neighbouring families and these included the Anglo Irish of the Pale to the south of their territory. There is no evidence that the O'Reillys were here embarking on a conscious strategy of integration with Anglo Irish families as a means of making themselves more acceptable to the Dublin government. As Ciaran Parker's essay suggests, it would be more accurate to say that the ethnic distinction between the O'Reillys and the families of Meath had long since been blurred, even though the reports of English officials on the interaction between the O'Reillys and the Pale tended to highlight differences between those who lived under Gaelic law and those who lived within the Pale. Government reports concentrated on the threat posed to the economic possessions of Anglo-Irish communities living in the Pale who were perceived as targets for plunder in the O'Reillys' quest for enhanced economic status. By the 1550s, such incursions into the Pale were liable to prompt retaliation from the Dublin government. While acts of aggression did occur, usually perpetrated by disaffected younger sons, that was only part of the relationship between Breifne and the Pale. There were long established contacts between Breifne and the Pale at all sorts of levels—trade, religion, the law. These connections operated independently of the promptings of the Dublin government for the most part. There was a traditional association with Trim in county Meath as a place of pilgrimage for the people of Breifne in the medieval period which survived into the sixteenth century.[25] The abbots of the Augustinian monastic house at Kells in county Meath were regularly supplied by the O'Reillys in the late fifteenth century.[26] Interaction between Breifne and the Pale was also evident in the significant merchant traffic which evolved. The Mac Bradys, a Gaelic merchant family, who owned one of the two principal castles in the town of Cavan in the sixteenth century were active in trading with the Pale. Cavan town had been a prosperous market before the end of the fifteenth century and the existence of 'O'Reilly's money' must have been a product of that trade. The very existence of the town of Cavan, an urban centre untypical of the economy of Gaelic Ireland, was itself an indication of the impact of the proximity of the Pale on the economic life of Breifne.[27] The economy of the region was thereby linked to the urban network of north Leinster which also included Ardee, Kells and Drogheda. Intermarriage between the O'Reillys and Anglo Irish families from north Leinster was not unusual in the later sixteenth century. Three of the sons of Maol Mordha, chief of the O'Reillys from 1536 to 1565, were married to women from the Pale. Sinead Betagh, first wife of Aodh Conallach, died in 1560. He subsequently married Mary Nugent, a daughter of Sir Thomas Nugent, and thirdly Isabella Barnewall of Trimleston. Pilib an Prior was married to a daughter of Christopher Nugent, baron of Delvin. A third brother, Eamonn, married Mary Plunkett, daughter of Robert, Baron Dunsany, and secondly Elizabeth Nugent, daughter of the baron of Delvin. One of the daughters of Maol Mordha O'Reilly was also married to a Plunkett, while the husbands of the remaining daughters were chosen from Ulster families. This level of marriage connections with families from the Pale may have been particularly prevalent among the dominant branch of the O'Reillys, and those social connections coupled with economic ties were significant for the direction of political development in Cavan.[28]

While the O'Reillys and other Cavan families looked south to the Pale as much as they looked north to Ulster, so also did some Anglo-Irish families in Meath and Westmeath look to Cavan as an area where they could profitably do business. The Nugents, barons of Delvin provide one sixteenth century example of how a family from the Pale could have extensive speculative land interests in both Cavan and Longford. Delvin was particularly successful in acquiring property in the barony of Clanmahon. O'Reilly jurisdiction in the region was disputed, allowing Delvin scope to profit from the lack of political control.[29] Delvin's interests may have been primarily economic, but successive barons of Delvin were in reality the local face of the English administration in the region. For their own political reasons, the barons of Delvin were anxious to show their support for the Dublin administration through military service in the localities. In 1535, for example, the then Baron Delvin was in the service of Sir William Skeffington defending the northern boundary of the Pale, specifically Trim, Kells and Navan.[30] English sources for the mid-1530s reveal that the O'Reillys too were supporting Sir William Skeffington in his opposition to the troublesome O'Connors of Offaly.[31] But it was the barons of Delvin who were most regularly called on to police the north midlands on behalf of the Dublin government.[32] Much of the interaction between the barons of Delvin and other Pale families and the O'Reillys was amicable and sometimes mutually beneficial, but the possibility of conflict in the fluid political situation of the sixteenth century was ever present. A dispute between the O'Reillys and the baron of Delvin in 1566 'respecting titles and demands between them and their countries' was arbitrated on by the lord deputy, Sir Henry Sidney, who insisted that O'Reilly should abide by the decisions of the lord deputy's commissioners.[33]

In 1553, in his role as commissioner, Sir Thomas Cusack's immediate concern in dealing with the O'Reillys was to curb their incursions into the Pale, where the property of the Plunketts had been a prime target. Cusack claimed to have achieved his aim of having the O'Reillys make restitution for the thefts they had carried out over the previous six years. Encouraged by his unprecedented, if short-lived, success in promoting reform among the O'Reillys, Cusack philosophised that

> the like hath not been that a man of such power as he is of, would redeliver without greater circumstance do the same, whereby it appeareth

that the poor and simple people be as soon brought to good as evil, if they were taught accordingly; for hard it is for such men to know their duties to God and to the king when they shall not hear preaching or teaching throughout all the year to edify the poor ignorant to know his duty.[34]

Neither the larger issue of the appropriate education of the Irish nor the more immediate problem of incursions by dissident members of the O'Reillys into the Pale were permanently resolved by Cusack, however. Subsequent lords deputy continued to concern themselves with the problem, and Sir Henry Sidney's indenture with Hugh and Edmund O'Reilly in 1566 included a clause that:

O'Reilly promises to dwell on the borders of this country and of the English parts, at the pleasure of the lord deputy during the war and rebellion of his brothers and John O'Neyll, in order that the English parts may be secured by his protection against the said rebels.[35]

When in the 1580s Sir John Perrott was reflecting on the reasons for the formation of the county of Cavan, he cited the spoils of the Pale as the principal explanation. Thus, the establishment of a county administration was perceived by the Dublin government as a way of controlling the unruly provinces through the implementation of 'good government'.[36]

III

While theoretical issues underpinning the Elizabethan government's reform strategies occasionally surfaced, administrators were more often pragmatists, seeking to achieve progress wherever feasible. All parties recognised the strategic significance of east Breifne, not least the Dublin administration. Recognising the near insurmountable difficulties in attempting to extend government control over the whole of Ireland, there was a concern that at the very least, the English of the Pale should be protected from attack from their Irish neighbours. Since the O'Reilly territory bordered on the Pale, the maintenance of peace and good order there was a primary concern. Anglicisation was seen as a key to the promotion of political stability which would bring peace there.

One of the developments which distinguished the sixteenth century from the medieval period was the new dynamism with which successive English chief administrators sought to change the political structures of Gaelic Ireland, which they perceived to be a source of strife. From the 1540s onwards, a dominant theme was that of the English administration's concern to negotiate agreements with the various Gaelic lords which would transform the

Gaelic lordships and the war lords who were their chiefs into English style landlords who held their land peaceably from the crown. This was the strategy now usually referred to as surrender and regrant. By 1562 the question of securing agreements with a number of individual Ulster lords, principally O'Donnell, O'Reilly and Maguire was being actively pursued. Queen Elizabeth's instructions to the earl of Sussex, lord lieutenant of Ireland, in July 1562 explained what was intended.

> You shall endeavour to stay O'Donnell, O'Reilly and Maguire in an assured opinion of our favour towards them for the advancing of them to honour ... and therefore to devise with them to repair hither and receive their lands from us as our gift, in such sort as the earls of Clanricard and Thomond did in our father's time.[37]

This strategy was designed to remove the need for the confrontational politics of the Gaelic system of tanistry, and replace it with English style landownership and inheritance structures. In theory, if the occasion for military confrontation could be removed by settling the method of succession, then Gaelic society could be demilitarised, and would be less of a threat to peace in the English areas of the country. Instead of the leader being selected on the basis of his being the most powerful eligible male, and that man having power vested in him by the freeholders of the lordship, the English system was one where the principal lord's authority was underpinned by his holding his land by grant from the crown. On his death a lord was to be succeeded by his eldest son, or in some cases another individual selected by prior agreement. The full implications of the surrender and regrant strategy were not realised for some considerable time, but it was a policy which continued to be pursued throughout the sixteenth century in various guises.

In the lordship of Breifne, the plan was to offer the chief of the O'Reillys the title of earl, and to encourage him to surrender his lands to the crown and received a grant of them valid in English law. His creation as earl was to be done with due pomp and ceremony. Sussex reported in July 1561 on the arrangements then in progress. The 'robes, collars and coronets' for O'Reilly and O'Donnell were ready, he recorded.[38] Evidently their appointment as earls was to be accompanied by the sort of trappings and ceremonies which might have been part of the investiture of a Gaelic lord. At any rate the English were aware of the need to recognise the concept of honour within Gaelic society.

The difficulty with the strategy of persuading lords to surrender their lands to the crown and to accept a regrant of those lands from the Queen, was that the O'Reillys could not be dealt with in isolation. Other Ulster lords, not least O'Neill, had to be dealt with also. Ciaran Brady's detailed analysis of the 'surrender and regrant' process in Breifne has illustrated the gradual realisation, by the parties concerned, of the difficulties inherent in the surrender and regrant scheme in the middle decades of the sixteenth century. The transformation from a Gaelic lordship system to an English style of political organisation and landownership could not be achieved in the short term. Furthermore, for surrender and regrant to be truly effective it had to be implemented on virtually a countrywide basis, so that those who adopted an innovative anglicised form of political organisation and inheritance would not be at a disadvantage as compared with those who continued to promote traditional Gaelic political strategies.[39] However, by its very nature 'surrender and regrant' arranagements comprised individually negotiated deals with particular lords drawn up as opportunities arose. The difficulty inherent in the scheme was that given the fragmented structure of Gaelic lordship society, the opportunity for a countrywide programme of surrender and regrant type agreements was not going to arise.

This is not to say that the English administration did not think in terms of grand plans, for such schemes existed at least in outline. One plan in the early 1560s was to divide the country into six regions, Ulster, Connacht, upper and nether Munster, Leinster and Meath, and there were to be provincial presidents in the various provinces.[40] Breifne had traditionally been considered part of Connacht, but for English administrative purposes it was to be excluded from the jurisdiction of the Connacht presidency. In keeping with a long standing view of the Dublin administration, it was also considered that O'Reilly should not be under the jurisdiction of any Ulster governor; evidence of the concern by the English administration that the O'Reillys should be supported in their attempt to maintain their independence from the overlordship of the O'Neills:

> O'Reilly, bordering upon Meath, and lying by situation of his country unfit for any of the other governments, is to be under the order of the principal governor, only he doth offer to give up his Irish tenure and to receive state tayly at the Queen's hands, with the creation of an earl, which were good to be received, and such services and duties to be reserved in the state as to the Queen's Majesty shall be thought fit which be to be levied and answered into the exchequer by order from the principal governor with 360 li for the bonnaght of the Gallowglas to be put upon him.[41]

Provincial presidencies were established in Connacht in 1569 and in Munster shortly afterwards, and remained in place in those provinces for the next 100 years.[42] Plans for an Ulster presidency were never brought to fruition, because of the Dublin government's failure to come to terms with the power of O'Neill in Ulster. Progress was made in the south of the province, towards establishing an English style system of government, when east Breifne was designated as the county of Cavan in 1579.[43] Soon afterwards a sheriff and other minor officials were appointed.[44] Although the practical implications of the move were negligible in the short term, by 1585 all of Ulster had been divided into counties, and plans to implement English common law procedures in the province were being discussed. That a treatise of 1586 called for these counties to be 'as well brought to the nature as to the name of shires' indicated that in practice the county administration had not yet begun to match the theoretical blueprint.[45] Some progress was achieved and Cavan was one of the counties in which the appointment of minor government officials such as sheriffs made some impact. In 1586, Archbishop Long of Armagh noted the enthusiasm of the inhabitants of Cavan for English law.[46] Given the long tradition of interaction with the Pale, at an economic, cultural and social level, the blending of different legal and cultural systems was not new to Breifne. A gradual process of anglicization was reinforced by more formal networks of government officials from the 1580s onwards, and occasionally, when the time was right, there was more direct intervention by the state in the affairs of the O'Reilly lordship.

The Dublin administration took measures to ensure that their attempts to deal with the rebellion of the troublesome Shane O'Neill in 1566 was not complicated by disturbances in Breifne. In November 1566, Aodh Conallach [Hugh] O'Reilly and his brother Eamonn [Edmond], were party to an agreement with the lord deputy, Sir Henry Sidney, that they would guard the border between Breifne and the Pale 'to protect the English parts against the rebels' who included O'Reilly's brothers, as well as Shane O'Neill.[47] Again in the autumn of 1579 the inhabitants of the Pale were faced with renewed threats from Ulster, this time from Turlough Luineach O'Neill. The newly formed county of Cavan was under threat from Turlough Luineach at the same time.[48] In such circumstances, it was not unusual for one faction of the O'Reillys to side with the O'Neills while another group sided with the Dublin government.[49] The objective of the Dublin government was to harness the assistance of those of the O'Reillys who had expressed loyalty to the Dublin government, in their opposition to O'Neill. The O'Reillys were fully aware of both the risks and the opportunities of their position. Each faction within the O'Reillys was a potential ally and also a potential enemy of both O'Neill and the Dublin government. On 3 September 1580 for example, Aodh Conallach O'Reilly sent evidence to the lord deputy, Arthur Grey, of his invitation to join forces with the 'rebel' O'Neill. O'Reilly accompanied this evidence with assurances that he would not join O'Neill and requested assistance.[50] His faction of the O'Reillys succeeded in winning the sympathy of Sir Nicholas Malby, who described O'Reilly in 1581 as 'the best Irish subject in the land' and expressed concern for the losses O'Reilly had suffered at the hands of Conn O'Neill.[51]

IV

The death of Aodh Conallach, chief of the O'Reillys, in 1583 prompted a succession crisis in Breifne. It also created an opening which the English administration sought to profit from. The man who died, known to the English as Sir Hugh O'Reilly,[52] had left four younger brothers along with four legitimate and at least seven illegitimate sons. His brother Eamonn was the taniste, and believed he was therefore entitled to succeed to the title of chief of the O'Reillys. Aodh Conallach's eldest legitimate son, Seaán ruadh, was the heir approved under the English common law system of primogeniture inheritance.[53] Despite some doubts, it was his candidacy which the English administration chose to support, as opposed to the claims of his uncle, Eamonn.[54] The third contender for the lordship was Seaán's younger brother, Pilib dubh, who had proved his abilities as a military style leader in the native Irish tradition during Aodh Conallach's last years. As recorded by contemporary commentators in the form of bardic poetry,

> He caused great burning throughout a land, thus was peace enforced, as a result of Pilib's deeds in battle, others do not seek restitution of their losses from him.

This poem, 'Ní ar aois meadhaighthear mac ríogh' [It is not age which is the measure of the successor of the king] was probably composed in 1583 when the O'Reilly succession was in dispute.[55] The poem stressed that 'virtue' and 'action' rather than age were the criteria which should influence the choice of leader. Under Gaelic law and custom, this was traditionally the case. And Pilib was reported to have proved his worth by his actions: 'a king who had been a vigorous warrior is put to shame in battle by your challenge'. This was probably a reference to Pilib's successes against the O'Neills, as recorded in the annals of Loch Cé for 1581: 'Philip son of Aodh O'Reilly, i.e. son of the O'Reilly, with his kinsmen and followers came up with them; and John Óg, the son of O'Neill, was killed there, and O'Neill's other son was taken prisoner, and four of his good cavalry were killed there also.'[56]

In another poem of about the same date, Pilib was described as the Cu Chulainn of Connacht, and drawing on the traditional image of the lord as spouse of his lordship, the poet claimed that Connacht

> hopes to be wooed by that son of O Raghallaigh,
> and Ireland wishes for the lips of a spouse,
> they always choose the younger.[57]

Although the O'Reillys influence in Connacht was no longer a reality when this poem was composed, the poet was not just recounting irrelevant tales of old. The audience for this poem would have known perfectly well what military successes Pilib had had, they would have understood the analogy with Cu Chulainn, and they would have known that the case was being made on behalf of Pilib against his own elder brother, Seaán, and his uncle, Eamonn. Other contemporary Gaelic sources give us another side to the story. The annals of Loch Cé for 1584 record that

> Sean, son of Aodh Conallach was made the O'Reilly by the foreigners, in the presence of the sons of Maol Mordha O'Reilly, who were senior to him, and the sons of Maol Mordha destroyed the entire country for that.[58]

In contrast to the poetry, there was no mention of Pilib here. For the annalist, the interests of the earlier generation, particularly the tánaiste, Eamonn, brother to Aodh Conallach, were paramount. In each case, however, there is a clear indication of both innovation and controversy; things were not being done in the traditional way. The insignificance of Pilib in both the annals and the records of the Dublin government at this time suggests that the message of the poetry about his achievements may have been largely propagandist.

The records of the English administration reveal another perspective on the 1583 succession dispute. In the summer of 1583, there was general support among officials for Seaán O'Reilly, being 'a gentleman of good behaviour and so well addicted to civility and good order as few we know of this nation' with few complaints of 'common disorders and outrages' against him or his followers.[59] Apart from the fact that he was the legitimate eldest son, the main case in his support was his Englishness:

> in respect of his honest trade of life he is most worthy of any man, for although he live in an Irish country yet hath he always maintained himself very civilly, liveth of his own lands and industry after the English manner, speaketh the English tongue, maintains no thieves nor idle men about him.[60]

The official argument was that this English style of living should be rewarded.

> If reward follow not there will be few or none hereafter that will imitate the same but follow their own barbarous manner in oppressing all that live under them, robbing all that dwell near them, and maintaining none but thieves and idle kerne about them to the oppression of all poor men that labour for their living.[61]

It is evident that the English administration were seeking to engineer political and social change through their support for Seaán O'Reilly. They had a low opinion of the principal rival, Eamonn O'Reilly, who was

base born, liveth after the Irish manner, hath very lewd sons and
followers that have greatly annoyed the Pale, and made no restitution
when it had been by order awarded ... speaketh no English though he
dwelleth nearer the Pale than the other.[62]

While expressed is such language, the English decision to support Seaán
seemed obvious. The reality was more complex. There was the practical
difficulty of Eamonn's very real support in east Breifne, and Seaán's relative
ineffectiveness as a Gaelic leader. Members of the privy council in Dublin
consoled themselves that Seaán was well connected through his father's and
mother's alliances, the marriage partners of his sisters, and the sept with
whom he had been fostered. On his father's side these allies included O'Donnell,
Maguire, O'Rourke and Mac Mahon, while on his mother's side there were
the Anglo Irish Betaghs of Moynalty. The marriage partners of his four
sisters included a Plunkett of Clonbrene, as well as Sir Hugh Magennis,
Conor Maguire and MacFarrell O'Reilly.[63] The privy councillors also claimed
to be reassured by the offers of assistance which Seaán had received from the
baron of Dungannon, from O'Donnell, Maguire and Magennis on his father's
death.[64]

The representatives of the Dublin administration were also concerned that
the tánaiste, Eamonn, would be brought to accept his nephew as chief of the
O'Reillys. Rather that force Eamonn to accept defeat, they devised a scheme
whereby he would continue as tanaiste until his death, and would receive 'an
increase of 40 li pension' to be paid by his nephew, the new O'Reilly chief.
When this proposal was made, Eamonn 'took breath, neither taking or refusing it till he should come into the country and have some experience of his
nephew's usage of him.'[65] The English officials had gone to some lengths to
try to accommodate Eamonn's political aspirations, but were constrained by
Seaán's absolute refusal to allow a division of the territory between them.
Displaying his mastery of the legalities of both English and Irish landholding,
Seaán was reported to have insisted that the territory could not be split,
arguing:

> by entail and custom that it may not suffer any division by sale, gift or
> other device whatsoever and that any act to be done by him in that
> behalf can be of no validity ... and therefore it resteth not in his power
> to make any larger portion to Edmond than he presently enjoyeth.[66]

When it suited his case, Seaán could resort to traditional Gaelic law and
custom in opposition to the objectives of both his local rivals and the English
administration.

Despite English military backing,[67] Seaán O'Reilly was not ultimately able
to withstand Eamonn's challenge to his position as chief of the O'Reillys and

by 1584 a deal was negotiated which effectively imposed on the O'Reillys the Dublin administration's strategy for limiting O'Reilly power.[68] The lords justice were in no doubt that a division of the O'Reilly territory among the rival contenders would ensure 'the captainry thereby be weakened, and made the fuller to be overruled by the state'.[69] An agreement was drawn up which gave recognition to the relative strength of the various parties involved. The old chief's eldest son, Seaán, was recognised as his father's heir and was given to expect English support of his position. In return Seaán agreed to drop his claim to overlordship over the entire O'Reilly territory. Instead, parts of Breifne were allocated to each of his principal rival contenders for the O'Reilly lordship. Of the seven baronies into which Breifne was divided, four were deemed to be under the jurisdiction of Seaán O'Reilly: Loughtee, Tullygarvey, Tullyhunco and Tullyhaw. He was then excluded from influence in the remaining three baronies. One of these, Castlerahan, was allocated to Eamonn in compensation for the abolition of the position of tanaiste. Another southern barony, Clanmahon, was divided among Seaán's other uncles and their male heirs. The barony of Clankee in the north east of the county was confirmed under the control of Pilib dubh O'Reilly, in recognition of his de facto power as a military force in that region.[70]

The English administration had, on paper at least, achieved its aim of restricting the power of any one individual among the O'Reillys. It was this immediate objective of 'divide and rule' which seems to have been paramount. As had been the case with the 'surrender and regrant' deal of the early 1560s, outward political appearances seem to have been paramount. The longer term need to establish recognition in English law for the landholding arrangements was scarcely considered. The indentures of agreement stipulated that these allocated territories were to be held from the crown in fee simple, but no sixteenth-century record survives of any of the lands in these baronies being granted by patent to any of the O'Reillys. In 1591 Seaán O'Reilly was still petitioning the Commissioners for Irish Causes to have the grant of the four baronies detailed in the indentures confirmed by letters patent, but his applications do not seem to have been acted upon.[71] Likewise, the challenges which the O'Reillys, in their altered circumstances, might face from O'Neill were not given adequate consideration.

Under the terms negotiated in the 1584 agreement, which carved up local political jurisdiction in Cavan and promised to secure titles to land, the rights of the occupiers of the land, sometimes termed freeholders, were provided for. The freeholders were the followers of the principal lords, and the 1584 deal marked a stage in the transformation of their status from that of supporter of a war lord to that of tenant of a landlord. They were to hold their lands from the O'Reillys by knight's service and the traditional exactions which they owed were to be commuted to fixed payments. Thus, instead of providing military service to a lord, and providing food and other supplies for soldiers in wartime, the freeholders were now to pay something more akin to

an annual rent to their lord. Those of the elite group within the O'Reilly sept
who were allocated jurisdiction over specific baronies in the 1584 composition
settlement were to pay an annual rent or tax in cattle to the crown in recognition of their holding the lands from the crown.[72] The extent to which any of
these arrangements came to be legally binding is debateable.

   A sheriff was appointed to administer the shire of Cavan and oversee the
collection of the crown rent of 300 cattle. The fact that the rent was paid for
some years indicates that the arrangement was at least partly accepted. Assizes
were held and English style justice was dispensed. Cattle raiding was cur-
tailed. It appeared that the 'composition' policy was effective there, as it was
to an even more significant extent in south Connacht. The sheriff of Breifne,
Henry Duke, a native of county Meath, born of English parents, reported a
transformation of the region. Whereas before, Breifne had been 'a country of
Rome runners ... robbers, spoilers and burners of her Majesty's good subjects
of the Pale so as neither merchant nor other could pass to the market unrobbed
... no man answerable to the law', now, he believed, all was reformed and the
inhabitants of Breifne were answerable to the assizes and quarter sessions, and
he optimistically asserted that the subjects were free of fear and danger, 'they
can leave their cattle abroad at night without stealing'. Furthermore, where
before no revenue was received by the crown, her Majesty's revenue was now
greatly enhanced.[73] These sentiments echoed the views of Patrick Barnewall,
Lord Trimleston, who reported to Lord Burghley in November 1586 on the
universal quiet of Ireland, the absence of cattle raids, and the obedience of the
Irishry.[74]

V

Despite the optimism of many in the Pale, there were still those in Breifne
who were discontented, and Henry Duke and his successors as sheriff in
Cavan were kept busy attempting to enforce the law. In October 1589 it was
reported by Patrick Foxe that the heads of Brian Mac Ferral Oge O'Reilly
and three others had been sent to Dublin by Mr Herbert, sheriff of Cavan.
The beheaded man was described as a notorious traitor, who had a price of
£20 on his head.[75] In 1592 the lord deputy's commissioners, Thomas Fleming,
baron of Slane, and William Bathe reported of their visit to county Cavan that

> we found the gaol very full of prisoners and multitudes of causes, all
> which we ended as shortness of time would suffer. Eight were con-
> demned whereof five were for several wilful murders all which suffered
> according to their deserts some of them being chief of the blood of the
> O'Reillys. It is thought good example of severe justice will terrify other
> malefactors to the quiet of that country.[76]

The O'Reillys did not necessarily approve of such law enforcement activities by the sheriff and the assize courts: and sometimes complained through official channels. Lord Burghley, in 1596, was taking seriously formal complaints made by the O'Reillys against the activities of Henry Duke, and his successor as sheriff, Edward Herbert.[77] If the county administration was to work, it was necessary that the common law be enforced, but it was also important that administrative officials should not antagonise those who had traditionally had jurisdiction in the area. One of the difficulties faced by a central government was that of controlling its agents in the localities.

Internal rivalries among the principal factions of the O'Reillys were controlled by the simple expedient of imprisoning Pilib O'Reilly in Dublin castle where he remained as a hostage from 1585 to 1592. This was done not so much as punishment for crimes he had committed but rather to prevent trouble he might cause if he were allowed to remain free. The strategy was not fully effective, for even though he was imprisoned, he was certainly not forgotten by his supporters. The sheriff, Henry Duke, complained in January 1588 that Pilib O'Reilly's followers, along with the freeholders and gentlemen of his barony of Clankee had rescued cattle which the sheriff's men had taken 'as a distress for the earl of Kildare's money'. According to the sheriff, Pilib's followers frequently claimed that the lord deputy would shortly release him.[78] The evidence of the poetry in support of Pilib also suggests that his early release was anticipated. A poem by Mac Con Ó Cléirigh, entitled 'Cionnus do mholfuinn Mac Ríogh' composed while Pilib was in prison argued that provided Pilib was released from the fetters of the English he would be a king designed for Breifne.[79] However, Pilib's imprisonment was a long term one. In September 1591 one of his petitions to the privy council seeking his release claimed that the six years he had spent in prison had impaired his health, that his goods were consumed, his tenants had fled, his lands were lying waste and his wife and children were destitute.[80] The case Pilib presented implied the continued functioning of a traditional model of Gaelic lordship within his territory, where the very presence of tenants and the productive use of land were dependent on the support provided by a lord. The traditional nature of Pilib's authority in Clankee is also suggested by the existence of poems in his praise. That some of them were written while he was in prison hints at the probable role of his wife, Rose Maguire, as patron of the poets, supporting Pilib's status in his absence in the traditional way.[81] He eventually escaped from prison, in December 1591, along with Aodh ruadh O'Donnell, an escape which may have been allowed to happen so as to strengthen the opponents of the O'Neills in Ulster. The escapees were among those who would have been regarded as among the natural military leaders of Gaelic Ulster.[82] Pilib had other sources of support also. After his escape, four Dublin merchants, Gerald Plunkett, Walter Sedgrave, James Taylor and James Betagh, his mother's and his aunt's relatives, were among those who were prepared to act as guarantor for him to appear before the lord deputy given twenty days notice. Even one of the most consistent opponents of the English administration among the O'Reilly elite had a network of contacts in the English Pale which were used to advantage as required.[83]

Partly because of the strength of Pilib's support in some of east Breifne, things had not gone well for his elder brother Seaán O'Reilly. Seaán's moral authority was probably never equal to his nominal position as chief among the O'Reillys. He was continually dependent on the English administration to bolster his position, and help was not always at hand, so that he was obliged to make compromises with the earl of Tyrone also. The outbreak of the nine years war in Ulster in 1594 threatened to engulf the O'Reillys in political controversies not of their own making. The Tudor attempts at peaceful reform in Ulster had undermined the political authority of the traditional elite, while encouraging their followers to demand increased autonomy. Meanwhile, the English garrisons intended for the support of the lords, in place of the traditional military component of the individual lordships, could not be relied on. Succession crises in peripheral Ulster lordships in the 1580s, not just in east Breifne, but also among the Mac Mahons and Maguires highlighted the difficulties those lordships faced in seeking to implement English style systems of political organisation, and left their nominal leaders weakened. The power struggle degenerated into rebellion throughout much of Ulster by 1594.[84]

Realising his vulnerability, as political unrest escalated in the early 1590s, Seaán O'Reilly continued to seek support from the Dublin government. On 24 May 1594 Seaán reported to the lord deputy that Hugh Maguire and Brian O'Rourke were both threatening to invade Breifne from one side, while on the other side all of Tyrone except the earl himself were ready to assault him.[85] However, the real threat to Seaán came from within the lordship, where Pilib, allying himself with the Ulster rebels against the Dublin government, continued as the dominant military leader of the O'Reillys. By the time of Seaán's death in 1596, having failed to win the practical support he needed from Dublin, and having belatedly allied himself to the earl of Tyrone, he was leader of the O'Reillys in name only.[86] His brother Pilib wasted no time in taking over as chief of the O'Reillys, and proudly declared that he would bring back tanistry and allow no other law.[87] Pilib's prompt assumption of power did not go unnoticed by the lord deputy and council.[88] However, the earl of Tyrone was still committed to the cause of the O'Reilly's ninety-year-old uncle, Eamonn, and in August 1596 O'Neill was acting as arbitrator among the various contenders for the title of O'Reilly.[89] Meanwhile, Sir John Norris, seconded from his position as president of Munster to serve as military commander in Ulster, discounted the claims of Eamonn. Instead, he stressed the importance of settling matters between Pilib and his nephew Maol Mordha, the eldest legitimate son and common law heir of Seaán O'Reilly. Norris considered this a matter of importance because Pilib was 'a person stirring and politic and bordering the Pale' who could be 'made either a good or ill neighbour to the subjects there'.[90] As had been the case with Eamonn in

1583, Pilib was considered to be a man with local support who should not be antagonised. Norris believed that strict primogeniture succession should only be supported if expedient. He considered that the present troubles of the region were the outcome of previous incompetence by the English adminis-tration and expressed a concern that the current problems of Ulster be re-solved by 'good government'.

The removal of Pilib O'Reilly from the political landscape later in the same year, was not the product of 'good government'. A poetic lament, prob-ably written at the end of 1596 by Lochluinn Mac Taidhg Óig Í Dhálaigh entitled 'Frémh gach uilc oidheach Flatha', is the composition of a man shocked by the violent death of the person he believed a rightful 'high king'.[91] In the autumn of 1596, Pilib dubh, newly created chief of the O'Reillys, died at the hands of some of the followers of Hugh O'Neill, earl of Tyrone, with whom he had been in alliance. The poem conveys something of the sense of shock which must have been experienced by Pilib's long time supporters:

> The land of the kings of the stock of Raghallach of older times com-pared with today is but a dream, such are the sad changes brought about [by the death of] the fair scion of the territory of fair Tulach.[92]

Presenting Breifne in its traditional context as part of the province of Con-nacht, the poet then related many injuries done to Ulster by Connacht in past times, and claimed that this injury inflicted by Ulster was sufficient to avenge them all. The poem was no mere collection of clichés. It was not just an abstract lament for a Gaelic warrior, but made specific political comments on the implications of Pilib's death. The poet noted that not just one territory was endangered. The Gall now had power they never had on the river Boyle and Shannon 'doors are open from the Boyne to Sligo'. Because of his death, 'the band of the Irish is surrendered'.[93] The poet was well aware of the strategic significance of the O'Reilly lordship, lying as it did between the Pale and the north west. And although his death was, in a way, a victory for the English, the hardest blow, for the poet, was that Pilib O'Reilly had been killed not by the English but by some of the Ulster Irish with whom most of the O'Reillys were collaborating in the nine years war. Just one month before his death Pilib O'Reilly had been appointed by Hugh O'Neill, earl of Tyrone to guard the borders of Ulster and the Pale.[94]

> Even had he fallen defending Ireland of the melodious waterfalls,
> his death could hardly have been more grievous,
> but the king of the sloping stronghold of Leamhain
> was slain by a treacherous design of fate.[95]

His was not a glorious death in an honourable field of battle. His death was treachery, the poem asserted.[96] Other views on the event are recorded among the state papers. The lord deputy reported that Pilib had been 'the earl of Tyrone's special counsellor, to contrive mischief in time of peace and as it were his right hand to execute it in time of war'.[97] Tyrone reported that he had taken distress from Breifne as punishment for O'Reilly incursions in the Pale, and when Pilib resisted this punishment he was killed.[98] The Four Masters, writing some thirty years after the event, recorded the death as an accident.[99] James Carney's suggestion that Pilib was probably 'killed in a fracas with some of O'Neill's followers whom O'Neill did not wish to punish', is probably correct.[100] The relationship between O'Neill and Pilib O'Reilly was fluid and ambiguous, and there was no agreed version of where the life and death of Pilib dubh O'Reilly fitted into the story of Breifne at the end of the sixteenth century.

When Pilib O'Reilly died in controversial circumstances soon after realising his ambition of becoming chief of the O'Reillys, he was succeeded by the ageing Eamonn, who became chief of the O'Reillys, in name at least, until his death in 1601. His advanced years precluded him taking any active part in the nine years war. In the circumstances, Seaán O'Reilly's eldest son, Maol Mordha, had the chance to assert himself. It was reported by Hugh O'Neill in June 1598 that Maol Mordha O'Reilly had banished the O'Reilly out of Breifne, and had taken his uncles, Eoghan and Maol Mordha, prisoner, and had taken all their goods and tenants, along with Eoghan's castle.[101] Maol Mordha, son of Seaán, was supported by the Dublin government and was himself a captain in the English army in Ulster. In August 1598, despite his reputation for 'loyalaty and valour', he was among the casualties at the Blackwater.[102] The nine years war had claimed yet another victim from among the O'Reilly elite, this time one who was serving on the English side at the battle of the Yellow Ford.

The last years of the century saw the O'Reillys becoming more deeply embroiled in the war, on both sides. By November 1599 there was a garrison of 1000 footmen and 100 horsemen based at Cavan town, and among the commanders of that garrison was Hugh O'Reilly, the task being to control and defend the O'Rourkes, Mac Mahons, Maguires and O'Reillys and keep their forces from joining the earl of Tyrone.[103] In January 1600 another of the O'Reillys who was serving in the English army, Captain John O'Reilly, defected from her Majesty's service taking with him his 100 well armed footmen.[104] In October 1600 an informant reported that Maol Mordha Mac Prior O'Reilly, who had charge of the powder at Port na Holla had gone to Tyrone in company with O'Reilly. They arrived too late, however, for the encounter between Hugh O'Neill and the lord deputy. The informant reported that they 'tore their glibbs in anger, but Tyrone bade them not doubt but they should have fighting enough'.[105] Richard Hadsor reported in October 1601 that O'Reilly and Captain Hugh O'Reilly had defected to the rebels, taking with them a company of soldiers armed and furnished by her Majesty. An informant later that year put the strength of the O'Reilly element in Tyrone's force at 400 footmen and 80 horsemen.[106] When Tyrone marched south to Kinsale in the autumn of 1601, the remnants of the military elite among the O'Reillys were instructed to remain behind and attack the pale as a diversionary tactic. On his return in January 1602, O'Neill was reported to be very angry at the O'Reilly's inactivity in his absence.[107] By April 1602, in the aftermath of the defeat of the combined Ulster and Spanish forces at Kinsale, the O'Reillys were quick to seek pardon from the English government for their part in the rebellion.[108] Those who sought pardons evidently believed that in the aftermath of the defeat of O'Neill and O'Donnell, their political future could be best secured by co-operation with the English administration.

VI

The O'Reillys had been drawn into rebellion largely because of the strategic significance of the territory they occupied. Internal conflicts within east Breifne had meant that those O'Reillys with political ambitions had regularly sought outside assistance in the pursuit of local supremacy. In consequence, they had become victims of the conflicting ambitions of the dominant Ulster lord, Hugh O'Neill, earl of Tyrone and the Dublin government. Neither those who sought to advance their particular ambitions by seeking government assistance, nor those who continued to operate within a more traditional Gaelic political world, had profited from the war which engulfed them all. Despite significant progress towards converting the O'Reilly lordship into the administrative unit known as county Cavan, establishing links between local political jurisdiction and loyalty to the crown, introducing common law methods of resolving disputes, and encouraging primogeniture succession, the outcome was the sort of large scale military encounter which all sides had hoped to avoid.

In the new century, east Breifne was included in the reallocation of lands under a formal scheme for the plantation of Ulster. Although some of the O'Reillys were favourably dealt with, they had lost their traditional political status. In the course of the seventeenth century, the native occupants of the region came to understand the term 'county Cavan', and the use of older terms like 'east Breifne' and 'O'Reilly's country' rapidly declined. Within a generation of the ending of the nine years war, the days when the O'Reillys were chiefs of their territory lived on only in the memory of the people, like the blind man, who in 1620 could recite accurately the poems recounting the exploits and singing the praises of the ambitious but ill-fated Pilib dubh O'Reilly.[109]

The Reformation in Kilmore before 1641

ALAN FORD

The process of religious change in early modern Ireland is still a mysterious one. The end result is known: the reformation failed to win over the native population; but precisely how or when this happened is persistently perplexing. Historians have provided confident assertions and broadly based explanations, particularly about the failure of the reformation. Unfortunately they seldom agree.[1]

One way out of this impasse is to shift the focus of attention from the general to the particular, from the national to the local: from Ireland to Kilmore. Elsewhere in Europe, the testing of historical generalizations about political and religious change against the detailed evidence from individual towns, cities and even parishes, has repeatedly forced historians to abandon broad brush-strokes and construct instead detailed and sometimes fragmentary explanatory mosaics. Indeed, such has been the concentration upon the county community in English history, that there has recently been a shift back to recognizing the importance of national institutions.[2] In Irish history, by contrast, the dominance of the central perspective has remained so total that the connections between the national and the local communities, indeed, the very existence and nature of local communities, has remained little explored.[3] As a result, the overarching generalizations about the reformation have scarcely been tested against detailed local studies.[4]

Part of the problem has been the too ready assumption that because the reformation uniformly failed to gain majority support in any region of Ireland, the reasons for, and the timing of its failure were also uniform. But uniformity was precisely what early modern Ireland lacked—it was riven by racial and religious, political and cultural divisions. Religious change, as a result, was a product of a complex and complicated interaction between a wide range of variables: catholicism and protestantism; survivalism and the counter-reformation; Irish and English cultures; Celtic and anglicized church structures; royal supremacy and papal jurisdiction; Gaelic, Anglo–Irish and new English political identities; and the contingencies of personality, to name but a few.

The interaction of these many variables produced a differentiated geography of religious change which can be studied at several levels: national, provincial, diocesan, and even, if the sources would permit it, parochial. At the

provincial level, a brief examination of the neighbouring ecclesiastical provinces of Dublin and Armagh illustrates the sharp contrasts in the nature and
pace of religious change in the late sixteenth and early seventeenth centuries.
In the province of Dublin, royal supremacy was enforced from an early stage
on a church structure which was firmly anglicized, with English-style courts
and administration, and a reformation policy that was firmly anglicizing. The
upper reaches of the ministry included many English emigrés while the parochial clergy, initially at least, included a significant number of conforming
local clergy. Such continuity meant that the pace of religious change was slow:
royal supremacy was grudgingly accepted, but the deep-seated conservatism
of the Anglo Irish limited the gains made by protestantism. It was not until
the 1570s and 1580s that this conservatism began to coalesce into firm recusancy
and withdrawal from the established church. By the 1590s divisions between
Protestant and Catholic were becoming increasingly sharp, as Protestant clergy
began to be confronted by counter-reformation trained opponents such as the
Jesuits.[5]

In the province of Armagh (in which Kilmore lay) with the exception of
the diocese of Meath and the part of Armagh that was within the Pale, the
church was largely loyal to Rome, firmly Irish speaking, Gaelic in its structures, and often subservient to the local native Irish chieftains. Religious
divisions were minimal, largely because of the failure of the reformation to
make any progress at all. However, the defeat of O'Neill in the nine years war
in 1603 and the plantation of Ulster following the flight of the earls in 1607,
were followed by a dramatic transfer of ecclesiastical power, as newly appointed Protestant bishops set about taking over the institutions and structures of the Catholic church. This newly established church had to take
urgent decisions about what it wanted to do with its Irish structures and its
approach to both settler and native Irish parishioners. The Catholic church
had, for its part, to survive, retain the allegiance of the people and rebuild an
alternative organizational structure. Thus changes which in Dublin province
had developed slowly over a period of a hundred years were compressed in
the planted dioceses of Armagh into a decade or two. In short, the very nature
of the church and the pace of religious change were utterly different in the
two provinces.

Even at the regional level, however, one must be wary of generalizations.
Within the ecclesiastical province of Armagh, at the end of the sixteenth
century, the distribution of ecclesiastical power, as measured by episcopal
appointments, was far from straightforward. Royal nominees held the three
sees close to Dublin—Meath, Down and Connor, and Armagh, but the remoter dioceses of Raphoe and Derry had been left vacant by the crown since
the 1560s. By contrast, on the Catholic side, both Armagh and Meath were
vacant, while papal appointees held Raphoe, Derry, Kilmore, and also Down
and Connor. Finally as an indication of the disorganisation on both sides, two
sees, Clogher and Ardagh, were unfilled by either pope or king.[6] As a result,

even within Ulster, religious change needs to be considered in a diocesan, as well as a provincial, context.

This study focuses on one strand of religious change in one Ulster diocese—the progress of the reformation in Kilmore during its first half century—in the hope of contributing one tessera to the mosaic of religious change in early modern Ireland. In many respects Kilmore was a typical Ulster diocese. Firmly Gaelic and loyal to Rome in the sixteenth century, and dramatically transformed by the collapse of Gaelic power and the plantation in the early seventeenth. It telescopes into a period of less than fifty years three distinct phases of the reformation: the 'pre-history' of religious change—the desultory efforts to enforce royal supremacy up to the end of Elizabeth's reign; a brief attempt at an 'indigenous reformation' after the appointment in 1603 of the first resident Protestant bishop, Robert Draper; and the 'plantation church', coinciding with the episcopate of Thomas Moigne, 1612–29, which saw the construction of an anglicized, settler church in tandem with the Ulster plantation. In another respect, however, Kilmore was markedly different from the general pattern of the Ulster reformation, in the addition of a fourth stage, in the period 1629–41, when Moigne's successor, William Bedell, attempted to reform the planter church and combine it with an indigenous reformation. Kilmore both encapsulates the various strategies and tactics employed by the Protestant church to foster the reformation, and at the same time provides a means of judging the success or failure of national religious policies at the diocesan level.

In the continuing debate over when and why the reformation failed, it has been argued that it would be premature to declare the reformation a failure by the early seventeenth century. Though the Protestant church had indeed signally failed to mount the necessary campaign of evangelization and education to win over the Irish population in the wake of the secular conquest of Ireland, the counter-reformation Catholic church also, it is argued, struggled to gain popular support. This left 'the majority of the native population outside the structure of the rival churches' clinging tenaciously 'to pre-Tridentine religious practice'. It was therefore not till the nineteenth century that the majority of the Irish people were incorporated within a Tridentine style Catholic church.[7] The response to this claim has been a call for more detailed investigation of the religious history of late sixteenth and early seventeenth Ireland in an attempt to discover whether or not changes of long-term significance were occurring. Karl Bottigheimer has argued that there was an important qualitative transformation in religious allegiance in this period and has cited the particular example of Kilmore and the experience of Bedell as evidence that a 'distinctive polarisation' had occurred by the early seventeenth century.[8]

I

The first two stages of the reformation in Kilmore can be briefly dealt with, since each proved abortive. Sixteenth-century Kilmore was a medium-sized Ulster diocese, bordering on the dioceses of Clogher to the north, Meath to the south-east, and Ardagh to the north-west. Though there was some Anglo-Irish settlement in the south east, its population was largely native Irish.[9] The dominant secular powers were the O'Reilly family of east Breifne, and the O'Rourkes, Magaurans and MacRannells to the north west. The pattern of religious life in the sixteenth century was relatively free from the tumultuous changes in allegiance and practice that characterised other Irish dioceses: Kilmore had a continuous succession of papally appointed bishops down to 1607; the Franciscan monastery at Cavan survived until as late as 1608; and the parish churches continued to be served, as in the medieval period, by the traditional local clerical families, such as the O'Farrells, Mac Bradys and O'Reillys. Kilmore was clearly part of the non-anglicised Irish Roman Catholic church.[10]

Kilmore's early involvement with the reformation is largely a product of geography. The diocese was on the periphery of Ulster, where the ambitions of the native Ulster lords and the Dublin government intersected. There is, as Bernadette Cunningham's essay shows, evidence that Dublin sporadically wished to extend royal authority, both civil and ecclesiastical, to Kilmore, and also that certain elements of the ruling secular and church elites in Kilmore toyed with the idea of such a shift in allegiance. The result is a Janus-like quality on the part of both civil and ecclesiastical leaders. In 1540 Bishop Edmund Nugent of Kilmore accepted royal supremacy, and subsequently there are hints at conformity on the part of two prominent clerical families, the Bradys and the O'Gowans.[11] The 1580s saw the culmination of royal attempts to assimilate Breifne, led by Lord Deputy Perrott, who promoted the new shire of Cavan, and persuaded the O'Reillys to accept an English system of landholding, and replace papal jurisdiction with royal supremacy.[12] Perrott tried to make the latter a reality by nominating Irish born and Irish speaking John Garvey, dean of Christ Church, Dublin, to the see of Kilmore in 1585.[13]

The efforts at assimilation repeatedly failed. When Bishop Nugent died about 1550, the crown did not nominate a successor. Garvey never resided as a bishop, or exercised any jurisdiction within Kilmore.[14] When he was promoted to Armagh in 1596 the crown again left Kilmore unfilled.[15] Finally, when the nine years war broke out in 1594, the land settlement collapsed when many of the O'Reillys chose the side of O'Neill.[16]

The defeat of O'Neill and his Irish allies in 1603 was the pivotal event which destroyed the old order and was followed by the extension of royal secular and ecclesiastical authority throughout Ulster. In 1605 a commission was issued for the redistribution of landholdings in Ulster, and in 1606 Lord Deputy Chichester, together with his attorney general, Sir John Davies, visited Monaghan, Fermanagh and Cavan holding courts and investigating titles to land.[17] From 1603 to 1607 six vacant sees in Ulster were filled by royal nominees.[18] As the bishops assumed office, they also took over the cathedrals, churches, income and administrative structures of the pre-existing Roman Catholic church.[19]

How was the newly established church to handle this Irish inheritance? Traditionally, the leaders of the Protestant church in Ireland had sought to impose an anglicized and anglicizing reformation. The church structures were to be modelled upon the English reformation and the clergy were to speak English and use the English liturgy, as in the province of Dublin.[20] The sheer rapidity of the extension of royal control over native Irish Ulster in the early seventeenth century, however, forced the government to look beyond existing models. Buoyed up by a brief upsurge in naïve official optimism about the malleability of the local population, it was hoped that the Ulster Irish would enthusiastically welcome the liberating authority of the Dublin government in civil and ecclesiastical matters.[21] The English privy council was especially anxious that, rather than concentrating official resources on enforcing conformity in the Pale and the Anglo-Irish towns, where recusancy was strongest, the Church of Ireland should focus its missionary efforts upon the 'backward', 'ignorant', rural areas, such as Kilmore and Ulster, where, it was believed, the simple people would be much more amenable to the Protestant gospel.[22]

English officials in Ireland encouraged this picture of Ulster as a primitive and shapeless society. Chichester saw it as a terra incognita for the church— 'confused and out of order, as if it were in a wilderness, where neither Christianity nor religion was ever heard of.'[23] Davies thought that 'all the people of that province [Ulster], at least the multitude, are apt to receive any faith', and, after his trip to Cavan in 1606 he pointed to the analogy of 1558 in England, suggesting that the Elizabethan priests in Kilmore would follow the example of their English Marian counterparts, and, by and large, accept the new regime.[24] All that was needed was for the new bishops to 'come and be a new St Patrick among them'.[25]

Efforts were made to provide just such missionaries. Resident bilingual bishops were provided for both Armagh and Kilmore.[26] Robert Draper, appointed to the latter in 1603, though probably English born, was an Irish speaker with extensive pastoral experience of the neighbouring diocese of Meath.[27] His episcopate was seen by the government as a fresh start, a chance to 'set on foot again these two long decayed and wasted bishoprics', and 'to reduce the country to love and follow God's true religion, when they shall hear it preached in their own language'.[28] Promising local students were sent at state expense to Trinity College, Dublin, including one Charles Brady a 'poor scholar from Cavan'.[29]

The success of Draper's mission is difficult to assess, due to the confusion and disarray in the Kilmore churches after 1603. The Protestant seizure of control over the essential structures, coupled with the sporadically intense persecution of Catholic priests by the government and the closure of monasteries, had a severely disruptive effect upon the Catholic ministry. No Catholic bishop was appointed between 1607 and 1625, not even a vicar apostolic; few records of appointments of parish priests survive from this era.[30] Instead an alternative, underground, Catholic church structure had slowly to be built up, moving away from a church-based religion to one founded on private observance.[31] On the Protestant side the capability of the established church under Draper was decidedly limited. There is no evidence that Draper appointed any new ministers to benefices. Davies's comments on those clergy the diocese did possess, and, indeed, on Draper himself, were dismissive.[32] Finally, evidence from an exchequer inquisition of 1619 suggests that over half the benefices in the diocese were vacant during the first nine years of James's reign.[33]

Behind this confusion two important battles were being fought, one over the allegiance of the clergy, the other over the loyalty of the laity. Davies's report on Cavan in 1606 implies that Draper relied entirely upon priests he had inherited from the Catholic church.[34] Furthermore, it is clear that under Draper's successor a significant number of the Protestant church's clergy came from families such as the Bradys or O'Gowans which had shown some interest in conformity in the sixteenth century.[35] Similar evidence for limited clerical conformity is found in other planted dioceses, suggesting that the benefices of the established church continued to appeal to some native Irish priests.[36] As for the laity, it appears that the Catholic clergy, particularly the Franciscans, who had been particularly influential in Kilmore, led a strenuous campaign in the Ulster dioceses to ensure that the local people were fully aware that 'the English service proceeded from the seducement of the devil'.[37] The counter-reformation determination to avoid heretical services would have been strengthened by the close links that existed between Cavan and the leading recusant Anglo–Irish families of Meath.[38]

There is little evidence of any coherent response to such Catholic efforts from the Protestant church in Kilmore under Draper. His episcopate was too short—he died in 1612—and his resources too limited for progress to have been made. Of Davies's Patrician missionary enterprise no evidence survives. Ambiguity rather than enthusiasm is the main characteristic of these halting efforts to create an indigenous church; an ambiguity, indeed, that extended even to the bishop's own family—Draper's wife was reported after his death in 1612 to have been a recusant.[39]

II

By the time of Draper's death the context of the reformation in Ulster had changed. The brief experiment in constructing a wholly indigenous church was over. The flight of the earls in 1607, their attainder, and the subsequent decision to plant six of the Ulster counties, including Cavan, offered the English authorities a chance to reshape radically the whole settlement of the province, both secular and ecclesiastical. This was a remarkable opportunity. Elsewhere in Ireland and England, basic ecclesiastical structures were immutable, inextricably bound up with secular and landed interests. Far from threatening these interests, the reformation usually strongly reinforced them. In plantation Ulster, however, no such restrictions existed, since the local landholders had been stripped of all rights, and the land, both ecclesiastical and secular, was in the hands of the king. As a result, the reformation in Ulster, it briefly seemed, might start with a tabula rasa.[40]

The chief architect of the Ulster church in the early stages of the plantation was the Scot, George Montgomery, appointed to the combined sees of Derry, Raphoe and Clogher in 1605, and translated to Meath in 1609. Montgomery used his considerable influence, both as plantation commissioner and as courtier, to secure the best possible deal for the church in the land settlement. Both Montgomery, and the project for the plantation, clearly envisaged the replacement of the traditional Irish church structure with a fully anglicized one. The most explicit indication of Montgomery's policy was contained in a document presented by him to the king in 1610: this summarised the nature of the traditional church in Derry, Raphoe, Clogher, Kilmore and Armagh, and also contained his blueprint for its new anglicized replacement.[41] The general tenor of his approach was that Irish customs were to be suppressed 'seeing this is a new plantation and erection of churches'. He did not ignore the native presence, but saw the role of the church in terms of bringing the indigenous inhabitants to 'civility and religion'. The means whereby this was to be done were threefold. First, 'by authority of ecclesiastical censure to punish the obstinate, and draw the people to conformity': in other words, the establishment of an English-style system of ecclesiastical courts, backed up where necessary by the civil arm. Secondly, a comprehensive system of schooling at all levels to further the acculturation of the next generation. Finally, Montgomery laid great emphasis upon the provision of a firm financial basis for the ministry. He suggested that the native Irish system of separate rectorial and vicarial tithes be scrapped, with the income being combined to provide support for one minister. Rather than retain the distinctive Irish financial organisation, Montgomery insisted that it be replaced by the English system of tithes and oblations. To improve episcopal income Montgomery urged that traditional demesne lands be separated from grants to settlers and reserved for the bishops, and further proposed that the termon land—the land traditionally associated with local churches and their clerical families—be granted to the bishops. This left ministers with no land of their own on which to build a house and farm, so Montgomery argued that the king should allocate land specially from escheated temporal holdings to provide for suitable glebes. Finally there was the question of whether the church should retain the existing boundaries of parishes, the product of many centuries of evolution, or should it designate new ones, more closely aligned to the new patterns of settlement. The first plans for the plantation, drawn up in 1609–10, envisaged that the land would be allocated in proportions, which varied in size from 1000 to 3000 acres, and that each proportion would be made a parish.[42]

These, however, were only paper proposals. They still had to be tested against the messy reality of early seventeenth-century Ulster. The results of that testing were mixed. Some proposals were fundamentally misconceived, and had to be abandoned. It was never feasible to transfer rectorial tithes to the incumbents in a diocese such as Kilmore where nearly all the rectories were impropriate, since this conflicted with the rights of the influential Anglo Irish and English farmers. As a result, the clergy had to be content with the vicarial tithes.[43] Similarly, while the proposal to redraw the parishes would in theory have ensured a perfect match between settlement and church, it would have resulted in a large number of decidedly small parishes, and required the building of an almost equally large number of churches. In the end, the existing parish structure, as Patrick Duffy's essay above explains, was retained. Kilmore, as a result, has a small number of large parishes, a pattern typical of the dispersed Gaelic church, in marked contrast to the smaller, more fragmented parochial structure of the Anglo-Norman areas.[44]

Some of Montgomery's proposals were, however, implemented. The bishops were endowed with the termon lands, and a system of church courts was established.[45] Other aspects of his plan for the Ulster church, however, ran into that all too familiar early modern Irish problem—the inability of the government to put its decisions into effect. While all agreed in theory with the king's noble desire to endow the church, in practice it was often difficult to prevent church lands slipping into the clutches of the settlers—where greed and altruism conflicted, the baser instinct usually won. There were, for instance, repeated difficulties in the Ulster plantation in ensuring that school lands were used for their stated purpose.[46] In Kilmore, the lands at least survived to provide an income for the schoolmaster, and a continuous succession of schoolmasters was appointed, but the schoolhouse, ordered to be built in 1611, was still unbuilt in 1622.[47]

It soon became apparent that the plantation created as many problems as it solved. It is true that by 1622 the bishop had an impressive income of over £230 sterling a year, and that the value of benefices in Kilmore was twice as large as in neighbouring Ardagh. However, the clergy in Kilmore were still much poorer than those in other planted dioceses.[48] Glebes proved a nightmare, severely disrupting the church's ministry. The government did not finally assign the glebes to ministers until 1626, and by then much of the land was illegally detained by local landholders.[49] The plantation commissioners, moreover, had allocated ministers lands which bore no relation to the location of their church.[50] Since clergy were supposed to build their houses on their glebes, they were faced with a choice between non-residence and homeless-ness.[51] In one Kilmore case, the minister's glebe was ten miles away from his church, in another it was in a different parish.[52] As Bishop Bramhall of Derry remarked in the 1630s, 'if all the Jesuits of the Church of Rome had conspired together to hinder the propagation of the gospel, they could not have con-trived it more effectually'.[53] The financial problems of the church were amply reflected in the survey of the diocese of Kilmore which was provided for the 1622 commissioners. The most telling evidence was the state of the church buildings. The cathedral was newly built with the help of £175 from recusancy fines, but otherwise there were only four churches in a reasonable condition, while a full thirty were recorded as ruinous or in bad repair.[54]

Hand in hand with the efforts to create an anglicised church went the transformation of the ministry in Kilmore. As settlers arrived from England and Scotland they brought with them Protestant ministers. Thus in 1611 a survey of the portion allotted to the Scot, Sir Alexander Hamilton, in south-ern Kilmore, recorded the presence of two tenants, their servants, six artifi-cers and a minister, thought the latter was 'not yet allowed by the bishop'.[55] In Kilmore much depended upon the bishop, since, unusually in an Irish diocese, the vast majority of the benefices were collative. When Draper died in 1612 a new bishop was nominated who fitted neatly into the colonial context. Thomas Moigne was an Englishman, educated at Cambridge and gaining his MA in 1597, who, after a normal academic career, decided in 1604 to emigrate to Ireland and seek preferment in the church there.[56] His timing was good. The church was expanding into new areas such as Ulster, and Moigne's chances of preferment were strengthened by his close family ties with those successful Irish adventurers, the Moryson brothers, Fynes and Richard. His rise was rapid: in 1605 he was made archdeacon of Meath, in 1608 dean of St Patrick's, and in December 1612 he was granted the see of Kilmore.[57]

Moigne, and the plantation, transformed the ministry in Kilmore. During his episcopate thirty-seven clergy are known to have been appointed. The majority—some thirty—appear to be of English or Scottish origin.[58] Fifteen of these thirty-seven ministers had been to university, and in the case of twelve of the graduates their university can be identified with some confi-dence. The six who had attended English universities had all been to Cam-bridge, five of them overlapping with Moigne. Thus Nathaniel Hollington matriculated at the puritan seminary of Emmanuel College, Cambridge, in 1602, while Robert Whiskins graduated in 1593 with a BA, and served for a time as curate and schoolmaster in Cambridgeshire.[59] Both came to Ireland as the plantation began: in 1613 Whiskins appears as vicar of Annagelliff and of Denn; in 1616 Moigne ordained Hollington and by 1618 he was vicar of Drumlane.[60] Both were recorded in 1622 as resident preachers, and both spent the remainder of their careers in Kilmore and neighbouring Ardagh.[61] An-other six ministers had been to Trinity College, Dublin.[62] Here Moigne was

on good terms with the professor of divinity, James Ussher, and was willing
to support students at the college by allocating them benefices without cure in
his dioceses.[63] Whilst the king had hoped that Trinity would provide the Irish
church with Irish speaking ministers, it did little to fulfil this role in the first
quarter of the seventeenth century. More typical of the Trinity student was
William Holliwell from Cheshire, who graduated from Trinity with an MA in
1621 and by 1622 had been appointed vicar of the neighbouring parishes of
Clonloher and Killargue.[64]

These clergy concentrated their pastoral efforts on their settler parishioners. It was in the areas of settlement that churches were repaired and built and
that English ministers resided. Thus by 1622 a church was being built in
Cavan town, with further new churches proposed for the plantation centres of
Virginia and Belturbet where, it was reported, 'there are a great store of
Protestants'.[65] Pluralism was also rife. In some cases the arrangement was at
least logical, involving the joining of adjacent benefices to ensure an adequate
income for the minister.[66] In other cases, however, the benefices were so far
apart, indeed even in different dioceses, that the minister had no hope of
serving the second cure himself.[67] As one observer remarked: 'it is the wages
is sought, not the work'.[68] Ideally, ministers sought to combine one parish
with plentiful English or Scottish inhabitants, where they resided, with one or
more others where the parishioners were wholly Irish and could either be
neglected or, at best, left to an Irish curate.[69]

The ties between clergy and planters were also evident in the extent of
clerical involvement in the plantation. A number of the English and Scots
ministers acquired considerable estates of their own. Moigne in 1627 bought
one of the original 2000 acre plantation proportions in the barony of Loughtee.
By the time of his death, his estate included a 'large and spacious castle'
together with a town with twenty four 'English like houses ... all inhabited
with English and British families', and a remote parish church which, it was
proposed, should be moved to the area 'where the greatest plantation and
British inhabitants do now reside'.[70] Faithful Teate, another prominent minister, acquired a freehold in Ballyhaise, where he was vicar.[71]

That the plantation produced a plantation church was hardly surprising.
As King James had himself observed in spelling out the role of the Protestant
church in Ulster, its primary aim was 'planting ... the gospel in those churches
for the comfort of our civil subjects that shall be settled there'. James had
gone on to specify a second task: that of 'reducing ... the natives unto His true
service'.[72] One obvious way of judging how effective the Church of Ireland
was in achieving these goals is by looking at the composition and distribution
of the ministry. It has been suggested that the state church in the native Irish
areas could succeed only by excluding rather than absorbing local clergy.[73]
Indeed, in many parishes the influx of English clergy marks a dramatic breach
in the native Irish succession of priests from the traditional clerical coarb and
erenagh families. In Drumlane, for example, the medieval incumbent had

repeatedly been drawn from the O'Farrelly family. After the appointment of Hollington the family association with Drumlane recurs, but the next O'Farrelly, recorded in 1631, is operating as a Catholic priest.[74] A similar pattern is recorded in the case of many of the families that repeatedly served in the medieval ministry in Kilmore but after the reformation appear exclusively in the records of the Catholic church.[75]

Yet continuity was not wholly lost: exclusion was not the inevitable result of reformation. Some native Irish clergy conformed. There were six native Irish clergy recorded in Kilmore during Moigne's episcopate.[76] Thomas, a representative of the Brady family, long associated with the parishes of Drung and Laragh, was appointed in 1620 by Moigne to the neighbouring Lavey.[77] Three clergy in 1622 came from the O'Gowans, prominent in the south east of the diocese: Nicholas senior, Nicholas Junior, and John (or Shane), who had converted from the Catholic priesthood.[78] Why did they choose to remain within the established church? The Bradys and O'Gowans already had an existing tradition of conformity.[79] In addition, the Cavan plantation had made relatively generous provision for native landholders—the Bradys had received almost 1700 acres of land—and it was in the native-Irish and servitor baronies of Tullygarvey, Castlerahan and Clanmahon that the local clergy generally ministered.[80]

The vital question is the role of such clergy in the church's ministry. In other areas of Ulster, native clergy tended to be treated as an inferior substratum, despised for their failure to meet 'civilised' standards, and left to look after the remoter, Irish speaking rural parishes, often as curates to non-resident English or Scots ministers.[81] Thus in Kilmore in 1622 Hugh McComyn, the rector of Drumgoon, was returned to the commissioners as a 'priest converted' living in 'a poor Irish house', who had been 'deprived for misdemeanours', with his living sequestrated to Francis Parker.[82] Even Bishop Bedell, Moigne's successor, complained that the wives of three of his clergy were recusants, while Bedell's son, William Bedell, also a minister in Kilmore, was dubious about the motives behind the conversion of native Irish clergy.[83] However, native conformists were not necessarily the backward-looking remnant of a dying survivalist church. Nicholas O'Gowan junior had attended the indisputably Protestant Trinity College, graduating in 1602 with a BA, and, conforming to the anglicising ethos of the Irish reformation, ending his days as Nicholas Smith, vicar of Ratoath in county Meath, where he resided in a well-repaired manse with a garden and four acres of enclosed pasture.[84] Nor was the assimilation of the Smith/O'Gowans transient: one branch of the family remained Protestant.[85] For every such example of native conformity, far more could be cited of continued loyalty to catholicism. Even within the O'Gowan family, the pattern is clear. At precisely the time that Nicholas Smith was studying at Trinity College, Bernard O'Gowan from the diocese of Kilmore was pursuing his studies in the counter-reformation centres of learning in Europe, finally entering the Irish College in Salamanca in 1603, aged twenty-five. Three other members of the family are recorded as Catholic priests in the early seventeenth century.[86] The depositions taken after the 1641 rising in Cavan record a plethora of O'Gowans choosing the Irish side in the rising, including Michael Smith, 'alias O Goan', of Oldcastle, described as 'son to parson Smith'.[87]

Though about twenty per cent of the ministry in Kilmore were native Irish during Moigne's episcopate, lay conformity appears to have been much rarer. The 1622 Commissioners lamented the 'almost empty' churches in Ulster.[88] Bedell reported in 1629 that the Irish and Anglo Irish in Kilmore were 'almost universally' Catholic, 'the Irish without exception'.[89] Bedell's son confirmed that there were several parishes where 'there was not one British or Protestant, save the minister's family', and pointed to the parish of Killinkere, which adjoined the diocese of Meath, as being entirely Catholic in 1631.[90] Does Killinkere represent the failure of the reformation to strike indigenous roots in Kilmore? There are three possible aproaches to answering this question, which lies at the heart of the debate over the Irish reformation. One could argue that the weaknesses of the Catholic and established churches were such that neither succeeded in effectively imposing their religious authority over the population of Kilmore. This, simply does not fit with the early seventeenth century evidence for religious allegiance. As James Kelly argues in his essay the bishops in Kilmore continued to struggle to impose Tridentine standards of behaviour, but there is no suggestion on their part that the prevalent Catholic observance in Kilmore was in any sense a half-way house between protestantism and the counter-reformation, or anything but loyal to the Catholic church.[91] Alternatively, it is possible to concentrate upon the strategies which the Catholic church used to survive the upheavals and persecution of the early seventeenth century, accepting that it had created by the 1620s a fully functioning alternative church structure with its own system of ecclesiastical justice and a priest in every parish, administering the sacraments to a loyal population.[92] A third approach focuses upon the weaknesses of the Church of Ireland and its inability to seize the evangelical opportunities open to it in the immediate aftermath of 1603.[93]

The relationship between the latter two approaches—the strengths of the Catholic church and the defects of the Protestant—is not simple. The failure of the Protestant mission and the success of the Catholic one were, it has been pointed out the necessary condition, but not the sufficient cause of each other.[94] The crucial period in Kilmore was the first three decades of the seventeenth century when Protestant and Catholic churches were constructed in parallel. At the beginning Sir John Davies, the attorney general, believed that the people of Cavan were open to receive any religion at all; by 1629 William Bedell, an acute observer, was quite clear that they were firmly committed to Catholicism.[95] Trying to disentangle what happened in between is complex. It is possible to suggest that, on the Protestant side, the speed of the transition from an Irish to an anglicized church structure created serious tensions between the church and the local population, which were exacerbated by the assumptions that settler clergy brought with them. The paradoxical result was that the very structures which were supposed to further and enforce the reformation in fact hindered its acceptance and alienated the native population.

The early modern established church had a number of interconnected points of contact with the laity, particularly in pastoral, financial and legal matters. The ministers provided spiritual and pastoral care for their flocks; in return their parishioners supported them by tithes and oblations—the fees they paid for services such as christenings and funerals. Underpinning this relationship was the formal system of ecclesiastical juridiction, dealing with a wide range of issues ranging from wills to morality to failure to pay one's tithes. In Ulster the relationship between Protestant clergy and people repeatedly broke down, as these points of contact became sources of friction. The overarching cause of the tension was the mismatch between the capacity of the Church of Ireland's ministry, limited only to the settlers, and its claim to be the national church, catering for all the population. Not only was its ministry unable to provide services for all those who lived in Kilmore but most of Kilmore's inhabitants had no desire to avail of such services, remaining loyal to the Catholic priesthood. While the people had no need of the Protestant clergy, those clergy needed the financial support of their nominal parishioners. In many cases the main interest which pluralist British ministers had in their native Irish parishes was to ensure that they secured their income from the tithes and dues.[96] This was also the case in other regions of Ireland.[97] What made Kilmore and the other areas covered by the Ulster plantation special was the speed of change from traditional Gaelic to the new English form of tithing, that is from a system based on payment in kind to payment in specie; and the failure to define what or how much could be exacted. The result was a repeated temptation, to which many ministers succumed, to exact both English and Irish tithes at unacceptably high levels.

This problem was recognised at an early stage, resulting in repeated attempts to regulate tithing. In 1609 the king ordered that tithes in Ulster be paid in kind.[98] Among the many government bills which were proposed for the 1613 parliament were ones to restrain 'the unjust exactions of ministers' and to ensure that tithes in the Ulster plantation were paid in money and that none were paid to Catholic priests.[99] In 1615 Lord Deputy Chichester attempted to regulate the exactions of the clergy by banning the imposition of tithes on milk and 'other like innovations' which he claimed were new not merely to Ireland but also to England. To Chichester the attitude of the clergy—'more zealous and sharp than moderate and cautious'—was a symptom of their much broader pastoral failure in Ulster:

> the ministers there are non-residents for the most part, as having few
> churches in reparation to serve God in, nor houses to dwell in, neither
> do they endeavour to build them any; yet nevertheless, intending their

profits most among the Irish ... they did farm their said tithe milk to certain kerns, bailiff errants and such like extortious people, who ... did ... take away the same rudely, to the extreme displeasure of the poor people whose daily food and blood it is, and with like envy to ministers of the gospel and their profession.[100]

Such tensions were of course a normal part of parish life throughout Europe, classically expressed in anticlericalism. But in Ireland the absence of adequate, often any, pastoral provision, and the employment of bailiffs, exposed the relationship as uniquely exploitative.

Following the 1622 commissioners' recommendations, the king ordered that 'old Irish customs and exactions of tithings and mortuaries, contrary to the use and law of England', be abolished and commuted into a monetary payment.[101] In 1624 an Act of State finally set down the 'tithes, offerings and other ecclesiastical duties' which could be taken by ministers in Ulster.[102] Official diktat, however, did not eliminate the problem. In 1629, a Protestant layman, Sir John Bingley, claimed that the ministers of the Church of Ireland 'do exact of their parishioners more fees and duties than is taken in England which is a great scandal'.[103] A major part of the problem was financial necessity: large sums of money were at stake. Faithful Teate, rector of Castleterra, Drung and Laragh, claimed that his proctor, Hugh Brady, 'was raised by him from poverty to a rich estate'.[104] Bedell's son claimed that one parishioner in Kilmore found that a failure to pay 3*d.* for tithe turf ended up costing him £5.[105] The imposition on the local people was all the more onerous because they had also to support the Catholic clergy. Indeed, from the point of view of Bishop Moigne, the collection of tithes was a straightforward battle between the Protestant and Catholic churches: 'the more that is taken away from the king's clergy, the more accrues to the pope's'.[106] Tithes and other dues, as a result, remained a major source of friction, and were the subject of lengthy and detailed complaint in the Irish parliament in 1640.[107]

Even apart from tithes the majority of the population had already been statutorily placed in a monetary rather than a religious relationship with the established church. The Elizabethan Act of Uniformity had imposed a fine of 12*d.* for each failure to attend the parish church, which was enforceable through the church courts. The peace which followed the end of the war in 1603 was seen by Irish churchmen and officials as providing them at last with the ideal conditions to enforce conformity with vigour.[108] Significant sums were raised by enforcing the 12*d.* fine, some of which were used to rebuild churches in both Cavan and neighbouring Fermanagh.[109] Sporadic government support for the enforcement of conformity, and its limited long term effects upon popular religious allegiance, led by the 1620s to recusancy fines being seen less as a genuine means of making people Protestant, and more as an additional source of revenue.[110] The 1622 Commissioners received a number of complaints on this issue. One grievance from Tyrone pointed out that the people are fined for not coming to church

> when as for the most part there is no church to come unto. And if there be, there is commonly none but an English or Scottish minister, whom the common people understand not, neither do they know, or were ever taught, what difference is in religion.[111]

Examples were given of the behaviour of one English minister, Felix Crane, then beneficed in Clogher, but subsequently appointed by Moigne to the vicarages of Rossinver and Killasnett in Kilmore. His native Irish parishioners complained about Crane on three grounds: his two bailiffs, James O'Callan and Cale Boye O'Heere, insisted on taking tithes in specie rather than in kind; he allegedly collected exorbitant fees—as much as 7s. 6d. to christen the child of Patrick McMorriertie; and despite the fact that forty of his parishioners had compounded with him to pay £12 sterling to avoid being presented for recusancy during the following two years, nevertheless he presented five of those who had paid, costing them a further £7.[112]

Tithes and recusancy fines were not the only sources of friction. The church courts, which had formed a key element in Montgomery's proposals, also bore heavily upon the local population. His successor as bishop of Derry did, it is true, attempt to control its impact by sitting in his own court on a weekly basis.[113] This was decidedly unusual: bishops almost universally left their courts in the hands of their chancellors, ecclesiastical lawyers who were granted a commission during the life of the bishop. This assured the bishop of income, but at the expense of direct control over his court. Had the commissaries been competent, moral and upright men, this would not have mattered, but often or, one sometimes gains the impression, normally, they were not.[114] Such failings were all the more serious because the peculiar religious imbalance in Ireland meant that the potential scope of these courts was much larger than in England. In England the ecclesiastical courts were perceived as performing a useful role in society and, though complaints were far from unknown, they were not sources of friction between church and people.[115] In Ireland, however the scope for resentment was much greater. The refusal of the Catholic population to come to church, and their resort to Catholic clergy for christenings, marriages and funerals, all immediately exposed them to prosecution in the church courts. Those in charge of ecclesiastical justice were thus faced with an irresistible temptation to harass the local population, since prosecutions brought with them fees and fines. In addition, the threat of prosecution could also result in illegal but equally profitable payments. The result was regular Catholic protests at the oppressive nature of the ecclesiastical courts and their officials.[116]

The theoretical justification for this system of discipline was that it was essential for the imposition of order which was both a normal part of any church settlement and especially important in the plantation church, since the church in Ulster had the additional role of ensuring that the population adjusted to 'civilised' norms of behaviour. The imposition of an anglicised church structure, together with the establishment of English settlers, and an English system of civil and ecclesiastical justice, would, it was hoped, gradually produce a native population that conformed not merely civilly but also religiously. Acting on the implicit assumptions of the superiority of English culture over Irish, it was assumed that with time the former would inevitably triumph over the latter. The problems with such assumptions were twofold: assimilation, where it happened, proved to be a much lengthier process than imagined; and civil and religious conformity proved to have no necessary connection. This was partly a result of the resilience of catholicism. It was also, however, a product of the very system that was designed to impose religious uniformity: its means frustrated its aims. The system simply could not cope with fatal combination of mass disaffection and corrupt officials.

III

The need for reform was pressingly evident by the 1630s and reform was exactly what Kilmore got, in the person of William Bedell. Bedell was born in Essex in 1571, went to Emmanuel, Cambridge's newly founded puritan college, and then followed a clerical career. Twice he was plucked from obscurity as an English country parson, first in 1607–10, to go to Venice as chaplain to the English ambassador, and again in 1627, when he was chosen to reform Trinity College, Dublin. Unlike most of his fellow Irish clerics he was culturally curious and relatively unprejudiced, positive about the syncretic approach of the Jesuit missionaries in the far east, familiar with the centralising thrust of Propaganda Fide, and even prepared to view positively the reformist activities of the Council of Trent.[117] Linguistically gifted, he translated the Book of Common Prayer into Italian and was an accomplished biblical scholar and open-minded theologian.[118] His experience of the complexities and intellectual richness of Italian catholicism during his time in Venice meant that, whilst he had retained his theological opposition to catholicism, he had long abandoned simplistic puritan views of 'popery' as a faith founded upon superstitious ignorance and antichristian whoredom.[119] Though genuinely diffident in terms of personal ambition, he was nevertheless a firmly committed, questioning, stubborn reformer, determined that the standards which he applied so rigourously to himself should also be adhered to by others.[120] The application of these attributes during his time in Ireland comprise one of the tests of the structures and assumptions that lay behind the Irish reformation, and particularly of the nature of religious allegiance in Kilmore and the possibility of restoring the balance within the Protestant ministry between the plantation and the indigenous churches.

As provost of Trinity College, Dublin between 1627 and 1629, he took on a college that was disorganised and factious and began the task of reshaping it, seeking to ensure that it fulfilled its original, and largely ignored purpose, of providing an Irish speaking ministry for the Church of Ireland.[121] After two years at Trinity, he was promoted in 1629 to the sees of Kilmore and Ardagh, and it was in Cavan that he spent the remainder of his ministry until his death in 1642. Bedell quickly laid down the essential elements of his reform pro-gramme: he was determined to eliminate the abuses from his ecclesiastical court, root out pluralism and pastoral incompetence amongst his clergy and he sought to strengthen the native Irish ministry by providing it with the men and the tools that it needed to proselytise the local population. As part of these missionary endeavours Bedell adopted an accommodating tone towards individual Catholics, preferring discussion and persuasion to denunciation and coercion.

Almost as soon as he arrived in Kilmore, Bedell encountered the 'clamour of the people' against the system of ecclesiastical justice. His own neighbours and tenants protested that they were forced to attend the courts without just cause, and only escaped by paying excessive fees. In particular the over-use of the sentence of excommunication had devalued its reformative power. Bedell became convinced 'that amongst all the impediments to the work of God amongst us, there is not any one greater than the abuse of ecclesiastical jurisdiction'. The ordinary people, Bedell argued, could spot the contradic-tion between the pious principles of the Protestant clergy, and the 'publicans and worldlings' of the church courts that 'so ... prey upon them'. The diffi-culty, however, lay in bringing the courts under episcopal control: the canon lawyers had 'engrossed all jurisdiction to themselves, and left to the bishops and ministry nothing but the name'. Bedell took decisive action, formally declaring, at a meeting of his diocesan clergy, that his chancellor's patent was null and void, and subsequently backing up his claims with extensive citations from canon law and ecclesiastical history. He sat personally in his courts, travelling throughout his diocese to administer justice and, he hoped, also to dispense pastoral counsel.[122]

At the start of his episcopate Bedell made the grand and unprecedented gesture of voluntarily resigning his twin see of Ardagh, so that it could be entrusted to a resident bishop.[123] He observed 'plainly I do thus think, that of all the diseases of the church in these times, next to that of the corruption of our courts, this of pluralities is the most deadly and pestilent'[124] and then set about ensuring that the Kilmore clergy followed his example. He admonished pluralist ministers to be resident in at least one of their parishes, and provide adequate curates for the others. He refused, when parishes became vacant, to collate non-resident clergy to them, and required that ministers as part of their formal institution should swear both to reside and to hold no other benefice. He tried to tackle the problem of distant glebes by Chichester's expedient of exchanging the old termon lands (which were generally near to the parish church) for the inconvenient glebes.[125]

Bedell also took great care to ensure that ministers were able to communicate with all their parishioners. Given a choice between an English and an Irish speaking cleric, Bedell prefered the latter, even if the former was otherwise better qualified. According to his son, he explained to English speaking clergy that 'though they had Saint Paul's gifts, yet he could not see how they would be able to do any good unless they had the language of the people'.[126] Seeking to provide ministers with essential religious texts in Irish, he set about translating the Old Testament, and having a single sheet, dual language catechism printed in Dublin in 1631.[127] The former task was a major enterprise. Bedell himself, with his expert Hebrew and recently learnt Irish, could supervise the project, but he relied for the actual task of translation upon two Irish scholars, Murtagh King (whom he provided with a benefice in Kilmore) and James Nangle, together with one of his servants who acted as amanuensis.[128]

Though firmly Protestant, Bedell, took a gentler line towards Roman Catholicism than some of his fellow Irish Protestants. At Trinity he had gained a reputation for contracting rather than expanding the differences between protestantism and Rome.[129] One of his first intentions on arriving in his diocese was to write to the Catholic bishop (recently made primate) who lived two miles away from him.[130] He was ever willing to engage in discussion with his opponents, and sought where possible to win them over to protestantism.[131] Both King and Nangle were converts to protestantism, Bedell ordaining the former and providing him with a benefice.[132] A Kilmore friar, Dennis O'Crean (or Crane), who had become a Protestant before Bedell arrived in Kilmore, was provided with the wholly native Irish living of Killinkere, where he preached to the people in Irish.[133] The case of the Sheridans best illustrates Bedell's methods. Denis Sheridan, from a prominent local family, initially became Protestant as a result of his upbringing in the household of John Hill, dean of Kilmore from 1619 until 1627. In 1634 he was ordained deacon by Bedell and at the same time collated to the vicarage of Killesher. Sheridan remained loyal to his bishop, even during the rising (it was in Sheridan's house that Bedell died in 1642), and went on to found a Protestant dynasty.[134] More relevantly, he was also a point of contact between Bedell and Cornelius (Cohonaght) O'Sheridan, to whom Bedell in 1636 wrote a brief theological treatise trying to win him over to Protestant views on grace, faith and works.[135] Bedell's efforts met with success, since Cohonaght went on to become a schoolmaster in the diocese.[136] Finally, another O'Sheridan, Owen, is also mentioned by Bedell's biographer Alexander Clogie as an Irish speaking minister.[137]

The image of Bedell as the saintly reforming bishop seeking single-handedly to tackle the abuses of the Church of Ireland, which pervades the semi-hagiographical biographies by his son, Clogie and Burnett, sometimes gives the impression that, had the Irish reformation been modelled upon Bedell's policies, it might have universally succeeded. Careful reading of the biographies and contemporary sources suggest that, though Bedell's reforming zeal was genuine, his ability to transform the assumptions and structures underlying the Protestant reformation in Kilmore was limited. Rather than changing the shape of the established church in Kilmore, he demonstrated its resilience and resistance to reform, fully justifying his inclusion in the pantheon of 'losers in Irish history'.

In each of the four main elements of his reforming policies he encountered setbacks and obstacles. His voiding of his chancellor's patent was a grand gesture, but of doubtful validity. The chancellor, Alan Cook, immediately challenged him in the archbishop's court, thence to the civil courts, beginning a long legal battle that was to end with the lord chancellor fining Bedell £100.[138] In the course of the legal struggle Bedell appealed for help to both James Ussher, archbishop of Armagh and William Laud, archbishop of Canterbury. He asked Ussher to sit in person on his case, rather than leave it to his chancellor, George Synge, a friend of Cook's.[139] He even, with typical tactlessness, warned Ussher that his own archiepiscopal court was riddled with the same abuses as the one in Kilmore.[140] While both archbishops were sympathetic they were aware of the power of the vested interests that Bedell was attacking and refused to intervene, warning him instead to desist.[141] In the end, after his fruitless legal odyssey, Bedell reached an uneasy compromise: Cooke refrained from recovering his fine from Bedell, and left the administration of the court in the hands of his registrar, a local official called Richard Ash, who in practice deferred to Bedell.[142]

Conflict between Bedell's principles and the institutionalised church recurred over his hostility to pluralism. Bedell was relatively fortunate in having considerable powers of patronage in his diocese and was able to use these to control who was appointed to benefices and to insist upon their residence. Difficulties arose, however, where patronage slipped out of Bedell's hands, or where clergy connived to avoid his stringent requirements. The case of William Bayly amply illustrates Bedell's problems. Two advowsons had been granted by Bishop Moigne to his brother-in-law, John Greenham, a lawyer and local land-holder. He in turn presented Bayly, a young Scottish cleric, and Bedell admitted him, with the usual caveat about pluralism. Bayly, however, sought to evade this by securing a dispensation (routinely granted in the Church of Ireland on payment of the requisite fee) from the court of faculties in Dublin, which allowed him to hold two more benefices provided they were within thirty miles of his first. He then, without Bedell's permission, was priested outside the diocese by the bishop of Kilfenora who was 'father in law to my friendly chancellor', as Bedell put it. Subsequently, he secured a presentation to the second of Greenham's vicarages, Denn, and when Bedell refused to admit him, got the chancellor of Armagh, George Synge, to do so. Bedell suspended him, but Bayly appealed (the illiterate Latin clearly suggested to Bedell the hand of Cook) to a variety of courts, concluding with the lord deputy.[143] When that came to naught, Bayly then sought to obtain the living of Murtagh King, first by claiming that it was in law void and in the presentation of the lord deputy and secondly, by having King persecuted in the High Commission court for ignorance, neglect of his cure, and having a Catholic wife and children. Bayly's continuing pressure on King led to the latter's imprisonment and eventual capitulation, much to the annoyance of Bedell, who sought to fight the case even against the wishes of the defendant. Bayly having obtained King's vicarage, Bedell then proceeded to call a meeting of his clergy and excommunicate him. Bayly appealed to the archiepiscopal court, at which stage records of the case cease.[144]

Bedell's attempt in 1638 to reform his clergy by calling a synod and passing twenty two reforming articles merely exacerbated his difficulties. Under the English Act for Submission of the Clergy convocations and synods required the royal approval before they could meet or pass articles. Bedell's synod was further cited as evidence of *praemunire*—infringing upon the jurisdictional rights of the monarch. Bedell had in fact a good case for his defence (indeed, better than he knew: there was in fact no equivalent of the English Act for Submission in Ireland), citing long forgotten historical precedents, and in the end he escaped censure, but not before he had given considerable ammunition to his opponents, including, in particular, Alan Cook.[145]

Bedell's theological openness caused further problems for him with the Calvinist establishment of the Church of Ireland, especially in two areas, his attitude towards catholicism and his theology of grace. From his first arrival in Kilmore he was pursued by rumours as to his doctrinal orthodoxy. Even Ussher wrote to Bedell voicing concern at the discontent that Bedell's attitude towards catholicism had caused.[146] Bedell was indignant: his approach was no different than he had taken at Trinity.[147] That, however, was a large part of the problem. Bedell had had repeated arguments while at Trinity with the professor of theology, Joshua Hoyle, a precise and rigourous Calvinist, who was intensely suspicious of the provost's 'Italianate' tendencies, suspecting him of that modish anti-Calvinist, indeed semi-papist, heresy, Arminianism.[148] Bedell did not realise the pervasiveness of such rumours until early in 1630, when he discovered that some of his clergy were considering leaving Kilmore for fear of being tainted by their new bishop's heterodoxy. He was even faced with one ordinand, who, before Bedell could examine him, presented Bedell with a list of twelve articles about which he first required satisfaction from the bishop.[149] Bedell had in the end to call a meeting of his clergy to scotch the rumours.[150] Even then, senior members of the Irish hierarchy deputed Bedell's neighbour, the bishop of Ardagh, to engage in a lengthy theological correspondence with him to test the orthodoxy of his views on grace.[151]

The sense that Bedell was out of step with conventional wisdom also hindered his efforts to promote Irish. Bedell's belief that Irish was an ancient and noble language was, to start with, contrary to the common assumption that it was a backward and barbaric tongue.[152] Even more seriously, his championing of the language brought him into conflict with the spirit of the Act for English Order Habit and Language, passed by Henry VIII's reformation parliament in 1537. This became the classic statement of the official insistence upon anglicization, and an underlying justification for the settlement of Ireland and the strategy of the plantation church. Bedell's flouting of such a basic principle caused resentment and opposition. He was suspected of having 'gone native', of being 'soft' towards the Irish and failing to uphold the use of English, one of the basic planks in the policy of assimilation.[153] Even the persecution of King was linked by one of Bedell's biographers to hostility within church and state to the translation of the Old Testament.[154]

What Bedell encountered regularly were the limits on the freedom of action of an Irish bishop. With his high vision of the episcopal role, correcting and admonishing a respectful clergy, and his pedantic armoury of historical precedents, confirming and supporting the exercise of his power, Bedell found it difficult to come to terms with the everyday restrictions imposed on him by the structures and realities of the Irish church. He resented the loss of his jurisdiction during the triennial archiepiscopal visitation; his chancellor's freedom from episcopal control; the dominance of the civil over the ecclesiastical courts, and the endless capacity for appeal from the latter to the former; the rights of the king to present to lapsed benefices; the power of the court of faculties to grant dispensations. In short, he felt that he was not in control of his own diocese. The result for Bedell was frustration. As he lamented to Laud in 1638: 'What likelihood is there of redress in the matter of non-residence and pluralities whereas, if they were all now dissolved, we have a forge that can (and will for money) presently make us as many more?'[155]

Frustration is the inevitable lot of all reformers. The critical question is the extent to which they manage to triumph over the obstacles put in their way. Any attempt at an overall assessment of Bedell's lasting achievement has been hindered by the fact that, after a dozen years of his ministry, the rising of 1641 destroyed the Protestant church in Kilmore. Indeed, the oft-told story of his treatment at the hands of his captors and, above all, the poignant scenes at his funeral, with their clear subtext of the triumph of his saintly and tolerant personality over the pervasive racial and religious bitterness of the rising, have, by concentrating upon the personal and the heroic, at the expense of the institutional and the prosaic, as much obscured as they have clarified his achievement.

It is possible to use the rising, and the depositions that arose from it, together with ecclesiastical records and the biographies of Bedell, as a means of testing the extent and durability of Bedell's achievements in one crucial area: the creation of an indigenous Protestant church. It has recently been suggested that the 1641 depositions can be used not merely to determine the extent of Protestant penetration of the native population, but that such penetration might well have been greater than has hitherto been supposed.[156] Since in the case of Kilmore, it would appear that indigenous protestantism was limited at the start of the 1630s, any progress by the time of the rising is in fact an index of Bedell's success in winning over the native population. Bedell's success in gaining native Irish to serve in the ministry of the Church of Ireland can be estimated with some accuracy. During his episcopate thirty eight clergy were appointed to Kilmore for the first time: of these, nine can be identified as native Irish.[157] While it does not represent any major breakthrough, the proportion of native Irish, at a quarter, was larger than that under Moigne.[158] At least Bedell was preserving and even building upon what gains had already been made, an achievement in itself, since in other Ulster dioceses the number of native Irish clergy was generally declining.[159] What is unclear is the relationship between ministerial and lay conformity. Close analysis of the Kilmore depositions reveals very few native Irish Protestants, and certainly does not suggest any significant Protestant advance amongst the ordinary people.[160] At most, the depositions suggest that Kilmore differed from other Ulster dioceses in two respects. First, no ministers were killed.[161] Secondly, some of the native Irish converts remained loyal to their new religion. Indeed, Bedell's biographer boasted that he knew of none 'that were converted and promoted by my Lord ... to any ecclesiastical function, that turned apostate ... save one Patrick Brady, minister'.[162]

Where the depositions *are* revealing is not in proving the strength of indigenous protestantism, but, on the contrary, in confirming the deep-seated hostility towards the Church of Ireland that had built up in Kilmore. Even amongst the families and relations of native Protestant clergy and converts there was support for the rising.[163] As for the mass of the Catholic population, the Cavan depositions[164] contain repeated indications of their resentment against the English plantation and the Protestant church which manifested themselves as the rebellion gathered momentum.[165] As one deponent summed it up 'their main reason for rising was to enjoy all their lands again, and have their conscience'.[166] Richard Parsons, a minister married to an O'Reilly, reported that he was hated by the Irish 'not merely as a minister but ... because he was an Englishman', and that the Irish aimed

> to shake off and root out the English government, and their very laws, customs, habit, language, the Protestant religion, and the whole race, lineage, posterity, seed and memorial both of the English and Scottish nations out of Ireland.[167]

Similarly, William Jameson of the parish of Drumgoon claimed that Patrick O'Gowen, a yeoman, had 'burned the church bible saying It was the word of the devil and that we were an unchristened people'.[168] George Creighton, vicar of Lurgan, confirmed the alienation caused by the church courts. He claimed that he had escaped assault because his parishioners professed to love him, because (as they said) he had not been grievous to them (no man ever lost a penny by him in the bishop's court, and none having ever paid to him what he did not owe) ... [169]

If one accepts such reports at face value it suggests that, beyond the short term and accidental political causes of the rising, there lurked real resentments which the Irish leaders were able to build on, where, indeed they proved able to control them. Certainly the dispossession of the English ministers was rapidly followed by the Catholic bishops and clergy taking back possession of the cathedral and the parish churches. [170]

The knowledge of what happened in the rising inevitably colours the historians' evaluation of the success or failure of Bedell's mission. Indeed, in the aftermath of 1641, even Bedell's own son cast a jaundiced eye over his father's success in gaining Irish converts, arguing that Bedell was sometimes led

to prefer many Irishmen, some of which were such as had been popish, and some priests and friars, who either by some injury or disgrace from those of their religion, or through poverty and desire for preferment (being once acquainted with the bishop's way and principles) were moved to desire conference with him; and so by degrees becoming converts ... they were by the bishop preferred, merely out of his zeal for the conversion of the Irish. But some of these men proved scandalous, returning again to their vomit; not by revolting to popery, but by breaking out into dissoluteness of life ... [171]

To sum up, though there was a persistent minority of native Irish clergy who served in Kilmore, and though Bedell did all that he could to encourage such ministers, he never managed to eliminate the instinctive English fear, evidenced even by his own son, that the native clergy were an unreliable fifth column, untrustworthy Protestants, inferior to the English and Scots ministry. Nor was clerical conformity parallelled amongst a significant section of the local population. As one Victorian commentator remarked: 'his love of justice won the esteem of our poor countrymen, though it could not seduce them from their religion'. [172] In this one can only echo the judgement of Bedell's son: 'It must not here be concealed that his success was not so answerable to his good intentions'. [173]

IV

During the first forty years of the seventeenth century the Irish state and the Irish state church experimented with virtually its full range of tactics and strategies to further the reformation in Kilmore. The Roman Catholic church structure and, where possible, ministry, was taken over, and, after a brief attempt to construct an indigenous established church, Bishop Moigne over-saw the building up of an anglicized, plantation church. In this Kilmore was similar to all the other Ulster plantation dioceses. The final and distinctive twist to the early history of the reformation in Kilmore was the vigorous reforming episcopate of Bedell, which acted as a litmus test of the resilience of the structures, loyalties and assumptions both of the new plantation church, and of the reconstructed Catholic church. The persistence of the attitudes of the plantation church, and the pattern of economic exploitation without any real pastoral provision, confirms that even under Bedell, the realities of the established church precluded or at least spancelled the essential 'campaign of evangelization and education to win over the Irish population'. The very structures and assumptions of the plantation church served as much to alien-ate as to convert, producing tensions and resentments which violently sur-faced as the rising 1641 gained momentum. Bedell, though unable to remedy it, identified the problem with his usual clarity:

> the popish clergy is double to us in number, and having the advantage of the tongue, of the love of the people, of our extortions on them, of the very inborn hatred of subdued people to their conquerors, they hold them still in blindness and superstition, ourselves being the chiefest impediments to the work that we pretend to set forward.[174]

APPENDIX: CHURCH OF IRELAND CLERGY KNOWN
TO HAVE SERVED IN KILMORE 1603–41

Where there is no other indication of nationality, it has been inferred from the minister's name. Such an approach can only produce approximate results. For the general principles involved in distinguishing between Scots and English, see R.J.Hunter and Michael Perceval-Maxwell, 'The muster roll of c.1630: Co. Cavan' in *Breifne*, v (1976–81), 206–21; for a basic list of Irish names see Edward MacLysaght, *Irish families: their names, arms and origins* (Dublin, 1957).

ENGLISH

Name	First appears in Kilmore	University	Name	First appears in Kilmore	University
Bostock, John	1612	Camb	Roycroft, William	1619	TCD
Whiskens, Robert	1613	Camb	Sarcott, Thomas	1619	
Parker, Francis	1615		Robinson, Laurence	1620	TCD
Andrews, William	1617		Barrett, Walter	1622	
Hollington, Nathaniel	1618	Camb	Evatt, John	1622	
Hill, John	1619		Holliwell, William	1622	TCD
Patrick, John	1619	TCD	Johnson, John	1622	TCD
Robinson, Thomas	1619	TCD	Metcalf, James	1622	

Name	First appears in Kilmore	University	Name	First appears in Kilmore	University
Slacke, James	1622	Camb	Hammond, William	1634	
Taylor, Robert	1622		Parsons, Richard	1634	
Groves, Thomas	1625		Stanhope, Edward	1634	
Bolton, William	1626		Vaux, Robert	1634	Camb
Crane, Felix	1626	Camb	Gonnys, Valentine	1635	
Teate, Faithful	1626	TCD	Margetson, James	1635	Camb
Bernard, Nicholas	1627	Camb	Cresswell, John	1636	TCD
Jones, Thomas	1627		Roberts, Thomas	1636	TCD
Moorhead, James	1627		Jones, Henry	1637	TCD
Dunsterville, Edward	1629	TCD	Rhodes, Godfrey	1637	Oxf
Hathersall, Henry	1632		Sotheby, Samuel	1638	Camb
Aldrich, William	1634		Hodson, John	1640	
Bedell, William Jun	1634				

25 appointed under Moigne
16 under Bedell

Note
New English are also included in this list, even where they have been born in Ireland: e.g. Henry Jones. A number of names are difficult to place: Barrett, for example could be a well established Irish or Anglo–Irish family. Vaux could also be Scottish, but Cambridge education would seem to indicate English. University can only be inferred in some cases from the coincidence of dates and absence of any details of an alternative career in lists of alumni such as those of Venn for Cambridge or Foster for Oxford.

NATIVE IRISH CLERGY

Name	First appears in Kilmore	University	Name	First appears in Kilmore	University
Smith, Nicholas Jr	1615	TCD	King, Murtagh	1632	
O'Gowan, John	1619		Reynolds, Bernard	1634	
Brady, Thomas	1620		Sheridan, Denis	1634	
McComyn, Hugh	1622		O'Sheridan, Owen	163?	
O'Siredok, Patrick	1622		O'Hogley, Cormac	1635	
Smith, Nicholas Sen	1622		Swiny, Hugh	1635	
Crane, Daniel	1631		McAuley, Manus	1641	TCD
O'Connolly, Terence	1631				

6 appointed under Moigne
9 under Bedell

Note
On the Reynolds family see Joseph Meehan, 'Notes on the MacRannals of Leitrim and their country' in *Journal of the Royal Society of Antiquaries of Ireland*, xxxv (1905), pp. 139–51.

SCOTTISH

Name	First appears in Kilmore	University	Name	First appears in Kilmore	University
Watson, Adam	1613		Bayly, William	1635	Glasg
Baxter, Martin	1618		Clogie, Alexander	1637	
Creighton, George	1619	Aberd	Coningham, John	1637	Glasg
Comyn, Alexander	1622	Edinb	Fraser, Walter	1639	
Frasor, Thomas	1629		Murdoe, David	1641	TCD
McWhidd, Alexander	1630		Wallace, William	1640	Aberd
Campbell, Archibald	1632				

5 appointed under Moigne
8 under Bedell

Note
Creighton is definitely Scottish: J.T. Gilbert (ed.), *A contemporary history of affairs in Ireland*, i (3 vols. Dublin, 1879), pp. 525–30; as is Bayly: E.S. Shuckburgh (ed.), *Two lives of William Bedell* (Cambridge, 1902), p. 345; and Clogie: Leslie, *Kilmore Clergy*, p. 340. Adam Watson's benefice was in the Scottish barony of Tullyhunco, and his patron was Francis Hamilton. McWhidd is an Hiberno–Scottish name: Alexander, however, was clearly associated with the Scottish settlers, both in Antrim and in Cavan: T.J. Barron, 'Alexander McWhidd *c.*1610–*c.*1690: the story of an heirloom' in *The Heart of Breifne* (1981), pp. 102–8. In the case of Alexander Comyn, while it is true that there was a native Irish family of McComyns living in Cavan, he did have an MA (and may be identified with a Scottish graduate) and was beneficed in a Scottish barony.

In the case of Scottish ministers the links with the university are somewhat tentative, given the absence of other identifying details in the lists of alumni that have been used. Nevertheless, it fits the general pattern of Scottish graduates serving in the Ulster church: A.F.S. Pearson, 'Alumni of St Andrews and the Scottish settlement of Ulster' in *Ulster Journal of Archaeology*, 3rd Series, xiv (1951), pp. 7–14.

WELSH

Name	First appears in Kilmore	University
Floyd, John	1639	
Price, Thomas	1638	TCD

NO CLEAR INDICATION

Name	First appears in Kilmore	University
Smith, John	1631	
Moore, Mathew	1625	

Faith, Family and Fortune: The Structures of Everyday Life in Early Modern Cavan

RAYMOND GILLESPIE

Towards the end of June 1646, a few weeks after the victory of the commander of the Irish forces in Ulster, Owen Roe O'Neill, at the battle of Benburb, the dominant faction in the confederation of Kilkenny led by the papal nuncio Rinuccini sent an envoy north to discuss how the military advantage might best be consolidated. He travelled north from Kilkenny to Birr and Multifarnham and then through Westmeath to arrive at the meeting point with the northern forces at Lismore in the southern part of county Cavan. Such a journey was not remarkable. What was unusual was that the delegate, unlike most foreign travellers through early modern Ireland, was not English but Italian. He was Dino Massari, dean of Fermo and secretary to the papal nuncio.[1] Most English visitors came to Ireland with preconceived views of the barbarity of native Irish society and held well established opinions as to how the Irish regions should be reformed and how their economic and social life could be regulated. As a result they often failed to perceive the realities of Irish life, preferring instead a series of stereotypes. Massari's visit provides a rather different perspective. It was not, however, an uncritical or unbiased one. On his first night in county Cavan, at Lismore, for example, he was tempted not to go to bed because the only accommodation he was provided with was a bundle of rushes and a blanket in the corner of a room with two other occupants. Similarly he did not approve of Irish drinking habits. He preferred to use his own silver cup rather than the large wooden mazzard type bowls used by his Cavan hosts. Despite a certain amount of distaste of some such practices his account provides a useful starting point in any attempt to understand the structures of everyday life in Cavan during the seventeenth century.

I

Perhaps the dominant element of Massari's account was his observations on the landscape, the stage on which everyday life was played out. Unfortunately his journey through Cavan was a rather restricted one. He confined himself largely to the south east of the county. Arriving at Lismore castle, where he stayed with Philip dubh O'Reilly for two nights, he then moved to Clogh Oughter where he remained for three nights. Finally he journeyed to Cavan town where he lodged one night with the Franciscans before journeying to Longford by way of Fenagh and joining with Owen Roe O'Neill's Confederate army in Roscommon. The area which he saw, the two southern baronies of Castlemahon and Castlerahan, was not the best land in the county. It was described in a survey of 1656 as mountainous, boggy and heathy and even if reclaimed would quickly revert to its natural state if not continuously worked. In the extreme south, towards county Meath the land was much better drained and suitable for sheep.[2] This topography was reflected in the building types which Massari saw. Houses were 'all built and covered with sods some three arms in length, others five or six, so well fitted together that neither sun nor rain no matter how heavy could penetrate them'. This tradition of using available turf for building was not confined to the native Irish. Those English and Scots who settled in the county as part of the scheme for the plantation of Ulster also appreciated the utility of using local materials. Captain John Ridgeway in Castlerahan, for instance, by 1613 had constructed for his tenants 'three thatched houses of one storey with walls of stone and clay'.[3]

As Massari travelled north towards Cavan town the landscape changed. The boggy land gave way to a hilly terrain dominated by drumlins with lakes between them. An earlier visitor, Lord Deputy Arthur Chichester, commented in 1606 that Cavan town was 'situated betwixt many hills'. In the 1630s the bishop of Kilmore, William Bedell, had described the county as 'consisting altogether of hills, very steep and high, valleys between them being most commonly bogs and loughs'.[4] This topography had given central Cavan its military importance for loughs when fortified using man made islands or crannogs were difficult to take. Massari saw what was probably the most impressive of these, Clogh Oughter castle, which he described as 'an impregnable fortress in the middle of a large lake'. It was approachable only by boat and hence could be held by a small garrison. In the sixteenth century these strongholds had been of considerable importance but they fell out of use in the seventeenth century as warfare moved from guerrilla warfare to European style set piece battles and it was Cromwellian artillery which finally demolished Clogh Oughter.[5] As residences they also became impracticable with the rise of a more commercial economy which the final section of this essay will describe.

Despite the hilly terrain studded with lakes the surveyors of the 1650s felt that central Cavan had potential. It was good for cattle raising and well provided with fuel both turf and timber and, in the opinion of the surveyors, some of the timber was suitable for building small houses.[6] This is reflected in the building styles which Massari observed. Arriving at the Franciscan friary in Cavan town he described it as 'a marvellous structure in the Ulster fashion, the church, cells, refectory and all other apartments being of wood roofed with sods'. Again in the 1613 survey of the Ulster plantation this was the region where houses were built 'of English frames'.

There were parts of Cavan into which Massari did not venture, the barony of Tullyhaw in the north west for instance. Few went there in the seventeenth century and it was little settled because of its mountainous nature.[7] Even the surveyors of the 1650s knew little of this area apart from its boundaries. This was a highland mainly of limestone which also had other mineral resources. These were exploited to some extent in the seventeenth century. In 1613 the surveyors of the Ulster plantation noted of Captain Culme's proportion, which lay in this area, that a 'quarry of limestone and building stone is on the place, good store of lime already burnt and of building stone digged'.[8] While such material could be used locally it was more difficult to transport resources out of this area. Despite this Sir Charles Coote had established an ironworks in this area, one of three located in counties Cavan, Fermanagh and Leitrim. The Dutch polemicist Gerard Boate claimed in the 1650s that they provided employment for 2500 or 2600 workers most of whom were English or Dutch.[9] Boate was probably over enthusiastic in his assessment of the importance of this venture which was destroyed in the 1641 rising but by the middle of the seventeenth century iron working had be reestablished in the area. By 1695 there was one iron works at Ballinamore and another at Swanlinbar by 1700, although this may have originated in the 1680s to judge by a later reference in an eighteenth century deed. This area also remained wooded long after the remainder of the county had been cleared.[10]

These purely topographical regions within the county formed the physical world occupied by the inhabitants of early modern Cavan. The less tangible world of the minds of those inhabitants, shaped by the interaction between communities is more difficult to describe. The area which Massari visited, in the south and east of the county, was distinguished by its contact with the pale and Dublin and to a lesser extent east Ulster. For example, by 1622 the barony of Clankee, which abutted onto Monaghan, had attracted a number of settlers, both natives and newcomers, from Clandeboy in north county Down.[11] To the south in Castlerahan and Clanmahon it was recorded that there were 'several palesmen' as settlers, and as the seventeenth century progressed they were joined by others, who built on their traditional contacts with the area by buying land from the early grantees in the plantation scheme. Luke Plunkett, the earl of Fingal, for instance, acquired the lands around Virginia in 1626.[12] There was, as the essays of Ciaran Parker and Bernadette Cunningham above have shown, a long tradition of such connections of landholding and Pale merchants had traded into southern Cavan since the fifteenth century which led O'Reilly to establish the market town of Cavan and even strike his own coinage. The north west of the county tended to look more towards west Ulster for its trade and settlers. This can be explained mainly in terms of the complex river systems which provided a way into Lough Erne and south Ulster. Belturbet became the gateway for such contacts. In the 1590s it had

been suggested that boats should be placed at Belturbet as a way of controlling access to Ulster. By 1613 the local landlord, Stephen Butler, was operating three boats varying in size from four to ten tons from Belturbet along the
south Ulster waterways.[13]

II

To regard the physical and human landscapes which Massari encountered in
the mid-seventeenth century as merely the product of natural forces or com-
munications routes would be to miss the significance of these landscapes
for contemporaries. The landscapes, as P.J. Duffy's essay shows, were part of
a wider mental world of both natives and settlers which was the outcome not
only of physical forces but political, social, economic and ideological ones
also. Placenames, for instance, not only identified points in the landscape but
explained why they were that way. Thus the early eighteenth-century tract
The genealogical history of the O'Reillys explained that Mullach na Mallacht
was so called because it was there that An Prior Balbh O'Reilly had been
cursed by the coarb of Madhog's chapel.[14] This process of naming was not
confined to places but was applied to families also. One branch of the O'Reilly's,
for instance, were known as An Caoch to distinguish themselves from others
since one of their ancestors had been blinded in war.[15] In 1611 the Dublin
administration founding a new settlement at Aghanure chose to give it a new
name: Virginia indicating a desire by government at least to see the region as
a new anglicised world. However old placenames were difficult to expunge
because of their explanatory power in the history of the landscape. This was
not confined to natives since in 1642 when the earl of Fingal wished to restore
Virginia to its former name even the newcomer Church of Ireland minister
was able to tell him what the older name was.[16]

For the native Irish population one of the most powerful ways of understanding the landscape was through the ideas of traditional catholicism. Such
religious beliefs are central to understanding the mental world of the inhabitants of Cavan. In the case of the native Irish it was traditional catholicism
which demarcated the world into sacred and profane areas and underpinned
this with stories, especially those of the activities of saints in the past. Massari
encountered this view when he visited Trinity Island in Lough Oughter.
There he found the ruins of a monastery of Premonstratensian canons which
still had a crucifix and a number of statues of saints. He noted that on leaving
the site 'I came on a well of the clearest water which as many of the islanders
told me had been miraculously discovered in the days of a saintly abbot when
his monks were suffering greatly from a want of water'. This cult of the holy
well was an important element in the traditional catholicism of early modern
Cavan. Most holy wells had a story of miraculous discovery by a saint and
were held to be especially holy places and hence formed the focus for local

pilgrimages. One description of a holy well at the church of Urney (half way between Belturbet and Cavan) in 1683 by a native, Patrick Bredin, recorded that at midsummer eve about twenty people gathered there to pray to a stone 'upon which was a face representing St Brigid'. Bredin was told by the pilgrims 'that St Brigid who built the church had left the stone in that heap and that they pay adoration to that stone in commemoration of the saint'.[17] Such pilgrimages were clearly amalgams of several traditions. Midsummer eve, for instance, seems to have no special connection with Brigid but was used as a pilgrimage date in other regions and the tradition of Brigid was merged with another tradition to produce this date. It was normal for pilgrims to make several rounds of the site saying a fixed number of Our Fathers and Ave Marias. Such sites seem to have been relatively common in the diocese of Kilmore. A partial list of the placenames of the diocese of the early seventeenth century mentions five but this must be seen as a minimum number given the fragmentary nature of the list.[18]

The presence of these wells points to one of the most important aspects of the popular religiosity of the native inhabitants of seventeenth century Cavan: the cult of the saints. These holy men and women may well have left traces in the landscape in the form of wells and marks on stones but they were not fossilised figures in the minds of contemporaries. Rather they acted as supernatural guardians and helpers in the contemporary world. Parishes and their inhabitants were placed under the protection of saints who were often assigned genealogies linking them to their localities. The identities of the local saints in any parish is difficult to establish although an early seventeenth century list of churches in the diocese of Kilmore does list a number of them associated with highly localised cults.[19]

Just as the saint was knitted into the local landscape through hagiographical legend so he or she was integrated into other activities in the community. The patron or pattern day involved much activity. The feast day of the saint was usually an occasion not only for prayer and pilgrimage but for other community events also. A 1608 survey of county Cavan noted that there was 'one fair held at Kilmore yearly the 3rd day of August being St Phelim's day' and 'fair Magheryhullage, St Patrick's day'.[20]

Saints were not simply linked to the physical world and the economic structure but to the social order also. In the late sixteenth century Aodh, son of Pilib O'Reilly, justified his position as lord of Breifne by appealing to the prophecies of Patrick, Columkille and Bearchan in which he, at least, saw himself approved of as lord of Breifne. In a more intimate way also the saint as a friend of God might be implored for aid. In one late sixteenth-century poem the poet implored the assistance of Columkille, 'Ciaran to be our protector' and Mary for the safe recovery of Pilib O'Reilly from an illness.[21]

This brief description of some of the elements of popular catholicism in seventeenth-century Cavan highlights one important feature: the immediacy of the religious experience. Religion was central to the understanding of every aspect of life from the physical landscape to the political and social structure. All these were the result of direct intervention of the supernatural power of God in the world. As the seventeenth century progressed such religious beliefs became increasingly politicised and the conflicts of mid-century following from the rising of 1641 were interpreted in a religious way by all the inhabitants of Cavan. Thus during the war of the 1640s the Catholic insurgents saw God as fighting on their side and after the battle of Julianstown in 1642 Philip O'Reilly could declare that the victory of the Irish forces was 'done by the hand of God'.[22] While the agents of the power of God, such as saints, might be distinctive of catholicism the basic ideas were shared with the Protestant settlers in seventeenth century Cavan. Protestants preferred to see God's will as revealed through the bible read by individuals rather than as manifested in specific times and places. Saints and other intermediaries formed no part of this world. Thus the will of Sir Stephen Butler of Belturbet proclaimed that he was 'hoping to be saved by the death and passion of Jesus Christ my only saviour'.[23] The rejection of this proposition by their Catholic neighbours was made manifestly clear by the burning of bibles at the market cross at Belturbet in the early months of the rising in 1641.[24]

The language chosen by Cavan Protestants, who as Alan Ford's essay shows were mainly settlers, to express the reality of religion was that of the providence of God. As with catholicism God was seen to act in the world to protect what Protestants chose to see as His people. Thus Mary Biggot of Virginia described in 1642 how Turlough O'Reilly came to burn the houses of Protestants in the town but 'howbeit it pleased God to command and work with the rebels to out rule him so that the most imminent danger was prevented'.[25] The mechanism of this providential intervention could sometimes be dramatic reversals of normal natural processes. After the drowning of Protestants at the bridge at Belturbet in 1642 strange visions and apparitions appeared on the river for up to a year, and all the fish were reported to have disappeared from the river.[26] The Church of Ireland minister at Ballyhaise, Faithful Teate, recorded how he and his son had been protected from the rebels and supplied with food by a ghostly messenger.[27] William Bedell, the son of the bishop of Kilmore in the 1630s, also recorded a number of portends before the rebellion: a multitude of rats and strange worms which appeared at Kilmore and a madman who prophesied the rising, although he was taken little note of at the time, was later thought to be 'very significant'.[28]

III

The indissoluble intertwining of immanence and transcendence which characterised the understanding of the world by the inhabitants of early modern Cavan meant that many of the structures of the religious world were reflections of social arrangements in the secular one. The world of patrons and saints as friends of God in an extended lineage of the heavenly family had particular appeal to the native Irish inhabitants of Cavan whose lives had traditionally been arranged around extended lineages. In this world the genealogy was important since it formed the basis of the social structure and acted as the guide for alliances and friends who could be relied on for support.[29] The continued significance of such family ties was reflected in the compilation of tracts such as the *Genealogical history of the O'Reilly's* first put together in the late seventeenth century and revised in the eighteenth century. This text is exceptional only in the level of detail which it recorded. Other less detailed O'Reilly genealogies had been complied as occasion demanded.[30]

The ties which bound this society together were not only those of kinship. Other forms of bonding were of equal importance. Fosterage, a practice whereby a child of one family was raised in the house of another, created a bond between families and godparenthood was another way of linking families. Thus, according to the *Genealogical history* it was the foster father of the Prior Balbh who was one of his chief advisors.[31] Gift giving was yet another way of creating bonds. In the sixteenth century the freeholders of Cavan had expressed their allegiance to their lord by rendering him food or money and in return the lord was expected to provide hospitality. In turn provincial leaders, such as the O'Neills, demanded their customary tribute from O'Reilly.[32] Although attempts had been made to curtail this practice by Sir John Perrott in his composition in the county in the 1580s, entertainment and gift giving remained important and valued social attributes. Thus An Prior O'Reilly was lauded in the *Genealogical history* as 'a great bestower, and that for three days he was bestowing money and horses' and when Brian O'Rourke of Breifne was beheaded in 1591 the annalists noted that 'there had not been for a long time any one of his tribe who excelled him in bounty, in hospitality, in giving rewards for panegyrical poems, in sumptuousness ...'. Such virtues were celebrated not only after death but were favourite themes of the poets in praising living lords.[33]

Such bonds of gift giving survived into the seventeenth century as a form of social cement which held society together when other social connections were being disrupted by new patterns of settlement shaped by the Ulster plantation. When Bishop Bedell arrived in Kilmore for the first time in the early 1630s he was greeted with gifts of horses, fat oxen and brawns. Convinced that the local inhabitants were attempting to bribe him he offered to pay for the gifts, an action which was received 'with indignation as a kind of affront'.[34] Massari, by contrast, responded favourably to the local custom, as he usually did. He received gifts and rather like a hospitable native lord distributed 'to the generals and colonels who had been to see me presents of sheep, young pigs, chickens, cheese, bread, wine, beer and whiskey according to the rank and position of the recipients'. For those lower on the social scale, such as the inhabitants of Holy Trinity Island there were 'some hundreds of blessed medals', and 'objects of devotion' for others.

Lineages and other socially created networks therefore formed the framework within which the native Irish in Cavan lived. It was these social structures which determined the pattern of violence, which usually consisted of
feuds within and between well defined kinship networks as one attempted to
assert superiority over others. Internal rivalries among the O'Reillys could be
problematic but in their case it was the power of the O'Neill's to the north
which offered the greatest threat. As the *Genealogical history* notes of one
episode 'O'Neill sent unto Maol Mordha demanding that he pay tribute or
else he would spoil and burn Breifne' and this was not an isolated incident.[35]
However it was not only those from outside who proved a threat since internal disputes among the differing branches of the O'Reillys was a continual
problem mainly because there was no dominant branch of the family to
maintain order. As Lord Deputy Chichester observed of the families of Cavan
in 1608

> the chief of them are the O'Reillys of which surname there are sundry
> septs most of them cross and opposite one to another ... [they] will not
> fear or obey their neighbours unless some one or two be made so
> powerful as to overtop and sway the rest.[36]

It is this lineage based social structure which, as Bernadette Cunningham's
essay shows, determined the pattern of allegiances in the late sixteenth century and allowed external groups, including the Dublin government, to gain
influence in the region.

IV

By the time of Massari's visit to Cavan in the mid-seventeenth century the
world dominated by extended lineages with a propensity towards violence was
under pressure from a number of sources, both internal and external, and
elements of it had already passed away. Two sets of external pressures contributed to the changing nature of Cavan society in the seventeenth century,
the first political and the second religious. Perhaps the most dramatic change
in the lives of the inhabitants of Cavan in the seventeenth century was a
political one. The defeat of O'Neill in 1603 after the nine years war dramatically increased the power of the Dublin administration in the county. The
presence of royal authority was hardly an innovation since the Dublin government had been active in trying to stabilise power relations in the county
during the sixteenth century. After 1603 and even more so after the plantation of Ulster the authority of the king and the common law became central
elements in determining the workings of society.

This was a world which many Cavan inhabitants could at least recognise
because of their links with the anglicised Pale. From the 1580s legal cases

involving parties from Cavan had been heard before the royal courts in Dublin. Indeed it was individuals from Cavan who attempted to upset the scheme for the Ulster plantation by challenging it under common law, using an Old English lawyer from the Pale to argue their case.[37] While the introduction of the common law may have been revolutionary in some parts of Ulster its evolution in Cavan represented the intensification of an already existing process, as Bernadette Cunningham's essay suggests. Assize judges, operating sporadically in Cavan in the 1590s and continuously from 1603, and other forms of courts such as chancery or even castle chamber provided an alternative to arbitration by a native lawyer under the control of a local lord for the resolution of disputes. Thus when in 1611 Richard Tyrell of Drumlaghan forcibly entered the lands of Cahal Mac Philip in Killibadrick in Cavan and assaulted Bryan Mac Cahal, one of Mac Philip's tenants, the result was a fine in castle chamber rather than a brawl.[38] While the spread of the institutions of the common law was rapid its full impact took somewhat longer to establish itself. Into the 1660s Cavan suffered from the effects of the survival of the older lineage system which perpetuated the idea of the feud and manifested itself in the raids of tories. By 1700 even this had disappeared as the authority of Dublin became more effective in the county.[39]

It was not only common law legal procedures which were embraced by Cavan inhabitants. Other aspects of the new political order were adopted also. By 1641 O'Reillys occupied prominent positions in the local government of the county and one was sheriff when the rebellion broke out in 1641. Another was the MP for the county in the Irish parliament.[40] For the O'Reilly's to retain influence in the county it was necessary to adapt to the new legal and political system. What is perhaps most striking about the process of adaptation to the new order is the acceptance of the king as their ultimate ruler and the royalism which developed from that. That royalism can be best seen in the conversations which the Cavan rebels had with the settlers in the early months of the 1641 rising and which were reported by those settlers in depositions taken by the Dublin government. Almost all the O'Reillys, at least in the early months of the rising, were concerned to explain that their rebellion was not against the king but in support of him and produced a forged royal commission to support their arguments. They feared that the king was about to fall under the control of the strongly anti-Catholic parliament in London, supported by the puritan administration in Dublin, which would force him to consent to anti-Catholic legislation. Indeed there were rumours circulating in Cavan on the eve of the rebellion that such legislation had been enacted. There were other rumours that the king, or in some versions the queen, had been imprisoned by parliament.[41] The loyalty of the O'Reillys to the crown is further underscored by the fact that in early November 1641, within a fortnight of the outbreak of the rising, nine of the most prominent O'Reilly's in Cavan wrote to the privy council in Dublin explaining their actions as being 'for the preservation of his majesty's honour'.[42] Of course not

all were staunchly royalist. A few depositions record an older political tradition in the shouts of 'God save king O'Reilly' on some occasions which
suggests that memories of the traditional power of the O'Reilly's had not yet
finally disappeared. Most, however, adapted well to the political and legal
world of the seventeenth century with its mechanisms for settling disputes
through the royal courts rather than by feud or local arbitration.

The second set of pressures which led to changes in the way in which the
social world of Cavan was organised in the seventeenth century were religious. Both the reformation and the counter reformation were not merely
movements of institutional reform but also fundamental shifts in the way in
which their adherents viewed the world. Both movements took increasing
hold in Cavan in the seventeenth century as detailed in Alan Ford's and James
Kelly's essays. The reform of catholicism, for example, involved not just a
reorganisation of parishes and an increase in the number of clergy but a new
attitude to what was holy. Traditional religious practices and devotion to local
patron saints came under attack from the new order. Many of the traditional
saints associated with particular holy wells and other sacred places were amalgams of various traditions and were often of dubious authenticity. These
provided a target for the counter-reformation clergy in Cavan during the
seventeenth century. A list of church dedications in the diocese of Kilmore
from the early eighteenth century suggests that the number of saints of local
origin had been replaced with more respected national figures such as Patrick,
Brigid and Columkille.[43]

Reform was most significant where the symbols of the sacred world met
those of the profane one: most dramatically in the sacraments. For Catholics
the most important of these was the mass. Tridentine norms required that the
mass was to be celebrated in particular holy places which were designated as
such and sanctified with relics, often concealed in the altar. Other places,
previously considered suitable for mass because of the traditional interrela-
tionship of sacred and profane worlds, were now deemed unsuitable for the
sacrament. Bishop Hugh O'Reilly in his relation of the state of the diocese of
Kilmore in 1629 ordered that the sacraments were to be administered with
'proper ceremonies' and explained that

> the Holy sacrifice of the mass was being celebrated either in the open
> air or in unbecoming places and the Most Holy Sacrament of the
> Eucharist was being administered to the faithful with great danger of
> sacrilege I ordered that ecclesiastical houses or neat oratories be erected
> in every parish.[44]

How successful this injunction was is not clear but other Ulster dioceses did
manage to construct churches. The speed at which these new religious ideas,
as opposed to the institutions they created, spread is not clear but by 1704

one Cavan scribe was at work transcribing copies of that most central of Tridentine works, the catechism, for circulation in the county.[45]

The sacramental reform became particularly important where it touched the social order. The Eucharist was administered only to those who were not in dispute with each other and could offer the peace. Thus the Church of Ireland vicar Murtagh King refused on one occasion to administer the Holy Communion 'saying he was not in charity'.[46] The cleric as a holy man was well placed to arbitrate and resolve disputes before they developed into a traditional style feud articulated by extended lineages. In the case of the Church of Ireland the church courts, discussed by Alan Ford, proved singularly ineffective in this matter but the Catholic clergy seem to have more effective in resolving disputes. Bishop O'Reilly reported in 1629 that 'to the great benefit, peace and quietness of the country I have frequently adjusted and settled the law suits and quarrels of the nobles, gentry and people' and 'by using various means I have banished from my territories thefts, robberies, drunkenness and various pests of the State'.[47] The techniques which O'Reilly used to achieve these results are not clear but in the 1640s some friars in Cavan did not hesitate to ritually curse those who indulged in gratuitous violence in the early weeks of the rebellion.[48] Equally, anything which perpetuated violence or feuds were regarded as barbarous. In 1672, for example, Oliver Plunkett, archbishop of Armagh attempted to stamp out the practice of attaching the nickname 'an caoch' to one branch of the O'Reillys to commemorate a blinding in war.[49] Quasi religious events, such as wakes, which might give rise to disorder were also condemned at the diocesan synod of Kilmore in 1687.[50]

While the ritual use of the Eucharist and arbitration by clergy could control the sort of violence which characterised a society based on extended lineages other measures of social control were also introduced by the counter reformation clergy. They attacked the roots of the problem of social conflict within Gaelic society by attempting to reshape the idea of marriage. This was much less of a problem among the settlers for the process of immigration had broken kinship networks among the settlers. Thus many who came from England or Scotland married not within already existing lineage networks but with new families, at least some of whom were native Irish. As Bishop Bedell observed many settlers 'married Irish women, their wives and children went to mass'.[51] Among the native population marriage was traditionally used to strengthen lineage networks, which often meant that marriage within the ecclesiastically prohibited degrees of kinship was part of the problem. So too was divorce as partners were jettisoned for reasons of expediency to make way for forging new alliances. The *Genealogical history* relates one story of a man whose father-in-law refused help when his father was in prison. The response of his wife was 'since you did not get help from my father leave me and take another wife with whom help will be got. And when there is peace let you have the wife you wish or the wife who has most right to you'.[52] While the detail of the story may be doubtful the principle was one which clearly struck a chord with contemporaries. In 1627 Bishop O'Reilly complained of 'frequent divorces' from which 'many scandals and disorders were arising' and he prohibited the practice. He also required that impending marriages should be announced to check on pre-existing relationships. An even more stringent set of rules governing the practice of marriage were set down by the synod of Kilmore in 1687.[53]

Tightening of regulations on marriage inevitably involved a more rigid division between illegitimate and legitimate children. In traditional society the boundary between legitimate and illegitimate children was at best blurred and both sets tended to inherit from their father. In the early seventeenth century Mulmore O'Reilly divided the land which he had obtained in the plantation scheme between four sons, one of whom was illegitimate.[54] By the later half of the century the position was rather different. When Eoghan O Raghallaigh composed the preface to his edition of the *Genealogical history* in 1703 he felt compelled to defend the fact that he had included illegitimate sons in the genealogies. 'Let no one think' he argued 'that it is from ignorance that I have pursued the history of those born illegitimately, whom the world at large calls family but as I found it before me with knowledgeable people' but he was clearly unhappy about the inclusions.[55]

V

The consequences of the changes in the social order forced by both the state and the various churches in the county were far-reaching but are perhaps best seen in the interrelated worlds of economics and landownership. In the sixteenth century a Cavan family held their lands by virtue of their genealogy. Greater lords had no claim on the lands of their freeholders but held their own mensal land by virtue of the chieftainship of the family. By the seventeenth century a man's landholding and social position was determined not by his family or his background but by the contracts or leases into which he entered. The report of Sir Nicholas Pynnar in 1619 reveals that a new hierarchy of landholding had developed in the county.[56] At the top were landlords who held their land by grant from the king under the terms of the plantation scheme. In turn these men had made contracts, or leases, with others to use the land for a fixed period of time in return for a rent which within a few decades of the beginning plantation was to be paid in cash rather than in produce. The terms and rents for these leases varied a good deal over the county depending on the balance of bargaining power between landlord and tenant.[57] Landlords often demanded that their tenants build or enclose land or introduce new types of livestock. In return the tenant had the use of the land for a specified period of time. In some cases, the freeholders, this was in perpetuity with no possibility of rent increases by the landlord. Most estates had a few freeholders who were intended to be substantial figures who would develop the estate and Pynnar noted that most freeholds were about 100 acres although they could range from 480 to twenty-four acres. Below the freeholders was a hierarchy of leaseholders who held their lands for terms of years, from three to forty one, or for named lives, usually three. Leaseholds were usually smaller than freeholds, from 186 to just four or five acres. Leaseholders and freeholders with substantial property usually sublet to others.

This complex social hierarchy based on agreements between landlords and tenants required cash to pay the rent. There were other demands for cash from the inhabitants of Cavan. Central government taxation grew in scale and in frequency during the seventeenth century, especially after the introduction of the annual hearth tax from the 1660s and as Alan Ford points out the established church also made demands. These developments required the native Irish to use cash to a greater extent than they ever had before. How quickly they adapted to this world is suggested by the 1638 will of Philip Mac Philip O'Reilly of Dromdomane in Cavan.[58] Philip listed debts to fifty-two individuals in cash amounting to £19. 7s. 10d. Four debts were significant sums of £1 or more but the vast majority were a few shillings owed to local people, residents in Cavan town, and in a few cases Dublin or Trim. It is clear that a credit network using money as the medium of exchange was well established by the 1630s.

One of the results of the expansion of a more commercialised economy was the development of a more developed marketing structure in the county. In particular occasional fairs, which were well suited to the cattle and live-stock trade and, to a lesser extent, more frequent markets were set up to meet the marketing needs of the local population. These were not innovations in the landscape. The market at Cavan town was already well established in the fifteenth century and there were smaller fairs reported in parts of Cavan before the plantation. From 1610 that network expanded so that by 1685 there were eight major fairs in the county some meeting on three occasions in the year and others on two although usually only for one day. Most of these were concentrated in central Cavan but in 1688 there were signs that the commercial economy was spreading into the more remote north west part of the county with the establishment of a market at Ballyconnell.[59] Not only did the number of fairs increase during the seventeenth century but it seems that the volume of business which was transacted also grew. Massari's impressions of the fair at Cavan town in 1645 suggest a substantial trade

> I went to see this great fair held in a field near Cavan. It is attended by crowds and great quantities of merchandise are brought thither by the people of the surrounding districts. I was amazed at the abundant supply, especially of animals of all kinds which were sold at an absurdly low price.

The impact of these economic changes of the seventeenth century should not be exaggerated in the case of Cavan. Contacts with the Pale since the middle ages had already taught the inhabitants of the county the basics of this sort of economic organisation based on money and contracts. By the middle of the sixteenth century there is some evidence that at least some of the O'Reillys were attempting to emulate the Pale custom of leases. In 1558, possibly under the influence of the church, Myles O'Reilly assigned land in Cavan town to Donagh MacBrady using an indenture rather like those in use in the Pale.[60] One indication of the rapidity of assimilation into the new order, at least at the upper social levels, is the scale of literacy in the county in the early seventeenth century. In a world ruled by contracts the ability to read and possibly to master the more advanced skill of writing was desirable. At the lowest social level it seems that few mastered even reading. Bishop Bedell estimated in the 1630s that not one in a thousand could read. Yet at the upper social level where the commercial changes had most effect the story was different. A petition of 1629 of the Catholic freeholders of the county contained eighty nine names of which only three were unable to sign.[61]

If it would be a mistake to overestimate the success of these economic changes of the seventeenth century it would be equally wrong to assume that there were no casualties as a result of the change. Changing family structures which reduced the status of illegitimate children and the decline of violence as a mechanism of social change reduced the career options for younger sons. There were also native Irish landowners who failed to adjust to the new world and lost out. They fell into debt and were forced to sell their land. In 1610 some 22.5 per cent of the land of Cavan had been set aside for native Irish grantees. By 1641 the proportion in native hands had fallen to 16.5 per cent of the county with Old English of the Pale acquiring most of the land which was sold. In many cases it was not the plantation but the market economy which destroyed the O'Reillys.[62] Those who failed to find a home in the new order for political, social or economic reasons saw continental Europe as a prospect. In 1609, for example, Shane O'Reilly who had fought on the English side of the nine years war, saw little prospect of advancement in Cavan since he was a younger son and he left to fight in Sweden.[63] Other Cavan families served in the Irish regiment of the Spanish Netherlands during the early seventeenth century.[64] There were other career paths which could be followed abroad, most notably the church. Two men from the diocese of Kilmore were among the first intake to the Irish college at Louvain, one already having been at Douai, and another was at Salamanca. One Cavan Franciscan served his noviate at Padua before progressing to Louvain to be ordained in the 1630s.[65] Such migration was not always permanent. Bernard Corcoran from Farnham explained in 1664 that at the time of the plantation his family had gone to Brussels to serve the Archduke Albert there and he had now returned to claim his inheritance. The return of some Cavan men from the European wars in the 1660s may at least partially explain the outbreak of toryism in the county in the early years of the Restoration.[66]

Part of the reason for that rapid assimilation of new political and economic structures was the continuity from the sixteenth century not only in ideas borrowed from the Pale but in the structure of agricultural organisation itself. The seventeenth century economy was much like its sixteenth century predecessor, based largely on cattle although some grain was grown in parts of the county for local consumption. The predominance of livestock is seen reflected in the diet of the inhabitants of the county which tended to be based on dairy products. When Monsignor Massari was invited to a banquet during his brief stay in the county dairy products were the main food item. On his arrival at Lismore, for instance, he was feted with 'three dishes of trefoil and three of butter with a large griddle loaf and a cheese of great circumference but only as thick as one's finger'.

The main economic change which the Ulster plantation scheme saw was the introduction of new breeds of livestock and a rise in population levels.[67] The plantation surveys suggest that the number of British adult males in Cavan increased from about 120 in 1611 to over 750 by about 1630 although as P.J. Duffy's essay points out these were very unevenly distributed.[68] This clearly had a significant impact on the labour supply which in turn served to increase agricultural output. This increased output could not be absorbed within the county and hence producers had to look elsewhere to dispose of their surplus in order to obtain cash for the rent and other demands. Apart from the local markets and fairs some looked to the large market of Dublin. One Cavan deponent after the outbreak of the rising in 1641 claimed that he had lost £40 of butter 'ready to be sent to Dublin' and a carrier lost six horses laden with butter.[69] Such trade was not all one way and luxuries from Dublin such as tobacco as well as more basic goods such as hops, stockings and cloth were beginning to penetrate into the county. By 1641 Belturbet had sufficient trade to support five merchants, two carriers, a baker, a gunsmith a feltmaker, a shoemaker, a tanner and an innkeeper although it still remained a small town indicating the still underdeveloped nature of the Cavan economy.[70] Bishop Bedell noted in the early 1630s when he arrived in his diocese that

> The only considerable town in the whole county was Belturbet which yet was but as one of our ordinary market towns here in England but having but one church in it ... the town of Cavan was not so big by one half as Belturbet. excepting these two towns there was nothing considerable in the county. Kilmore itself was a mere country village but so thinly inhabited that nowhere in the whole parish any street or part of a street.[71]

Bedell's comments help to place the economic changes of the seventeenth century in context. The economic developments in Cavan were less dramatic than in some other parts of the country as its position adjacent to the Pale ensured that the inhabitants of Cavan were already aware of the world of contracts, money and trade before their full impact became apparent. That, however, should not minimise the significant economic expansion which the early part of the century saw with the corresponding growth in marketing provision.

VI

The seventeenth century therefore saw dramatic changes in the nature of the structures of everyday life in Cavan. There was a shift from a lineage dominated lordship society imbued with a traditional catholicism to a world governed by the rules of the common law, the ideas of Tridentine catholicism and protestantism were both promoted and a rapidly commercialising economy dependent on markets and contracts formed the cement which held society together. By 1700 most of the political and landed elite who had ruled Cavan in 1600 were gone and had been replaced by a new social group. In some respects that process of social change, particularly the displacement of landowners, can be described as a revolution but in others it was very far from that. While some of the traditional O'Reilly elite suffered a significant decline in status, Cavan's position as a buffer between the pale and Ulster ensured that many of its inhabitants already understood how to cope with the commercial and legal changes which characterised the seventeenth century. In that sense the seventeenth century experience of social and economic change— including those brought about by the Ulster plantation—was an intensification of the existing situation, although one which occurred very rapidly indeed. In the context of religious belief and practice the changes of the seventeenth century did not constitute a revolution in themselves but laid the foundations for profound long term changes in Cavan society. While the counter-reformation rules on sacraments began to be enforced in the seventeenth century it took more time, as James Kelly's essay shows, before the full impact of the counter reformation came to be felt in south Ulster. To call the events of the seventeenth century a revolution is to simplify the local experience of a series of different, through interrelated, developments all moving at differing speeds and hence giving Cavan its own unique personality.

The Formation of the Modern Catholic Church in the Diocese of Kilmore, 1580–1880

JAMES KELLY

The organization of the Catholic church in the diocese of Kilmore along the lines set out in the reforming sixteenth-century council of Trent proved a complex and prolonged process extending over several centuries. The first steps were taken in the late sixteenth and early seventeenth centuries, but these were negated by the ferocity of the Cromwellian assault on catholicism in the 1650s. Considerable progress was made towards revitalising the church in the 1670s and 1680s despite acute factional differences in the diocese, but the enactment of the penal laws following the Williamite wars seriously set-back the process once more. The Catholic church remained beset by legal, pastoral, organizational and financial difficulties for much of the next three quarters of a century. A number of initiatives were taken to address these problems from the mid-eighteenth century, but they were localised and not always successful. However, foundations upon which a more permanent edifice could be built were laid in these years, and these combined with the repeal between the late 1770s and mid-1790s of religious disabilities against the Catholic church to pave the way for the rapid advances that were a feature of the early and mid-nineteenth century. The diocese acquired a new administrative centre; new churches were built; a seminary was established, and new devotional practices cultivated. Despite this progress, the church still faced major problems in the shape of survivalist catholicism and an adverse priest to people ratio, and the triumph of Tridentine catholicism was not assured until the Great Famine weakened adherence to popular heterodoxy and resulted in a dramatic improvement in the priest to people ratio.

I

The late sixteenth century was an extremely difficult period for the Catholic church in the diocese of Kilmore. The state sponsored reformation authorised the confiscation of the monasteries and religious houses, which had for centuries ministered to large parts of eastern Cavan, while the reduction of the Brady clan irrevocably altered the political, social and religious landscape in which it operated. The region corresponding to the diocese of Kilmore escaped the sustained attention of the Tudor monarchy until the last quarter of the century but the inquisition of 1590, the nine years war and Jacobean confiscations resulted in the loss of churches as well as of monastic lands. The Tudors aspired to replace catholicism with protestantism, and with this object in view much, though by no means all, of the confiscated church property was transferred to the Church of Ireland.[1]

As a result of these events, the Catholic church in the region entered the seventeenth century virtually without a fabric or resources. Its churches were either in ruins or in the possession of the Church of Ireland; some of its priests had converted and ministered as Protestants; others were pursued and mistreated. Ostensibly, circumstances were tailor made for an *en masse* movement to the Church of Ireland, but this, as Alan Ford's essay shows, did not happen. Priests continued to minister, and though Catholics were reduced in many instances to using mass rocks and private residences for sacramental purposes, the Catholic church in the diocese proved sufficiently resilient to enable it to survive these difficult years and it soon possessed a greater number of clergy and adherents than the Church of Ireland.

This was all the more remarkable because Kilmore was bishopless between 1607 and 1625. The bishop of the diocese during the very difficult years of the 1580s, 1590s and early seventeenth century was the Franciscan, Richard Brady. He was able to exercise his jurisdiction without hindrance at the outset of his episcopacy. But following the appointment of John Garvey as Church of Ireland bishop of Kilmore in 1585, the suspicion of the authorities that he was a papal envoy who acted as go-between between the duke of Parma, Spain and the O'Neills led to his arrest and imprisonment on a number of occasions. Effective administration was impossible in these circumstances, and the task was exacerbated by Brady's ill-health which caused him to resign the see in 1607.[2]

Bishop Richard Brady left the diocese in a disorganized and depressed state, and there is little evidence of improvement in the fifteen years that followed. No successor to Bishop Brady was appointed. Instead the administration of the diocese was entrusted to a non-resident vicar general. Given the impoverished state of Kilmore, this was not unexpected, but it was hardly in the diocese's best interests. Despite this, the church continued to function, albeit in a restricted manner. Priests trained abroad; the Franciscans defied all attempts to remove them, and the mass continued to be celebrated in secret.[3] When William Bedell took charge of the diocese on behalf of the Church of Ireland in 1629, he acknowledged that, despite their contrasting recent experiences, the Catholic church was stronger and more vibrant than the Church of Ireland.[4] According to Bedell, there were thirty-two Protestant minsters and sixty-six priests in the united dioceses of Ardagh and Kilmore in 1630. Moreover, great strides were being taken towards establishing a parish structure along the lines laid down by the Council of Trent. Bishop Hugh O'Reilly's

(1625–8) instruction that chapels of some sort be built in every parish attests to the new found sense of confidence and expectation.[5]

Credit for these advances belongs to the priests of the diocese, to the relaxation in the enforcement of the recusancy laws in the later years of James I's reign, and to the new found confidence of the Catholic Church in the 1620s which was given vivid expression in a spate of ecclesiastical appointments.[6] Though it was not until 1625 that Ulster dioceses were assigned resident bishops, the appointment of Hugh O'Reilly to Kilmore gave the diocese an energetic and able pastor. O'Reilly spent only three years in charge before he was promoted to the archbishopric of Armagh, but in these years he directed his energies to the eradication of the 'confusion and deviation from ecclesiastical discipline' that was a feature of church life prior to his appointment. He was unable to combat all problems, but his ambition to establish a *domus ecclesiasticus* in every parish, his attempts to discipline his priests (who numbered about twenty) and to ensure that those who entered the priesthood were 'suitable', and his endeavours to administer confirmation and to enforce Tridentine marriage law represented the first sustained attempt to run the diocese according to the precepts of the Catholic reformation enunciated at Trent. Bishop O'Reilly's reforming zeal was not welcomed by all; he met with resistance from some of his clergy for personal (he was taciturn and punctilious) as well as political reasons. His administration was also hampered by the continuing financial problems of the diocese; it was described as the poorest in the ecclesiastical province of Armagh in 1630.[7]

Deprived of its traditional sources of income by confiscation, and unable to secure a sufficiency by way of alms from the downwardly mobile Catholic population, both O'Reilly and his successor, Eugene MacSweeney, appealed to Rome. In 1630, MacSweeney (supported by O'Reilly, who continued to reside in county Cavan) petitioned the pope for the restoration to Kilmore of the tithes collected in the diocese on behalf of the Augustinians of Kells and the Benedictines of Fore.[8] Nothing came of this, but MacSweeney did not give up. With the backing of Archbishops O'Reilly (Armagh) and Queeley (Tuam), he sought Roman approval for the union of the dioceses of Kilmore and Ardagh, and when this too did not bear fruit, he sought a translation to the wealthier diocese of Derry where he had served as vicar apostolic prior to his promotion to the bishopric of Kilmore. Once again, MacSweeney met with disappointment. Though he and his metropolitan were convinced that Kilmore was too poor to maintain a resident bishop, Rome was not persuaded of the wisdom of his plans to ease his difficulties and no changes were authorised.[9]

Despite his repeated requests for a transfer to Derry, MacSweeney did not neglect the administration of Kilmore in the mid and late 1630s. This was not trouble free as intermittent bouts of persecution, which obliged him to go into hiding, and the self interest of 'certain contumacious clerics and ... laymen' encouraged clerical indiscipline. In these circumstances, it was simply not possible to provide anything resembling a comprehensive religious service, but the presence in the diocese in 1636 of twenty-eight parish priests and an unknown number of Franciscan regulars represented a considerable improvement on the situation as it was at the beginning of the century. Moreover, there are grounds for believing that matters continued to improve unless MacSweeney's attendance at a provincial synod of bishops in May 1637 and his continuing attention to administrative and theological issues is misleading.[10]

If, poverty excepted, prospects for the Catholic church in the diocese of Kilmore in the 1630s looked brighter than they had done in decades, the outbreak of rebellion in Ulster in 1641 altered the environment utterly. Both MacSweeney and O'Reilly were quick to appreciate the opportunity it offered them to improve the material and religious standing of their church. MacSweeney was present at the provincial synod convened by O'Reilly at Kells on 22 March 1642, and gave his support to the decrees of the assembly which deemed the rebellion a 'just war', directed bishops to contribute to the financing of a Catholic army, anticipated the restoration of confiscated church property and the commencement of unrestricted Catholic worship, and urged the convening of a council (which took shape in the form of the Confederation of Kilkenny) to oversee and to direct the war effort.[11]

Given its active involvement in the formation of the Confederation of Kilkenny, the failure of the coalition of Old English and native Irish interests that comprised the confederacy to secure a favourable diplomatic or military outcome in the 1640s bode ill for the Catholic church. It had resumed possession of much of the property confiscated in the sixteenth century. Like most of the clergy, Archbishop O'Reilly and Bishop MacSweeney perceived what took place in the 1640s as a religious war, and they continued to align themselves behind the uncompromising stance taken by Rinuccini, the papal nuncio, at a synod convened at Clonmacnoise in late 1649, though it was clear by then that the rebellion and the Confederation had failed to achieve its military and religious goals.

The arrival in Ireland in August 1649 of Oliver Cromwell and the New Model Army changed the course of Irish affairs completely. An attempt was made at a meeting of bishops at Jamestown, county Leitrim, in August 1650, attended by O'Reilly and MacSweeney, to salvage something out of the ruins, but it was without effect.[12] A year later, the two bishops convened another synod of bishops and clergy of the province of Armagh at the remote location of Trinity Island in Lough Oughter on the Cavan–Leitrim border, close to where O'Reilly and MacSweeney had taken up residence, to discuss matters of ecclesiastical organization as well as how best to counter the Cromwellian regime. But the moment was unpropitious for any initiatives of this sort.[13] The Cromwellians' authority in the kingdom was so complete by the early 1650s there was nothing the bishops could do to turn events in their favour; their priority now had to be simply to survive.

II

The 1650s proved one of the darkest decades in the history of the Catholic church in Kilmore. The efforts made between the 1620s and the 1640s to create a definably Tridentine church in the diocese were undone and the church was reduced to a level of disorganization it had not previously experienced. The immediate source of difficulty was the Cromwellian decree of 1653 expelling all Catholic clergy. Perhaps a third went into exile; many of the remainder were obliged to embrace a peripatetic lifestyle and to minister secretly. As a result, the parish system put in place in the early seventeenth century broke down, and the religious service available to the laity was reduced to a shadow of what was available previously.[14] It is not clear how many priests remained in the diocese of Kilmore, but those that declined the option of exile were obliged, in the words of Bishop MacSweeney, 'to roam through the wilderness and maintain and live in woods and caves, hungry, thirsty, cold and badly clothed to assist the scattered flocks'.[15] Things might have been even worse. Kilmore was the only diocese in the country to retain a residential bishop throughout the 1650s. Bishop MacSweeney was too old and infirm to travel abroad with the result that he spent most of the decade in a safe house on the slopes of Slieve an Iarainn on the Cavan–Leitrim border. Because his infirmity rendered him immobile, his continued residence was supposedly connived at by the Cromwellian authorities, who showed little restraint in their treatment of able-bodied clergy.[16] At least six and, possibly, ten priests from the diocese of Kilmore were arrested and imprisoned between 1654 and 1658.[17]

Despite assertions to the contrary, MacSweeney's infirmity was not so incapacitating that he could not function. He sought and was given special faculties by the pope in 1656 or 1657 on foot of a report he sent to Rome describing the miserable state of the church in the country.[18] However, he was unable to do much more than appeal to others to act and he was in no position to take advantage of the relaxation in the repressive atmosphere from 1658. He did not, for instance, attend the provincial synod of Armagh held at Conelly, county Longford, in October 1660 at which the doctrines and decrees of the Council of Trent were reaffirmed and an attempt was made once again to give direction to the church in the province.[19]

Such direction was necessary because the environment in which the church now operated in Kilmore as elsewhere, while an improvement on that of the early and mid-1650s, remained unfavourable. In the summer of 1663, for example, a gentleman informant swore a series of examinations implicating Bishop MacSweeney and Archbishop O'Reilly in a conspiracy to bring 25,000 soldiers to Ireland to restore 'the spiritualities and temporalities' of the Catholic church, while in the following year three priests of the diocese were arrested and held captive in a Dublin prison.[20] To compound matters, the church remained in a weakened and rudderless state. The number of clergy in the diocese had fallen by more than forty per cent since the 1630s (from twenty-eight in 1636 to sixteen in 1660),²¹ and in the absence of firm leadership (MacSweeney was variously described as 'old, sick and unable to work' and as 'completely unfit and debilitated'), responsibility for administering the diocese rested with the clergy alone.²² They faced formidable financial and personnel problems. Officially, Kilmore was equal with Meath, Derry, Clogher and Armagh in that each diocese agreed to commit an equal sum to a fund for overseas burses for clerical students at the synod of Clonelly, but the confiscation and redistribution of forty-three per cent of the land in county Cavan in the 1650s had further attenuated the resource base upon which the church could draw.²³ In addition, the number of clergy remained low. According to Archbishop O'Reilly, there was only seventeen priests in the diocese in 1662, which almost certainly meant that large numbers of people in the region seldom came into contact with a priest.²⁴ In an attempt to alleviate these pastoral problems, Archbishop O'Reilly requested the pope in 1663 to appoint either Bernard Geaghran or James Gowan as vicar apostolic to aid MacSweeney who was now 'incapable of attending to his duties'. He also recommended Gowan and Thomas Fitzsimons, another leading priest in the diocese, as suitable candidates for promotion to a full bishopric, but his repeated requests did not elicit the positive response he invited.²⁵

While Rome deliberated, the mental and physical health of Bishop MacSweeney, who was now in his eighties, continued to deteriorate. By July 1665, he was, Archbishop O'Reilly reported to Rome, completely bedridden and living like an anchorite on whiskey and brandy provided by priests who supported his continued administration of the diocese. The only part of him, O'Reilly observed sardonically, still alive was his tongue, which he used to make clear that he would neither nominate a vicar general nor accept one nominated by others.²⁶ From Archbishop O'Reilly's vantage point this was intolerable, and having failed with his plea to Rome in February 1666 to have Bernard Geaghran appointed vicar to the 'helpless' MacSweeney, he intervened personally and oversaw the appointment of Dr Thomas Fitzsimons to the position in June.²⁷ It proved a disastrous decision. Though learned and well thought of by a number of bishops, Fitzsimons was so actively disliked by MacSweeney and his clerical supporters that Kilmore was quickly riven by faction. The precise course of events is not clear, but the combination of Fitzsimons' impolitic manoeuvring, the determination of MacSweeney and his supporters not to co-operate, and the bishop's increasing age and erratic behaviour made for a highly unstable situation. By 1668, MacSweeney was so incapacitated he could no longer recite the divine office; and it may be that it was encroaching senility rather than obstinacy or contumacy that lay at the root of his increasingly erratic behaviour. In 1668–9, for example, when Archbishop O'Reilly (who was in France) directed his vicar general and that of Dromore to prepare a canonical process to dismiss Terence O'Kelly, the vicar general of Derry, for openly maintaining a mistress, the delegates were im-

peded, deprived of their commission, and threatened with excommunication
by MacSweeney who sided with O'Kelly. O'Reilly was infuriated by this and
by MacSweeney's subsequent attempt to secure sanction for his behaviour by
convening a provincial synod to approve his actions. To make matters worse,
relations between Fitzsimons and MacSweeney had become so embittered
that the bishop 'excommunicated him [Fitzsimons] and had him denounced
throughout the whole diocese'. Not to be outdone, Fitzsimons responded by
excommunicating MacSweeney. Such an unedifying drama could not be allowed go on and Bishop Patrick Plunkett of Meath was delegated to investigate. However, before he reached Slieve an Iarainn MacSweeney died; a week
later Fitzsimons was confirmed as vicar general of the diocese in somewhat
confusing and controversial circumstances.[28]

The death in 1669 of both Bishop MacSweeney and of his most powerful
critic, Archbishop O'Reilly, represented a good opportunity for the Catholic
diocese of Kilmore to overcome the disunity and administrative inefficiency
that was endemic to the diocese in the 1660s. The restoration of the religious
fabric of the diocese after the calamitous events of the 1650s was retarded by
the poor leadership and internecine squabbling that characterised diocesan life
then. Shortage of money also played its part though, in this respect, Kilmore
was better placed than Ardagh, Dromore and Raphoe which were then the
poorest dioceses in the Armagh province.[29]

The confirmation of Dr Fitzsimons as vicar general and the appointment
of Oliver Plunkett as archbishop of Armagh in 1669 heralded a pastorally
more expansive era in Kilmore diocese. Archbishop Plunkett had a high
opinion of Fitzsimons. He had recommended him repeatedly to Rome in the
early 1670s as 'a learned and exemplary man and a good theologian and
canonist'—one of the 'three ablest men in the province'—who was well de-
serving of promotion to a bishopric or to the vicar apostolicship of either
Kilmore or Derry.[30] Fitzsimons merited this praise; he worked with and supported the archbishop as he endeavoured to combat the myriad of abuses and
factional disagreements that were all too prevalent in the archdiocese at this
time.[31]

One of Plunkett's first undertakings, after he had convened a provincial
synod at Clones in 1670 at which the thrust of the decrees and doctrines of
the Council of Trent was reaffirmed, was to undertake a visitation of his
suffragan dioceses. The severest problem he encountered in Kilmore was the
alignment of the clergy into two factions behind Thomas Fitzsimons and
Bernard Geaghran which effectively tore the diocese 'apart'. In his report to
Rome, Plunkett claimed to have settled 'all the clerical disputes' and while
this is not correct, they certainly abated for a time.[32] The pastoral and administrative operation of the diocese improved as a consequence, as the identification of several Kilmore clergy as suitable candidates for promotion in 1671
implies.[33] This was facilitated by an increase in the number of ordinations,
and the resulting increase in the number of secular clergy in the diocese to

twenty-six by 1675.[34] Much of the credit for this belongs to Fitzsimons, on whose behalf twenty-one priests petitioned Rome in April 1675 to request that he was raised to the bishopric, but despite this and Archbishop Plunkett's repeated entreaties, Rome declined even to make him a vicar apostolic.[35]

Plunkett was thankful that this was so a short time later when Fitzsimons' increasingly unpredictable behaviour, following an attack of dysentery in 1674, compelled the archbishop to intervene in Kilmore's affairs once again. Plunkett's intervention was prompted by an appeal from three priests Fitzsimons had deposed in a manner contrary to canon law. The archbishop found in favour of the priests, but Fitzsimons refused to cede to his metropolitan. Unable to ignore such a blatant act of defiance, Plunkett determined to remove the recalcitrant vicar general from office, in the course of which process he gleaned that Fitzsimons had a drink problem and that he had infringed a series of church rules by offering dispensations for cash. In his stead, Plunkett transferred responsibility for running the diocese to sixty year-old Bernard Geaghran, who was made vicar general, and gave him thirty-eight year-old Bernard Brady, a vicar forane, as his assistant.[36] All three, but particularly Plunkett, had to withstand a series of abusive allegations by Fitzsimons who took his deposition very badly. Matters became so acrimonious, that Rome deputised the neutral figure of Archbishop John Brenan of Cashel to investigate and to report on affairs in the diocese. He found in favour of the primate, which prompted Rome to determine in 1678 that it was in the best interests of the diocese that its administration was taken out of the hands of Fr Geaghran and vested in those of Patrick Tyrell, the Franciscan bishop of Clogher.[37]

The decision to vest the administration of Kilmore in the hands of the bishop of Clogher rather than in those of a bishop for the diocese, was received with disappointment in some quarters.[38] However, it did not dissuade Thomas Fitzsimons from pursuing his vendetta. In 1675, shortly after his deposition in Kilmore, he had endeavoured to foment opposition to Bishop Tyrell among the clergy of Clogher by claiming that bishops could not be appointed without 'postulation and election'. Archbishop Plunkett, whose view of Fitzsimons had altered utterly as a result of events, was appalled by this further evidence of his 'contumacy, dissension and schism', and he was confirmed in his low opinion when Fitzsimons sought in vain in 1678 'to stir up the priests and people of Kilmore' to resist Tyrell's 'taking possession' of the diocese on the grounds that his 'letters of appointment were null and void because of the suppression of some words'. Fitzsimons endeavoured to perpetuate the quarrel, but his death in Brussels in 1680 irrevocably weakened his cause for though an 'ambitious friar', the Franciscan John Brady and his colleague, Phelim O'Neill, sought to assume the mantle left by Fitzsimons, they received little support and little inconvenienced Bishop Tyrell.[39]

With the conclusion of the Fitzsimons affair, the way seemed clear for the diocese of Kilmore finally to overcome the disorganization and division that were a feature of the Catholic church in the diocese since the 1650s. There were positive signs. The number of known ordainations for the diocese in the 1670s registered an increase on the known figure for the 1660s.[40] Furthermore the provincial synod held at Ardpatrick in 1678 (several of whose decrees were a response to events in Kilmore) represented a further attempt to give effect to the decrees and decisions of the Council of Trent and to eradicate the administrative, jurisdictional and doctrinal abuses that continued to blight the church in the region.[41] However, neither Tyrell nor his vicar general, Edmund O'Reilly, the parish priest of Crosserlough, were given much opportunity to make their mark, as the 'Popish Plot' (1678–81), in which Tyrell was implicated, inaugurated a period of repression singularly unconducive to religious reform. Tyrell successfully evaded arrest, but Edmund O'Reilly was incarcerated for a time in Cavan gaol.[42]

If the repression associated with the 'Popish Plot' once again interrupted efforts to revitalise the Catholic church in Kilmore, the more relaxed atmosphere of the 1680s allowed considerable progress to be made. The number of priests admitted to orders remained at an encouraging level; there were renewed calls for the appointment of a bishop to administer the diocese; and, most strikingly, a diocesan synod was convened by Bishop Tyrell in June 1687. The document which resulted amounted to a comprehensive statement of intent by those charged with running the diocese of their resolve to organize it along Tridentine lines. The forty-three statutes that comprised the synod's deliberations were divided into eight sections, and they dealt with such issues as the conduct and behaviour of clergy, the administration of the sacraments, marriage law, legacies and reserved sins. Together, they provided the priests of the diocese with a comprehensive code far in advance of that available in most dioceses, but there was to be little opportunity to put it into effect as war and politics once again took centre stage.[43] The events of James II's reign (1685–8) and the Williamite wars brought the Protestant interest in Ireland face to face once again with the prospect of annihilation, and left a bitter legacy of religious suspicion that convinced them of the necessity of a comprehensive code of laws which protected them against the threat of Catholic religious and political domination.

III

The individual charged with guiding the diocese of Kilmore through the difficult years of the 1690s and early eighteenth century, when the Protestant interest in Ireland endeavoured to secure its position against Catholic *revanchism*, was Bernard Brady, the parish priest of Laragh. He was made vicar general on the translation of Bishop Tyrell to the diocese of Meath in 1689. Brady had assisted Bernard Geaghran when the latter was vicar general in the 1670s, and though legally he should have gone into exile following the implementation of the Bishops' Banishment Act in 1697, he chose to stay in the diocese. Little is known of the workings of the church in these years, but it is safe to assume that it was an uncomfortable period. But repression like power is relative, and the fact that no attempt was made to replicate the intense coercion of the 1650s, that members of the Franciscan order continued to minister, that eight priests are known to have been ordained for the diocese in the 1690s, and that others like Terence Smith acquired faculties which enabled them to say mass and to hear confessions in any parish, allowed the church in the diocese to continue to operate in the years immediately following the surrender at Limerick.[44]

The influx of a significant number of presbyterian settlers into the region almost certainly contributed to the church's problems, but the disorganized state of the Church of Ireland meant that there was no threat of proselytisation.[45] Furthermore, the 1703 *act for registering the popish clergy* from which provided for one priest for each parish enabled the diocese to maintain forty priests from 1704 which was considerably greater than the number available during most if not all of the seventeenth century. This is not to say there were not serious problems. For instance, an unregistered priest was liable to be transported, as happened to Philip Brady in 1704. At least one other was imprisoned for a short period.[46] Furthermore, priests were at the mercy of zealous officials; in 1706, the egregious sheriff of county Leitrim, George St George, was prompted by an invasion scare to summon all priests in the county to present themselves to the authorities.[47] It is unlikely that all obeyed, but the threat of imprisonment or worse remained a real fear in the minds of most priests in the early decades of the eighteenth century.

Though the penal laws provided Irish Protestants with a potentially decisive array of powers with which to disrupt if not to destroy the Catholic church in Ireland, the treatment meted out to the clergy of Kilmore in the early eighteenth century, when the enforcement of the penal laws was at its most intense, was not unendurable. For instance, the 1709 act which provided that registered priests should take the oath of abjuration was widely ignored. This elicited a threat from the grand jury of county Cavan during the mid-1710s, when fears of a Jacobite inspired descent were high, that it would take legal sanction against sixteen defiant priests and those who offered sureties on their behalf, but no action was taken. The same was true in county Leitrim.[48]

The failure to enforce the penal laws rigorously means that Philip O'Connell's dark and unconditional remarks on the impact of these laws on the Catholic church in Kilmore must be severely qualified. That said, the church was put on the defensive organizationally and pastorally in the early eighteenth century, though the paucity of information makes it difficult to establish a clear picture. One fact that is clear is that the number of priests ministering in the diocese contracted sharply in the first two decades of the eighteenth century. This is not surprising. Seventy per cent (twenty-eight out of forty) of the priests that registered in accordance with the 1703 act were aged fifty or above, and since it was the policy of the state to prevent their replacement, numbers were bound to decline in the short term.[49] It is not possible to trace this process precisely, but the fact that Bishop Hugh MacMahon maintained in 1714 that there were twenty-five parish priests and an unspecified number of Franciscans in the diocese, that twenty-seven names were appended to a petition presented to Rome in 1715 soliciting the elevation of Michael Smith to the bishopric and that twenty-three priests signed a memorial in support of Bishop MacMahon in 1723 would point to the conclusion that there was a decline of about one-third in the number of secular clergy in the diocese in the two decades following registration, and that some priests were obliged to take responsibility for more than one parish.[50] The prohibition on Catholic schools and Catholic bishops meant that recruitment was also a problem, for though there was a network of Irish seminaries on the continent, the cost remained a major obstacle. Bishop MacMahon provided a number of small burses at the Irish College in Paris from a legacy bequeathed for this purpose; a number of others became available at a later date, but for most of the time the steady trickle of intending clerics were ordained *titulo missionis*.[51]

As this implies, next to repression the primary causes of Kilmore's problems was the poverty of the Catholic population. The underdeveloped state of the region economically was underlined by the series of famines and crises that buffeted the population in the first half of the eighteenth century. Furthermore, the paucity of Catholic gentry, highlighted by the fact that no Catholic from the counties of Cavan, Leitrim or Fermanagh secured a licence to carry arms, meant there was no wealthy lay elite in the region in a position to endow the church.[52] What money the church secured had to come from an impoverished laity, and they had precious little by way of surplus they could make available for religious purposes. This also partly accounts for the continued recourse to mass rocks in the region and the peripatetic existence of virtually all the regular (Franciscans mainly) and some secular clergy in the diocese.[53] Given these circumstances, it is reasonable to conclude that the sacramental service available to much of the Catholic population in Kilmore in the early eighteenth century was rudimentary and irregular.

This conclusion is supported by the fact that the maintenance of clerical discipline, which was of such central concern to the Tridentine church, proved difficult. There was no repetition of the extraordinary acts of defiance perpetrated in the 1670s. But the ease with which Conor McLoughlin, who registered as parish priest of Cloonclare in 1704, moved without permission to Oughteragh; the preparedness of Philip Tully, the parish priest of Kilmore, to present a petition to Rome in 1723 critical of the administration of Bishop MacMahon, and the reluctance of MacMahon in 1714 to discipline an apostate priest, Philip Brady, provides a perspective on the scale and nature of the problem.[54] Bishops and those exercising ecclesiastical jurisdiction felt constrained in their exercise of authority lest it attracted unwelcome official notice. As a result, single-minded and disinterested priests could get away with serious acts of indiscipline.

Bishop MacMahon was posed with these problems by Rome's decision, on the death of Bernard Brady in 1710, to return the administration of the diocese of Kilmore to the bishop of Clogher. We know little of Brady's twenty-one year stewardship of the diocese, but the criticism implicit in the request advanced by Fr Michael Smith in 1704 that a vicar apostolic should be appointed, and in the letter signed by a number of leading clergy and laity in 1711 calling on Bishop MacMahon to resume responsibility for the diocese suggests that he was not as attentive as some wished.[55] MacMahon, who as bishop of Clogher (1711–14) and archbishop of Armagh (1714–37) had charge of the diocese for seventeen years was a brave and energetic pastor, but he was greatly constrained in what he could do by the temper of the time and by his wider responsibilities as archbishop. He also faced opposition from within the diocese from the supporters of Fr Smith who convened a 'diocesan synod' at Slieve Glah in Lavey parish in 1715 to voice their concern at the increasing age of the diocesan clergy and to request Rome to elevate Smith to the bishopric.[56] Their action was almost certainly prompted by MacMahon's decision to hand over the running of the diocese to Michael O'Reilly, a young priest in his twenties, who was believed to possess 'superior talents'. It is difficult at this remove to get a sense of O'Reilly's contribution, but his role in the foundation of the 'Dominican convent of Cavan', and the presence of curates in a number of parishes in the 1720s suggests that he oversaw a visible increase in clerical numbers. Moreover, evidence for the construction of masshouses suggests that a sizeable number of parishes were equipped with unostentatious, and probably quite modest sized buildings where the people and priests could congregate for worship.[57] The relaxation in the repressive intent of the authorities this reflected was not missed in Rome where a decision was taken in 1728 to resume the appointment of bishops to the diocese for the first time since the death of Eugene MacSweeney in 1669.

The Rome-trained Dominican, Michael MacDonagh, was consecrated bishop of Kilmore in December 1728. MacDonagh, who was highly regarded by his superiors, arrived in Ireland in 1730 and took charge of a diocese that showed only tentative signs of coming to terms with the penal laws. It was a challenging posting for one so young (he was only thirty), but MacDonagh was given appropriate faculties to enable him to operate in the taxing environment to which he was appointed.[58] One of the challenges the new bishop had to negotiate was the permanent unease of the sizeable Protestant and Presbyterian communities in the diocese. This rarely spilled over into confrontation, but Protestant suspicion that Catholics were intent on mischief remained acute throughout his episcopacy.[59] This obliged MacDonagh to keep a low profile; he divided his time between Dublin, where he resided with the Dominican sisters, and Kilmore which he visited during the summer months. When he travelled, he did so *incognito* and frequently in disguise, but even this did not secure him against unwelcome attention. In 1739 he and the Dominican provincial, John Fottrell, were arrested in county Londonderry.

Both were soon released, but the £200 reward offered for his apprehension convinced him that it was in his interest to leave the country for a time.[60]

MacDonagh spent the whole of 1740 in Rome. It was a timely visit as he had been sharply criticised for his failure to reside permanently in Kilmore though the diocese did not possess an episcopal residence. He evidently gave a good account of himself, because he secured the restoration of the diocesan chapter of Kilmore and a benefice in Liege to ease his pressing financial worries. As he was on his way back to Ireland in the early summer of 1741, he was invited to take part in a meeting convened by the papal nuncio at Brussels aimed restricting access to both the regular and secular priesthoods. This was now a matter of pressing concern because the combination of unconfined admission to ordination and the continuing poverty of the country had resulted in a palpable rise in tension between the two branches of the clergy as they both scrambled for the limited alms available, to an increase in the level of abuses and to a concomitant decline in ecclesiastical discipline. In view of MacDonagh's previous support of the regular clergy, his involvement with the campaign to persuade the pope of the necessity of confining access to the priesthood is unexpected, but this combined with his detailed reports on the dangers posed to the Catholic church by the charter schools established in the 1730s for the conversion of Catholic children to deflect attention from the criticisms directed at him. He had not reached Ireland when Pope Benedict XIV limited the number of candidates each bishop could ordain *titulo missionis* to twelve, and on his arrival he once again took up residence in Dublin.[61]

The inability of the diocese of Kilmore to offer either an adequate income or a suitable residence, combined with the gradual deterioration in his own health, provided MacDonogh with compelling reasons to continue to choose Dublin rather than Kilmore as his place of residence.[62] Another was provided by the intensification of anti-Catholic activity in the mid-1740s in response to the Jacobite invasion of Scotland and England. MacDonagh avoided incarceration on this occasion, but he had to cope with repeated allegations of high treason, to change his place of residence twelve times in two months to evade detection and to operate under a pseudonym. The charge of treason may seem severe, but it was to be anticipated since MacDonagh had served as confessor to the young Pretender in the late 1720s.[63] Of greater significance to the Catholic church in Kilmore was the disimprovement in his health, which precluded him giving the diocese the attention it so badly needed. His decision, in 1746, to travel to Portugal for health reasons took him further away from the diocese it was his charge to administer. He was never to return because he died in Lisbon on 26 November.[64]

The premature death of Michael MacDonogh was a source of genuine regret to those he had encountered during his lifetime. He was a kindly man, disinclined to be disputacious, who did what he could in unfavourable circumstances to revitalise the Catholic church in the diocese of Kilmore. Lack of documentation makes it impossible to establish his precise actions during

his annual summer visitations, but his fellow Dominican and successor Law-
rence Richardson maintained he instructed his clergy to catechise, established
confraternities of the most holy name of Jesus throughout the diocese, inaugurated regular clerical conferences to discuss theological and other pertinent
issues, enforced Tridentine law on marriage and endeavoured to eliminate the
practice of consuming alcohol at funeral breakfasts.[65] This must be treated
with some scepticism. MacDonogh spent more time out of the diocese than in
it, and it strains credulity to believe that the diocese hosted four theological
conferences each year or that it was capable of maintaining a confraternity in
every parish, as Richardson claimed. Because of its continuing poverty and
the spasmodic enforcement of the penal laws, Kilmore possessed few attrac-
tions for talented and ambitious clerics. There is little or no evidence other
than the *relatio* penned by the unreliable Richardson that MacDonogh's eight-
een-year episcopacy produced anything like the series of pastoral reforms
attributed to him; rather his episcopal career attests to the length of the pall
cast over the Catholic church in the diocese by the penal laws. Viewed in
simple numerical terms, the diocese appears not to have fared badly. According to Bishop Richardson there were thirty-seven priests in the diocese in
1750, which was just three less than the number registered in 1704.[66] But
simply to focus on the number of priests occludes the impact of sixty years of
mal-administration and intermittent oppression. By the mid-eighteenth century, the Catholic church in Kilmore had experienced a number of attempts
over a 150-year-period to disrupt and to destroy it; it is hardly surprising that
it emerged from the experience in the second half of the eighteenth century in
a weakened and enervated state or that its rehabilitation was a prolonged and
complex process.

IV

His difficult experiences notwithstanding, the episcopacy of Michael MacDonagh
was a turning point in the history of Kilmore diocese because he was the last
bishop personally to experience repression. This makes it all the more unlikely that he implemented all the reforms attributed to him by Bishop
Richardson. As an active opponent of the moves to restrict admissions to the
religious orders, it was in Richardson's interest to exaggerate the contribution
of his Dominican predecessor. He also had personal motives. Like MacDonagh,
Richardson was not disposed to reside in Kilmore, as he made clear in 1750:
'all the Catholics are compelled to live in low and wretched dwellings, as are
also the parish priest ... No bishop has had a permanent residence there
within living memory. Even the visitor or traveller finds it difficult to obtain
a suitable place for a night's rest or refreshment'.[67] There is more that a hint
of special pleading in Richardson's description. He aspired to the archbishopric
of Dublin, and this combined with his antipathy to the archbishop of Ar-

magh, Michael O'Reilly, who was one of the *zelanti* most eager to restrict admission to the regular clergy, to ensure that he never became permanently resident in Kilmore. He did undertake regular visitations (sometimes two or three in a year) during which he chaired theological conferences of the diocesan clergy, directed them to catechise the population on doctrinal points, encouraged the confraternity of the most holy name of Jesus 'against blasphemy, perjury and unlawful oaths', sought to enforce Tridentine regulations on marriage and funerals and authorised the maintenance, for the first time, of parish registers.[68] This is not an unimpressive list, but as already indicated one cannot take Richardson's testimony at face value. For this reason it is very difficult to judge precisely what was happening in the diocese during his six-year episcopate. If the evidence of the surviving parish registers is an accurate guide the fact that only one register (Castlerahan, 1751) dates from his episcopacy suggests that the gap between his intentions and his achievement was substantial. It is certainly unlikely, given the opposition to his appointment in the diocese, that he had the full co-operation of the clergy.[69]

If Bishop Richardson's impact on Kilmore was less than the impression he sought to convey and more than he was given credit for by critics who contended that he should take up residence 'and attend his own sheep which stand in great need of instruction',[70] his episcopacy did represent the beginnings of a new era. He was the first ecclesiastic with responsibility for the diocese in decades who was not pursued and threatened with incarceration and exile. Moreover, the diocese was now adequately supplied with priests. There were thirty-seven priests in the diocese in 1750, which was enough to ensure that every parish or union of parishes had a priest and that a small number also had a curate. The main problem in this regard, Richardson reported to Rome in 1749, was their advanced age, but this was eased in 1752 when he was given permission to ordain six applicants above the quota laid down in 1741.[71]

The reform programme identified by Bishops MacDonagh and Richardson was continued by Andrew Campbell (1753–69). A priest of the diocese of Armagh, he chose to continue the tradition of not residing in the diocese and of delegating its administration to a vicar general during the long stretches that he was elsewhere. Campbell travelled to Kilmore for three months each year, during which time he endeavoured to expand on the organizational initiatives undertaken by his immediate predecessors.[72] This is most clearly illustrated by the introduction by the parishes of Lurgan (1755), Castletara (1763) and Killinkere and Mullagh (1766) of registers.[73] The significance of this can be overestimated, but taken in tandem with the religious census of 1766 which recorded that the diocese had forty-two secular and nine regular clergy, it provides further evidence of the growing strength and confidence of the Catholic church in at least parts of the diocese.[74] Much of the credit for implementing these reforms belongs to energetic parish priests like William McLean (who commenced the register at Castlerahan) Bartle MacCabe (who introduced the parish register to Killinkere) and his brother Alexander (who did likewise in Lurgan).[75]

This represented a reasonable beginning to a thoroughgoing structural reorganization of the diocese, but Campbell's successor, the Franciscan Denis Maguire (1770–98), allowed the momentum to dissipate. It is striking that no parish commenced keeping a register during his twenty-eight year episcopacy; indeed Castlerahan's ceased in 1776 and was not resumed until 1814.[76] Maguire had served as bishop of Dromore for three years before his translation to Kilmore in 1770, but unfortunately for the diocese, given the continuing current of ill-feeling between regulars and seculars, he allowed his loyalty to his order take precedence over his duty to his diocese. The church in Kilmore continued to grow during his episcopacy and slowly to put the memories and experiences of the penal laws behind it, but Maguire (who was from the parish of Kilesher) would have achieved more if he had lived in the diocese rather than in Enniskillen and if he had made an effort to assuage rather than to exacerbate rivalry between secular and regular clergy.[77]

The greatest achievement of Maguire's episcopate was the establishment of a network of chapels. O'Connell claims his episcopate marks the end of the era of the 'mass rock' and that 'Bishop Maguire took an active part in the erection of suitable churches', but there were larger forces than Bishop Maguire at work.[78] In the first place, it is unlikely that a network of masshouses—undifferentiated and unadorned structures such as were to be found in the parish of Mullagh[79] and elsewhere in the country—did not already exist throughout the diocese. Secondly, the improvement in the economy of the region which followed the embrace of linen spinning and commercial agricultural production brought money into the region which meant that the Catholic population had more disposable income. Furthermore, though denominational animosities remained alive in a diocese in which twenty-eight per cent of the population (according to the 1766 religious census) and the bulk of the social elite was Protestant, and Protestant landlords were prepared to evict sitting Catholic tenants in order to replace them with others of their own faith, there was a qualitative lessening of animosity which facilitated Catholics acquire land on which to build chapels. In the main, these were simple, clay floored, thatched-roofed, mud-walled structures, sometimes cruciform but more usually undifferentiated, of varying size and capacity. For example, the chapel erected in the parish of Drung in 1780 was a long, clay-built cabin with a capacity of five hundred, whereas that constructed in Killinkere lower in 1785 was a simple, small, mud-walled structure, roofed with rushes and open at both ends so people gathered outside could see the priest. Some of the smallest churches could shelter as few as twenty people.[80]

Such structures could not and did not provide accommodation for all of the seventy-two per cent of the diocese's population that were nominally Catholic. Bishop Maguire maintained in his 1794 *relatio status* that the reason many parents did not send their children to church to be catechised was their poverty, but this is hardly the full story.[81] Undoubtedly, some people did not go to church because they did not think they had appropriate attire; but others did not have a chapel conveniently close to their place of residence; while still others cannot have perceived attendance at church as necessary because they possessed a rich spiritual life that encompassed visits to holy wells (like that near the ruins of the old church in the parish of Lurgan) and patterns, and a diverse range of cures, folk remedies and sympathetic magic. The church authorities disapproved of these practices as they reiterated in the provincial synod held at Drogheda in August 1781 when they directed 'prelates ... to exert their zeal and prudence' to extirpate 'such scandalous enormities'.[82] It was possible for the church to make a more sustained assault now than at any time since assemblies such as these and wakes had first attracted hostile notice in the early seventeenth century, because every parish had its own pastor and, in cases where the incumbent was old or sick, a curate. The quality of the priests too appears to have improved, if Bishop Maguire's 1794 report is an accurate guide; however they were not in a position to impose their will on the Catholic population as the continuing practice of clandestine marriage bears witness.[83]

By the date the 1794 *relatio* was transmitted, Bishop Maguire had appealed to Rome and secured permission to appoint a co-adjutor—Fr Charles O'Reilly, the parish priest of Drumgoon—who succeeded him as bishop in 1798.[84] Though Maguire had been able to administer free of the threat of repression, all was not well in the diocese; his practice of giving the best parishes to friars excited such deep and bitter opposition that on one occasion in 1784 his horses were killed and his house set on fire while he slept.[85]

In the 1790s, acts of violence multiplied. The radicalizing tide of revolutionary ideas that wafted their way from France led to a striking increase in civil disorder and to the temporary alienation of the people from the hierarchical church. Like his episcopal colleagues, Maguire was deeply hostile to the democratic doctrines enunciated by radicals like Tom Paine and Wolfe Tone because, he maintained, they promoted irreligion and encouraged 'abuses against public peace and order' which erupted into violent outrage during the anti-militia riots of 1793 and contributed to sectarian clashes in 1794 in which more than thirty people died. They also encouraged anti-clericalism, prompting sections of the Catholic population in the diocese in 1793 to bind themselves by oath not to contribute to the maintenance of their clergy.[86] These were problems the church did not need because the outbreak of the French Revolution and the closure of the Irish colleges there had already posed a serious question over the future education of candidates for the priesthood. Charles O'Reilly represented Bishop Maguire in the discussions that culminated in the foundation of a seminary at Maynooth, and consonant with the disposition of most of those on the episcopal bench to co-operate with the government, he was a party to the ratification by the Ulster bishops in July

1798 of an address in which they urged their priests to be loyal and excommunicated those guilty of participating in the rebellion.[87]

The revolutionary violence that took place in county Cavan in the summer of 1798 mirrored the intensification in sectarian animosity between Catholic and Protestant in the region in the 1790s. This was not in the interest of the Catholic Church which, according to the return sent Lord Castlereagh in 1800, now possessed fifty-two priests—comprising thirty-nine parish priests, eleven curates (mainly attached to wealthier and more urbanized parishes like Lurgan, Castlerahan, Lavey, Laragh, Drumgoon, Urney and Carrigallen) and two who were unattached. There had been a striking improvement, too, in the financial circumstances of the diocese in the three preceding decades. Kilmore was not a rich diocese by any means, but parish priests whose annual income in 1800 ranged from a low of forty to a high of eighty guineas and a bishop who could anticipate 140 guineas a year were well-off by contemporary standards.[88]

V

The Catholic church throughout Ireland commenced the nineteenth century much better circumstanced that it had commenced either the seventeenth or eighteenth centuries. The repeal of the bulk of the penal laws between 1778 and 1793 meant that it could now function free of the threat of legal repression, while the foundation of Maynooth College gave the bishops direct control over the training of their own clergy. In Kilmore, it was possible for the diocese to provide a fuller religious service to a greater number of the Catholic population than was the case in centuries. Moreover, the ambience in which worship took place continued to improve. Most of the chapels built in the diocese in the eighteenth century were little more than commodious mud-walled cabins with a table or mound of sods for an altar, clay floors and little or no decoration or furniture. Mud-walled edifices continued to be built and maintained, but the era of the unassuming masshouse was fast drawing to a close. The 1790s witnessed the construction of a stone-walled and slate-roofed parish church in Templefort and a thatched, stone-walled chapel at Derrylin in Knockninny.[89]

The two bishops who administered the diocese in the early decades of the nineteenth century were James Dillon(1800–06) and Farrell O'Reilly (1807–29). Little is known of either;[90] but the process of diocesan reconstruction that was a feature of the second half of the eighteenth century was continued though it showed little real vigour in the thirty years they had command of the diocese. This is well illustrated by the fact that only two parishes (Kilsherdany (1803) and Urney and Annagelliff, 1812) commenced keeping registers during this period. However, circumstances remained conducive to reform. The number of ordinations nearly doubled the number of clerical deaths: in the two decades 1800–20, there were sixty-three ordinations compared with thirty deaths; while in the twenty years 1821–40 the respective figures were eighty-nine and fifty-one.[91] On first glance, this might be expected to have produced a marked improvement in the priest to people ratio, but this was slow in coming. From fifty two in 1800, the number of priests climbed marginally to fifty-four in 1822 and than sharply to eighty in 1835. This resulted in a significant number of parishes acquiring curates on a permanent basis.[92] However, it was not enough to offset the more than threefold rise in population that had taken place since the mid-eighteenth century, with the result that the priest to people ratio in the diocese stood at 1:3007 in 1835, the second worst figure in the province of Armagh.[93] On a more positive note, the quality of priests continued to improve. Most priests came from farming backgrounds,[94] and if their theological training in Maynooth was unadventurous, their commitment to duty and their obedience to their superiors was greater than that of their continentally-trained predecessors. Old habits proved persistent, however, and there remained a core of factious, inattentive and drunken priests, who appear as but pale shadows beside able and energetic pastors like James Magauran, later bishop of Ardagh, Tom Maguire, the famous preacher and controversial-ist, and Patrick Maguire, Bishop O'Reilly's co-adjutor from 1817.[95]

Though not as disturbed as the neighbouring diocese of Clogher, clerical factionalism was a persistent feature of religious life in Kilmore in the early nineteenth century. In 1817, when the Franciscan priest, Patrick Maguire was nominated by Bishop O'Reilly to serve as his co-adjutor, a public protest in Cavan town was addressed by Fr Michael O'Reilly of Kilmore parish who spoke against the nomination and sharply criticised the bishop's administra-tion of the diocese. This had the potential to escalate into an acrimonious and debilitating row, but this was avoided by lay intervention on the side of episcopal authority.[96] The evangelical Protestant revival may also have had an impact. One of the leading patrons of this movement in Ireland was Lord Farnham, the influential Cavan peer. He encouraged evangelical activity in the diocese, which resulted in the conversion of some Catholics.[97]

The activities of Protestant evangelicals greatly troubled the Catholic laity and clergy of Kilmore who had grown increasingly confident following the repeal of the penal laws and the improvement in the fabric of their church. Their confidence was to increase further in the 1820s as a consequence of their participation in the Catholic Association and the landmark election in the county Cavan constituency in 1826. County Cavan was one of the most committed and enthusiastic centres of Catholic Association activity in the country. Nearly every parish followed the lead provided by Bishop O'Reilly, his co-adjutor and the bulk of the parish priests and curates and contributed generously to the Catholic Rent. The increased assertiveness of the Catholic population, and the concomitant rise in sectarian tension served to cement further the bond between priests and people. It was no accident that Daniel O'Connell addressed the electors of county Cavan in June 1826 from a platform raised in the chapel yard in Cavan town, or that priests electioneered actively in a brave but ultimately unsuccessful attempt to triumph over their Tory and anti-emancipationist opponents.[98]

Patrick Maguire, Bishop O'Reilly's coadjutor, did not live to witness the passion and excitement of the 1826 election. He died in April, and was succeeded just over a year later by James Browne, the Wexford-born professor of scripture at Maynooth.[99] Two years later, Browne succeeded to the vacant see on the death of O'Reilly. Browne was thus familiar with the challenges that awaited him as bishop. Following his consecration, he moved from Drung where he had served as parish priest while co-adjutor, to the more central location of Coothill in the mensal parish of Drumgoon from where he commenced what was to become one of the formative episcopates in the history of the diocese of Kilmore.

James Browne was a highly intelligent, committed and hardworking pastor who kept discipline on the growing number of priests he commanded through regular visitation and a firm hand. He possessed a clear and distinct vision of what was necessary to transform Kilmore into an effectively run diocese. One of his priorities was to lay down a code of behaviour for his clergy. The key event in this process was the diocesan synod held in October 1834 which approved specific resolutions affirming the authority of the bishop over the clergy, regularising the troubled relationship between parish priest and curate, and instituting an explicit code of conduct and deportment for priests. Measures providing for the proper administration of the sacraments, particularly marriage, and the sanitising of wakes and local pilgrimages were likewise authorised in a further assault on popular heterodoxy. The purpose of these decrees was to put rules in place within which a Tridentine church could operate. The object was to create a more efficient institution, and to this end Browne instructed the additional priests he acquired to serve in those areas of the diocese in which there was greatest need and endeavoured to keep all his priests doctrinally informed by convening theological conferences and by establishing parish libraries of religious literature. He also endeavoured, but with less success, to get them to keep parish registers; a substantial number of parishes (twenty-six) did commence registers during his episcopacy, but nine others did not do so till after his death in 1865. Despite this, Bishop Browne oversaw the reduction in the priest to people ratio within the diocese from 3000:1 to 2765:1 in the decade 1835–45, as the number of pastors in the diocese approached ninety for the first time. He also oversaw an acceleration in the process of church construction and refurbishment as the church struggled to provide the 240,000 people that comprised the Catholic population of Kilmore in 1845 with places for worship.[100]

Church building had continued apace during the episcopates of James Dillon and Farrell O'Reilly. It is not possible at the moment to establish precisely the number of churches built and refurbished during these years, but those that were constructed were generally more substantial than their predecessors. Many, like that built in Mullagh in 1801, in lower Killinkere in 1810 and in Kilmainham Wood in 1817 were thatched and quite modestly sized, but the most striking feature of the early nineteenth century was the increase in the number of stone built churches. The largest (80 by 43.5 by 29 feet) was built in Cavan town in 1823 at a cost of £1000. It was a plain, rectangular edifice but it symbolised the triumph of stone and slate over mud and thatch, and attested to the mounting confidence and wealth of the Catholic population in the diocese. Throughout Browne's episcopacy, energetic priests in the diocese did what they could to raise the money to fund the construction of similar, but generally smaller, churches. The size and cost varied according to the wealth of the parish and the ambition of the parish priest. The larger and more costly tended to be built in the wealthier eastern parishes; for example, the church built in Castlerahan in 1834 cost £2000; whereas that built at Derrylin in Knockninny in 1838 cost £600 and that at Drumbeg some time earlier cost a mere £80. Most were barely furnished, if at all, but the fact that Browne could report to Rome in 1836 there were eighty stone built churches in the diocese (thirteen of which had been built in the previous seven years) attests to the rapid pace of construction. It was not necessary to maintain this pace throughout Browne's long episcopacy, but by 1865 thatched churches were a rarity and attention had switched to the provision of appropriate church furniture and internal decoration.[101]

In Kilmore, as in all other dioceses, the pace of reform continued to vary from parish to parish. On the whole, the wealthier, eastern parts of the diocese made faster progress than their poorer western counterparts, but the rather erratic geographical distribution of the introduction of registers and the impact of dynamic pastors like Tom Maguire of Inismagrath, who spearheaded an ambitious programme of church building in the parish of the same name, cautions one against being geographically deterministic on this complex issue.[102]

Geography was a central concern of Bishop Browne. On his appointment in 1829, he had taken up residence in Cootehill. But Cootehill is located in the north-eastern corner of the diocese, which was not an ideal location from which to administer the diocese. So like Bishop O'Higgins of Ardagh, Browne determined to move to a more central location and fixed on Cavan town, which was larger and more populous than Cootehill, as a more appropriate diocesan capital. His 'grand design', enunciated to the people of the diocese in a pastoral letter in 1838, involved building a seminary and bishop's residence in the town and once he had announced his intentions he did not delay putting them into action. He purchased a 'splendid house' near the Catholic church, refurbished it, renamed it St Augustine's academy and had it ready to admit students in 1839. Though conceived as a preparatory college for students for the priesthood who would attend Maynooth (104 made the transition), students other than future seminarians attended Kilmore Academy. Four years after the opening of the College, Browne availed of the death of the parish priest to take command of the parish of Urney and Annagelliff and to install himself in the bishop's quarters in the Academy building. This was a decisive moment in the history of the diocese. As Donal Kerr has observed: 'It gave the diocese a centre and focus and stability'.[103]

Central to Bishop O'Higgins's design for the diocese of Ardagh was the construction of a grand cathedral in Longford town. Browne did not possess an equally ambitious plan for Cavan, but he was conscious of the inadequacy of the church in the town to diocesan needs and he determined to enlarge it. Construction was delayed by the Famine, but the addition of a nave and chancel between 1853 and 1862 and the re-dedication of the building gave the administrative centre of the diocese a church more appropriate to its needs.[104]

By this date, as Margaret Crawford's essay shows, the Great Famine had taken its heavy toll on the population of the diocese. Cavan and Leitrim were among the counties worst hit by the Famine with a casualty rate of perhaps as much as twenty per cent. Bishop Browne was not inactive in attempting to organize succour for those in distress, but in keeping with the moderate and non-confrontational stance he had taken on the National Schools issue in the 1830s (when he did not oppose interdenominational education), on repeal in the 1840s (when he gave his priests free rein but declined to become involved himself), and on the Queen's Colleges issue, he maintained a low profile. He perceived himself as a pastor rather than a politician, and in view of the sizeable Protestant and presbyterian populations in the diocese and the sectarian discord in the region it was an understandable and, perhaps, a wise stance.[105]

Among the tens of thousands of people who died from contagion in county Cavan in the 1840s were five priests. However, their loss was more than offset by the Famine-inspired decline in the Catholic population, with the result that Bishop Browne had more priests than he needed in the post-Famine period.[106] In others respects too, the Famine actually facilitated the reforming process Browne sought to advance. According to the Commissioners of Public Instruction, church attendance in four parishes around Virginia in 1834 was just below forty per cent. This figure was almost certainly increasing as a consequence of the wave of church building and pastoral reforms being undertaken by Browne. However, it is unlikely that it came anywhere near present day figures before the Great Famine because of the continuing strength of traditional and heterodox religious observances, and the disinclination of the poor to go to church on a regular basis. This obstacle was greatly reduced by the death and emigration in the 1840s of a substantial percentage of the labourers, cottiers and small farmers whom the Catholic church nationally had failed to win over to its way of thinking in the pre-Famine period; their decimation in the 1840s thus fortuitously strengthened the hold Tridentine Catholicism, which was most warmly embraced by the middle classes, had on the religious life of the country. By the 1860s, the priest to people ratio in Kilmore was 1:1887, and it was to improve further in subsequent decades.[107]

If Browne had no reservations about reforming the diocese in accordance with the decrees of the Council of Trent, he was less easy with the ultramontane catholicism espoused by Paul Cullen, who was appointed to the archbishopric of Armagh in 1849. This emerged clearly at the National Synod of bishops convened at Thurles in 1850 when Browne supported Archbishop Murray's plea for the acceptance of the Queen's Colleges. Cullen espoused an uncompromising brand of Roman Catholicism Browne found uncongenial. His instinct was to diffuse conflict and to identify a middle way between contending parties rather than, like Cullen, to impose his own will and his ultramontane views. Cullen for his part had little time for Browne, though he could find little wrong with his pastoral endeavours.[108]

As mentioned above, Browne's main undertaking in the 1850s was the reconstruction of St Patrick's church in Cavan town, but he also active on other fronts. He encouraged the Society of St Vincent de Paul, confraternities which promoted religious knowledge, and the cult of the Sacred Heart. He also introduced the Poor Clare Sisters, who established a convent school in Cavan town in 1861 and an orphanage in 1865.[109] By this date, Browne's episcopacy was drawing to a close. In the thirty-six years that he had personal responsibility for the diocese he had effected major changes. He had, it is true, taken charge of the diocese at an apposite moment. By the early 1820s, the church in the diocese had enjoyed nearly seventy years freedom from repression, while economic growth over the same period meant there was more money in the diocese. Moreover, Browne's predecessor's had laid down firm foundations on which he could build. None of this should be allowed take away from Browne's own achievements as a pastor and an administrator. He perceived that the diocese of Kilmore could be transformed into a virtual model of the Tridentine church, and he pursued this goal with quiet but unflappable determination throughout his episcopacy and, in the process, did more than anybody in three centuries to make it a reality.

VI

Though James Browne's achievements as bishop of Kilmore were enormous, much remained to be done. A reoccurrence of the clerical factionalism that had so blighted the diocese before he took charge in 1829 threatened to rear its ugly head when the moment came to appoint a co-adjutor in 1863,[110] but it was checked by the appointment of Nicholas Conaty in 1863. Politically and religiously, Conaty's views were closer to Cullen's than to Browne's, as Gerard Moran's essay will show, but he was a capable and efficient administrator who shared Browne's commitment to the improvement and reform of the church in the diocese. Conaty ably continued Browne's work in the areas of clerical discipline and organization, church refurbishment and construction, education (he replaced Kilmore Academy with a diocesan seminary and introduced both the Christian Brothers and the Sisters of Mercy) and in the promotion of devotional practice.[111] It was a strategy that continued to pay dividends. By 1890, the diocese of Kilmore had more than one hundred priests and was an active contributor to foreign missions.[112] The trials and tribulations of successive bishops and vicars in the sixteenth, seventeenth and eighteenth centuries seemed but a distant memory. In practice, however, the goals and objects of Conaty bear sustainable comparison with those of Hugh O'Reilly in the early seventeenth century and with Michael MacDonagh in the eighteenth. The attempt to organize the Catholic church in the diocese of Kilmore along Tridentine lines is the *leitmotif* that unifies the history of that organization between the sixteenth and nineteenth centuries. In Kilmore as elsewhere in the country, it was long delayed because the political and economic circumstances were unconducive and, it must be added, because some priests, vicars general and bishops put their own comforts and ambitions before that of their church.

Poverty and Famine in County Cavan[1]

MARGARET CRAWFORD

Poverty and famine are synonymous with pre-Famine Ireland. Travellers, politicians and economists observed Irish men and women in a state of extreme destitution; some described it, many tried to explain it, while others looked for a remedy. Furthermore, by the nineteenth century the science of statistical and social enquiry had gathered momentum with the result that we now have numerous documents from which we can tease out information on the economy and society of this period. As a consequence of this intense scrutiny historians have inherited a wealth of documentation on the poverty of the Irish.

For county Cavan the best known sources for evidence on the conditions of the people are the *Statistical Survey of the County of Cavan* of 1801 by Sir Charles Coote,[2] the Ordnance Survey memoirs of the 1830s,[3] the census of Ireland for 1841 and 1851,[4] and the report of the Devon Commission on the occupation of land in the early 1840s.[5] In addition, the Poor Inquiry of 1836,[6] provides even more intimate details on many aspects of the life of the poor. Together, these documents paint a very clear picture of pre-Famine Cavan. We know of the numbers of people inhabiting the county, the number and condition of their housing. We also know about their clothing, their diet, their wage rates, the extent to which they used money or barter, the terms of their tenure, and much more besides.

I

In 1821, when the first complete census of Ireland was taken the population of the county exceeded 195,000. Over the next twenty years it increased by 24.7 per cent to reach almost a quarter of a million (243,158) in 1841. The Famine decade, however, witnessed a change in the pattern. During the ten year period 1841 to 1851 the population fell by almost one-third (28.42 per cent), so that in 1851 there were fewer people in the county than in 1821. Population decline continued during the next decade though on a reduced scale. Thus the total population was almost twelve per cent (11.6 per cent) less by 1861.

The sex ratio altered slightly during this decade too. Over the period 1821 to 1851 females slightly outnumbered males in a ratio of 100 males to 101 females. During 1851 to 1861, however, the position was reversed so that the ratio was ninety-eight females to 100 males. This phenomenon has been noted in other parts of the country. One explanation centres on domestic industry. In county Cavan home produced linen cloth, which relied heavily on female labour, had long been an important supplement to family incomes.[7] But as domestic spinners contracted in the face of competition from factory spun yarn after 1830, so women lost their economic importance and consequently had to seek work elsewhere. Female migration to Irish cities as well as further afield to work in factories or seek employment as domestic servants accounts for some of the decline in female numbers, though the occupations of the majority of Cavan females who migrated is unknown.[8]

Some areas of the county sustained greater population decline than others. Of the eight baronies in county Cavan, five lost about thirty per cent of their population between 1841 and 1851, while the remaining three lost 27.8, 24.1 and 19.2 per cent respectively.

Table 1: Population decline in the baronies[9] of county Cavan 1841–51

Baronies	Population 1841	Population 1851	Percentage Decline	Persons/ Square mile 1841	Persons/ Square mile 1851
Castlerahan	40909	28097	31.3	368	250
Clankee	38892	26606	31.5	387	264
Clanmahon	28674	19952	30.4	337	235
Loughtee Lower	15851	11245	29.0	343	243
Loughtee Upper	36440	27660	24.1	346	266
Tullygarvey	37532	25955	30.8	400	277
Tullyhaw	24992	20207	19.2	175	142
Tullyhunco	19868	14342	27.8	307	224

The barony with the lowest decline was the wild and mountainous region of Tullyhaw. The difficult terrain had limited ability to sustain a dense population, even before the Famine crisis. Prior to the Famine it supported approximately half the number of people per square mile compared with any other barony. Thus a combination of the hilly terrain and the wet climate forced those living in this inhospitable environment to eke out a pastoral-based existence, which furthermore, required a small labour force. The Famine, therefore, made less of an impact and so population decline was of a lower order in this western area. The availability of dairy produce and oatmeal further softened the failure of the potato crop.

Yet Cavan as a whole, along with Fermanagh and Monaghan experienced the steepest decline of all the Ulster counties, with a drop of almost thirty per cent occurring in each. Elsewhere in the province falls of a lower magnitude were recorded.[10] Although a county of few and small towns because the terrain made transportation difficult, nevertheless, like the rest of Ulster the proportion of town dwellers in Cavan rose, simply because urban populations declined less than the population in the countryside.[11]

Of the 69,094 people who vanished from the county between the 1841 and 1851 censuses we do not know exactly how many died or how many emigrated. Of those who died we do not know how many died of disease and how many died of starvation. What we do know is that of those who perished, more died of disease than of starvation. Mortality among children and the aged was greatest and, women survived better than men.

II

The people of the county were housed in two types of building, those made of clay and those constructed of stone. The topography of the land dictated the type. Lieutenant Taylor, surveyor for the Ordnance Survey of the parish of Drung, in the barony of Tullygarvey, noted that 'the habitations of the tenantry depends very much on the substratum of their soil. If unstratified rock [was] the prevailing formation the cabins [were] built of clay, if stratified they [were] formed of stone.'[12] In those areas where clay cabins predominated the general appearance of the region was one of wretchedness. Lieutenant Beatty, surveying for the Ordnance Survey parts of Clanmahon barony, provided more detail. He recorded that the mud cabins were thatched, had small glass windows, were one story high and usually contained only two rooms, occasionally three, though conditions within the cabins lacked comfort and cleanliness.[13] In his estimation only one-sixth of the cabins were of stone implying that five-sixths were of mud.

The Poor Inquiry also gives the impression that mud cabins dominated the landscape. Of the Cavan responses to the question about housing, mud cabins were listed by two-thirds of the respondents. A more precise approach was adopted by the Census Commissioners. In each census from 1841 to 1861 they attempted to measure the quality of housing by evaluating the materials used in the construction of the house, counting the number of rooms and the number of windows. The fourth or lowest class consisted entirely of mud and contained only one room. Third class was also built of mud with between two and four rooms and had windows. To achieve second class status a house had to have from five to nine rooms with windows, while a first-class dwelling was determined by superiority to the preceding three classes. The results for county Cavan are shown in table 2.

With the exception of one barony, Tullyhaw, third class housing exceeded fourth class. Together, the third and fourth class housing accounted for eighty-two per cent of all habitations, third class making up forty-seven per cent and

Table 2: Quality of housing in county Cavan 1841–61

Year	1st Class	2nd Class	3rd Class	4th Class	Total
1841	390	7022	19416	14136	40964
1851	585	8451	17448	3595	30079
1861	702	9671	15733	2220	28326

Source: *Census of Ire.*, 1841, 1851, 1861

fourth class thirty-five per cent. Assessed against pre-Famine Ulster the poorer quality Cavan housing stock is evident. In the province as a whole forty-three per cent of housing fell into the third-class category and thirty per cent was fourth class. Thus, as shown in table 3, compared with the four provinces county Cavan was more akin to Munster and Connacht than Ulster.

Table 3: Percentage of third and fourth class housing in the provinces of Ireland and county Cavan in 1841

		Cavan	Ulster	Leinster	Munster	Connacht
1841	3rd class	47	43	43	34	39
1841	4th class	35	30	26	45	50
Total	(3rd & 4th)	82	73	79	79	89

There was little difference between the third and fourth class homes in the census classification, but by virtue of the fact that many Cavan cabins had a second room they were rated as third rather than fourth class, giving the impression of relative improvement. Comments, however, attest to the misery of the peasantry's conditions. Mr Pierce Morton sent a very vivid description to the Poor Inquiry about the housing in the parish of Kildrumferton:

> The cabins are of stone, mud walls, or sods, as happens to be most convenient; seldom glazed or plastered; badly thatched; the floor of clay, which, as well as the walls, is, for the greater part of winter, wet with rain falling through the roof: the family sleeping on some dried rushes or straw thrown on the floor in the chimney-corner, as the warmest place in the house, with stools placed to keep the bed from taking fire: their own clothes thrown over them to assist the scanty bed-clothes.[14]

The furnishing of the cabins was very rudimentary. A few had bedsteads but the majority had nothing better than straw for sleeping upon. A few stools, sometimes a table, tins to drink from and a pot for cooking potatoes, constituted their furnishings.

III

After housing, clothing was one of the essentials of life. Both the Ordnance Survey memoirs and the Poor Inquiry indicate that clothing was made of very coarse friezes, corduroy and homespun woollens. Lieutenant Beatty presented a very colourful account stating 'the people of different districts and counties are known by the colour of the frieze they wear as the clans of Scotland are distinguished by their plaids.'[15] As a rule the men dressed in grey frieze, occasionally blue, the colour of women's clothing, however, was not recorded. The Poor Inquiry gives the impression of a peasantry very poorly clad. Numerous reporters make terse statements that clothing should be more accurately described as rags. The parish priest of West Annagh used just two words to describe the dress of the people in his district: 'half naked';[16] other comments state 'clothing [is] miserable in the extreme'.[17]

Worthy of note are the different perceptions of respondents to the Poor Inquiry on the living conditions of the labouring classes. Rosy pictures were presented by justices of the peace, members of parliament and gentlemen. John Young Esq, listed as a member of parliament, reported that clothing was generally respectable: 'coarse blue cloth and grey frieze [were] in common wear, and a person of either sex without shoes and stockings [was] rarely to be seen.'[18] Parish priests and some clergy of the Protestant faith, on the other hand, have left us in no doubt about the ragged condition of peasant clothing. It could be argued that the clergy were closer to the labouring population, attending to their parishioners' spiritual needs and the major crises in their lives, and consequently have left us a more accurate account.

IV

Being clothed and housed the people of Cavan had also to be fed. The monotonous fare of potatoes and milk were the dominant items of the diet. Without exception, potatoes were eaten daily in every household and at every meal. Additional items, such as milk, usually buttermilk, oatmeal and herring appeared from time to time, depending on the season of the year and disposable income. To quote Kevin O'Neill's colourful language in his study of Killashandra 'the potato fulfilled an almost magical combination of needs for the Cavan farmer.'[19] The potato was nutritious and when eaten in large quantities provided the entire family with a wholesome diet. In addition, potato offal fed the pig, which was reared to pay the rent, and furthermore was most suitable for the crop rotation system.

Table 4 shows the percentage of parishes recording the various items of food eaten in Cavan along with figures for the border counties of north Louth/south-east Ulster, and the whole of Ireland.

Every parish recorded the consumption of potatoes, seventy-four per cent noted either milk or buttermilk, thirty-one per cent oatmeal and so on. We can refine the data further by estimating the regularity of consumption and combining the results with the frequency a food was eaten to produce a variety score. The technique for processing the data is explained elsewhere.[20]

Table 4: Percentage frequency of foods recorded in the Poor Inquiry

	Co. Cavan	N. Louth/SE Ulster	Ireland
N=	35	57	1569
Potatoes	100	100	100
Milk Products	74	68	74
Oatmeal	31	28	28
Fish (Herring)	14	37	26
Butter	9	2	10
Bacon/meat	9	5	4
Bread	-	4	8
Tea	-	2	2

Source: Figures derived from *Poor Inquiry (Ireland)*, H.C. 1836 (36) xxxi, Appendix D.

Suffice here to say that county Cavan scored a low value of 863 reflecting the poor variety of the diet there. To give an impression of how county Cavan fared in comparison with other counties the variety index scores of the remaining counties in Ireland are presented in table 5.[21]

Table 5: Variety index of labouring class diet in Ireland by county

Ulster		Leinster		Munster		Connacht	
Antrim	1384	Carlow	950	Clare	1016	Galway	1032
Armagh	1149	Dublin	1450	Cork	969	Leitrim	1230
CAVAN	863	Kildare	1593	Kerry	911	Mayo	1024
Donegal	1098	Kilkenny	1115	Limerick	861	Roscommon	806
Down	1343	King's Co.	1148	Tipperary	956	Sligo	1052
Fermanagh	1239	Longford	811	Waterford	812		
Londonderry	1395	Louth	843				
Monaghan	1026	Meath	1034				
Tyrone	1239	Queen's Co.	1119				
		W'meath	957				
		Wexford	1286				
		Wicklow	1288				

Source: See Clarkson and Crawford, 'Dietary directions' p. 178.

Travellers to Ireland and investigators of social conditions regarded the potato and buttermilk regime of the poor as frugal. Potatoes were looked upon as food fit only for animals. In nutritional terms, however, the redeeming feature of the diet was the large quantities of potatoes consumed, washed down with sizeable amounts of skimmed milk or buttermilk. The daily menu consisted of between ten and fourteen pounds of potatoes and one to two pints of buttermilk. We know from the Poor Inquiry that in Loughtee Barony the diet of labourers was primarily potatoes and buttermilk. Furthermore, a figure of from two and a half to three stones of potatoes was recorded as the daily consumption by a family in the 1830s. By weighting consumption within the family, and allowing for one pint of buttermilk as the daily intake, a nutritional analysis of this diet can be calculated as shown in table 6.

Table 6: Nutritional analysis of a diet recorded in
Loughtee barony for a labouring man per day in 1830s[22]

	Protein g.	*Energy* kcal.	*Value* / MJ
Potatoes 4000 g.	56	3200	13.4
Buttermilk 600 ml.	20	204	0.8
Total	76	3404	14.2

While county Cavan labourers fared less well compared with their peers in surrounding counties,[23] nevertheless, in nutritional terms they were not un-dernourished even when evaluated against recent dietary recommendations of between forty and sixty grams of protein daily and an energy requirement for heavy labouring of 3000 to 3500 kilocalories.[24]

v

At the beginning of the nineteenth century many households of county Cavan engaged in agrarian and industrial pursuits. Agriculture and linen manufac-ture were carried on side by side. Women spun and men weaved chiefly in the autumn and winter. In the spring and summer crops were cultivated and harvested. Small farms proliferated. By the 1840s the number of holdings of five acres or less amounted to approximately two-fifths of all holdings.[25] Prior to the Famine sub-division of farms was commonplace so that by the mid-century tiny parcels of land of as little as an acre or less were leased. Several contemporary commentators connected poverty to this practice. Lieutenant Taylor, for example, attributed the wretchedness and desolation of the parish of Drumgoon to 'the deplorable system of agriculture and the minute subdi-vision of farms which so unhappily prevails.'[26] His colleague Lieutenant Beatty made the same observation.

Charles Coote in his *Statistical survey of county Cavan*, presents a very clear picture of the crop rotation programme. In the barony of Loughtee he noted that 'flax always follows potatoes and is succeeded by oats. If wheat [is sown], it is only after a summer fallow, and but in a small proportion, and the crop by no means repays the expense so well as oats, as the produce is trifling, and the grain impoverished.'[27] This pattern of tillage management prevailed throughout the county. After the requirements for tillage crops were met, any remaining land was in grassland. In some areas, such as the west of the county, the land was unsuitable for intensive cultivation. There cattle were reared, primarily black cattle. Pig rearing was also important for the household economy. Potato scraps and dairy offal provided cheap feedstuff and pigs sales made a major contribution towards rent payments. On the eve of the Famine potatoes, oats and flax were the chief produce, with a little wheat, barley, rye and clover. Taylor noted that by the 1830s agriculture was, 're-duced to the lowest possible state of depression'.[28] Nevertheless, during the Famine period tillage crops continued to be cultivated. However, since no complete quantitative data existed for Ireland until 1847, when agricultural statistics were first recorded, we have no accurate way of judging county Cavan's agricultural output prior to the Famine. Data for the Famine years show that oats were the chief crop followed by potatoes. However, low potato acreages were recorded because of blight, 1847 standing out as a particularly poor year, shown in table 7.

Table 7: Acreage under main crops in county Cavan 1847–51

Year	Wheat	Oats	Barley	Rye	Potatoes	Flax	Total
1847	3531	99753	515	785	5206	1625	111415
1848	5413	97492	617	2203	16236	1526	123487
1849	5460	103043	390	2240	12980	2182	126346
1850	3934	100282	382	1488	20811	5107	132004
1851	2657	101854	214	1345	22175	8942	137187

Source: Agricultural Statistics (Ireland) 1847–51

At the turn of the nineteenth century linen was manufactured on a cottage industry basis. Coote attributed the prominence of linen manufacture in the county to the fragmentation of the land, and indeed economic conditions at the beginning of the nineteenth century reflect those found in some English regions in an earlier era where industries were needed to supplement the rural economy. Joan Thirsk, writing about industries in the countryside in the seventeenth century, described the west Yorkshire dales where, because of subdivision of land, 'the tenants [were] much increased in number ... and the tenements became so small in quantity that ... they could not maintain their families were it not by ... industry in knitting coarse stockings.'[29] Similarly in Cavan, subdivision of land over a long period, combined in the Cavan case with poor agricultural land, created economic and social conditions which compelled agrarian workers to supplement their farming activities. The manufacture of linen proved an ideal complement.

After 1825, however, 'domestic spinning and weaving did not survive in its fullest form'.[30] The competitiveness of the Lagan Valley following the advent of factory spinning, and later weaving, damaged the cottage industry. Nevertheless, there were still yarn markets in remoter rural areas of county Cavan, and home spinning and weaving continued for a time, because the rapidly increasing labour force were willing to accept lower wages for their labours, as well as increasing the number of hours worked. Thus, the expanding population was trapped in a declining industry. Wage rates dropped, and in response labourers worked harder in an effort to keep up earnings. To add to their vulnerability, the labouring population was subsisting on one crop, the potato. This was a high risk strategy, which for the Irish had a catastrophic outcome when the potato crops failed in successive seasons during 1845–9.

Kevin O'Neill has drawn attention to the difficulty of assigning occupational titles to the agricultural community.[31] One person could simultaneously be tenant farmer, a wage labourer and a conacre tenant. What is clear, however, is that between 1790 and 1830 the number of agricultural labourers increased rapidly. By 1841 fifty-three per cent of the employed population stated that they were engaged in agriculture and of these 64.5 per cent were recorded as agricultural servants and labourers, and 35.27 per cent as farmers. In county Cavan there were three types of labour contracts, farm service, cottier agreement and wage labour. Farm service was the most secure though the most restrictive; wage labour held the greatest insecurity. The cottier agreement emerged from incomplete monetisation. The farmer exchanged for labour, often on a yearly basis, a small potato plot, on which the cottier could cultivate the year's food requirements. Money was not required for this arrangement.

Remuneration for labour took several forms. Wages could be in cash, or in provisions or in lieu of rent or a combination of two or more of these. When evaluating levels of wage rates these factors have to be considered as also does the sporadic nature of agricultural labouring. In Cavan, as in many regions of rural Ireland, under-employment was endemic. Work and wages frequently were on a daily basis, and so while daily rates may not have fluctuated, income over the year could vary considerably. Using data from the Poor Inquiry (1836) Harris has mapped on a county basis the number of days worked, the average daily wages over the whole year, and the average winter daily wages, extracts of which are presented in table 8.[32]

The results show that in county Cavan the average number of days on which agricultural work was available numbered only 150, representing less than half a year. Cavan daily wage rates were among the lowest in Ulster at eight pence in winter and ten pence during the rest of the year. Thus Cavan was more comparable with the counties in Leinster than Ulster. However, as already indicated, wage rates formed only part of the picture. Other types of labour payments, such as provisions and rent in lieu of labour were important supplements to the household income.

Table 8: Average daily wages and number of
days worked in agricultural labour 1836

	Winter Wages (pence)	Rest of Year (pence)	Days work Available
Leinster	8.27	9.72	140
Munster	7.00	8.66	130
Connacht	6.25	8.50	100
Ulster	10.11	11.44	170
Cavan	8.00	10.00	150

Source: Extracted from Ruth-Ann M. Harris, *The nearest place that wasn't Ireland: early nineteenth century Irish labor migration* (Iowa, 1994), p. 48. See also *Poor Inquiry Ireland*, appendix H, H.C. 1836 [41] XXXIV, p. 12.

In recent years economists and historians have examined this practice as a means of evaluating the degree of underdevelopment in pre-Famine Ireland. Lynch and Vaisey proposed an alternative method for analysing the pre-Famine economy.[33] They identified two distinct sectors, a modern monetised sector practised in the maritime east, and a backward subsistence sector in the rest of the country. The theory has been much critised primarily for being too geographically determinant. There is no doubt, however, that both monetarised and non-monetarised economies existed, though not regionalized in the way Lynch and Vaisey suggest, rather they occurred side by side. What did exist was the production of food for subsistence requirements. The need for food compelled labourers into the land market. Either they rented land from a landlord, or middleman or alternatively they held land from a tenant farmer, sometimes in the form of conacre arrangement. Payment for a stake in the land varied. A money rent or labour in lieu of rent was agreed upon.

The Poor Inquiry commissioners recognised that labour was remunerated in a variety of ways. Consequently they requested respondents to record whether wages were paid in cash, in provisions, in lieu of rent for a conacre holding, or a combination of two or more of these methods.[34] From this information we can calculate a crude measure of monetisation. Joel Mokyr has developed a technique for this purpose. He used a simple numbering scheme whereby a score of three was given when only one medium of payment was stated. When a combination of two or more methods of payment was listed a judgement had to be made to weight the score according to the more common form. Thus if a respondent recorded that the labourers in his district were paid in both provisions and cash though more commonly with cash, money would score two and provisions one, and if all three were listed without greater emphasis to one each would then score one.[35] Table 9 shows the results of applying this technique to county Cavan, the province of Ulster, and Poor Law Unions in the surrounding area.

This exercise highlights the preference in county Cavan for remunerating labour in exchange for rent rather than cash when compared with Ulster and the surrounding poor law unions, though within Cavan itself, a cash wage was the most common, exceeding payment in lieu of rent by a small margin.

An alternative way of developing this theme is to examine to what degree labour was paid for through the medium of cash, that is solely by money, mainly by money, or a cocktail of cash, provisions, and in lieu of rent. Usingthe same data from the Poor Inquiry Liam Kennedy assembled the information in this way for Ulster and found that, 'labour was paid largely or extensively in the form of money'.[38]

Table 9: Medium of wage payment

	Cash	Provisions	Rent
Ulster (all) [36]	1.92	0.75	0.33
Cavan	1.14	0.74	1.12
Bailieborough (PLU)[37]	1.39	0.56	1.06
Castleblayney & Carrickmacross (PLU)	1.21	0.75	1.00

Source: Poor Inquiry (Ireland) 1836 (Appendix D); Joel Mokyr Why Ireland starved: a quantitative and analytical history of the Irish economy, 1800-1850 (London, 1983), p. 23; Margaret Crawford, 'Dietary considerations in pre-Famine Louth and its environs' in Raymond Gillespie and Harold O'Sullivan (eds), The borderlands: essays on the history of the Ulster-Leinster border (Belfast, 1989), pp. 117-18.

Table 10: Degree of monetisation (percentage) *c.*1834

	Money only	Mainly Money	Mixed Payments	No Money
Cavan	3	21	68	8
Inner Ulster	17	41	42	-
Outer Ulster	9	44	47	-
Ulster	13	43	44	-

Source: Poor Inquiry (Ireland) 1836 (Appendix D); Kennedy and Ollerenshaw Economic history of Ulster, p. 34.

However, as table 10 demonstrates, there were discernible differences in the levels of monetisation in what Kennedy terms Inner Ulster (Antrim, Down, Armagh and Londonderry) and Outer Ulster (Cavan, Monaghan, Tyrone, Fermanagh and Donegal), the inner sector having a high percentage of payment in cash alone. This exercise provides yet another indicator of Cavan's poverty in the pre-Famine era.

VI

For those who did not hold land or could not obtain labour and hence fell into a poverty trap the last resort was the workhouse. Set up in 1838, the Irish poor law provided a network of workhouses throughout the country, one in each of 130 unions.[39] Three workhouses were located in the county, Bailieborough, Cavan, and Cootehill, and a further five unions had territory in the county.[40] The Bailieborough and Cavan unions were both declared in November 1839 and the workhouses opened to paupers in March 1842. Cootehill union was declared earlier, in August of 1839, though the workhouse was not opened until September 1842. Cavan workhouse was the largest of the three, with accommodation for 1200 paupers. Cootehill held 800 and Bailieborough 600.[41]

There were three ways of obtaining admission into the workhouse. The officers of the union preferred applicants to arrive at the workhouse gate on the morning of the weekly board meeting, when their case was considered. Between board meetings a pauper could apply to the parish warden for an admission ticket to present to the workhouse master. Provisional admission was also given at the discretion of the master of the workhouse until the next board meeting. Details of name, age, trade and religious denomination were recorded. Paupers were then washed and their clothing replaced by workhouse uniforms. Finally, a medical examination was carried out by the workhouse doctor, primarily to prevent the entry of disease into the workhouse. This screening was not always diligently carried out, frequently it was no more than a vaccination check.[42] At the board interview the role of the guardians was to ascertain that the applicant was really destitute, that he or she had neither land or relatives able to support him or her.

Life in the workhouse was extremely harsh. The overall running of the system was according to the 'less eligibility' principle. The scheme was designed to make life inside the workhouse so unpleasant as to discourage the poor from entering unless really destitute. Once a pauper was accepted by the board of guardians, classification took place. This was a two stage process; firstly paupers were separated according to age, sex, and ability to work, secondly, according to their state of health. There were five groups of paupers: males above the age of fifteen years, females above the age of fifteen years, boys aged between two and fifteen years; girls in the same age range and children under two years. A particularly cruel aspect of this classification was the separation of children from their parents at the age of two. Children between two and seven years were supposed to have access to their mothers, 'at all reasonable times', but from seven years old only one private interview per day was allowed with parents.

All inmates were expected to work, with the exception of the physically and mentally ill. Furthermore, the authorities believed that this employment should be of an irksome nature. The purpose was to discourage inmates from remaining in the workhouse. Corn grinding and oakum picking were common occupations. Not all paupers were unskilled. Many had a trade and some boards utilized their skills. Tailors and shoemakers were two examples of such crafts. Cootehill workhouse, however, employed a master tailor at the rate of nine shillings per week without rations for a twelve hour day for half the year and eleven hours per day for the remainder.[43] Some workhouse officials were lax and did not enforce employment of paupers. Failure in this area 'was perhaps the greatest single inadequacy in the internal management of the Irish workhouse.'[44] Many commissioners on their routine inspections found idleness, as well as filth and disorder.

The Irish commission was very concerned that the diet served in the workhouses did not exceed in quantity or quality the fare eaten by the Irish peasantry outside. Strict guide-lines were laid down, once again on the 'less eligibility' principle. Before stipulating the menus, enquiries were made in numerous districts throughout the country. From the responses received from assistant commissioners it became apparent that setting a dietary scale was going to be a difficult task. To quote Sir George Nicholls, one of the Irish poor law commissioners:

> It would perhaps be in vain, even if it were desirable to seek to make ... the diet of the inmates of the Irish workhouse, inferior to those of the Irish peasantry. The standard of their mode of living is so low, that the establishment of one still lower is difficult.[45]

A second dietary criterion was that the menu had to be sufficient to maintain health (table 11). Workhouses full of sick paupers because of inadequate food would increase the running costs.

Table 11: Pre-Famine workhouse dietary

Breakfast	Dinner
7 oz oatmeal (as stirabout)	3½ lb potatoes
1 pt buttermilk	1 pt buttermilk
or ½ pt new Milk	or ½ pt new Milk

Reduced food rations were used to punish misdemeanours. Pauper misdemeanours were classed into two categories—disorder and refractory. Refractory crimes were regarded as the more serious of the two. In the case of disorderly behaviour, punishment was usually of the order of extra work— one hour per day for two days, and dietary penalty of no buttermilk or milk for that time. Punishment for refractory 'crime' was often solitary confinement for twenty-four hours or longer depending on the severity of the offence. An offender could be clothed in a distinctive punishment uniform during the time of his or her punishment. Cavan, Cootehill and Bailieborough minute books are peppered with cases of minor misdemeanours frequently punished with twenty-four hours of solitary confinement and reduced food rations on alternate days for a limited period. Solitary confinement required the sanction of the board of guardians before being carried out. Children under the age of twelve years were exempt from solitary confinement, but boys under fifteen years could be disciplined by corporal punishment. The vast majority of disciplinary problems were resolved within the workhouse, only particularly serious offences were referred by the board of guardians for trial. Abuses of the punishment system did occur and cases of extreme cruelty to paupers have been recorded, but these were exceptions. On the whole, paupers suffered hardship through neglect and incompetence rather than physical violence.[46]

VII

This system of poor relief was placed under greatest strain during the Famine of the late 1840s. The crop failure in 1845 did not immediately precipitate alarm. Millions of Irishmen regularly endured annual semi-starvation during the hiatus between one season's crop of potatoes and the next. Time soon revealed the enormity of the catastrophe. The dependence of the vast majority of the labouring population upon the potato left them totally destitute. They had little choice but ultimately to seek admission to the workhouse, when the only alternative was starving to death outside. The workhouses, therefore, became inextricably involved in the Famine crisis.

Table 12: Paupers admitted to the county Cavan Workhouses 1845–51

	1844	1845	1846	1847	1848	1849	1850	1851
Bailieborough	850	724	1616	1906	4705	6098	5842	2476
Cavan	1084	991	2146	3141	4970	12820	4002	2366
Cootehill	1330	983	1585	2029	3583	9768	4379	2167
Total	3264	2698	5347	7076	13258	28686	14223	7009

Source: The Annual Reports of the Poor Law Commissioners 1843–52

Initially the authorities were reluctant to plan for the crucial role they were compelled to play in the crisis. As Helen Burke noted, the annual report of 1846, prepared at the height of the Famine, contained ninety-eight paragraphs but it was not until the ninety-fourth that passing reference was made to the failure of the potato crop with comment on an alternative dietary strategy.[47] Helen Burke has suggested three reasons for this complacency. First, the headquarters of the Irish poor law was still in London.[48] Secondly, the crop failure was viewed as an extreme episode of the normal annual food shortage and thirdly, in times of extreme distress, the poor law scheme was not regarded as an agency for support.

Meanwhile, at local level alarm at the accelerating crisis was being expressed by the poor law guardians. In the autumn of 1845 contractors for the provision of potatoes and grains requested to be released from their contract prices because potatoes were becoming too expensive. Similarly grain prices were rising rapidly also, making the agreeed terms uneconomic. In November, Mr J. Reilly, the supplier to the Cavan workhouse, 'gave notice to the Board expressing his inability to supply the establishment with potatoes and oatmeal pursuant to the terms of his tender'.[49] Guidance had already been sought from the Dublin administrators on modifying the dietary regime. On 27 October, 1845 a general order was issued by the poor law commissioners authorising the guardians to, 'depart from the established dietaries by substituting the use of oatmeal, rice, bread or other foods in lieu of potatoes, whenever the guardians may deem it advisable to do so.'[50] By early summer the food crisis had deepened to such an extent that at the board meeting of 26 May 1846 the clerk was ordered to advertise for a supplier of Indian meal.[51]

The introduction of this new food was controversial. In July there was a complaint at the Cavan board of guardians meeting about 'the impropriety of ... doing away with Indian meal without giving regular notice to the guardians, and moved that [it] be used in future according to half Indian meal and half oatmeal.'[52] A hint as to the reason for removing Indian meal from the menu is found in the minutes of the next week. At that meeting the medical officer was asked to give his opinion of the Indian meal diet. He responded that during the months of the Indian meal menu paupers were complaining of violent and sudden attack of the stomach and bowels which he attributed to the Indian grain. He recommended, therefore, that the offending food be removed from the menu. The subject caused considerable agitation, and the clerk was instructed to write to the poor law commission for guidance. As we now know the root of the problem was a combination of insufficiently ground meal and a population unaccustomed to that particular grain. Indian corn is particularly hard and required steel grinders to render the grain to a fine meal. A sample menu of the Famine years from the Cootehill workhouse was as follows:

Breakfast:	*Dinner*
4 oz oatmeal	12 oz bread
4 oz Indian meal	1½ pt soup or 2/3 pt buttermilk
1 oz rice	
2/3 pt buttermilk	

Source: Cavan County Library, Cavan, Minute book of the Cootehill poor law board of guardians, 8 July 1848.

Fraud permeated through the system, though documented facts are not easily uncovered. Hints of misappropriation of food appear in the Cootehill minute book in 1848 when a stocktake of food revealed that 17 cwts and 15 lbs of oatmeal were missing.[53] In the previous year a nurse in the hospital was accused by a pauper patient of giving away three loaves of bread for which she received three pence. The nurse was particularly unpopular with the paupers, and so the charge was not sustained on the grounds that it was 'frivolous and vexatious'.[54]

The financial difficulties of the unions had a direct bearing on the quality of the workhouse diets. The entire system was financed by rates levied locally according to value of property. As the grip of famine tightened, more and more rate payers defaulted. Consequently the flow of income declined to a trickle, resulting in many unions becoming bankrupt. Contractors frequently refused to supply food, and the diet deteriorated because guardians' cheques were not honoured. Evidence to this effect abounds in correspondence between the boards of guardians and inspectors to the poor law commissioners. A resolution of the Cavan board of guardians indicates that because of

> the extraordinary increase of paupers admitted into the poor-house during the existence of the calamity which has afflicted the country, has completely exhausted the funds, and the establishment is consequently indebted to the contractors in a very considerable sum, about £800, while the arrears likely to be collected does not exceed £250 ... Under these circumstances the contractors have refused further supplies, and unless funds be raised for the immediate expenditure, it will be necessary, however painful ... not only to close the house, but actually to put out the unfortunate paupers.[55]

VIII

As the impact of the Famine increased, it became apparent that the workhouse system could not cope with the influx of destitutes. The concept of free relief rations was unthinkable. However, as many Irish labourers did not receive a money wage for their labour, the introduction of food rations for money was impossible. A task of work was therefore necessary in order for a scheme of relief to commence. As early as April 1846, extraordinary presentment sessions were held in the chief town of each of the eight baronies of county Cavan.[56] One of their roles was the assessment of applications for public works schemes, which in turn were passed on to the Board of Works. Public works schemes were not new to Ireland; they had been used during previous periods of hardship. When it became apparent that a second potato failure was imminent a new public works act entitled, 'An act to extend and consolidate the powers ... by the commissioners of public works in Ireland' was passed in the autumn of 1846. County Cavan was one of the first Ulster counties to participate in the scheme. Within six weeks more than 15,000 in the county were employed on schemes, rising to 25,500 by February 1847.

Table 13: Average number of persons employed on public works
6 October 1846-26 December 1846 and 30 January 1847

Week:	1	2	3	4	5	6	7	8	9	10
Antrim	85	257	–	500	–	407	38	53	–	255
Armagh	–	–	–	98	217	435	525	843	1905	2302
Cavan	72	789	1027	796	1277	16240	17507	18523	20503	20503
Donegal	–	–	–	–	–	533	757	786	1804	1804
Down	–	–	242	–	–	166	166	199	429	429
F'agh	–	–	–	349	1369	2563	4538	4140	5996	5996
L'derry	–	–	–	–	–	1359	1954	3337	4933	4933
Monaghan	–	–	–	289	2131	3362	4262	5589	6650	6650
Tyrone	–	–	–	–	–	336	1001	2131	2715	2715

Source: Relief of distress in Ireland, Board of Works, H.C. 1847 (764) l, and H.C. 1847 (797) lii.

By 1847 distress was unabated. Workhouses were full and the administration of the public works schemes was breaking down. Frequently workers were unpaid for their labours and consequently were unable to purchase food. Furthermore, in the county there was a falling off in the earnings of workmen because they were

> unable to earn more than 8d or 10d per day. Two scanty meals [was] all they could get per day, one half of the day's wages or 4d for each meal ... A four penny loaf not quite 1½ lb. to a family of six or eight persons for their morning meal, and the share which the man could get [was] very inadequate to give him the strength and support for the day's work.[57]

Frequently, many weeks' wages were unpaid; and with alarming regularity in some parts of the country workers were found dead from starvation.[58]

By the summer of 1847 the government realised that both the workhouse system and the public works schemes were failing to cope with the increasing numbers of Famine victims. A change in policy was reluctantly agreed. A Temporary Relief Act, more popularly called the Soup Kitchen Act was reluctantly introduced in 1847. Eligibility was strictly scrutinised. Three categories could apply for relief:

1 Destitute poor who were disabled because of age, infirmity or insanity

2 Destitute poor who were disabled because of severe illness or accident and so were unable to provide for themselves or their families.

3 Poor widows having two or more dependent legitimate children.

In the county Cavan poor law unions of Bailieborough, Cavan and Cootehill approximately one third of the population received outdoor relief during the summer of 1847. When compared with some of the neighbouring unions the Cavan figures are sizeable (see table 14).

IX

More people died of disease than starvation during the Famine years, nevertheless the image of death from starvation has survived as a sharper and more

Table 14: Number of persons who received outdoor relief
April–September 1847 (10 Victoria c. 7)

	Maximum No. of Persons supplied with food in any one day	Proportion % to population of persons relieved
Bailieborough	19247	39
Cavan	29523	30
Cootehill	24857	37
Ardee		18
Armagh		16
Navan		36
Oldcastle		37
Granard		29
Enniskillen		12

Source: *7th Report of the Relief Commission*, Supplementary Appendix.

emotive picture. Dysentery and diarrhoea were endemic in the county prior to Famine. The crisis added to the incidence. Furthermore, fever exacerbated the misery, though it was no respecter of class or status of health. As the medical profession noted;

> a previous state of good health had not much influence in warding off the disease; for although it weighed heavily on the poor, ill-fed portion of the population, whose constitutions were in fact so debilitated as to be unable to resist fever or any other form of disease that might present itself, we have observed it in some of the healthiest portion of the people ...'[59]

Drs Halpin and Mease of Cavan town observed that fever very frequently set in after recovery from starvation, and change of diet did not appear to exercise any perceptible influence on it. The most obvious difference between the rich and the poor who caught fever was in level of mortality. The poor had a better chance of survival. Doctors, clergy and philanthropic workers suffered most. In county Cavan, many prominent and professional men died from fever. Cunningham names physicians, surgeons, an apothecary and clergy who succombed to fever, highlighting the vulnerability of this group.[60]

Fever was two distinct species of disease, typhus and relapsing fever. They were the most lethal fevers raging during the Great Famine. Both were transmitted by the common louse. As the starving masses congregated in urban centres so both typhus and relapsing fever spread with alarming rapidity. Typhus organisms caused extensive damage to the blood vessels, particularly of the skin. Consequently the skin acquired a characteristic spotted red/purple coloured rash. Patients complained of headache, agonizing pains, raging temperatures, delirium and stupor.

Relapsing fever had a more sudden onset than typhus. As its name suggests, it was an intermittent fever. The infection was acquired most commonly through the skin via a scratch, and having gained access to the host, circulated in the blood stream. During fever crises the organisms were profuse in the blood, but their numbers fell as the fever relapsed. Several relapses occurred before the fever finally dissipated. The phases of relapsing fever usually lasted seven days and were accompanied by rigor, sickness, vomiting and, in some patients, jaundice; hence the popular names of 'gastric fever' and 'yellow fever'.

Table 15: Admissions and deaths in county Cavan fever hospitals, 1845–50 (Cootehill, Cavan, Virginia, B'borough and ten temporary hospitals)

	1845	1846	1847	1848	1849	1850
Admissions	468	546	3342	4033	2844	1140
Deaths	35	36	247	478	470	172
Total county Cavan fever deaths						
County deaths	245	407	1214	1820	1615	493

Source: *Census of Ire., 1851* Deaths vol. i & vol. ii

Commenting on the pattern of the fever epidemics, Sir William Wilde noted that, though mortality among males was higher than females, morbidity was greater among women.[61] He also observed that children were particularly vulnerable, 'to an extent far greater then any previous records of fever have elicited'.[62] The high mortality in Milltown hospital in Cavan union, certainly was attributed to a combination of overcrowding and high numbers of children initially ill with fever but were 'carried off by a complication of diseases.'[63] When members of the professional classes fell victim to fever their chances of survival were less than those of the poorer classes. However, within poor families typhus and relapsing fever were more likely to afflict the entire family. In better class homes fever was confined to an individual who did not infect other members of the household.[64] The ability of the rich to isolate themselves when ill in their spacious living accommodation contained the spread of the disease among this group. Cases of purpura (purple discolouration of the skin) or scurvy did not occur in immediate connexion with fever, but purpura was frequently observed by Cavan doctors suggesting at least pre-clinical scurvy.[65]

X

Mr and Mrs S.C. Hall travelled frequently in Ireland. Following their tour in 1840 they published the now famous *Hall's Ireland*. Of county Cavan they wrote succinctly if not flatteringly:

> The county of Cavan possesses no features of striking or peculiar character, and in natural beauty it is far surpassed by the adjoining counties of Meath, Fermanagh and Armagh. This inland county is bounded in the north by the county of Fermanagh, on the west by that of Leitrim, on the east and north-east by Monaghan and on the south by parts of the counties of Longford, Meath and Westmeath. It is divided into the baronies of Castleraghan, Clonmahon, Clonkee, Upper and Lower Loughtee, Tullagarvey, Tullaghunco and Tullaghagh. Cavan and Belturbet are the only towns of size.[66]

From the criteria we have just examined it is clearly apparent that a large proportion of the population of county Cavan was poor and getting poorer as the early decades of the nineteenth century progressed. The Great Famine thus hit very hard an already impoverished people.

The Emergence and Consolidation of the Home Rule Movement in County Cavan, 1870–86

GERARD MORAN

The history of the home rule movement in the 1870s and 1880s has tended to be charted by the weaknesses and strengths of the organisation at a national level. Only recently have historians begun to examine its contribution to the evolution of local societies. As a result they have discovered contrasts between the national and local situations and indeed variations between regions themselves. It would appear that the home rule movement was not a homogeneous entity and only when detailed studies are undertaken for all parts of the country can a true assessment of the movement be undertaken at a national level. Different factors affected the development of the movement, depending on its location, local influences and power groups. Nowhere is this more evident than in Cavan.

An examination of political life in Cavan before 1874 reveals some important features of the county. Between 1832 and 1868 the Conservatives monopolised the parliamentary representation. Apart from Sir John Young, a Peelite MP between 1847 and 1857, and Captain E.J. Saunderson, a Liberal who was in effect a Protestant who advocated land reform, all its representatives were Conservatives. While the Great Famine had destroyed the repeal/independence opposition movement during the 1850s and 1860s it failed to have much effect on the Conservative party since the Tories held the majority of the Irish seats in 1852 and 1865. This was particularly clear in Cavan in the 1850s and 1860s.[1] Access to the county's parliamentary seats was controlled by three landowning families. The Farnhams, who owned 26,000 acres in the county, were the strongest political power broking family controlling one-fifth of the Cavan electorate, along with the Saundersons and the Annesleys.[2] Five of the eight county representatives between 1832 and 1868 came from these families. This was not unusual as nearly all the Ulster constituencies were controlled by their principal landlords which was a powerful disincentive to new political movements taking root there. The difficulties which all nationalist movements encountered in Ulster can be noted in the carve up of seats by the landlords: only seven constituencies were contested at the 1865 general election and this declined to six at the 1868 election. Not until the 1874 election and the implementation of the 1872 Secret

Ballot Act was the province opened up to electoral contests, there were seven-teen contests in Ulster, but even then the home rule movement was reluctant to fight many of the seats.

Furthermore, of the sixteen elections before 1868, only three were con-tested: 1852, the 1855 by-election and 1857. This paucity of electoral contests in the 1860s had one important effect, namely the absence of electoral vio-lence, which was a common feature of electioneering in most other constitu-encies.[3] As Cavan passed from one power group to another—from the Conservatives to the nationalists—there was little conflict. This was assisted by the increase of the number of polling stations in the county after 1872 from three to eighteen which helped to diminish violence on election day as large crowds no longer congregated at the few centres.[4]

Cavan differed from the other Ulster counties in that its population was mainly Catholic. In the 1871 census 80.4 per cent were Catholics, similar to many southern counties, such as Kildare (86 per cent) and Wicklow (80.6 per cent).[5] A high proportion of its male population were electors: 17.3 per cent in 1871, slightly above the Ulster average of 16.3 per cent. By 1891 65.9 per cent of all males could vote, compared to 62.1 per cent for the rest of the province.[6] Most of the electorate, however, was Protestant. Only after 1885 did a major change occur in the religious composition of the electorate in both Cavan and Ulster generally. Up to the early 1880s Catholics in Cavan were only a small majority of the electorate, but the 1884 Franchise Act, which trebled the number of voters, gave them an unassailable position. Cavan became a testing ground for new political and religious ideas, both for Catho-lics and Protestants, and hence was often described as 'the gateway to the north'. In the 1820s and 1830s it became the centre of the struggle occasioned by the 'Second Reformation', largely because of Lord Farnham's support and commitment to that movement.[7]

To break into this world of landed, Conservative dominated interest was a major challenge to the emerging nationalist movement of the late nineteenth century. Cavan nationalists suffered from a lack of direction up to 1865, largely because their natural leaders, the Catholic clergy, failed to provide any leadership. As James Kelly's essay has shown, during the episcopate of James Browne, bishop of Kilmore between 1829 and 1865, the church devoted its energies to ecclesiastical affairs rather than national politics.[8] Thus the clergy took a passive approach to electoral affairs, except in the 1830s when they supported emancipation candidates, such as Charles Coote of Cootehill and Robert Henry Southwell, and during the 1850s when they championed the claims of Anthony O'Reilly and M. O'Reilly Dease.[9] However, the clergy had little impact on the electoral process. Their nominees were not elected because the clergy's involvement had been opportunistic rather than having a longer term strategy.

By contrast with the earlier part of the century, Cavan was the only Ulster county in which the clergy played a major role in political affairs between

1868 and 1885. Cavan was the only Ulster county where the clergy became politically active, largely due to the election of Nicholas Conaty as bishop of Kilmore in 1865. Conaty was an ardent supporter of the National Association which was established in 1865. Other Kilmore clerics followed his example. They included Frs Francis O'Reilly, Bailieborough; John O'Reilly, Virginia; John Boylan, Crosserlough and Patrick O'Reilly, Drumlane. All played prominent roles in the home rule movement in the 1870s. While Conaty's leadership was important in this process there were other factors in the clergy's political awakening including the decision of one Cavan MP, Colonel Saunderson, not to support Gladstone's church disestablishment proposals.[10] The clergy were only aware of this on the eve on the 1868 election contest in Cavan. While this allowed them insufficient time to nominate an alternative candidate it did force them to establish structures which provided the clergy with a way of influencing future political developments. Conaty presided over a Liberal meeting which agreed to set up a county club. The local clergy provided the basis for parish sub-committees, and Revd Patrick Galligan became its secretary.[11]

By the end of the 1860s the clergy's political influence was evident: no major demonstration could take place without their support and participation. The failure to hold an Amnesty meeting in Cavan in the autumn of 1869, when fifty-two nationwide demonstrations were organised in support of the release of the fenian prisioners, is a case in point. While Conaty himself supported the amnesty principle and in December 1868 wrote to the Amnesty Committee enclosing a £1 subscription and agreeing to sign their petition, he could not mobilise his priests on the issue.[12] Amnesty for fenian prisioners was not an issue which concerned the people or priests of Cavan. Fenian influence in the county during the 1860s was minimal and no attempt was made to organise an amnesty demonstration in Cavan.[13]

By contrast the highly successful tenant right meeting which took place on 1 November 1869 in Cavan town was attended by thirty-one priests. A demonstration expressing sympathy with the pope's temporal difficulties also occurred in Cavan town on 8 December 1870 when Conaty and forty-five priests were present. While this gathering expressed support for the pope, some speakers, like Nesbitt of Ballinamore and H.P. Kennedy, also referred to Ireland's problems with England.[14]

While clerical support was important for the tenant right meeting the popularity of the cause also contributed to its success. The land question affected all sections of Cavan society and contingents from every parish converged on Cavan town for the November 1869 demonstration, carrying banners which said, 'A fair rent and good security' and 'fixity of tenure at fair rents'. However a close examination of the meeting indicates deeper political overtones than were overtly apparent and aided in developing a nationalist philosophy in the county. Many wore green sashes, a common feature during nationalist demonstrations in favour of repeal and amnesty. Bands played national airs such as 'O'Donnell aboo' and 'St Patrick's Day' and some banners carried potent political messages such as 'God save Ireland' and 'Ireland for the Irish'.[15] The demonstration resulted in the establishment of the Cavan Tenant League, controlled by the larger farmers and whose aim was to ensure that Gladstone's land bill would satisfy them. This pattern was repeated in other parts of Ulster in the early 1870s after the failure of the 1870 Land Act to meet the expectations of farmers, and in particular its failure to define the 'Ulster custom'. These Farmers' Defence Associations were closely associated with the Liberal party.[16]

In Cavan the Tenant League remained in existence after the passage of the 1870 Land Act although it changed its name in January 1871 to the Cavan Farmers' Defence League. Its objectives were now to ensure that farmers secured the maximum benefits from the legislation and to initiate a fund to support all farmers who required legal assistance. Its political functions were to scrutinise the parliamentary voters lists to ensure that all eligible farmers had the vote and it also campaigned for secret ballot legislation.[17] Many of these voters were Catholics and eventually would support the newly formed home rule movement. Thus the Cavan Farmers' Defence League assumed the responsibilities of a local political organisation. Most areas had Liberal and Conservative organisations, but the nationalists failed to establish such a network because of poor organisation and lack of money. While some members opposed the League's political objectives, Fr John Whelan, its principal promoter, argued that farmers would only secure benefits from parliament when they could ensure that their MPs supported their needs. Thus the Cavan Farmers' Defence League had strong political aims which were not determined by landlord actions, as occurred in other areas.[18] Its leading figures were Philip Smith, JP from Artina; Thomas Brady of Lisboduff and John F. O'Hanlon, editor of the *Anglo–Celt*.

In May 1870 Isaac Butt founded the Home Government Association in Dublin. The Association thus had one principal aim: to establish a parliament in Dublin. In its early stages a small group of Protestant Conservatives supported the party, being disillusioned with the English political parties and hoping that an Irish parliament would be more sympathetic to their grievances. The first Cavan people associated with the party were John Tute of Belturbet and T.C. Sixsmith of Cavan town, whose names appear as members of the committee in August 1870. Bishop Conaty endorsed the federal parliament concept in September and while he had reservations about the home rule movement, probably because of Protestant involvement, he did allow his priests support the new party.[19] Cavan was the only Ulster county in which the home rule movement made advances during Isaac Butt's leadership, largely because of Conaty's neutral stand. It remained the bastion of the home rule movement in the province, often referred to as 'the gateway to Ulster' until 1883 when the next stage of advancement occurred with Tim Healy's election in Monaghan.

The Home Government Association developed rapidly in Cavan; the *Anglo–Celt* stated that the appearance of the home rule idea was the most important event to take place during 1870, even more significant than Gladstone's Land Act.[20] The County Cavan Home Rule Association was formed on 1 November 1871 and its leading personalities included Richard Ryan, MD; Charles J. Fay, solicitor and James Fitzpatrick, a poor law guardian for Mountnugent.[21] New members were enrolled, but the Association was largely inactive during 1871 and early 1872 since it lacked clerical leadership. Few clergy seem to have joined since they placed their faith in the London parliament, hoping that Gladstone would deliver a satisfactory solution to the controversy over the provision of university education for Catholics which was the single most important issue affecting the church in 1870. Friction also existed with the Cavan Farmers' Defence League and its attitude annoyed the Home Rule Association.[22] Most farmers wished to remain outside the mainstream political organisations fearing that party politics would divide the club's membership.

In its early days the Cavan Home Rule Association was centred around Bailieborough and little activity was reported from Cavan town: the exception being a demonstration on the 30 September 1872, which Conaty opposed and which was denounced from the altar because it had been organised in secret.[23] By late 1872 the Association had members in nearly every parish in Cavan, as well as Meath, Leitrim and Monaghan, but its base remained in Bailieborough and it was commonly referred to as the Bailieborough Home Rule Club. It was more radical than other such clubs. Most, such as the Edenderry Home Rule Association, the Queen's County Independent Club and the Wexford County Independent Club were legacies of the tenant right movement of the 1850s and were more interested in agrarian matters than in promoting an aggressive parliamentary programme.[24] Unfortunately little co-operation existed between these local bodies and the head office in Dublin, let alone among the clubs themselves. Even within county Cavan different objectives meant there was little contact between the Bailieborough club and those established in Cavan and Ballyconnell before the 1874 general election.

Nevertheless the Cavan Home Rule Association had an important function. As the home rule party was primarily a Dublin centred organisation with a council dominated by Dublin based members, it often neglected its provincial members. Local clubs boosted morale and gave the movement a presence outside of Dublin. In this way the Cavan association helped in the development and consolidation of the party in the county. Its monthly meetings were uneventful, confined to supporting home rule candidates fighting by-election contests in other parts of the country and calling for organisation within the county so that a home rule candidate would be elected at the next general election.

A number of events in 1872–3 contributed to the advancement of the Home Rule Association in Cavan. One was the Galway by-election petition in

June 1872, when Judge Keogh attacked the Galway clergy for their involvement in the contest. The result was an unprecedented show of Catholic unity
with demonstrations in almost every parish in the country at which Keogh
was condemned and collections made to defray the court costs of the unseated
home rule candidate, Captain Nolan.[25] Cavan typified the mood: Bishop Conaty
and his clergy condemned Keogh's attack and the Nolan defence fund was
established with the bishop contributing £5. Anti-Keogh demonstrations followed in Cavan on 17 June, Ballyjamesduff on 29 June and Cootehill on 1
July.[26] Catholics questioned their traditional link with the Liberal party because the authorities had prosecuted Bishop Patrick Duggan of Clonfert and
a number of priests. The attack on Keogh in parliament was led by Isaac Butt
which convinced bishops, such as Conaty, that the home rule party, despite
its Protestant background, could be trusted and was more sympathetic to
Irish Catholics than the Liberals.

As a result, some clergy attended the first major home rule demonstration
in the county at Swanlinbar on 15 August, chaired by Edward Maguire of
Gortoral House. The local parish priest, Fr Peter Whelan, sanctioned the
meeting and he and his curate, Revd B. O'Reilly, were present. The speeches
at the meeting reveal two contrasting views within the movement: the chairman stating that home rule should not lead to the break up of the empire,
while P. Kane, a poor law guardian from Ballyconnell, said that their minimum demand should be the restoration of the Irish parliament at College
Green and that no parliamentary candidate should be supported who did not
express clear support for this demand.[27]

This meeting formed part of an attempt to expand the Association into
the provinces, in the hope that support would be secured in the aftermath of
the Galway by-election affair. Success in Cavan was seen as crucial for this
expansion and meetings were held in Kingscourt, Swanlinbar and Bailieborough
between August and October. Leading national party members addressed
these demonstrations with Philip Callan, MP for Dundalk speaking at Kingscourt. The Bailieborough meeting on 30 October attracted a crowd of 8000
since A.M. Sullivan from the central council was the principal speaker. Sullivan
spoke about Ireland's right to home rule, asking why England supported
Italy's right to independence while refusing to grant it to Ireland. He also
urged that Cavan return a representative to parliament who would espouse
home rule principles.[28] A noticeable feature of these meetings was the absence
of the clergy, although Fr Kelly from Kingscourt sent his apologies, suggesting that although there was some sympathy for the movement it did not
command universal acceptance. This reflected Bishop Conaty's own attitude:
while being sympathetic to the Association he still was not prepared to give
total support.

Thus the closing months of 1872 indicated progress for the home rule
movement in Cavan and attempts were made to improve local organisation by
dividing the county into regional units although this was a short-lived change.

The foundation of the Cavan Liberal club on 28 January 1873 proved to be a reverse for home rule fortunes. The Liberal party competed with the home rule movement for members, but more importantly it was supported by the clergy. At least ten priests attended its inaugural meeting, including Fr Edward Sheridan, the administrator of Cavan town. Again this reflected Bishop Conaty's position: a continuing reliance on Gladstone to secure the political objectives of the clergy. An additional concern for the home rule movement was the membership of leading members of the Cavan Farmers' Defence League, such as Philip Smith, JP, indicating that they were also supporting the Liberals.[29]

Such a powerful alliance of the church and farmers behind the Liberals was temporary. The Liberal administration's failure to provide adequately for Catholic education in its Irish university bill in March 1873, greatly angered the Catholic community in Cavan. Before the bill was introduced into the house of commons, Conaty devoted his lenten pastoral to the need for a Catholic university. Thus Conaty felt let down by Gladstone and the Cavan clergy's support for the Liberals ended. Over the next twelve months they directed their support to the home rule movement.[30] The Cavan Farmers' Defence League also quickly swung behind the home rule party because of their agrarian policies. By April 1873 the home rule movement in Cavan indicated that it would wholeheartedly support fixity of tenure and changes in the 1870 land act, resulting in the farmers supporting its candidates.[31] Thus home rule had secured a strong base for itself in Cavan, just before the 1874 general election.

The dissolution of parliament on 23 January 1874 caught the home rulers throughout Ireland completely unprepared. A shortage of funds and no proper regional organisation meant that in most parts of the country the party had to rely on local groups to select their representatives. Central office informed the constituencies that it was unable to assist and left the selection up to them. The Catholic clergy were invited to help in the selection process, resulting in different criteria being used in most constituencies.[32]

While Cavan held good prospects for the home rule party it was not without its problems: in the main psychological. Two Ulster by-elections had been contested between 1870 and 1874—Monaghan in 1871 and Derry City in 1872, yet both had been major disappointments. Even the 1872 Secret Ballot Act, which should have limited landlord influence, had little impact in the Derry election.[33] These events gave rise to a nervousness and lack of confidence as a result of previous failures which was noted in Cavan, as elsewhere. Nationalists indicated that the sitting MPs, Saunderson and Annesley, did not represent their views and accused the former of betraying them. The *Anglo–Celt* pointed out that while Saunderson was a good, benevolent landlord, his parliamentary actions had disgraced the county.[34] The nationalist press insisted that the Cavan electors would have to remove those who had misrepresented and humiliated them.[35] In the three southern provinces of

Ireland the home rule issue dominated the 1874 contest but in most of Ulster the land question was the main issue, with the exception of Cavan where home rule dominated the debate.[36] This was largely because of the well-organised local home rule clubs in Cavan: three branches were in existence, Bailieborough, the most active club, Cavan and Ballyconnell.

From an early stage Joseph Biggar signified his intention of contesting Cavan and on 28 January he was nominated by the Ballyconnell Home Rule Club.[37] Biggar was a good choice on a number of grounds. He was well-known within the party since his unsuccessful candidacy at the 1872 Derry city by-election and was supported by Archbishop John MacHale of Tuam and the bishop of Down and Conor, Patrick Dorrian, which secured him the backing of the Kilmore clergy. Being a Belfast presbyterian, it was hoped his co-religionists would support him, although they had traditionally espoused the Liberals. However, Biggar did not ingratiate himself with the Cavan Presbyterian community. Their opposition to home rule outweighed their desire for a co-religionist as their parliamentary representative.[38]

The nomination procedure in Cavan was the most democratic in the country because the selection of the home rule candidates was not confined to one particular interest section. Various groups including the Cavan Farmers' Defence League, the Cavan Home Rule Club and the local clergy were involved. However it was Conaty and the local priests who were instrumental in uniting the different strands when it appeared that the popular vote might split.[39] A meeting of delegates from each parish, organised by Fr Peter Galligan from Cavan and with Conaty's sanction, assembled on 30 January in Cavan town.[40] The meeting was convened early (the election itself did not take place until 16 February) to ensure that the nationalists were not overtaken by events as they had been in the previous election of 1868. A united approach was now being adopted within the county and this was further endorsed by the resolutions which reflected the interests of the three groups in attendance. These resolutions centred on home rule, denominational education and land reform. It contrasted with other counties, such as Longford, where the resolutions merely reflected the control of one specific interest group.[41] This bonding together of the various constitutional interests in the county, largely under the influence of Bishop Conaty, ensured not only that the nationalists were united but also that militant nationalist organisations, such as fenianism and ribbonism, were marginalised. In the 1850s and 1860s some secret agrarian activity took place in Arva and Ballyconnell and ribbonism existed in the county up to the 1880s but none of these reached the scale seen in other parts of Ireland.[42]

While the Cavan meeting was referred to as an assembly of Liberal electors, it was in reality a home rule convention. Philip Callan, home rule MP for Dundalk, attended to advise on organisation and electoral procedure, adding credence to this opinion. Conaty insisted that all would abide by the decisions of the meeting, but declared that only candidates who espoused denominational education, reform of the grand jury system and home rule would be selected. Biggar had incorporated these into his election address, and was unanimously chosen. Charles Fay also supported these principles and was selected as all other contenders were opposed. This was a further endorsement of home rule as Fay was a leading member of the Cavan Home Rule Association.[43]

The clergy's acceptance of home rule is clear from the fact that Bishop Conaty nominated its two candidates, and the assenting electors included Frs Francis O'Reilly of Bailieborough and Patrick O'Reilly of Drumlane.[44] Clerical participation was also evident at the demonstrations which Biggar and Fay addressed. Each was chaired by the local parish priest and the surrounding clergy attended.[45] In the run up to the poll both candidates addressed meetings in Cavan, Killashandra, Bailieborough, Cootehill, Virginia and Mountnugent and on the day before the election a demonstration was held at Mullagh, in the centre of the property of the sitting Liberal MP, Col. Saunderson. Prominent party members, such as Denis B. Sullivan, John O'Connor Power and Philip Callan, were sent from Dublin to strengthen the campaign. Head office obviously regarded the Cavan election as important, for no other constituency received such help.

Cavan had become one of the most radical home rule constituencies in the country, as seen at a meeting of the Kingscourt voters on 1 February. Biggar and Fay had to pledge that they would pursue an independent line and vote 'against the present government, and against every government opposed to the concession of legislative independence ...'. They also promised to resign their seats if their constituents at any time adjudged them to have failed to carry out their duties.[46]

The decision of the sitting Conservative MP, Lord Annesley, to retire from politics forced the Conservatives to switch their allegiance to the Liberal, Colonel Saunderson. While all non-resident voters were encouraged to return to Cavan and vote for Saunderson, it was a forlorn attempt to retain the seat. Saunderson was continuously jeered during a speech at Stradone on 8 February and made no attempt to flirt with home rule, as happened in other south Ulster constituencies with large Catholic populations.[47]

Biggar and Fay appear to have been supported only by Catholic electors. The priests' overt support for home rule angered many Protestants and Saunderson, as a Protestant candidate advocating land reform, secured most of the Protestant farmer vote. Clerical influence over the Catholic population should not be underestimated. As the election took place on a Monday the Catholic clergy had the opportunity to exhort their congregations to vote for Biggar and Fay at mass on the day before the contest. Conaty also issued a pastoral letter on the day before the election calling on his flock to vote only for the home rule candidates. While the Conservatives exaggerated this point, many priests did use the pulpit for electoral purposes.[48]

The result of the poll was predictable. Fay headed the poll with 3229 votes, with Biggar comfortably taking the second seat with 3079 and Saunderson in third place with 2310 votes. Celebrations took place all over the county when the result was announced.[49] Two home rule MPs had been elected and 1874 became a major turning point in Cavan's political history. The county remained firmly in nationalist control for the remainder of the century as reflected in the continuous electoral successes which were achieved against Conservative opponents. Thus while Cavan may have had difficulties with its nationalist identity up to 1874, it had certainly atoned. For the first time the numerical strength of its Catholic population was manifest. Charles Fay was the only Catholic MP elected in Ulster and for the first time in the nineteenth century the county had returned a Catholic representative.

The victory reawakened nationalist pride throughout Ulster and indicated that they should have a more positive approach to the political process.[50] While historians have highlighted the home rule success in Louth as the greatest triumph of the 1874 election, the Cavan victory was just as significant because it proved to contemporaries that the home rule movement could make gains in Ulster.[51] However such rejoicing was quickly cooled by the harsh realities of political life. The election in Cavan drove Protestants over to the Conservatives. Moreover, no Ulster county, except Monaghan, could use the Catholic clergy to unite the divergent strands of nationalism, and only in 1883 did the Monaghan clerical network prove to be an electoral advantage.[52]

Biggar and Fay were among the forty-six home rule MPs who met in the City Hall, Dublin, on 3 March to discuss tactics for the coming parliamentary session. Difficulties emerged as to the rules which the different constituencies had imposed on their representatives' parliamentary behaviour, and the Cavan attitude was most inflexible. The nationalists were unwilling to reverse the pledge which Biggar and Fay had given at Kingscourt regarding independent opposition. Both MPs felt the rule was too harsh, allowing no flexibility to play constructive roles within the home rule party. They thus informed the Dublin meeting that they were unable to involve themselves fully in the movement.[53] This threat forced the revocation of the pledge at a public meeting in Cavan on 18 April; Biggar and Fay could now take a fuller part within the home rule movement.[54] However the episode reveals that Cavan wanted its representatives to be answerable to them. They were to be the servants of and not the masters in the constituency. The discipline which the Cavan nationalists adopted was not to be relaxed now that they had gained control of the county.

The confidence engendered in the county by the electoral success of the home rule movement was noticeable over the next few months. Meetings were convened which were addressed by the more advanced nationalists within the party, such as John O'Connor Power, the newly elected MP for Mayo.[55] A major demonstration, the first since the election in February, was held on 1 August in Cootehill, when over 30,000 people gathered to hear local speakers. The large attendance indicates the rapid progress the movement was making in the county. Resolutions in favour of a native Irish parliament and expressions of support for Butt, Biggar and Fay were passed. Another such meeting followed in Belturbet on 31 August attended by the two county MPs and six priests. Fay and Biggar accounted for their parliamentary activities over the previous six months, further evidence that Cavan representatives were now the servants of the constituency.[56]

By now the home rule movement in Cavan was a more pragmatic and professional organisation than in other parts of the country. After the election many local branches in other regions disappeared, but this did not occur in Cavan. In 1874 steps were taken to register voters and the county was divided into eight districts with paid agents in each area.[57] The electoral majority in Cavan was only 200 and the home rulers wanted this increased to over 1000, making it a safe nationalist constituency. Electoral division courts sat every September and October and the political parties supported or opposed the claims of potential voters. In the early 1870s the Conservatives paid much attention to the Cavan lists, but they lost interest when a majority of the electorate seemed to favour home rule. By 1879 Cavan and Fermanagh, were the only counties where the Conservatives had not appointed registration agents.[58] The electoral advantage of these moves were probably limited as a decline in the electorate occurred between 1874 and 1880: from 6225 to 6,096.[59] However this had no major influence on the relative voting strengths of Catholics and Protestants since all nationalist voters were already on the lists.

Not only did the home rule party consolidate its position in Cavan, it also assisted in the attempts at expansion into the adjoining Ulster counties. Cavan nationalists attended home rule meetings in Ballygawley, county Tyrone and in August eight home rule demonstrations were held throughout the province in an attempt to broaden its geographical base.[60] Its success in Cavan had given an important, but temporary, lift to Ulster nationalists. However the long term effect in Ulster was negligible because apart from the establishment of branches in Belfast and Derry no other clubs came into being.

The unavailability of the local newspapers for the period after 1874 makes it difficult to monitor the day-to-day activities of the movement, the only hints being the coverage provided by the national newspapers. Unfortunately these do not provide weekly or monthly accounts and the Cavan Home Rule Club was only mentioned when major demonstrations organised. Nevertheless the Club continued to function and to keep the home rule principle alive in the region. Major demonstrations were held especially when Fay and Biggar gave their annual addresses to their constituents or when meetings in favour of home rule principles took place, such as that for the Butt land bill on 23 April 1876. These were major social as well as political occasions with bands playing national airs to which the inhabitants of each townland or parish marched together, led by the clergy.[61] This discipline ensured that no unruly scenes occurred and the perpetrators of any crime could be quickly recognised and dealt with.

The Cavan Home Rule Club was one of the most active groups in Ireland in 1875 and 1876, along with the clubs from Wexford and Edenderry.[62] Its strength lay in its decision to be a complete nationalist movement concerned with Irish grievances and not confining itself to the single issue of home rule. Resolutions favouring Catholic education, amnesty and tenant right, as well as home rule were passed by the Club. This broadened its support within the community for no one group had a stranglehold over the party. No other county displayed this level of democracy within the home rule movement.

The transformation in Cavan politics after the 1874 election is evident in the attitude towards the parliamentary representatives. Biggar and Fay were among the first parliamentarians to address their constituents each year: defending their voting record and outlining the party's policies. Meetings were held in Bailieborough, Cootehill, Killeshandra and Kingscourt and this contrasted with the approach of the previous representatives who only met their constituents at election time. Other counties, such as Mayo and Meath, regarded as radical home rule constituencies, also adopted this system. Several parishes in Cavan, like Bawnboy, commended their parliamentary representatives' activities.[63]

The clergy had an important role in this changed political environment, evident from their continued presence at the public demonstrations.[64] They were active in the County Cavan Home Rule Club with Frs Francis O'Reilly of Bailieborough, Patrick O'Reilly of Drumlane and Peter Galligan of Cavan the most prominent. When Patrick O'Reilly became its chairman in November 1875 the Club was renamed the Cavan Home Rule and Farmers' Club in an attempt to enlarge its support as it still had little attraction for the farming community since tenant farmers had a greater interest in land policy than in the national question. This countered the attraction of the Liberals and Conservatives, whose candidates in Ulster constituencies in the 1860s and 1870s advocated agrarian reform.[65] The Club now pursued both an agrarian and a political role, sending representatives to land conferences, such as that in Dublin on 23 October 1876.[66]

Despite the crucial role of the clergy in this organisation they maintained a distance from some of the home rule activities such as the meetings organised by the party to support an amnesty for fenian prisioners. No priest attended the Cootehill amnesty meetings of August 1875 and August 1876, which Charles Fay and a number of local nationalists addressed, calling for the release of the remaining political prisoners.[67] These events highlight the tolerance of the different sections of the party towards each other. Resolutions were passed encompassing all the major Irish grievances. These demonstrations made people more aware of the movement's principles and encouraged them to join thus spreading the party's influence throughout the county.[68] One of the largest of these demonstrations took place at Kilnaleck on 14 April 1879, when 12,000 people heard Biggar and Fay account for their parliamentary actions. Charles Stewart Parnell gave the most rousing speech stating,

'Time was on their side, and their English enemies could not fight against time'. He called on the people to elect representatives who would serve Ireland.[69]

While some home rule branches in the county, influenced by the clergy, followed Issac Butt's moderate stance others, such as the Bailieborough branch, continued to hold advanced views on the national question. While it was the first home rule branch in Ulster, it was also the first club to support Biggar's radical policy of obstruction of parliamentary business. A demonstration in late August 1877, denounced Butt's conciliation policy and praised the obstructionist conduct of Parnell and Biggar.[70] The clergy were not present at this demonstration, suggesting that they did not yet control this branch. Eventually the Cavan clergy supported obstruction stating there were occasions when it was justified. However, they regretted the divisions between Biggar and Butt, feeling that it did nothing to further the home rule cause.[71]

The consolidation of the home rule movement in Cavan was not without its difficulties. While the Cavan MPs remained loyal to the party some members became disillusioned because of its parliamentary failures and the refusal of some of its MPs to support the party's bills.[72] This disenchantment affected the local branches and was partly responsible for the temporary demise of the Bailieborough club, which was inactive during 1877. It was reactivated with the founding of the Bailieborough Home Rule and Tenant Right Association on 20 June 1878. Its policies centred on home rule, fixity of tenure and denominational education. Revd Dr O'Reilly, its president, was its inspiration and the local clergy played a leading role in its formation. It refused to support parliamentary representatives who allied themselves to either of the English parties.[73] Public meetings were held throughout the county, the first on 19 September, when Fay and Biggar addressed their constituents. Once again the home rule party had structures in place for the 1880 general election.

The 1880 election in Ireland was dominated by the land question which was given prominence by the Land League's activities and widespread distress and poverty. While the agrarian question advanced the home rule party at the election, especially in Connacht, it had not yet taken hold in Cavan and played no role in Cavan politics. This was despite the severe hardship caused by heavy rains and the flooding of the Erne basin which resulted in many farmers being unable to pay their rents on the Annesley estate. It was November 1880 before the first Land League branch was formed in Cavan at Bailieborough.[74] Cavan was not dependent on the motivating and organising influence of the League, as structures for the choosing and the promotion of nationalist candidates already existed.

The sitting MPs, Biggar and Fay, were unanimously approved at the meeting of the county electors in Cavan town on 15 March.[75] Cavan was one of the few counties where the two factions within the party did not oppose each other as it was feared that any internal division would lead to the

Conservatives taking a seat. Again the Catholic clergy were the unifying force. The county had come a long way since the 1874 election and the clergy and nationalists did not want to lose these advances. Everybody was confident that Biggar and Fay would be returned comfortably and national attention was thus focused on other constituencies, unlike the 1874 election. Even the Conservatives felt that the county was under home rule control leading to indecision which benefitted the nationalists.[76] In 1879 the Conservatives had abandoned voter registration and now confusion reigned as to whether they would nominate a candidate. Indeed Captain Somerset Maxwell, heir to the Farnham estate, was nominated only two weeks before the election although the Conservative campaign was a vigorous one. The low key contest was seen in the relatively lack lustre approach which the local home rule movement adopted. Unlike the 1874 contest no major tour of the county was made and demonstrations were confined to the larger towns, such as Cavan and Killeshandra. No prominent national home rule figures appeared at demonstrations in the county.

From the outset the electoral significance of the clergy was evident: when Fay and Biggar arrived in Cavan they first called on Dr Conaty at Cullies. Seven priests, including the administrator, Revd Michael Fitzpatrick who was chairman, attended the home rule meeting in Cavan town on 30 March.[77] However the clergy only supported Biggar after he renounced a statement he was supposed to have made in Cork regarding the assassination of Queen Victoria. Biggar also encountered difficulties because of his support for Revd Isaac Nelson, a presbyterian home rule minister, in the Leitrim election, with Conaty threatening that he would not recommend him to the Cavan electors.[78] In the end, however, Conaty and Philip Smith, a justice of the peace from Artina, did nominate Biggar and Fay. During the election the clergy acted as organisers and chairmen of the demonstrations, and in some cases, such as Fr Fitzpatrick at Castleterra, escorted the electors to the polling stations.[79] Fay headed the poll with 3097 votes, with Biggar taking the second seat with 3061 votes, well ahead of Somerset Maxwell. Overall, sixty-three nationalists were elected, twenty-seven of whom were committed Parnellites and the remainder moderate home rulers.

Fay was elected because of clerical support and the failure of the more radical Parnellites to nominate an alternative candidate. As Vincent Comerford points out, the 1880 election resulted in the moderate home rulers, including Fay, being left without a rallying point. The radical obstructionists, including Biggar, used the agrarian question to their advantage. Biggar addressed demonstrations all over the country, including the meeting at Irishtown on 21 April 1879 at which the Land League was founded.[80] However, Fay and the other moderates were forced to make some gesture towards the land issue without ever being totally sincere, as when Fay attended an anti-eviction rally at Mountnugent on 25 March 1880.[81] With the election over Fay could renege on his feint promises. The 1880 contest was the last occasion that people like Fay could behave in such a manner. By the 1885 general election the situation had changed dramatically and Parnell and his party not only controlled the issues to be discussed, but also the process which selected the candidates.[82] The position of moderate representatives such as Fay was also becoming more insecure as their activities were being closely monitored by the nationalist newspapers who quickly indicated any indiscretion. Criticisms from local groups were printed in these newspapers and these alerted nationalists in other parts of the county to the performance of their representatives.[83] Thus Fay's actions were constantly scrutinised to ascertain the true level of his support for home rule. This became even more intense with the establishment of *United Ireland* in 1882, a newspaper controlled by Parnell and his supporters and edited by William O'Brien.

While Fay was not a Parnellite supporter his parliamentary and constituency activities between 1874 and 1880 indicate that he was a political moderate who wished to see the party advance by tying together all the nationalist strands within the country. He participated in parliamentary obstruction when he considered it necessary and was supported by all nationalists in Cavan up to 1880. The first indication of a rift with his constituents occurred in January 1881 when the Land League branches in Cavan, Killeshandra and Laragh passed resolutions condemning Fay's parliamentary absences, especially when the land question was being debated. They called on him to be more attentive in his duties or else to resign so that a representative who had their confidence could be elected.[84] Fay denied the charges maintaining he had done nothing wrong and stated

> I sit in the house not as a mere delegate or mouthpiece, but as an independent Irish gentleman, bound to act as my conscience dictates, and that as long as I am true to my pledges at the hustings, no elector or body of electors has a right to pass a resolution condemnatory of me.[85]

By this stage Fay had lost the confidence of a substantial body of the Cavan electors and effectively became a member without a constituency. The events of 1880, when Parnell was elected leader of the party, forced moderate home rulers such as Fay, Errington in Longford, Patrick O'Brien of King's county and Mitchel Henry of county Galway to reconsider their positions. Most came from that section of the movement most opposed to Parnell, the landowners who had deserted the party during his leadership. They had neither the dedication nor the determination to accept the centralised approach which Parnell forced on the party. Fay, however, did not leave when the twelve whig members seceded from the party in January 1881, but in April he signed his own political death warrant by supporting the 1881 land bill, when the official party line was to abstain in the vote.[86] He was now an outcast within the party and as late as 1885 in Cavan the very mention of his name was met with derision. His split with the party can be noted in that he was absent from the house of commons on thirteen of the fifteen occasions on which Irish issues were being debated.

Fay's situation was indicative of the changing patterns within Irish nationalism in the 1870s and 1880s. What had been acceptable in 1874 was no longer appropriate in the early 1880s as the direction and fundamentals of constitutional nationalism changed course. The change marked the emergence of a modern political party which was not centred on individual needs or that of a particular region, but rather on the benefits for the party and country itself. This can be seen during the 1885 election when neither of the home rule candidates for Cavan, Biggar and Thomas O'Hanlon, had connections with the county; the former being from Belfast and the later from Derry city. Those who were unable to conform to the new structure had no alternative but to leave. While attempts were made by local nationalists to have Patrick O'Reilly, a poor law guardian from Scrabby, nominated his name was withdrawn because the central organisation was intent on having Biggar and O'Hanlon selected.[87]

While the Land League may not have had an influential part in electoral affairs in Cavan in 1880 it quickly developed a role, leaving a mark on Ulster politics which continued well into the next century. It mobilised the Catholic population in support of nationalism, moving them away from their espousal of the Liberals and in the process providing the leadership previously offered by the Catholic clergy.[88] The Land League became the local organisational unit for the home rule party and by the time the National League replaced it in 1882 it had already moulded the Catholic population into an effective force for Parnell.

October 1882 marked a major change in the organisation and development of the home rule movement in both Cavan and Ireland generally. Since 1880 Parnell and his party had relied on the Land League for funding and practical support. There were disadvantages with this: the main aim of the Land League was agrarian rather than political. The fear existed that the League could quickly and easily turn away from the nationalist party, as its leadership was composed of fenians whose sympathy with constitutional politics was, to say the least, suspect. For this reason Parnell used the opportunity of the Land League's proscription to launch his own political organisation, the National League, on 17 October 1882. The primary objective of the National League was the promotion of political affairs with the agrarian issue of secondary importance. Nowhere was this more important than in the selection and promotion of parliamentary candidates at election time. Under National League rules each branch was entitled to send four representatives to vote at the county selection meeting.[89] With the establishment of the National League, Cavan once again was to the forefront in its advancement of the nationalist cause in Ulster. Of the thirty-eight League branches in existence in Ulster in December 1882, thirteen were in Cavan, making it by far the best organised county. These included Drumgoon, Ballymachugh, Killinagh, Scrabby and Drumlane.[90] By July 1883 the number of League branches in Cavan had increased to twenty-two branches, but all branches were in rural areas and by the middle of 1884 none had been established in Cavan town or any of the other urban centres. By October 1885, forty two branches had been established in the county. This growth can be seen as the result of local concern to select their own parliamentary candidates since only affiliated branches were entitled to select the party's candidates. The development of the National League helped centralise the selection of the home rule candidates at election time. No one interest group could dominate the selection process as had occurred in many areas in 1874 and 1880. It put in place a uniformity which had been evident in Cavan since 1874, when the clergy and laity acted jointly in the selection of candidates.

The League's advancement in Cavan was assisted by Bishop Conaty's positive attitude. He encouraged his priests to become actively involved and Gabriel Kelly has identified nine clerics who were presidents of National League branches in their areas.[91] Clerical participation was important for a number of reasons. It ensured that no radical groups gained control of local branches as had occurred with the Land League. It also allowed the clergy to pursue an active political role within the county, and in particular to involve themselves when parliamentary candidates were being selected. Twenty-six priests attended the Irish Parliamentary party convention on 18 October 1885 which selected Biggar and Thomas O'Hanlon as the candidates for Cavan.[92]

The 1884 Franchise Act played a major role in ensuring that the county remained under nationalist control. There were two constituencies—east and west Cavan—at the 1885 general election. The act resulted in an increase in the electorate from 6096 in 1880 to 19,029 in 1885. The vast majority of the new voters were small tenant farmers and labourers who supported home rule. In west Cavan 79.9 per cent of the population of 65,449 were Catholic and 81.8 per cent in east Cavan.[93] Except for west Donegal, where 90 per cent were Catholic, these constituencies had the highest proportion of Catholics in Ulster. The National League maximised this vote by ensuring that electors paid their rates to prevent them from being disenfranchised. This meant that the Conservatives felt there was little point in channelling their energies into a futile exercise. At the 1885 election Thomas O'Hanlon was returned unopposed in west Cavan. Samuel Saunderson contested east Cavan as a Conservative, though it was more of a gesture than a threat to the nationalists. Biggar comfortably won the seat with 6425 votes against 1779 for his opponent. At the 1886 general election both nationalist candidates were elected unopposed, indicating the unassailable position of the movement in Cavan.

The development and consolidation of the home rule movement in Cavan in the 1870s and 1880s was largely influenced by the fear that any split in the nationalist ranks would permit the Conservatives to take over part of its representation.[94] Thus a vigilant attitude prevailed and the Catholic clergy ensured that a united approach was adopted at election time. Bishop Nicholas Conaty's political pragmatism was important in this respect. The emergence of the home rule movement coincided with the demise of the Liberal party in the county and the emergence of the Irish Parliamentary party. The decline in Liberal fortunes in the rest of Ulster was less spectacular and even after 1886 it survived in some rural regions of the province. In Cavan, Catholics had an effective and well-run home rule party. The Liberals failed to attract any of this vote because they appeared to be soft on the constitutional question and even among labouring groups this became the most important issue. Thus Cavan's political transformation in the two decades after 1870 was much more akin to developments in the three southern provinces of Ireland than to the direction of political change in the rest of Ulster. In this, as in other aspects of Cavan life, it shows its role as straddling two rather different worlds.

Cavan in the Era of the Great War, 1914–18

EILEEN REILLY

The period of the First World war, 1914–18, is one of great importance in the evolution of Irish society. The culmination of the struggle for home rule, and the threat of civil war over that issue, the Easter rebellion of 1916, and its effect on the character of Irish nationalism, the growth of Sinn Féin and the subsequent fight for Irish independence are all issues which have been extensively studied by Irish historians. However, Irish involvement in the First World War is a topic which is only recently receiving the attention it deserves.[1] This essay will examine the development of county Cavan during this period, the inter-related themes of how Irish involvement in the war affected the county, and how the county responded to the war effort. To understand these themes Cavan provides an interesting case study. Geographically, it was part of Ulster, but was it part of Ulster ideologically? Did Cavan show the level of commitment to the war which Ulster as a whole has been credited with, usually in contrast to the supposed apathy of the other provinces?

During the first half of the war, Cavan like most of the counties in Ireland, contributed strongly to the war effort, in terms of recruits, public support for the war, and charitable organisations who worked on behalf of soldiers and their dependants. Nationalists and unionists, who had been pitted against one another in the years previous to the outbreak of war, served on the same committees, spoke at the same meetings, and supported the cause, although admittedly for different reasons, the nationalists with home rule within sight, the unionists for reasons of tradition, loyalty, and fear of the future. As the war continued the character of Irish nationalism underwent many changes, particularly after the 1916 rising, and the subsequent growth of Sinn Féin. Priorities changed, from active sympathy with, and commitment to the war effort, to insular concern with the struggle for independence. This divergence of commitment is clearly apparent in the case of Cavan, as with most counties with a large nationalist population. The total population of Cavan, according to the 1911 census was 91,223 persons of which 81.5 per cent were Catholic, 14.2 per cent were Church of Ireland, 3.1 per cent were Presbyterian, 0.9 per cent were Methodist.

As David Fitzpatrick has observed 'The promise, or threat of home rule was the driving force behind every substantial faction in Irish politics from 1870–1916'.[2] In the period immediately preceding the First World War tension had been growing over the issue of home rule. Nationalists became jubilant as it became apparent that their goal was within their grasp. Unionists were becoming increasingly defensive, and then aggressive, with the formation of the Ulster Volunteers, to fight against home rule. Nationalists swiftly formed their own volunteer corps in response. Unionist opposition to home rule in Cavan was traditional. In 1882, Colonel Edward Saunderson, of Castle Saunderson in the county, urged Orangemen 'to drill, arm and don uniforms' against the combined nationalist threat of the Land League, and the campaign for home rule.[3] An analysis of the character and contents of Cavan's weekly newspapers, the *Anglo–Celt*, and the *Irish Post*, the former nationalist in tone, the latter unionist, during the period 1912–14, reveals the growing polarisation between the two groups. The *Anglo–Celt*, was owned and edited by Mr J.F. O'Hanlon. During 1912, his editorials heaped scorn and ridicule on unionist drilling and demonstrations. One such demonstration at Omagh on January 5th 1912, was expected, according to O'Hanlon,

> ... to have a hundred thousand men in attendance. Despite the fact that special trains were run from every Ulster county, the number dwindled down to one fifth the original estimate ... No fire, no thunder, no nothing ... And so ended the great demonstration which was to have driven terror into the advocates of home rule![4]

Who were these advocates of home rule? The Irish Parliamentary Party, as David Fitzpatrick has pointed out, 'formally existed only at Westminster. It had no provincial branches, no rank-and-file party members, no formal party hierarchy ... The busiest advocates of home rule were members of the numerous and active local government bodies', the county councils, urban and rural district councils, town commissioners, and boards of guardians of poor law unions.[5] In addition to Cavan's county council, there were four urban districts, West Cavan, East Cavan, Cootehill, and Belturbet. There were seven rural districts covering the county, Baileborough, Bawnboy, Castleraghan, Cavan, Cootehill, Mullahoran, and part of Enniskillen no. 2 district.

Other social and political organisations where Home Rulers were to be found were, for example, the United Irish League, the Ancient Order of Hibernians, the Gaelic League, the Evicted Tenant's Association, the Town Tenant's League, and the National Foresters, all of which had a healthy existence in Cavan during this period. The United Irish League had been founded at the turn of the century to defend the interests of the tenant farmer, but by this time had outlived the grievances of land purchase, and had developed a distinct political shape, nominating and selecting candidates for the parliamentary party. Local papers all over Ireland reported in detail the proceedings of various political and socio-political groups. The *Anglo–Celt* was no exception. During 1912, fifty-one branches of the United Irish League appeared in weekly notes. The affiliated fees for the League in Cavan in 1912 were £129, compared to £53 for Monaghan, £72 for Meath, £36 for Longford, and £66 for Leitrim. Twenty-one branches of the Ancient Order of Hibernians (AOH) were represented in the newspaper also; the AOH had during the nineteenth century 'acquired a sinister reputation as the Roman Catholic counterpart of the Orange Order', but by 1912 it was a 'direct competitor of the United Irish League's as principal launching-pad for political office in nationalist Ireland'.[6] Many parishes in Cavan were represented in the pages of the *Anglo–Celt* by both groups.

However scornful the *Anglo–Celt* was, there was quite a lot of unionist activity in Cavan during this period. In January, 1912, a notice appeared in the paper from the 'West Cavan Women's Unionist Association', 'established to oppose home rule and to preserve the Union'. The work of this association involved sending leaflets to 'friends in England, America, and the Colonies ... that will help them understand the true condition of affairs in Ireland'. The motto of the organisation was, not surprisingly, 'Union is strength'.[7] The editor labelled this action as dissemination of slander against nationalists, and went on to offer the opinion that this move 'should be checkmated ... the nationalist women of Ireland should be similarly employed'.[8] In February, Lord Farnham (Arthur Kenlis, eleventh Baron Farnham), addressed a meeting of the Women's Unionist organisation in Killeshandra, his brother, Colonel the Honourable Henry Edward Maxwell, JP and DL, of Fortland, county Cavan, presided over a meeting of Orangemen in Dublin, and a new Orange Hall was opened in Killegar, in the county.[9]

In April 1912, the third Home Rule Bill was introduced in the House of Commons. Four hundred delegates from Cavan were reported to have attended a home rule meeting in Dublin.[10] Editorials opined that the Bill was sure to pass and included comments from Protestants who were favourable to the measure. Mr Samuel Young, nationalist MP for East Cavan, a native of county Down, resident in Belfast, and eighty-nine years old in 1912, was quoted as saying that home rule would 'produce peace and contentment' and 'concentrate the energies of the entire population on useful industries'.[11] Attendance at the National Convention included clergy from all over Cavan, and members of the various councils and organisations within the county.[12] A similar attendance was reported at a 'magnificent demonstration at Clones' in favour of home rule, where the number was estimated at fifty thousand.[13] The *Anglo–Celt* noted with glee the low profile of the unionists in Cavan at this time, and in particular the small attendances at the annual 'Twelfth' celebrations, and the absence of the leading lay Orange members, such as Lord Farnham and Col. Maxwell. Most of the speakers at the celebrations, according to the reports carried by the paper, were clergymen who proposed resolutions to 'resist to the uttermost' the Home Rule Bill.[14] As tension rose between the two groups, it was noted that Lord Farnham's statue had been tarred, the piers of Kingscourt Protestant church were vandalised, and meetings were held by branches of the United Irish League in sympathy with the 'victims of

"Belfast bigotry" ', which were attended by the nationalist MP for West Cavan, Vincent Kennedy.[15] News of the planned Solemn Covenant was greeted as the 'abject cave-in by the Ulster "leaders" on the question of that armed resistance of which they have been speaking'.[16] Home rule meetings noted that from an Ulster unionist point of view, Cavan, Monaghan, and Donegal no longer seemed to be in Ulster; 'Ulster is now confined to four counties of Antrim, Down, Derry, and Armagh'.[17] At a unionist meeting in Enniskillen, Mr H. Horner, KC, crown prosecutor for Cavan, prophesied that home rule would turn Ulster into 'a scene of sullen discontent, poverty and civil war'.[18] The occasion of the Solemn Covenant itself was characterised by the editor of the *Anglo–Celt* as merely fist-shaking.[19]

However, there were some instances of conciliation between the two sides. In October 1912, Mr Thomas Lough, a county lieutenant and a MP, wrote from his home in Killeshandra, a letter to the London *Times*, which was also published in the *Anglo–Celt*. In this piece he stressed the nonsectarian nature of this 'Ulster village', and the prosperity engendered by the establishment of a cooperative there. He went on to assure Protestants that they had nothing to fear from home rule which he defined as 'the cooperation of Irishmen directed towards improving the condition of the country'. This was followed by the establishment, in November 1912, of a Cavan branch of the Irish Protestant Home Rule Association.[20]

Despite this, Lord Farnham representing Cavan unionists, continued vigorously campaigning against home rule. In a speech to the House of Lords, in February 1913, he alleged that nationalist farmers were terrified that home rule would result in further land agitation, and that the only demand for home rule came from the Ancient Order of Hibernians. During the following months, Cavan unionists addressed several local meetings. Lord Farnham spoke to the unionist clubs of Cavan, and to the Unionist Women's Association. Other speakers included Col. the Hon. H.E. Maxwell, Sir James Stronge, Armagh, and Captain Bryan Cooper. The unionist paper, the *Irish Post*, carried detailed reports of these meetings. Mr Horner, KC spoke at another Unionist meeting of the 'preparation for desperate resistance' being made to oppose home rule.[21] By the end of May, the *Anglo–Celt* reported that Unionist clubs were drilling at Corglass, an estimated 120 members attended, and were addressed by Lord Farnham who was reported as saying that home rule 'could only be defeated by their own grim determination not to have it under any circumstances'.[22] A further report of this drill meeting resulted in a writ being served on the *Anglo–Celt* for alleged libel, on behalf of Col. the Hon. H.E. Maxwell.[23] The *Anglo–Celt* continued its derisory tone in reporting unionist activities.

> The speeches at the 'Twelfth' of July meetings in Cavan and Monaghan this year were the tamest that have been delivered from these platforms for years ... The gathering for Cavan this year was expected

to reach record proportions; yet in the procession there were all told, only 1833 men and boys.[24]

Unionist activity in the county was, however, growing stronger with each month that passed. In November 1912, intelligence notes for the county estimated the number of unionist clubs at twelve, with a membership of 1425. By May of 1913 this had risen to sixteen clubs in the county, with a total membership of 1949. The Ulster Volunteer Force was founded in January 1913. In September 1913, intelligence notes report the following figures for county Cavan. There were seven district centres for the UVF; Cavan, with 570 members, Cootehill had 400, Castlesaunderson had 590, Bailieborough with 400, Derrylane had 450, and Stradone, with 220. Total membership of the UVF in Cavan at this point was 2630. In comparison, Monaghan had a total of 1209 members, Fermanagh had 2090, and Donegal had 1,178 members.[25] However, two months later, in November 1913, numbers had increased significantly. Cavan now had a total membership of 3041. It was also believed by the police that the UVF in Cavan had arms numbering 1619.[26]

Home rule supporters responded with a meeting in Cavan in November, the sixth such meeting that year in the county, at which an estimated forty thousand men attended. Speeches by MP's such as Vincent Kennedy, J. McVeagh, and Hector Morrison were reported in detail, as was a speech by the owner and editor of the *Anglo–Celt*, J.F. O'Hanlon, in his capacity as a member of the Cavan urban district council. The presence of each branch of the United Irish League and AOH, together with the name of each member who attended, were also recorded in a four page special report in the *Anglo–Celt*.[27] By the end of the year, articles explaining the new nationalist movement, the National Irish Volunteers, founded on 25 November, were appearing in the newspaper, with editorials commenting on the certainty of an Irish parliament in the coming year.[28] This air of certainty continued in the early months of 1914, despite the increasing activity of the Ulster Volunteers. In January, a speech by Lord Farnham was quoted in the *Irish Post*.

> Remember that the people in county Cavan have got to do their utmost to put their whole moral and spiritual courage and feeling in the Ulster Volunteer Force, and to do their utmost to make it a success and a real disciplined military force.[29]

The monthly reports of the County Inspector noted that the Ulster Volunteers were 'drilling vigorously' in January, and also reported that an attempt was made to injure Lord Farnham. He, and Mr T.J. Burrowes of Stradone were returning home from a Volunteer drill when they discovered barbed wire stretched across the road at a height of three and a half feet. The attempt was unsuccessful as Lord Farnham stopped his motor car before striking the wire.[30] The Inspector's reports for the following months consist-

ently noted the heightened activity of all societies in the county, particularly
the Ulster Volunteers, who in March carried out 'target practice at Farnham,
Macken, Killeshandra, and Rathkerry'. A camp of instruction was also held at
Farnham from 7 to 14 of March, 'for the purpose of receiving instructions in
drill. 230 section and squad leaders were present'. Political and party feelings
were described as acute, particularly in the wake of the action of the military
officers at the Curragh, which 'the unionists and the Ulster Volunteers are
quite jubilant over ... whilst the nationalist press refer to them as rebels'.[31] By
March, however, the National Irish Volunteers were beginning to make their
presence felt in the county, organised by Lt. R.B. Sheridan of Mountnugent.
One of the first branches was set up in Belturbet, with one hundred members
enrolling at its inaugural meeting. Knockbride West followed suit, with ninety
members joining at the first meeting. Drung Corps was described in the
Anglo–Celt notes as being composed 'of men from the UIL ranks'.[32] While the
formation of corps of National Volunteers in the county was celebrated in the
Anglo–Celt, its tone of derision in relation to the Ulster Volunteers continued.
The following is in relation to the camp of instruction, noted above.

> Colonel Nugent, DSO, an ex-officer of the King's Own Rifles ... is
> now 'Commander' of the Cavan battalion of the Carsonite Volunteers
> ... it would now seem ... that these men to the full strength of 120 in
> a county with a population of 91,173, met at Lord Farnham's last
> week.

By the end of March, intelligence reports estimated the strength of the Ulster
Volunteers in the county at 3406, with 2676 assorted varieties of rifles between them. By the summer months the strength of the National Volunteers
was reported as being 6366, armed with revolvers and shotguns.[33] Members
of the latter were described by the County Inspector in his monthly report for
May, as being ' ... the sons of farmers and labourers ... and in the town shop
assistants and corner boys.'[34] Feelings were becoming more bitter and strained,
particularly after the third reading of the Home Rule Bill in the House of
Commons at the end of May 1914 which gave added impetus to both sides.
Despite the tension, the July anniversaries passed off without disorder.[35] Early
in August the First World War began. 'The political tension was at once
relieved' in the county, 'all parties with the exception of Sinn Féin supporting
the government'.[36] The National Volunteers responded positively to Redmond's
call to support the war effort. Cavan army reservists were given a hearty
send-off when leaving to join their respective regiments. An estimated 400,
which seems quite high in relation to later police reports, many of whom were
reported to be members of the National Volunteers, left Cavan on 7 August to
the air of 'A nation once again'.[37] The *Anglo–Celt* supported wholeheartedly
Redmond's 'magnificent offer' that 'the nationalist and Ulster Volunteers will
hold Ireland for the empire against the enemy', and hoped it would 'end an

age-old quarrel'.[38] Notes from various branches of the National Volunteers reported that 'to a man they were prepared to fight on foreign service provided the Home Rule Bill was placed on the Statute Book'.[39] Lord Farnham was active in recruiting from the Ulster Volunteers.[40] He himself had been a lieutenant colonel in the North Irish Horse Yeomanry, an acting lieutenant colonel in the Royal Inniskillling Fusiliers, a lieutenant in the 10th Hussars, and had served in the Boer war. His father had been a captain in the county regiment, the Royal Irish Fusiliers, and his brother, Col. H.E. Maxwell, had also served in the Boer war.[41] Intelligence notes reported that

> All classes displayed a strong patriotic and anti-German feeling, and joined irrespective of creed and politics in giving a hearty send-off to reservists and recruits when leaving to join the army. Nevertheless considerable unrest prevailed alike in the unionist and nationalist ranks as to the action the government would take with regard to the Home Rule Bill.[42]

The placing of the Home Rule Bill on the Statute Book in September 1914 was celebrated by the county's nationalist population. Public meetings were held to advocate recruiting, many clergy supporting the defence of Belgium, while lay leaders supported Redmond.

> The present war is popular with all classes save a few Sinn Féiners, and there is not the slightest sympathy with the Germans so far as can be ascertained; all sections working cordially together to raise funds for the assistance of dependants of soldiers and sailors engaged in the war.[43]

The County Cavan War Relief Fund was set up in response to the Prince of Wales appeal, by Lord Farnham, Thomas Lough, MP, and Mr J. Maxwell Greene. Notice of the fund was carried and supported by both papers. Initially, lists of subscribers included most of the gentry of the county, but was also supported by nationalist leaders.[44] The ladies of the county set up their own organisation, the County Cavan Women's Patriotic Committee, to organise fund-raising events, make clothing to send to soldiers at the front, and organise first-aid classes. The conveners of the first meeting of this committee were largely the wives of the gentry, Lady Farnham, Mrs Thomas Lough, the Hon. Mrs Burrowes, the Hon. Mrs Maxwell, Mrs and Miss Whyte-Venables. However wives of nationalists were also represented, for example, Mrs Vincent Kennedy. They decided to organise local committees 'which should be as representative as possible of all sections' to carry out the aims of the organisation, and held regular meetings and fund-raising activities throughout the following months. The Roman Catholic bishop of Kilmore, Dr Finegan, publicly supported the work of the committees, and 'appealed to each woman and girl in county Cavan' to become involved in the organisation.[45] In return, the bishop's appeal for Belgian refugees was supported by the committee, £840 being raised by collections in all churches.[46]

Despite this effort by both communities, some notes of doubt and dissension were to be heard. Some elements of the National Volunteers were becoming anxious at the lack of trust by the government in their intentions. O'Hanlon, owner and editor of the *Anglo–Celt*, and member of the Cavan urban council, in a speech to Volunteers at Killeshandra, encouraged recruitment to the army, but quoting a letter from Fr Osborne, Arva, 'Beware of brand-new friends who were former enemies'. He also declared that speaking for 'the men of county Cavan', they would have 'none of that class', men like Lord Powerscourt or Lord Fingall, put in charge of the Volunteers.[47] Questions were being raised on all sides as to why the National Volunteers were not armed, yet supporting the war effort, while Ulster unionists 'who have been perambulating Ulster with their machine-guns' should not be asked to go to the front.[48] The delay in sending Ulster unionists to the front was as a result of their campaign for their own unit, the 36th Ulster division, which did not arrive in France until October 1915. In contrast, many of the National Volunteers had been sent over with the 10th and 16th divisions, as part of the original expeditionary force, in September 1914. Intelligence reports estimated that 12,000 Ulster Volunteers throughout the province had joined the army by the end of September 1914.[49] A front-page report of a recruiting meeting held in Arva by Lord Farnham appeared in the *Anglo–Celt* in September.

> On Friday evening Lord Farnham attended near Arva for the purpose, he said, of enrolling members of the local Ulster Volunteers in Lord Kitchener's new army. The gathering was very small and lack of enthusiasm was the prevailing feature. His lordship spoke at length but only three young men from the entire district gave in their names.[50]

Meanwhile, there were some incidents of anti-enlistment activity noted in the monthly reports of the County Inspector, for September and October. A

> few despicable Sinn Féiners in the little town of Ballinagh ... posted up anti-recruiting notices ... but no evidence can be obtained against them ... The Sinn Féiners have distributed anti-enlistment leaflets which have a considerable effect in keeping young men from joining the army.[51]

Since the beginning of the war, according to police reports in October, 238 reservists had joined up. Of these, 153 were National Volunteers, 55 were Ulster Volunteers, and 30, 'whose politics are not ascertainable'. In terms of recruits, 210 men joined the army. Of these, 47 were National Volunteers, 71 were Ulster Volunteers, and 87 'whose politics are unknown'. Also reported was the fact that approximately 150 men from the county left for America during the past month in response to a report that the government were going to enforce the Militia Ballot Act.[52] Dissension was becoming apparent in the ranks of the National Volunteers, between moderate nationalists who supported Redmond, and advanced nationalists, a minority, who opposed Irish involvement in the war. This resulted in a split within the Volunteers, the National Volunteers remaining loyal to Redmond, the Irish Volunteers opposing his policy. As the *Anglo–Celt* observed

> With regard to the action of the few Dublin malcontents who have endeavoured to disrupt the movement and whose sole object is to vilify John Redmond and the Irish party, it is well understood that so far as this company is concerned their action has not had the slightest effect and that their programme and policy has not a single adherent. This company will have nothing to do with them or their pro-German and unpatriotic programme.[53]

This commitment to Redmond was followed by nearly every corps in the county during the following weeks. However, dissidents were at work. Intelligence notes for the month of November reported the activities of one Archie Heron, an organiser of 'the Sinn Féin, anti-recruiting and pro-German movement'.

> He delivered a speech at an indoor meeting at Ballinagh, of an anti-recruiting nature; and he visited Kilcogy, Ballyhaise, and Tullyvin sub-districts. On the 20th Nov., I executed a search warrant at the house of B. McCabe, Cavan, where Heron was staying, and seized a large amount of anti-recruiting and seditious literature, as well as letters from Bulmer Hobson, and Heron's letters. Heron subsequently disappeared and has not been traced.[54]

He went on to estimate that there were 1400 'Sinn Féiners', or those opposed to Redmond's policy in the county.[55]

Meanwhile, reports were starting to appear in the *Anglo–Celt* regarding Cavan men at the front. Battalions of the Royal Irish Fusiliers, Royal Munster Fusiliers, Irish Guards, and Inniskilling Fusiliers, were part of the British Expeditionary Force. Cavan soldiers were represented in all of the above regiments, especially the county regiment, the Royal Irish Fusiliers. The first and second battalions of the latter were sent to the front as part of Kitchener's army, the third and fourth battalions were militia, Armagh and Cavan respectively, located in Armagh with home defence and draft finding duties. The sixth to eighth battalions became part of the 10th Irish division, while the ninth battalion, formed from Armagh, Monaghan, and Cavan Ulster Volunteers, became part of the 36th Ulster Division, which was sent to France in October 1915.

The first casualty was reported in September, Second-Lieutenant Eric Dorman-Smith, son of Mr E.P. Smith, Cootehill, wounded at Troisville while serving with the Northumberland Fusiliers.[56] The first fatality reported was a son of Mr. E. Coyle, Cavan, killed at the front while serving with the Royal Irish Fusiliers, at the battle of Mons. Both were nineteen years old.[57] A reported fatality, a son of Ex-Colour Sergeant J. Horgan, Belturbet, serving with the Royal Irish Fusiliers, actually narrowly escaped death at the battles of Mons and Marne. He wrote to his father that he had met two other Belturbet men, Reynolds and McPartlan, serving with the Inniskilling Fusiliers.[58] Other casualties included Samuel Cowan, Ballinagh, of the Irish Guards, wounded at Marne, and Patrick Farrelly, Cavan, of the Inniskilling Fusiliers, wounded at Mons.[59] A nephew of the Protestant primate of Ireland, Second-Lieutenant J.C.B. Crozier, Royal Munster Fusiliers, was killed in action. His family lived at Knockfed, Cavan.[60] The lists of dead and injured from the county, reported in the newspapers, grew steadily as the war continued. The names of the county's gentry families were well represented, but so too were the names of former National Volunteers. Nonetheless, recruiting continued to be 'particularly brisk, hardly a day passing that from six to ten young men do not come in for service' in Cavan.[61]

> Recruiting is becoming brisk at Cavan military barracks just now, the number for this week, 9th to 16th inst. enrolled by Capt. Johnston, R.I.F. being 34 and for the first four days of the present week, 19, a large number coming from Bailieborough and Newtownbutler districts. Since the war began 268 in all have joined the colours ... 22 enlisting in August, 114 in September, 58 in October, and from the first of November until yesterday, 74. One of the best recruiting districts is Killeshandra, while Belturbet and Ballyjamesduff have also contributed their quota. Nearly all the men were members of the National Volunteers.[62]

The following year witnessed a decline in recruitment in the county. The total number of recruits for the year was 453, and this was achieved only with great effort on the part of those responsible for recruitment.

A large proportion of Cavan's population was engaged in agriculture. Of the total of specified occupations, given as 37,634, in the 1911 census, those engaged in agriculture numbered 27,634. The war had had a positive effect on agriculture. From 1913 to 1916, the agricultural wholesale price index had risen by sixty per cent. The agricultural instructor for the county, Mr J. Hanley, delivered lectures to farmers on improved methods of farming, while the editorials of the *Anglo–Celt* reflect as much a preoccupation with agriculture as with the war effort, and more so as the war continued. Editorial subjects included, for example, 'How to have more food', 'The war and the crops', 'Food and the Kaiser', and 'Farmers do your duty'.[63]

Police reports for the year dealt with the topic of recruitment, or the lack of it, on a monthly basis. As early as February the County Inspector recommended that troops be stationed at the vacant barracks in Cavan, in order to encourage recruitment.

> It is believed that if troops were stationed here, especially with a band, and moved about the county, it would give great stimulation to recruiting ... Recruiting is at a standstill and was greatly hindered by the interference of a pro-German called McTab at a public recruiting meeting here on 19th March ... It is my strong opinion that troops ought to be quartered at the barracks here ... Recruiting for H.M. Army does not appear to be so brisk in this county as elsewhere, and there are plenty of able-bodied young fellows who have not joined. A party of R.I. Fusiliers with band made a tour through here recently, but no recruit was obtained ... Hundreds of strapping young farmer's sons are still at home.[64]

The decline in recruitment was due to a number of factors, the realisation of what the sacrifices of war meant, with reports of increasing casualties and wounded from the county. The membership of the National Volunteers fell, due to enlistment and demoralisation, to 3675 members, compared to 6366 the previous year. The growth in popularity of the Irish Volunteers, estimated to number 295 members in February 1915, and steadily increasing.[65] The Irish Volunteers 'capitalised upon rural resentment at government regulation of profitable wartime agriculture', and the threat of conscription. The fact that Cavan had a high proportion of her population involved in profitable agriculture was a further deterrent to recruitment.[66] However, the war effort continued in other directions. The Women's Patriotic Committee had sent over 3,000 garments to the front, and had collected £450 for soldiers' dependents.[67] Nonetheless, recruitment was still the primary consideration. During the summer months an energetic drive for recruits was made. Meetings, with troops and bands, were held at Cavan and Blacklion in May, and at Cavan, Cootehill, and Bailieborough in June.[68] In July a full page advertisement for recruits appeared in the *Anglo–Celt*. Circulars were also distributed, which resulted in fifty recruits according to the paper.[69] The *Irish Post* featured an article on a patriotic Mrs Lynch of Arva, whose eight sons were all in the army.[70] By August, the County Inspector reported that,

> A strong local effort is being made to obtain recruits for H.M. Army in this county, led by Mr Lough ... Local committees have been formed in county places, and the Central Recruiting Council has arranged a tour of their motor bus with a military band. The barrack here has at

last been occupied by 200 men of the R. I. Fusiliers, the county regiment, and this will give a great stimulus to recruiting.[71]

Lough spoke at a war meeting in Cavan during August 1915, which was attended by unionists and nationalists, lay and clerical. He gave the following recruitment statistics for the year; January, thirty; February, forty-two; March, 40; April, fifty-two; May, forty; June, thirty-two; July, twenty-eight; a total of 521 recruits, which is much higher than the figure of 453 given in police reports for the entire year. This latter total was broken down into National Volunteer recruits, 193, Ulster Volunteers, 114, and those not known as Volunteers, 146; Catholics, 313, Protestants, 140.[72]

By October, the ninth battalion of the Royal Irish Fusiliers, made up of Ulster Volunteers from Armagh, Monaghan, and Cavan, as part of the 36th Ulster Division, commanded by Cavan man, Major-General Nugent, former commander of the Cavan Ulster Volunteers, had landed in France, and by November was fighting in the trenches of no-man's-land. Meanwhile, the 16th Irish Division, including the fifth and sixth battalions of the Royal Irish Fusiliers, was fighting on the eastern front, and played a major role in the battles of Suvla.

In September, the County Inspector reported that the recruiting drive had met with little success, 'The young men of this county will not go until they are brought', an ominous foreboding of conscription.[73] Meanwhile the Irish Volunteers continued to grow, four branches existing in October 1915. They continued their anti-recruitment work, an organiser, Alfie Monaghan, was arrested for making an anti-recruitment speech, which had the result of increasing membership.

> Many young men home on leave were persuaded not to return. If persuasion wasn't sufficient, then stormier methods were often used. many a soldier lost his rifle when on leave.[74]

By the end of the year the United Irish League was trying to reorganise, having declined in numbers, with eighteen branches out of affiliation. At its county convention in November, the speeches were in favour of recruitment, but opposed to compulsion. The County Inspector noted that numbers enlisting had 'been a little livelier' towards the end of the year, due to drives by local committees, but that 'the farmer's sons are holding back in numbers'.[75] In December, a letter appeared in the *Anglo–Celt* from Henry Gloster Armstrong, who offered £1 to each of the first 100 recruits to join the Royal Irish Fusiliers on or after 1 January 1916. This offer was extended in June to the first 200 to join.[76] The County Cavan Recruiting Committee continued its efforts to stimulate enlistment. Vincent Kennedy MP spoke at the first recruiting meeting of the year, of Gloster Armstrong's offer as the 'treasured ... gift of an old Cavan man who was proud of the county regiment'. Lough appealed to the National Volunteers to enlist 'before compulsion was to be used'.[77] The *Anglo–Celt* in its effort to support recruitment published a list of men from Belturbet, taken from the national school register, who were serving with the forces, and those who had been killed. Fifty men had joined the Royal Irish Fusiliers, three had been killed. Seventy men altogether had joined up, in regiments as diverse as the Norfolks, the Inniskillings, the Royal Irish Rifles, the Connaught Rifles, the Navy, and the Irish Guards. There were a total of four fatalities altogether from the fourteen regiments given.[78]

By the beginning of 1916 the issue of conscription began to be discussed in earnest in the press. Editorials of the *Anglo–Celt* with headlines such as 'Why Ireland objects to conscription' became commonplace, setting out the records of service and support that the county had provided since the beginning of the war.

> Not that nationalist Ireland has been lacking in its contribution to the war, for even on the testimony of Lord Kitchener himself, the result of voluntary enlistment of this county has far exceeded anything he expected ...

This argument was set against the example of the 'armed' unionist force, who had been ready to fight against home rule, according to O'Hanlon, yet not for Britain.[79] The County Inspector continued to report recruiting to be very slack in the early months of the year.

> All efforts to get the farmer's sons to come in have been fruitless ... Recruiting for the army during the past month has been very bad ... Recruiting for the army is still very slack—the farmer's sons holding back.[80]

The rebellion in Dublin at Easter focused attention dramatically away from the war. The County Inspector submitted a detailed report of the state of the county.

> The one topic of conversation is the rebellion in Dublin and elsewhere, and on all sides one hears nothing but condemnation expressed. The Sinn Féin Irish Volunteers—so far as can be ascertained—made no move to take part in the rising, nor can it be proved so far that any individual member was present at or assisted in that proceeding ... There was no circulation of seditious leaflets or newspapers.[81]

The *Anglo–Celt* carried reports of the rising on 29 April. In these initial reports of 'the rebels', Sinn Féin was not mentioned and Roger Casement was seen as the major figure involved. Just as newsworthy in these early reports was the worry that trade would be disrupted, and that Belfast would take advantage of this, also that the *Anglo–Celt* itself now had to be printed in Belfast.[82] The editor confidently asserted that the rebels policy while quite 'broadly national' was 'quite chaotic from the practical standpoint. Comparatively little notice was taken of them throughout the country'.[83] News of the executions of the leaders of the rising elicted quite a different response. O'Hanlon in his editorials called on the military authorities to dispel the rumours of secret trials and executions.

> There would be some explanation of the severity practised here if the mass of the Irish people were in sympathy with the revolt, if the young Irish reserve battalions had been false to their trust, if anywhere in Ireland, there was anything but an impotent minority that approved the insanity of the insurrection ... But the conditions are the very reverse of all that.

By the end of May, however, he noted changes in feelings, the rebels now being described in milder terms as 'misguided'. Ten arrests had been made in the county following searches, by one hundred Inniskilling Fusiliers, in Crosserlough, Mullahoran, and Ballintemple, resulting in deportations to prison camps.[84] Intelligence notes reported the arrest of one Cavan man, Peter Paul Galligan, of Ballinagh, a commandant in the Irish Volunteers, who had seen active service in Enniscorthy during the rising. He was sentenced to death, but the sentence was commuted to five years penal servitude.[85] War news became increasingly peripheral over the summer months, despite such major battles as that of the Somme. Fourteen officers and 518 men were killed from the 9th battalion of Royal Irish Fusiliers, within the 36th Ulster Division, during the first two days of the Somme, the Division distinguished itself during this and following battles, resulting in practical decimation of its ranks by the autumn. The first battalion of the Royal Irish Fusiliers, part of the original expeditionary force in 1914, had 120 causalities on the first day, the 2nd battalion suffered fatalities of 550, while the 7th and 8th battalions of the regiment, serving with the 16th Division, had to be amalgamated due to heavy losses, the Division suffering causalities of over 4000, especially during the battles of Guillemont and Ginchy in September.[86]

The issues that concerned those at home were domestic ones. War news was relegated to small insignificant columns, usually derived from other newspapers. Topics of concern were the rising and the government's response to it, Lloyd George's attempt at an Irish settlement which included partition of Ulster. Articles urged nationalists to be patient and hold out for unity, the decision by the nationalist conference which met in Belfast in July, to agree to short-term exclusion being denounced as foolish and hasty. Nationalists were not united on the issue. In June, police reports reflected this division.

The people seem to have turned from the topic of the Sinn Féin rising and now give their attention to the question of Home Rule negotiations in progress. Feeling on the subject is divided—many influential people taking the side of the northern bishops against exclusion—and this attitude is backed up by the local paper, the *Anglo–Celt*, which has a large circulation. On the other hand, a considerable number are in accord with the decision of the Belfast Conference, and resolutions have been passed by public boards and branches of AOH adhering to Mr Devlin's policy.[87]

Meanwhile, from May onwards recruiting was described consistently as 'at a standstill', 'practically nil' 'in spite of the fact that there are thousands of young men in the county who could be spared'.[88] In all reports it was suggested that it was the farming class which was holding back. J.M. Wilson, a southern Unionist from county Longford, toured the country during this period, collecting information about attitudes towards the war of both unionists and nationalists. In 1916 he reported that in Longford;

The small farmer has been brought up to think it beneath his dignity to serve in any of His Majesty's forces and I quite confidently say that recruiting from that element is perfectly nil. From the labouring class there has been a very fair number and I have discovered symptoms of intense jealously between the labourers and the farmers owing to the refusal of the latter to enlist and I confidently assert that a compulsion Bill would be welcome as a whole by the labourers who would rejoice to see the farmers able to serve![89]

A parliamentary report giving particulars of men of military age in Ireland was compiled in 1916. It was estimated that there were 12,990 men of military age in county Cavan. Of these, 7623 were considered indispensable due to their occupations, and a further 2025 were deemed physically unfit. The remaining 3037 were available for military service. They estimated that only 314 had joined up from September 1915 to September 1916, a total of 1120 had joined from the outbreak of the war to September 1916, but this figure included reservists as well as recruits.[90]

Intelligence notes for September reported little activity amongst the political societies.

Even with regard to Sinn Féinism nothing has been said or done. There have not been any opportunities, during the last month of showing sympathy in connection with it. No public meetings of any kind have been held. I have been making enquiries regarding the likelihood of trouble should conscription be applied to Ireland; I find that—so far as the disturbed (or Sinn Féin) district of this county is concerned; then there is little probability of it.

In October, four branches of Sinn Féin existed in the county, with a membership of 108. Six branches of the Irish Volunteers, with a membership of 177, operated in the county.[91] Both groups held a torchlit procession on the anniversary of the Manchester Martyrs in Ballinagh in November.[92]

As noted, little attention was paid to the exploits of the Irish and Ulster Divisions during the previous months, domestic political issues dominating the news. However, the Somme was not far removed from political questions of the day. The Ulster Division as a whole lost 5500 men, killed, wounded, and missing, and as the casualty lists were published, 'a hush of mourning fell upon' the unionist population. 'The sacrifice was not in vain, for it confirmed that no British government would ever force Ulster unionists to accept Dublin rule', that is, it seems, with the exceptions of Cavan, Donegal, and Monaghan.[93]

Preoccupations in the early months of 1917 centred on food shortages and how to increase production, in both UIL notes and editorials of the *Anglo–Celt*, farmers were urged to concentrate on tillage and Dr Finegan devoted his Lenten address to the same subject. Expectations grew that the war was nearing its end, the west Cavan executive of the United Irish League called for Irish representation at the peace conference as early as February.[94] Moderate nationalists became increasingly impatient with regard to the home rule issue, calling on the Irish Party to be more active and assertive. This concern was reflected in the resumption of the activities of the United Irish League and the Ancient Order of Hibernians, which had been on the wane during the previous two years. The extreme nationalists were active also. In May intelligence notes reported the

> visit of suspect John Milroy to Cootehill and neighbouring districts ... to further the interest of the Sinn Féin candidate for East Cavan, in the event of a vacancy arising in that constituency, gave the fillip to the Sinn Féin Movement, which continued to make progress during the remainder of the year. In June there were but four Sinn Féin clubs with a membership of 108. In December these numbers had increased to 53 and 2623 respectively. The Ulster Volunteers numbered 2505, and the National Volunteers 3253. Both inactive. The Irish Volunteers had a membership of 177.[95]

By 1918, however, intelligence notes were reporting a lesser figure of twenty-seven Sinn Féin clubs. This figure corresponds to reports of Sinn Féin activity in the *Anglo–Celt*. It may be that the strength of Sinn Féin was initially overestimated or that reorganisation of the movement within the county amalgamated smaller groups.

It is not surprising that Sinn Féin expected an election in East Cavan. The occupier of that seat, Samuel Young, was ninety-five years old. They were to get their opportunity within twelve months. A Sinn Féin candidate Joseph McGuinness, was elected in May 1917 for the South Longford constituency. On 29 July, Peter Paul Galligan was released from prison, and accorded a hero's welcome by twelve Sinn Féin clubs on his return to Cavan. This was followed by an announcement by the Cavan Sinn Féiners that they intended to capture all council and other seats of power within the county.[96] Also in July, the Twelfth celebrations took place for the first time in two years, with the Unionists vowing to support vigorously the Military Service Act, and once again vowing not to accept home rule. Many of the lay unionist leaders were absent, including Lord Farnham and his brother Col. H.E. Maxwell, both serving overseas.[97] The pre-war tension over home rule was once again building up. Instead of the Irish Party, however, Sinn Féin became more and more representative of nationalist opinion in the county. The moderate nationalists continued to try to hold their supporters. Meetings were held throughout the county, addressed by John Dillon MP, and Vincent Kennedy MP. These meetings received extensive coverage in the *Anglo–Celt*, often accompanied by pictures. Little coverage was given to the war except in relation to its end, food production, and Ireland's political future. In November, the nationalist forces clashed. The Irish Party held what was to be a huge meeting at Belturbet, to be addressed by Kennedy, and O'Hanlon. However, Sinn Féin stole its thunder by holding a meeting on the same day in Bailieborough, addressed by Arthur Griffith and Eamonn de Valera.[98] By the beginning of 1918, there were twenty-seven Sinn Féin clubs reported in the county, compared to the combined total of eighteen of the United Irish League and the Ancient Order of Hibernians.

Sinn Féin continued its organizing activities, identifying itself with food shortages as an issue relevant to daily life, and strongly supporting the anti-conscription campaign. Conscription had ceased to be a mere threat and the Bill was passed in Westminster on 16 April. The Irish Party also opposed conscription, and withdrew from Westminster. They were supported by local government bodies, but were accused of being weak and ineffectual with regard to conscription and of yielding to partition, by Sinn Féin. An anti-conscription protest meeting on 20 April at Cavan was attended by an estimated 8000, at another in Virginia, attendance was estimated between fifteen and twenty thousand.[99] This was followed on Sunday 21 April by an anti-conscription pledge taken at all churches. On the same day, the death of Samuel Young, who had represented the county in parliament since 1892, was announced. Sinn Féin's opportunity had arrived. J.F. O'Hanlon was selected as the candidate for the Irish Parliamentary Party. Not only was he well known as an urban councillor and outspoken nationalist, he also had the resources of the United Irish League, the Ancient Order of Hibernians, and the *Anglo–Celt* to aid his campaign. Arthur Griffith opposed him as the Sinn

Féin candidate. At the end of May, Sinn Féin leaders were arrested, including Griffith and de Valera, and meetings were prohibited, as a result of the 'German plot'. Election work was carried on by many of the Catholic clergy of East Cavan, including those of Cootehill, Shercock, Virginia, and Castlerahan. However, Dr Finnegan forbade them to appear on public platforms. While novenas were being offered all over the country during this month, for an end to the war, Cavan people concentrated all their attention on the by-election. Griffith beat O'Hanlon in the by-election although only by one thousand votes.

Not only were the nationalists actively opposing the threat of conscription, so too were many Protestants in the county, particularly the farming class, that class, Catholic and Protestant, which had been the despair of recruiting officers. One anti-conscription meeting held in Upper Killinkere appealed to

> Orangemen to form defence committees and show that if the worst came to the worst they will cooperate with their Catholic neighbours and fellow countrymen to retain in the soil the last remnant of an already insufficient and dwindling population.[100]

Intelligence notes reported the increase in strength and numbers of Sinn Féin, and estimated that its adherents outnumbered those of the Irish Parliamentary Party by three to one.[101] The plans to introduce conscription to Ireland were eventually abandoned in the face of fierce opposition, and a voluntary recruiting scheme was established in its place in August, with as poor results as previously. By November the war was over. This was greeted with a sigh of relief by the press in Cavan, but also with an air of impatience and anxiety for Ireland's political future. The conscription crisis had consolidated the change in Irish nationalism. Sinn Féin overwhelmed the Irish Parliamentary Party in the general election in December, winning seventy-three seats including both seats in Cavan, Arthur Griffith and Peter Paul Galligan representing the county.

The period of the war had witnessed many changes in the county. The outbreak of the war had relieved the tension over the home rule issue. For a period, nationalists and unionists buried their differences in a cooperative war effort. Each group had its own reasons. Redmond had committed the nationalists to the policy of supporting the war, at home and abroad. The unionists, by tradition and declarations of loyalty, were equally bound to the war effort, but also by their fear of, and opposition to home rule, and the desire to prove their loyalty. The face of nationalism changed irrevocably during the period of the war. The parliamentary party lost its previously unchallenged position of authority, while the extreme nationalists, represented by Sinn Féin, with their anti-war policies, gained in strength and authority. The county had sent many of its young men, Protestant and Catholic, nationalist and unionist, to fight and die on battlefields far away. According to the papers of Col. Maurice

Moore, only 260 former National Volunteers returned to Cavan after the war.[102] Only four battalions of the county regiment, the Royal Irish Fusiliers, existed at the end of the war. The first battalion, sent to France as part of the expeditionary force, had fatalities of over 1000 men, the usual number of a complete battalion. The ninth battalion, Cavan, Armagh, and Monaghan unionists, lost 700, excluding casualties. 'In all 3181 men of the regiment died in the war, and perhaps five times that number were wounded'.[103] This does not take into consideration all the other regiments where Cavan men were to be found, nor those who enlisted outside the county, or the country.

When those who survived returned they found a very different situation. The unionists had been abandoned by their Ulster brethren, willing to accept exclusion from a Dublin parliament, and from Cavan among other counties. Those former National Volunteers found that opinion had swung against them and what they had been fighting for. The issue of home rule became obsolete as Sinn Féin dedicated itself to a fully independent Ireland. Over the four years of the war, both unionists and nationalists had largely abandoned support for, and sympathy with the war effort. Farmers and their sons, Catholic and Protestant, had refused to enlist. Overall, the war became peripheral as more immediate domestic concerns dominated. For those who returned, nationalist or unionist, there was little space for them in the new scheme of things. Ulster unionism glorified its war sacrifices, but Cavan had been clearly abandoned by Ulster unionism, and unionists in the county found that they had more in common with their southern counterparts, isolated, and politically ineffectual. Nationalism, riding high on the wave of now popular antiwar policies, had no place for those who had answered the call to arms for the home rule cause. They were as peripheral and neglected then as they have been in Irish historiography since.

Notes

ABBREVIATIONS

A.F.M.	John O'Donovan (ed.), *Annals of the kingdom of Ireland by the four masters* (7 vols, Dublin, 1851)
A.L.C.	W.M. Hennessy (ed.), *The annals of Loch Cé* (2 vols, London, 1871)
Ann. Clon.	Denis Murphy (ed.), *The annals of Clonmacnoise, being annals of Ireland from the earliest period to AD 1408* (Dublin, 1896)
Ann. Conn.	A.M. Freeman (ed.), *Annála Connacht: the annals of Connacht* (Dublin, 1944)
Arch. Hib.	*Archivium Hibernicum*
A.U.	W.M. Hennessy, Bartholomew Mac Carthy (eds), *Annála Uladh, annals of Ulster* (4 vols, Dublin, 1187–1901)
B.A.S Jnl.	*Breifne Antiquarian and Historical Society Journal*
B.L.	British Library, London
Cal. Carew	*Calendar of the Carew manuscripts, 1515–1625* (6 vols, London, 1867–73)
Cal. S.P. Ire.	*Calendar of state papers relating to Ireland, 1509–1670* (24 vols, London, 1860–1911)
Coll. Hib.	*Collectanea Hibernica*
H.C.	Parliamentary papers, House of Commons series
H.M.C.	Historical Manuscripts Commission
N.A.	National Archives, Dublin
N.L.I.	National Library of Ireland, Dublin
P.R.O.	Public Record Office, London
R.I.A. Procs.	*Proceedings of the Royal Irish Academy*
R.S.A.I. Jn.	*Journal of the Royal Society of Antiquaries of Ireland*
S.P.O.	State Paper Office
TCD	Trinity College, Dublin

INTRODUCTION *Raymond Gillespie*

1 Philip O'Connell, *The diocese of Kilmore; its history and antiquities* (Dublin, 1937), p. xxiii.
2 See, for example, the comments in Raymond Gillespie and Gerard Moran (eds), '*A various country':essays in Mayo history, 1500–1900* (Westport, 1987), pp. 13–14.
3 For an examination of this idea in another south Ulster–north Leinster context see Raymond Gillespie and Harold O'Sullivan (eds), *The borderlands: essays on the history of the Ulster–Leinster border* (Belfast, 1989).
4 For the details see David Hempton and Myrtle Hill, *Evangelical protestantism in Ulster society, 1740–1890* (London, 1992), pp. 86–90.
5 J.C. Beckett, *Protestant dissent in Ireland, 1687–1780* (London, 1948), pp. 55–8.
6 O'Connell, *Kilmore*, p. xii.
7 O'Connell, *Kilmore*, pp. xxxviii–xlviii, the quotation is on p. xliv.

8 W.E. Vaughan and A.J. Fitzpatrick (eds), *Irish historical statistics: population, 1821–1971* (Dublin, 1978), p. 317. For estimates of pre-Famine migration J.H. Johnson, 'The distribution of Irish emmigration in the decade before the Great Famine' in *Irish Geography*, xxi (1987–8), p. 82.

9 For an example of this sort of re-creation W.H. Crawford, 'Economy and society in south Ulster in the eighteenth century' in *Clogher Record*, viii (1975), pp. 241–58.

PERSPECTIVES ON THE MAKING OF THE CAVAN LANDSCAPE
P.J. Duffy

1 W.J. Smyth, 'The making of Ireland: agendas and perspectives in cultural geography', in B.J. Graham, L.J. Proudfoot (eds), *An historical geography of Ireland* (London, 1993), p. 399.

2 David Lowenthal and H.C. Prince, 'The English landscape' in *The Geographical Review*, liv (1964), p. 310.

3 Seamus Heaney, 'The sense of the past' in *History Ireland*, i, no. 4 (1993), p. 33.

4 See P.J. Duffy, 'Conflicts in heritage and tourism' in Ullrick Kockel (ed.), *Culture, tourism and development* (Liverpool, 1994), pp. 77–86.

5 Lowenthal and Prince, 'The English landscape', p. 325.

6 For example Henry Glassie, *Passing the time in Ballymenone* (Dublin, 1982).

7 Pat Sheerin, 'The narrative creation of place: the example of Yeats', in Timothy Collins (ed.), *Decoding the landscape* (Galway, 1994), p. 151.

8 Sir James Perrott, *The chronicle of Ireland, 1584–1608*, ed. Herbert Wood (Dublin, 1933), p. 84 and Bernadette Cunningham's essay in this volume.

9 Ciaran Brady, 'The O'Reillys of Breifne and the problem of "surrender and regrant"' in *Breifne*, vi, no. 23 (1985), pp. 233–62.

10 Perrott, *Chronicle of Ireland*, p. 114.

11 The Revd George Hill in his *Historical account of the plantation in Ulster* (Belfast, 1877), suggested that the use of English terms of liquid measurement, such as pints and pottles, for land areas in Breifne possibly was a reflection of longstanding English commercial influences from the pale, (p. 112).

12 P. O Gallachair (ed.), '1622 survey of Cavan' in *Breifne*, i, no. 1 (1958), p. 61.

13 Oliver Davies, 'The castles of county Cavan' in *Ulster Journal of Archaeology*, 3rd ser., xi (1948), p. 115.

14 Quoted in Philip O'Connell, *The schools and scholars of Breiffne* (Dublin 1942), p. 77.

15 *The plantation of Ulster* (Dublin 1984), p. 14.

16 Sir William Wilde, *Memoir of Gabriel Berenger* (Dublin, 1880), p. 36.

17 P.J. Duffy, 'Farney in 1634: an examination of Thomas Raven's survey of the Essex estate' in *Clogher Record*, ix, no. 3 (1983), pp. 245–56.

18 Robinson, *Plantation of Ulster*, p. 87.

19 O Gallachair, '1622 survey', p. 67.

20 P.J. Duffy, 'The evolution of estate properties in south Ulster 1600–1900' in W.J. Smyth and Kevin Whelan (eds), *Common Ground, essays on the historical geography of Ireland* (Cork, 1988), pp. 90–9.

21 T. Jones Hughes, 'Landholding and settlement in the counties of Meath and Cavan in the nineteenth century' in Patrick O'Flanagan, Paul Ferguson and Kevin Whelan (eds), *Rural Ireland modernisation and change 1600–1900* (Cork, 1987), p. 105.

22 Jones Hughes, 'Landholding and settlement', p. 130.

23 P.J. Duffy, *Landscapes of south Ulster, a parish atlas of the diocese of Clogher* (Belfast, 1993), pp. 1–24.

24 Thomas McErlean, 'The Irish townland system of landscape organisation' in T. Reeves Smyth and Fred Hammond (eds), *Landscape archaeology of Ireland* (B.A.R. British series 116, Oxford, 1983), pp. 315–39.

25 See W. H. Crawford, 'The significance of landed estates in Ulster 1600–1820' in *Irish Economic and Social History*, xvii (1990), p. 61.

26 Duffy, *Landscapes of south Ulster*, pp. 19–20.

27 See Donncha O Corráin, 'The future for Irish placenames' in Art O Maolfabhail (ed.), *The placenames of Ireland in the third millennium* (Dublin, 1992), pp. 33–45.

28 See Jones Hughes, 'Landholding and settlement', p. 128.

29 Sheerin, 'Narrative creation of place', p. 153.

30 See Catherine Nash, 'Embodying the nation—the west of Ireland landscape and Irish identity' in Barbara O'Connor and Michael Cronin (eds), *Tourism in Ireland: a critical analysis* (Cork, 1993), p. 108; also David Brett, 'The construction of heritage' in O'Connor and Cronin (eds), *Tourism in Ireland*, p. 180.

31 Brian Graham, 'Heritage conservation and revisionist nationalism in Ireland' in G.J. Ashworth and P.J. Larkham (eds), *Building a new heritage—tourism, culture and identity in the new Europe* (London, 1994), pp. 147, 156.

32 See, for example, Virginia Crossman and Dympna McLoughlin, 'A peculiar eclipse: E. Estyn Evans and Irish studies' in *The Irish Review*, xv (Spring 1994), pp. 75–95.

CAVAN: A MEDIEVAL BORDER AREA *Ciaran Parker*

1 *A.F.M., A.U.,* 1128; This event is included under the year 1126 in *Miscellaneous Irish annals (A.D. 1114–1437)*, ed. Séamus Ó hInnse (Dublin, 1947).

2 See Katharine Simms, 'The O'Reillys and the kingdom of east Breifne' in *Breifne*, v no. 19, (1979), p. 318, n. 9.

3 *A.F.M.,* 1155, 1161, 1162; *A.U.,* 1161; Eamonn de hÓir (ed.), 'Annála as Breifne' in *Breifne*, iv, no. 13 (1970), p. 62.

4 See A.J. Otway-Ruthven, *A history of medieval Ireland* (London, 1968), pp. 62–3.

5 G.H. Orpen (ed.), *The song of Dermot and the earl* (Oxford, 1892), lines 1740, 1788, 1909.

6 *A.F.M.,* 1184; *A.L.C.,* 1198.

7 *A.L.C.,* 1186.

8 G.H. Orpen, *Ireland under the Normans* (4 vols, Oxford, 1911–20), iii, p. 32.

9 Orpen, *Ireland under the Normans*, iii, p. 32; Oliver Davies, 'The castles of county Cavan: part 1' in *Ulster Journal of Archaeology*, 3rd ser, x (1947), pp. 77–8. They may have been built in association with an unsuccessful attack on the Uí Ruairc in 1196 (*A.L.C.,* 1196).

10 Oliver Davies and D.B. Quinn (eds), 'The Irish pipe roll of 14 John, 1211–12' in *Ulster Journal of Archaeology*, 3rd ser. iv, supplement (July 1941), pp. 22–5. There is no evidence to support Professor Otway-Ruthven's argument that the castles were built by de Lacy prior to his forfeiture. (Otway-Ruthven, *Medieval Ireland*, pp. 89–90).

11 Davies, Quinn (eds), 'The Irish pipe roll, 1211–12', p. 44.

12 *A.L.C., A.F.M., Ann. Clon.,* 1220; de hÓir, 'Annála as Breifne', p. 63. For a discussion of the origins of Clough Oughter Castle see Connleth Manning, 'Clough Oughter Castle' in *Breifne*, viii, no. 1 (1990), pp. 20–38.

13 W.W. Shirley (ed.), *Royal and other historical letters illustrative of the reign of Henry III* (2 vols, London, Rolls series, 1862), i, pp. 500–3; *A.F.M.,* 1226.

14 *Ann. Clon., Ann. Conn., A.F.M., A.L.C., A.U.,* 1233; de hÓir, 'Annála as Breifne', p. 63.

15 *Ann. Conn., A.F.M., A.U.,* 1250.

16 *Ann. Conn.*, 1255.
17 de hÓir, 'Annála as Breifne', p. 63.
18 *Ann. Conn., A.L.C., A.F.M., A.U.*, 1256; de hÓir, 'Annála as Breifne', pp. 63–4. Of these annals the most detailed descriptions of the battle and of the events leading up to it is contained in the *Ann. Conn.*
19 On Eoghan na féasóige's death in 1449 he was described as lord of the two Breifnes. (*A.U.*, 1449.)
20 James Carney (ed.), *A genealogical history of the O'Reillys* (Cavan, 1959), pp. 73, 115.
21 Carney, *Genealogical history*, pp. 75, 116.
22 *Ann. Conn., A.F.M., A.L.C., A.U.*, 1293, 1298; Carney, *Genealogical history*, pp. 73, 114.
23 *Ann. Conn., A.F.M., A.U.*, 1317; de hÓir, 'Annála as Breifne', p. 65.
24 *Ann. Conn.*, 1350, 1342; *Ann. Conn., A.F.M., A.U.*, 1370, 1391.
25 Otway-Ruthven, *Medieval Ireland*, p. 216, n. 75.
26 James Mills (ed.), *Calendar of the justiciary rolls or proceedings in the court of the justiciar of Ireland. 1305–1307* (Dublin, 1914), p. 186.
27 Seamas Pender (ed.), 'The O Clery Book of Genealogies' in *Analecta Hibernica*, no. 18 (1951), p. 109.
28 de hÓir, 'Annála as Breifne', p. 65; For the history of the friary see Aubrey Gwynn and Neville Hadcock, *Medieval religious houses: Ireland* (London, 1970), p. 245.
29 *Ann. Conn., A.F.M., A.U.*, 1369; de hÓir, 'Annála as Breifne', p. 66.
30 H.J. Lawlor (ed.), 'A calendar of the register of Archbishop Sweteman' in *R.I.A. Procs.* , xxix, sect. C (1911), pp. 233, 237–41.
31 Carney, *Genealogical history*, pp. 62, 105.
32 *Ann. Clon., Ann. Conn., A.F.M., A.U.*, 1328; de hÓir, 'Annála as Breifne', p. 65.
33 James Graves (ed.), *A roll of the proceedings of the king's council in Ireland, 16 Richard II* (Rolls series, London, 1877), pp. 192–6.
34 P.R.O., E.101/242/4.
35 *Ann. Conn., A.F.M, A.U.*, 1336.
36 Carney, *Genealogical history*, pp. 63, 106. For the Tuites' lands in southern Cavan see A. J. Otway-Ruthven, 'The partition of the de Verdon lands in Ireland in 1332' in *R.I.A., Procs.*, lxvi, sect. C (1967), p. 411.
37 Carney, *Genealogical history*, p. 11.
38 Carney, *Genealogical history*, pp. 62, 106.
39 *Ann. Conn., A.F.M.*, 1358.
40 *A.F.M., Ann. Conn.*, 1413; The Breifne annals states that this was in retaliation for the capture of Tomás Óg's brother Seán. (de hÓir, 'Annála as Breifne', p. 67).
41 *A.F.M.*, 1453; In the early fifteenth century they had also fought for the Uí Ruairc, Mac Raghnaill and Mac Diarmada. (*Ann. Conn.*, 1405, 1416, 1434.)
42 *Ann. Conn., A.F.M., A.U.*, 1460; de hÓir, 'Annála as Breifne', p. 69.
43 Edmund Curtis, *Richard II in Ireland and submissions of the Irish chiefs* (Oxford, 1927), pp. 200–1.
44 See the genealogical table in Ciaran Parker, 'The O'Reillys of east Breifne' in *Breifne*, viii, no. 2 (1991), p. 177.
45 *Misc. Ir. Annals* ed. Ó hInnse, 1396.
46 *Misc. Ir. Annals* ed. Ó hInnse, 1396, 1397.
47 *Ann. Conn., A.F.M., A.L.C., A.U.*, 1400; *Misc. Ir. annals*, ed. Ó hInnse, 1401, 1402; de hOir, 'Annála as Breifne', p. 67.
48 *Ann. Conn., A.F.M., A.U.*, 1418; de hÓir, 'Annála as Breifne', p. 67.
49 *Ann. Conn.*, 1422; de hÓir, 'Annála as Breifne', p. 68; D.A. Chart (ed.), *Primate Swayne's register* (Belfast, 1935), pp. 88, 90.
50 *Ann. Conn., A.F.M.*, 1428; de hÓir, 'Annála as Breifne', p. 68.
51 *A.F.M.*, 1430.

52 Henry Piers, *A chorographical description of the county of West-meath in 1685* (Meath Archaeological and Historical Society, 1981), p. 119. I am indebted to Dr Katharine Simms for this reference.

53 H.F. Berry (ed.), *Statute rolls of the parliament of Ireland, reign of King Henry VI* (Dublin, 1907), p. 43.

54 See K.W. Nicholls, *Gaelic and gaelicised Ireland in the later middle ages* (Dublin, 1972). p. 119.

55 Edward Tresham (ed.), *Rotulorum patentium et clausorum cancellariae Hiberniae calendarium* (Dublin, 1828), p. 141.

56 Berry, *Statute rolls ... Henry VI*, p. 451.

57 For a discussion of these coins see W.A. Seaby and M. Dolley, 'Le money del O Raylly' in *British Numismatic Journal*, xxxvi (1967), p. 116; and the comments of Michael Dolley in Art Cosgrove (ed.), *A new history of Ireland: ii, medieval Ireland* (Oxford, 1987), pp. 822–3.

58 *Ann. Conn., A.F.M., A.L.C., A.U.,* 1447; de hÓir, 'Annála as Breifne', p. 69; 'The annals of Ireland from the year 1443 to 1468 translated from the Irish by ... Duald Mac Firbis' in *Miscellany of the Irish Archaeological Society,* i (Dublin, 1846), p. 219.

59 *Ann. Conn., A.F.M., A.L.C., A.U.,* 1449; 'The annals of Ireland', p. 222.

60 See the genealogical table in Parker, 'The O'Reillys of east Breifne', p. 177.

61 Edmund Curtis, 'Richard, duke of York as viceroy of Ireland, 1447–1460' in *R.S.A.I. Jn.,* lxii (1932), p. 167.

62 *A.F.M., A.U.,* 1450.

63 'The annals of Ireland', pp. 232–3.

64 *A.F.M., A.U.,* 1460; de hÓir, 'Annála as Breifne', p. 69.

65 *A.F.M., A.U.,* 1468.

66 *Ann. Conn., A.F.M., A.U.,* 1470.

67 *Ann. Conn., A.F.M., A.U.,* 1475.

68 *A.F.M.,* 1469.

69 *Ann. Conn., A.F.M.,* 1427; de hOir, 'Annála as Breifne', p. 68.

70 Carney, *Genealogical history,* pp. 70, 112.

71 *Ann. Conn., A.L.C., A.F.M., A.U.,* 1491; de hOir, 'Annála as Breifne', p. 70.

72 *A.F.M.,* 1485.

73 *A.F.M.,* 1492, 1494.

74 *Ann. Conn., A.F.M., A.L.C., A.U.,* 1514; de hOir, 'Annála as Breifne', p. 71.

75 *A.F.M.,* 1524.

76 *Ann. Conn., A.F.M., A.L.C.,* 1526; de hOir, 'Annála as Breifne', p. 71.

77 Ciaran Brady, 'The O'Reillys of east Breifne and the problem of "surrender and regrant" ' in *Breifne,* vi, no. 23 (1985), p. 239.

78 *Ann. Conn., A.F.M.,* 1536, *A.L.C., A.U.,* 1535; de hOir, 'Annála as Breifne', p. 71. The annals differ on the date of death.

79 Tresham, *Rotulorum patentium et clausorum cancellariae Hiberniae calendarium,* p. 196.

80 Tresham, *Rotulorum patentium et clausorum cancellariae Hiberniae calendarium,* p. 227; *A.F.M.,* 1503.

81 Tresham, *Rotulorum patentium et clausorum cancellariae Hiberniae calendarium,* p. 182. For a brief discussion of the links between the Betaghs and the Uí Raghallaigh, see Parker, 'The O'Reillys of east Breifne', p. 175.

82 *Ann. Conn., A.F.M., A.L.C., A.U.,* 1349.

83 *A.F.M.,* 1485, 1489.

THE ANGLICISATION OF EAST BREIFNE *Bernadette Cunningham*

 1 *Cal. S.P. Ire., 1574–85*, pp. 184, 170; Ciaran Brady, 'The O'Reillys of east Breifne and the problem of "surrender and regrant"' in *Breifne*, vi, no. 23 (1985) pp. 233–62.
 2 Marriage networks are one indication of political alliances. For mid-sixteenth century O'Reilly marriage links with both the O'Neills and O'Donnells see Eamonn de hÓir (ed), 'Annála as Breifne' in *Breifne*, iv, no. 13 (1970), p. 73; for links with the O'Ferralls, de hÓir, 'Annála as Breifne' p. 74.
 3 Katharine Simms, 'Warfare in the medieval Gaelic lordships', in *Irish Sword*, xii, no. 47 (1976), pp. 99–100; K.W. Nicholls, *Land, law and society in sixteenth century Ireland* (Dublin, 1976), p. 11.
 4 *Cal. Carew, 1515–74*, p. 240.
 5 For a detailed discussion see Katharine Simms, *From kings to warlords* (Woodbridge, 1987), pp. 41–59.
 6 *A.F.M.*, 1506, 1510.
 7 *A.F.M.*, 1520.
 8 *A.F.M.*, 1502.
 9 *A.F.M.*, 1504.
10 *A.F.M.*, 1492; He also received support from the earl of Kildare, Art Cosgrove (ed.), *A new history of Ireland: ii, medieval Ireland* (Oxford, 1987), p. 633.
11 *A.F.M.*, 1506.
12 *A.F.M.*, 1510.
13 *A.F.M.*, 1512, 1514; De hÓir, 'Annála as Breifne', p.71; On Kildare's role see Colm Lennon, *Sixteenth-century Ireland: the incomplete conquest* (Dublin, 1994), pp. 74–7.
14 *A.F.M.*, 1524, 1526.
15 *A.F.M.*, 1536, 1510.
16 James Carney (ed.), *A genealogical history of the O'Reillys*, (Cavan, 1959), pp. 40–2; T.W. Moody, F.X. Martin, F.J. Byrne, (eds), *A new history of Ireland: ix, maps, geneaologies, lists* (Oxford, 1984), pp. 164–5.
17 *A.F.M.*, 1537.
18 *A.F.M.*, 1552. *Cal. Carew, 1515–74*, p. 240.
19 Nicholls, *Land, law and society*, pp. 7–8.
20 *A.F.M.*, 1485.
21 *A.F.M.*, 1494, 1496, 1502, 1512.
22 Brady, 'Surrender and regrant', p. 247.
23 The activities of the Magaurans are not recorded in the Annals of the Four Masters after 1543. For the overall trend in Gaelic society see K.W. Nicholls, *Gaelic and gaelicised Ireland* (Dublin, 1972), pp. 10–11; Nicholls, *Land, law and society*, p. 7.
24 Brady, 'Surrender and regrant'; Simms, *From kings to warlords*, pp. 112–14, 136–7.
25 *A.F.M.*, 1447. See also Ciaran Parker's essay above.
26 Aubrey Gwynn and Neville Hadcock, *Medieval religious houses: Ireland* (London, 1970), p. 181. John O'Reilly, abbot of St Mary's, Kells, was made bishop of Kilmore in 1465; Philip O'Reilly was abbot in 1494; Dermot O'Reilly was abbot in 1523.
27 M. Dolley and W.A. Seaby, 'Le money del O Raylly [O'Reilly's money]' in *British Numismatic Journal*, xxxvi (1967), pp. 114–17.
28 De hÓir, 'Annála as Breifne', p. 72; P.R.O., SP63/102/116 (1583); Carney, *Genealogical history*, pp. 28, 37; Brady, 'Surrender and regrant', pp. 251–2; Philip O'Connell, *The diocese of Kilmore* (Dublin, 1937), pp. 279–318.
29 See. P.J. Duffy, 'The evolution of estate properties in south Ulster, 1600–1900' in W.J. Smyth and Kevin Whelan (eds), *Common ground: essays on the historical geography of Ireland* (Cork, 1988), pp. 93–4, esp. fig. 5.4.
30 *Cal. Carew, 1515–74*, p. 63.
31 *Cal. Carew, 1515–74*, p. 123.

32 *Cal. Carew, 1515–74,* pp. 261, 263.
33 *Cal. Carew, 1515–74,* p. 376.
34 *Cal. Carew, 1515–74,* p. 240.
35 *Cal. Carew, 1515–74,* pp. 376–7.
36 *Cal. S.P. Ire, 1588–92,* p. 82.
37 Instructions to Sussex, P.R.O., SP63/6/41, 3 July 1562.
38 *Cal. S.P. Ire., 1509–73,* p. 176, 17 July 1561.
39 Brady, 'Surrender and regrant'.
40 *Cal. Carew, 1515–74,* pp. 330–44.
41 *Cal. Carew, 1515–74,* p. 338.
42 N.P. Canny, *The Elizabethan conquest: a pattern established, 1565–76* (Hassocks, 1976), pp. 93–116.
43 P.R.O., SP63/66/65, 31 May 1579; SP63/67/9, 17 June 1579; SP63/67/12i, 6 June 1579.
44 *Cal. S.P. Ire., 1588–92,* p. 82.
45 As late as 1586 Sir Henry Bagenal was making recommendations that Ulster should be shired, *Cal. S.P. Ire., 1586–88,* pp. 72–3.
46 P.R.O., SP63/117/7, 3 June 1586.
47 *Cal. Carew, 1515–74,* pp. 376–7.
48 *Cal. S.P. Ire., 1574–85,* pp. 183–6; P.R.O., SP63/69/76, 31 Oct. 1579.
49 *Cal. S.P. Ire., 1574–85,* p. 195.
50 P.R.O. SP63/76/5, 3 Sept. 1580.
51 *Cal. S.P. Ire., 1574–85,* p. 320, 21 Sept. 1581.
52 Aodh Conallach O'Reilly had been knighted by Sir William Drury in 1579 at the time arrangements were being made to shire Cavan, P.R.O., SP63/67/12, 26 June 1579.
53 Carney, *Genealogical history,* p. 28.
54 P.R.O., SP63/102/64 June 1583; SP63/102/80; SP63/103/3 July 1583; SP63/104/69 Sept. 1583; *Cal. S.P. Ire., 1574–85,* p. 451.
55 James Carney (ed), *Poems on the O'Reillys* (Dublin, 1950), poem 14, lines 1841–4.
56 *A.L.C.,* 1581.
57 Carney, *Poems on the O'Reillys,* poem 8, lines 993–6.
58 *A.L.C.,* 1584.
59 P.R.O., SP63/102/60, 4 June 1583.
60 P.R.O., SP63/102/64, 4 June 1583.
61 P.R.O., SP63/102/64.
62 P.R.O., SP63/102/64.
63 P.R.O., SP63/102/116.
64 P.R.O., SP63/103/3, 2 July 1583.
65 P.R.O., SP63/104/69, 12 Sept. 1583.
66 P.R.O., SP63/103/3, 2 July 1583.
67 P.R.O., SP63/105/58, 7 Nov. 1583.
68 *A.F.M.,* 1583, and O'Donovan's note *d* to that entry. A division of east Breifne had been the lords justice's intention even before the death of Aodh Conallach in 1583, see P.R.O., SP63/100/50, 25 March 1583.
69 P.R.O., SP63/100/50.
70 Brady, 'Surrender and regrant', pp. 246–7; *A.F.M.,* 1583, note *d*; P.R.O., SP63/111/43. 6 Aug. 1584; SP63/113/9, 4 Dec. 1584.
71 *Cal. S. P, Ire., 1588–92,* p. 540.
72 Brady, 'Surrender and regrant'.
73 *Cal. S.P. Ire., 1586–88,* pp. 264–64, 19 Feb. 1587; Brady, 'Surrender and regrant', p. 247.
74 *Cal. S.P. Ire., 1586–88,* pp. 207–8.

75   P.R.O., SP63/147/36, SP63/147/37, 24 Oct. 1589.
76   *Cal. S.P. Ire., 1588–92*, p. 539.
77   *Cal. S.P. Ire., 1596–97*, p. 181.
78   *Cal. S.P. Ire., 1586–88*, pp. 466–7, 9 Jan. 1588.
79   Carney, *Poems on the O'Reillys*, poem 4.
80   *Cal. S.P. Ire., 1588–92*, p. 362, 10 Sept. 1590; see also P.R.O., SP63/160/31, 10 Oct. 1591.
81   Carney, *Poems on the O'Reillys*, lines 2312–28; Bernadette Cunningham, 'Women and Gaelic literature, 1500–1800', in Margaret MacCurtain and Mary O'Dowd (eds), *Women in early modern Ireland* (Edinburgh, 1991), esp. pp. 148–52; a parallel military role was played by Fionuala MacDonnell (Inion Dubh), mother of Aodh ruadh O'Donnell, in defending her son's rights during his imprisonment; Ciaran Brady, 'Political women and reform in Tudor Ireland' in MacCurtain and O'Dowd, *Women in early modern Ireland*, p. 78.
82   The lord deputy considered that Pilib was 'likely to prove the best or the worst subject that has left Dublin Castle these 40 years', *Cal. S.P. Ire., 1588–92*, p. 462; Ciaran Brady, 'Sixteenth-century Ulster and the failure of Tudor reform', in Ciaran Brady, Mary O'Dowd and Brian Walker (eds), *Ulster, an illustrated history* (London, 1989), pp. 97–98; Paul Walsh (ed.), *The life of Aodh Ruadh Ó Domhnaill.* (2 vols, Irish texts society, London, 1948–57) i, pp. 13–43; ii, pp. 54, 208–9.
83   *Cal. S.P. Ire., 1598–99*, p. 13, 12 Jan. 1598.
84   Brady, 'Sixteenth-century Ulster and the failure of Tudor reform', pp. 95–9.
85   *Cal. S.P. Ire., 1592–96*, p. 251, 24 May 1594.
86   Brady, 'Surrender and regrant', pp. 260–1.
87   P.R.O. SP63/180/10, 4 June 1595 (recte 1596); *Cal. S.P. Ire., 1596–97*, p. 35.
88   *Cal. S.P. Ire., 1592–96*, p. 529, 8 June 1596.
89   *Cal. S.P. Ire., 1596–97*, pp. 70, 72.
90   *Cal. S.P. Ire., 1596–97*, p. 105.
91   Carney, *Poems on the O'Reillys*, poem 11.
92   Carney, *Poems on the O'Reillys*, lines 1297–1300.
93   Carney, *Poems on the O'Reillys*, lines 1449–60.
94   *Cal. S.P. Ire., 1596–97*, p. 102.
95   Carney, *Poems on the O'Reillys*, lines 1133–6.
96   Carney, *Poems on the O'Reillys*, line 1436.
97   *Cal. S.P. Ire., 1596–97*, p. 102, 4 Sept. 1596.
98   *Cal. S.P. Ire., 1596–97*, p. 150, 18 Oct. 1596; see also p. 146, 10 Oct. 1596.
99   *A.F.M.*, 1596.
100 Carney, *Poems on the O'Reillys*, p. 202.
101 *Cal. S.P. Ire., 1598–99*, p. 178.
102 *Cal. S.P. Ire., 1598–99*, pp. 224, 237, Aug. 1598.
103 *Cal. S.P. Ire., 1599–1600*, pp. 328–30.
104 *Cal. S.P. Ire., 1599–1600*, p. 439.
105 P.R.O., SP63/207 pt.5/84, 4 Oct. 1600.
106 *Cal. S.P. Ire., 1601–03*, pp. 133, 172–3.
107 *Cal. S.P. Ire., 1601–03*, p. 283, 13 Jan. 1602.
108 *Cal. S.P. Ire., 1601–03*, p. 360, 10 April 1602.
109 Carney, *Poems on the O'Reillys*, pp. xii–xiii.

THE REFORMATION IN KILMORE BEFORE 1641 *Alan Ford*

1 Brendan Bradshaw, 'The Edwardian reformation in Ireland' in *Arch. Hib.*, xxxiv (1977), pp. 83–99; Brendan Bradshaw, 'The Elizabethans and the Irish' in *Studies*, lxvi (1977), pp. 38–50; Brendan Bradshaw, 'Sword, word and strategy in the reformation in Ireland' in *Historical Journal*, xxi (1978), pp. 475–502; N.P. Canny, 'Why the reformation failed in Ireland: une question mal posée' in *Journal of Ecclesiastical History*, xxx (1979), pp. 423–50; K.S. Bottigheimer, 'The failure of the reformation in Ireland: une question bien posée' in *Journal of Ecclesiastical History*, xxxvi (1985), pp. 196–207; Aidan Clarke, 'Varieties of uniformity: the first century of the Church of Ireland', in W.J. Shiels and Diana Wood (eds), *The churches, Ireland and the Irish* (Studies in Church History, xxv, Oxford, 1989), pp. 105–22; S.G. Ellis, 'Economic problems of the church: why the reformation failed in Ireland' in *Journal of Ecclesiastical History*, xli (1990), pp. 239–65.
2 J.S. Morrill, *The nature of the English revolution* (London, 1993), pp. 182–3.
3 Raymond Gillespie and Gerard Moran, 'Introduction: writing local history' in Raymond Gillespie and Gerard Moran (eds), *'A various country': essays in Mayo history 1500–1900* (Westport, 1987), pp. 11–23; T.C. Barnard, 'The political, material and mental culture of the Cork settlers, 1650–1700' in Patrick O'Flanagan and C.G. Buttimer (eds), *Cork: history and society. Interdisciplinary essays on the history of an Irish county* (Dublin, 1993), pp. 311–12; for a stimulating discussion of the relation between the national and the local from a later period and a different perspective, see Marilyn Silverman and P.H. Gulliver (eds), *Approaching the past: historical anthropology through Irish case studies* (New York, 1992), pp. 3–56.
4 The one major exception is James Murray's research on the reformation in the diocese of Dublin: 'Ecclesiastical justice and the enforcement of the reformation: the case of Archbishop Browne and the clergy of Dublin' in James McGuire, Kenneth Milne and Alan Ford (eds), *As by law established: the Church of Ireland since the reformation* (Dublin 1995), pp. 33–51. For a useful study of the developments of the Catholic church in Ulster see J.J. Silke, 'Some aspects of the reformation in Armagh province' in *Clogher Record*, xi (1984), pp. 342–63.
5 Ciaran Brady, 'Conservative subversives: the community of the pale and the Dublin administration' in P.J. Corish (ed.), *Radicals, rebels and establishments* (Historical Studies xv, Belfast, 1985), pp. 11–32; Aidan Clarke, 'Colonial identity in early seventeenth century Ireland' in T.W. Moody (ed.), *Nationality and the pursuit of national independence* (Historical Studies xi, Belfast, 1978), pp. 57–71; Colm Lennon, *The lords of Dublin in the age of reformation* (Dublin, 1989), pp. 128–218.
6 F.M. Powicke and E.B. Fryde (eds), *Handbook of British chronology* (2nd ed., London, 1961), pp. 352–61, 383–92.
7 Canny, 'Why the reformation failed', p. 450.
8 Bottigheimer, 'Failure of the reformation', pp. 196–7, 200–1.
9 P.J. Duffy, 'The evolution of estate properties in south Ulster 1600–1900' in W.J. Smith and Kevin Whelan (eds), *Common ground: essays on the historical geography of Ireland* (Cork, 1988), p. 93.
10 Philip O'Connell, *The diocese of Kilmore: its history and antiquities* (Dublin, 1937).
11 James Morrin (ed.), *Calendar of the patent and close rolls of chancery in Ireland* (3 vols., Dublin, 1861–3), i, 57; Aubrey Gwynn and R.N. Hadcock, *Medieval religious houses: Ireland* (London, 1970), p. 196; R.J. Hunter, 'The Ulster plantation in the counties of Armagh and Cavan', unpublished M.Litt. thesis, TCD, 1969, p. 442.
12 Ciaran Brady, 'The O'Reillys of east Breifne and the problem of "surrender and regrant" ' in *Breifne*, vi, no. 23 (1985), pp. 233–62; D.B. Quinn (ed.), 'Calendar of the Irish council book 1 March 1581 to 1 July 1586' in *Analecta Hibernica*, no. 24 (1967), p. 146.

13 Charles McNeill, 'The Perrot papers' in *Analecta Hibernica*, no. 12 (1943), pp. 11, 14–15; P.R.O., SP63/123/1 (*Cal. S.P. Ire., 1586–8*, p. 36).

14 Nor did he anticipate securing a significant income from the see. He only accepted it on condition that he could retain his deanery and other benefices *in commendam*: McNeill, 'The Perrot papers', p. 11; for his duties as a privy councillor see: P.R.O., SP63/128/98 (*Cal. S.P. Ire., 1586–88*, p. 283); *Cal. S.P. Ire., 1586–88*, pp. 13, 30, 60, 132, 221, 267, 328; *Cal. S.P. Ire., 1588–92*, pp. 142, 173; John Hagan (ed.), 'Miscellanea Vaticano-Hibernica' in *Arch. Hib.*, v (1916), pp. 164–5.; W.M. Brady, *The episcopal succession in England Scotland and Ireland, A.D. 1400 to 1875* (3 vols, Rome 1876–7), i, p. 281; see also Brian McCabe, 'An Elizabethan prelate: John Garvey (1527–1596)' in *Breifne*, vii, no. 25, (1987–8), pp. 594–604.

15 P.R.O., SP63/170/42 (*Cal. S.P. Ire., 1592–6*, p. 127); P.R.O., SP63/190/38 (*Cal. S.P. Ire., 1592–6*, p. 541); Powicke and Fryde, *Handbook of British chronology*, p. 358; J.B. Leslie, Biographical succession lists of Kilmore (Representative Church Body Library, Dublin, MS 61.2.11) [hereafter cited as Leslie, Kilmore clergy], pp. 7–8.

16 Brady, 'Surrender and regrant', pp. 261–2.

17 T.W. Moody, F.X. Martin and F.J. Byrne (eds), *A new history of Ireland: iii, early modern Ireland* (Oxford 1976), pp. 193–4.

18 Clogher, Derry, Dromore, Kilmore and Ardagh, Raphoe: Powicke and Fryde, *Handbook of British chronology*, pp. 352–61; J.C. Erck (ed.), *A repertory of the inrolments on the patent rolls of chancery in Ireland, commencing with the reign of James I* (1 vol, 2 parts, Dublin, 1846, 1852), i, pt. 1, pp. 30, 59.

19 See, for example, the efforts of the new bishop in Derry, Raphoe and Clogher, George Montgomery to gain control of his sees: A.F. Alexander (ed.), 'O'Kane papers' in *Analecta Hibernica*, no. 12 (1943), pp. 79–111; for the date of the document, see Alan Ford, *The protestant reformation in Ireland, 1590–1641* (Frankfurt, 1987), p. 182.

20 Ford, *Protestant reformation*, pp. 45–8.

21 P.R.O., Philadelphia Papers, 31/8/199/36 (*Cal. S.P. Ire., 1603–6*, pp. 389–90); P.R.O., Philadelphia Papers, 31/8/199/86 (*Cal. S.P. Ire., 1606–8*, p. 137); John McCavitt, ' "Good planets in their several spheares"—the establishment of the assize circuits in early seventeenth century Ireland' in *Irish Jurist*, n.s., xxiv (1989), pp. 258–9.

22 P.R.O., Philadelphia Papers, 31/8/199/36 (*Cal. S.P. Ire., 1603–6*, pp. 389–90); P.R.O., Philadelphia Papers, 31/8/199/86 (*Cal. S.P. Ire., 1606–8*, p. 137).

23 *Cal. S.P. Ire., 1606–8*, p. 64.

24 P.R.O., SP63/218/53 (*Cal. S.P. Ire., 1603–6*, p. 468); Henry Morley (ed.), *Ireland under Elizabeth and James the first* (London 1890), p. 361.

25 P.R.O., SP63/218/53 (*Cal. S.P. Ire., 1603–6*, p. 468).

26 P.R.O., SP63/217/63 (*Cal. S.P. Ire., 1603–6*, p. 317); P.R.O., SP63/215/92 (*Cal. S.P. Ire., 1603–6*, p. 86); another Irish speaker, Dugald Campbell, was nominated for Derry, but died before consecration: P.R.O., SP63/161/52, f. 119v; W.M. Brady, *Clerical and parochial records of Cork, Cloyne and Ross* (3 vols, Dublin, 1863–4), i, p. 65.

27 He is probably to be identified with the Pensioner who entered King's College, Cambridge in 1563 and gained his M.A. in 1571: J. Venn and J.A. Venn (eds), *Alumni Cantabrigienses, part I: from the earliest times to 1751* (4 vols., Cambridge, 1922–7); Sir Geoffrey Fenton suggests (though his phrasing is open to differing interpretations) that Draper was English: P.R.O., SP63/215/92 (*Cal. S.P. Ire., 1603–6*, pp. 86–7); but Davies thinks that he was Irish born: Morley, *Ireland under Elizabeth and James*, p. 377.

28 P.R.O., SP63/215/92 (*Cal. S.P. Ire., 1603–6*, pp. 86 f.; Erck, *Repeatory of the patent rolls*, i, pt. 1, pp. 30, 59; M.C. Griffith, *Irish patent rolls of James I* (Dublin, 1966), p. 13.

29 H.F. Berry (ed.), 'Probable early students of Trinity College, Dublin (being wards of the crown), 1599–1616' in *Hermathena*, xvi (1911), pp. 25–7.

30 Powicke and Fryde, *Handbook of British chronology*, p. 390; but see O'Connell, *Kilmore*, pp. 394–5; very few records survive of the appointment of Catholic priests to Kilmore for two decades after 1603: F.J. McKiernan, 'Kilmore priests' in *Breifne*, vi, no. 24 (1982); F.J. McKiernan (ed.), *Diocese of Kilmore: bishops and priests 1136–1988* (Cavan, 1989).

31 See the example of the Franciscan friars moving into private houses after their house in Cavan was closed in 1608: P.F. Moran (ed.), *Spicilegium Ossoriense* (3 vols., Dublin, 1874–84), i, p. 208.

32 Morley (ed.), *Ireland under Elizabeth and James*, p. 377.

33 N.A., MS RC9/1, pp. 98–101.

34 Morley (ed.), *Ireland under Elizabeth and James*, pp. 377–8.

35 See below, pp. 83; though it is not clear if these clergy conformed during or after Draper's episcopate.

36 P.R.O., SP63/222/96 (*Cal. S.P. Ire., 1606–8*, p. 214); Bodleian Library, Oxford, Carte Ms 61, f. 344; Ford *Protestant reformation*, pp. 159–69; P.R.O., SP63/231/4 (*Cal. S.P. Ire., 1611–14*, p. 3); Griffith, *Patent rolls*, p. 226.

37 P.R.O., SP63/232/21 (*Cal. S.P. Ire., 1611–14*, pp. 429–31); TCD, MS 567, f. 42v; Canice Mooney, 'The Franciscan first order friary at Dungannon' in *Seanchas Ardmhacha*, i (1954–5), pp. 72–3.

38 Hunter, 'Ulster plantation', pp. 58–9, 445–6.

39 James Ussher, *The whole works*, ed. C.R. Elrington and J.H. Todd, (17 vols., Dublin and London, 1847–64), i, app. v, p. lvii.

40 For an outline of the scheme, Philip Robinson, *The plantation of Ulster: British settlement in an Irish landscape, 1600–1670* (Dublin, 1984).

41 *Dictionary of National Biography*, sub George Montgomery; B.L., Cottonian MS Titus B XII, ff 669–675v, printed in E.P. Shirley (ed.), *Papers relating to the Church of Ireland (1631–9)* (London, 1874), pp. 25–37; and partially printed in T.F. Colby (ed.), *Ordnance survey of the county of Londonderry* (Dublin 1837), pp. 49–54.

42 T.W. Moody (ed.), 'Ulster plantation papers, 1608–13' in *Analecta Hibernica*, no. 8 (1938), p. 286; George Hill, *An historical account of the plantation in Ulster* (Belfast, 1877), p. 91; Michael Perceval-Maxwell, *The Scottish migration to Ulster in the reign of James I* (London, 1973), pp. 80–90.

43 TCD, MS 560, pp. 135–83.

44 P.J. Duffy, 'Geographical perspectives on the borderlands', in Raymond Gillespie and Harold O'Sullivan (eds), *The borderlands: essays on the history of the Ulster-Leinster border* (Belfast, 1989), pp. 12–13.

45 Robinson, *Plantation of Ulster*, pp. 70–1; TCD, MS 550, pp. 139–40.

46 Robinson, *Plantation of Ulster*, p. 83; Hunter, 'Ulster plantation', pp. 629–37.

47 For details of schoolmasters, see Hunter, 'Ulster plantation', pp. 636–7.

48 TCD, MS 550, pp. 139–183; the average value of benefices in Ardagh was £10 per annum, in Kilmore, just under £20 a year.

49 TCD, MS 550, pp. 144–5.

50 B.L., Add. MS 4756, f. 20.

51 E.S. Shuckburgh (ed.), *Two biographies of William Bedell, bishop of Kilmore* (Cambridge, 1902), pp. 103–4.

52 TCD, MS 550, pp. 146–7, 152–3.

208

Notes to pages 81–3

53 Shuckburgh, *Bedell*, p. 104.
54 TCD, MS 550, pp. 139–83.
55 Perceval-Maxwell, *Scottish migration to Ulster*, p. 325.
56 Venn, *Alumni Cantabrigienses*, sub Thomas Moigne.
57 He was consecrated in January 1613: Erck, *Repertory of the patent rolls*, i, pt. 1, p. 253; Griffith, *Patent rolls*, p. 237; H.J. Lawlor, *The fasti of St Patrick's, Dublin* (Dundalk, 1930), p. 47.
58 Tracing the origins of clergy is not always possible: in many cases the historian has to rely upon the evidence of the surname. See appendix pp. 96–8.
59 Venn, *Alumni Cantabrigienses*.
60 Leslie, Kilmore clergy, pp. 114, 143—Leslie's early date for Hollington is not supported by surviving documentary evidence.
61 Leslie, Kilmore clergy, pp. 114, 143; TCD, MS 550, pp. 146–7, 152–3.
62 Trinity: William Holliwell, John Patrick, Thomas Robinson, Laurence Robinson, William Roycroft, Faithful Teate see G.D. Burtchaell and T.U. Sadleir (eds), *Alumni Dublinenses* (London, 1924).
63 TCD, Ms 568, p. 153; Ussher, *Whole works*, xv, pp. 272–3.
64 Burtchaell and Sadleir, *Alumni Dublinenses* sub. Halliwell; Leslie, Kilmore clergy, pp. 112, 204.
65 TCD, MS 550, pp. 144–7; see also R.J. Hunter, 'The English undertakers in the plantation of Ulster, 1610–41' in *Breifne*, iv, no. 16 (1973), p. 495; on the fate of the Virginia church see R.J. Hunter, 'An Ulster plantation town—Virginia' in *Breifne*, iv, no. 13 (1970), pp. 50–1.
66 This was more frequent in the poorer north west of the diocese: Clonloher and Killargue, for example, were commonly held together: Leslie, Kilmore clergy, p. 112.
67 James Slacke, for instance, was vicar of Kinawley and Killesher in the county Fermanagh part of Kilmore, which he held as a non-resident with the rectories of Cleenish and Enniskillen in the diocese of Clogher until his death in 1634: Leslie, Kilmore clergy, p. 230; J.B. Leslie, *Clogher clergy and parishes* (Enniskillen, 1929), p. 132.
68 Ussher, *Whole works*, xv, p. 536.
69 Shuckburgh, *Bedell*, p. 40.
70 *Inquisitionum in officio rotulorum cancellariae Hiberniae* (2 vols, Dublin, 1829), ii, 22 Car. I, 23 Car. I; Hunter, 'English undertakers', p. 486.
71 Hunter, 'Ulster plantation', p. 495.
72 P.R.O., Philadelphia Papers, 31/8/201, pp. 373–4 (*Cal. S.P. Ire., 1608–10*, pp. 245–6).
73 Clarke, 'Varieties of uniformity', p. 115.
74 Leslie, Kilmore clergy; McKiernan, *Diocese of Kilmore* p. 58.
75 Leslie, Kilmore clergy; McKiernan, *Diocese of Kilmore*.
76 See appendix to the essay, pp. 96–8.
77 McKiernan, *Diocese of Kilmore*, pp. 41, 49, 55, 69, 104, 117; Leslie, Kilmore clergy, p. 277; TCD, MS 550, pp. 148–9.
78 See the O'Gowan incumbents listed for the following parishes in McKiernan, *Diocese of Kilmore*: Ballintemple, Crosserlough, Killinkere, Kilmore, Kilsherdany, Lara, and Mullagh; TCD, MS 550, pp. 146–9.
79 See above p. 76.
80 Robinson, *Plantation of Ulster*, app. 4; Moody, 'Ulster plantation papers 1608–13', pp. 204–5; see S. O'R. Mac Bradaigh, 'The Mac Bradaigh chiefs of Teallach Cearbhuill' in *Breifne*, vi, no. 24 (1982–6), p. 358; the strong native presence in Cavan was accentuated by the limited success of the plantation in attracting English

and especially Scots settlers: B.L., Cottonian MS Titus B X, f. 195 (*Cal. S.P. Ire., 1608–10*, p. 521).
81 See Ford, *Protestant reformation in Ireland*, pp. 168–70.
82 TCD, MS 550, pp. 144–5.
83 Ussher, *Whole works*, xv, p. 535; see below p. 95.
84 N.A., MS RC 9/1, p. 103; Burtchaell and Sadleir, *Alumni Dublinenses*; Ussher, *Whole works*, i, app v, p. lxix.
85 *A.F.M*, iv, p. 1189, note b.
86 M.J. O'Doherty, 'Students of the Irish College Salamanca (1595–1619)' in *Arch. Hib.*, ii (1913), p. 21; McKiernan, *Diocese of Kilmore*, pp. 151–3.
87 TCD, MS 832, ff 15–17, 95, 67.
88 B.L., Add. MS 4756, f. 19v. The only precise indication of native lay conformity in the Ulster plantation comes from a parish in Armagh in 1622, when the minister reported that a mere 2.4 per cent of Irish households attended the protestant church: N.L.I., MS 18,646.
89 Shuckburgh, *Bedell*, pp. 300, 297.
90 Shuckburgh, *Bedell*, p. 129.
91 Hagan 'Miscellanea Vaticano-Hibernica', pp. 80–4.
92 TCD, MS 550, pp. 139–40.; Hagan, 'Miscellanea Vaticano-Hibernica', pp. 80–4; P.J. Corish, *The Catholic community in the seventeenth and eighteenth centuries* (Dublin, 1981), p. 28.
93 Canny, 'Why the reformation failed', passim.
94 Clarke, 'Varieties of uniformity', p. 105.
95 See above p. 77, below pp. 94, 96.
96 Shuckburgh, *Bedell*, p. 40.
97 For example, Mary O'Dowd, *Power, politics and land: early modern Sligo 1568–1688* (Belfast, 1991), p. 112.
98 P.R.O., Philadelphia Papers, 31/8/201, pp. 373–4; (*Cal. S.P. Ire., 1608–10*, pp. 245–6).
99 *Cal. Carew, 1603–24*, p. 160.
100 P.R.O., Philadelphia Papers, 31/8/200, pp. 176a–178 (*Cal. S.P. Ire., 1615–25*, p. 23).
101 G.J. Hand and V.W. Treadwell (eds), 'His majesty's directions for ordering and settling the courts within the kingdom of Ireland, 1622' in *Analecta Hibernica*, no. 26 (1970), p. 211; c.f. Orders and directions for the Church of Ireland, 1622, P.R.O., SP63/237/35, ff 73v–74 (*Cal S. P. Ire., 1615–25*, p. 416).
102 R.R. Steele (ed.), *A bibliography of royal proclamations of the Tudor and Stuart sovereigns* (2 vols, Oxford, 1910), ii, p. 27.
103 P.R.O., SP63/248/46 (*Cal. S.P. Ire., 1625–32*, p. 442); see also the similar complaint by an English minister in Ireland, Henry Bell: P.R.O., SP63/276/21 (*Cal. S.P. Ire., 1647–60*, pp. 276–7).
104 TCD, MS 832, f. 7.
105 Shuckburgh, *Bedell*, p. 123.
106 Ussher, *Whole works*, xv, p. 272.
107 *Journals of the house of commons of the kingdom of Ireland* (28 vols, Dublin, 1753–91), i, pp. 150–1.
108 Ford, *Protestant reformation*, pp. 42–9; John McCavitt, 'The lord deputyship of Sir Arthur Chichester in Ireland, 1605–16', unpublished Ph.D. thesis, Queen's University Belfast, 1988, ch. 7.
109 TCD, MS 550, p. 139; P. Ó Gallachair, 'A Fermanagh survey' in *Clogher Record*, ii, no. 2 (1958), p. 294.
110 The classic example of this is the proposal by the earl of Cork in 1632 to use recusancy fines to support the Irish army: H.M.C., *12th report (report on the Cowper*

(Coke) Mss), pp. 482–3; T.O. Ranger, 'The career of Richard Boyle, first earl of Cork, in Ireland, 1588–1643', unpublished D.Phil. thesis, Oxford University, 1959, pp. 270–2; on the enforcement of conformity in general, see R.D. Edwards, 'Church and state in the Ireland of Michéal O Cléirigh 1626–1641', in Sylvester O'Brien (ed.), *Measgra i gcuimhne Mhichil Ui Chléirigh* (Dublin, 1944), pp. 1–20.

111 TCD, MS 808, f. 47.

112 Leslie, Kilmore clergy, p. 307; Leslie, *Clogher clergy*, pp. 173, 233; N.L.I., MS 8014/X

113 P.R.O., SP63/231/4 (*Cal. S.P. Ire., 1611–14*, p. 3).

114 George O'Brien (ed.), *Advertisements for Ireland being a description of the state of Ireland in the reign of James I* (Dublin, 1923), p. 15; James Bliss and W. Scott (eds), *The works of the most reverend father in God, William Laud* (7 vols., Oxford, 1847–60), vii, p. 121.

115 For examples Ralph Houlbrooke, *Church courts and the people during the English reformation 1520–1570* (Oxford, 1979); M.J. Ingram, *Church courts, sex and marriage in England, 1570–1640* (Cambridge, 1987).

116 TCD, MS 853, f. 81; *Cal. Carew, 1603–24*, p. 305; P.R.O., SP63/269/108 (*Cal. S.P. Ire.,1625–60*, p. 161); *Journals of the house of commons of … Ireland*, i, pp. 150–1.

117 Lambeth Palace Library, London, Ms 595, pp. 55–6; William Knowler (ed.), *The earl of Strafford's letters and despatches* (2 vols, Dublin, 1739–40), i, p. 148; Ussher, *Whole works*, xv, p. 535.

118 William Bedell (tr.), *Il libro delle preghiere publice … secondo l'uso della Chiesa Anglicana* (London, 1685); H.J.M. Mason, *The life of William Bedell, D.D., lord bishop of Kilmore* (London, 1843), pp. 66, 75.

119 See in particular his judicious treatment of the text Revelation 18.4, 'Come out of her my people', in Nicholas Bernard, *The judgement of the late archbishop of Armagh* (London, 1659), pp. 33–102.

120 Bedell was well served by biographers: his son, William, and step-son-in-law, Alexander Clogie, both wrote near-contemporary MS lives which were edited in the nineteenth and early twentieth centuries: Alexander Clogy, *Memoir of the life and episcopate of Dr William Bedell*, ed. W.W. Wilkins (London, 1862); William Bedell, *A true relation of the life and death of the right reverend father in God William Bedell, lord bishop of Kilmore in Ireland*, ed. T.W. Jones (Camden Society, London, 1872). Gilbert Burnett further burnished Bedell's image as the type of an apostolic bishop in his *The life of William Bedell, D.D. bishop of Kilmore in Ireland* (London, 1685). In addition to Monck Mason's 1843 treatment there are two useful modern vignettes: E.G. Rupp, *Just men* (London, 1977), pp. 93–111; Aidan Clarke, 'Bishop William Bedell (1571–1642) and the Irish reformation' in Ciaran Brady (ed.), *Worsted in the game: losers in Irish history* (Dublin, 1989), pp. 61–9.

121 Ford, *Protestant reformation*, pp. 104–7, 140–1.

122 Ussher, *Whole works*, xv, pp. 466–70; Shuckburgh, *Bedell*, pp. 36–8, 302, 337, 348.

123 Shuckburgh, *Bedell*, pp. 43–4, 102.

124 Ussher, *Whole works*, xv, p. 535.

125 The completion of this plan was thwarted, however, by the 1641 rising: Shuckburgh, *Bedell*, pp. 40, 102–4, 107–8.

126 Shuckburgh, *Bedell*, p. 41.

127 Shuckburgh, *Bedell*, pp. 125, 131–4.

128 Shuckburgh, *Bedell*, pp. 55–6, 131–4.

129 Shuckburgh, *Bedell*, p. 26.

130 Shuckburgh, *Bedell*, p. 299.

131 Shuckburgh, *Bedell*, pp. 126–30.

132 Shuckburgh, *Bedell*, pp. 56, 131–2: though note the contradictory evidence about when King converted.
133 Shuckburgh, *Bedell*, pp. 129, 318; Ussher, *Whole works*, xv, pp. 471, 534, 536.
134 McKiernan, *Diocese of Kilmore*, pp. 141–51; Shuckburgh, *Bedell*, p. 70; Leslie, Kilmore clergy, p. 230.
135 Shuckburgh, *Bedell*, pp. 126–9.
136 TCD, MS 832, f. 148.
137 Shuckburgh, *Bedell*, p. 134; he does not appear in any of the official church records.
138 Shuckburgh, *Bedell*, pp. 121–2.
139 Ussher, *Whole works*, xv, p. 458.
140 Ussher, *Whole works*, xv, p. 468; Shuckburgh, *Bedell*, pp. 117–18.
141 Ussher, *Whole works*, xv, pp. 458, 474–5; Shuckburgh, *Bedell*, pp. 314–16.
142 Shuckburgh, *Bedell*, pp. 51, 123.
143 Shuckburgh, *Bedell*, pp. 340–2.
144 Shuckburgh, *Bedell*, pp. 344–7; for another example of the difficulties which his refusal to countenance pluralism caused, see Bedell's battle with his dean, Nicholas Bernard: Shuckburgh, *Bedell*, pp. 110, 317–18; Ussher, *Whole works*, xv, pp. 532–8.
145 Shuckburgh, *Bedell*, pp. 110–14, 349–50, 354–5, 357.
146 Ussher, *Whole works*, xv, p. 473.
147 Ussher, *Whole works*, xv, p. 485.
148 Charles McNeill (ed.), *The Tanner letters* (Dublin, 1943), pp. 99–100; Shuckburgh, *Bedell*, pp. 26–7, 324; Ussher, *Whole works*, xv, p. 464.
149 Ussher, *Whole works*, xv, pp. 464–5.
150 Ussher, *Whole works*, xv, p. 459.
151 Printed in part in Shuckburgh, *Bedell*, pp. 371–96; for the full correspondence see Bodleian Library, Oxford, Tanner MS 458, f. 188 et seq.
152 Shuckburgh, *Bedell*, p. 295; T.C. Barnard, 'Protestants and the Irish language, c. 1675–1725' in *Journal of Ecclesiastical History*, xliv (1993), pp. 245–6.
153 Shuckburgh, *Bedell*, pp. 29, 41, 130f.
154 Shuckburgh, *Bedell*, p. 144.
155 Shuckburgh, *Bedell*, p. 347.
156 Michael Perceval-Maxwell, *The outbreak of the Irish rebellion of 1641* (Dublin, 1994), p. 23.
157 Of the remainder, 16 were probably English, two Welsh, 8 probably Scottish; one name is not clearly identifiable with any nationality: see appendix to the essay.
158 See above, p. 81–2.
159 Ford, *Protestant reformation*, p. 171. Native Irish ministers, of course, did not necessarily define the limits of the Irish speaking ministry or enthusiasm for the indigenous reformation: one minister, Thomas Brady, who served as vicar of Lavey 1620–1641, according to Bedell could not read Irish at all: Ussher, *Whole works*, xv, p. 537; on the other hand, some clergy educated at Trinity under Bedell, though not Irish, were nevertheless committed to the language: see the cases of Henry Jones and Thomas Price: Leslie, Kilmore clergy, pp. 28, 38; Barnard, 'Protestants and the Irish language', p. 248.
160 The full list of local protestants that can be constructed from the depositions (TCD, MS 832 unless otherwise stated) covering Kilmore is: Thomas Brady, minister (ff 66, 108v, 122, 132, Gilbert, 412); James Nugent, minister (Gilbert, 412); Cochonacht Sheridan, schoolmaster (Gilbert, 412); Richard Ashe of Lisnamahon (ff. 1, 68, 83, 108v, 116v, 138, Gilbert, 412); Henry Ashe of Cavan (Gilbert, 412); John Smith (Gilbert, 412); Nicholas Smith (Gilbert, 412); Michael Smith of Oldcastle (f.95; Shane O Goan, curate of the parish of Kill (f. 63v); Hugh Brady of Culluntroe (f. 108v); James Fitzgerald of Kill (f. 68v); William Gilpatrick (TCD, MS 831, f. 14).
161 See Richard Parsons's deposition: TCD, MS 832, f. 91.

162 Shuckburgh, *Bedell*, pp. 129 f; Clogie may be referring to Thomas Brady, above n. 156; certainly Cochonacht O'Sheridan, Richard Ash, both closely assocated with Bedell, joined the rebels: see above, n. 156.

163 For example John Sheridan, 'brother to Mr Sheridan the minister', TCD, MS 832, f. 132; the son of parson Smith, above, n. 87; Cochonaght Sheridan, above n. 135.

164 In fact of course Kilmore diocese also included parishes that were in Leitrim and Fermanagh: the depositions for these parishes have also been examined.

165 TCD, MS 832, ff 56, 61v, 69, 76, 91, 113.

166 TCD, MS 832, f. 98.

167 TCD, MS 832, f. 88.

168 TCD, MS 832, f. 63v.

169 TCD, MS 832, f. 148; J.T. Gilbert (ed.), *A contemporary history of affairs in Ireland from 1641 to 1652* (3 vols, Dublin, 1879–80), i, p. 529. Creighton was spared because he was Scottish.

170 TCD MS 832, ff 77v, 104v, 121v.

171 Shuckburgh, *Bedell*, pp. 42–3.

172 Matthew Kelly, *Dissertations chiefly on Irish church history*, ed. Daniel McCarthy (Dublin, 1864), p. 61.

173 Shuckburgh, *Bedell*, p. 42.

174 McNeill (ed.) *Tanner letters*, p. 104.

FAITH, FAMILY AND FORTUNE *Raymond Gillespie*

1 For Massari's description of his time in Cavan see 'My Irish campaign' in *Catholic Bulletin*, vii (1917), pp. 112–14, 179–82, 246–40. All subsequent quotations from Massari come from this source.

2 R.C. Simington (ed.), *The civil survey, 1654–6* (10 vols, Dublin, 1931–61), x, p. 75.

3 H.M.C., *Report on the manuscripts of the late R.R. Hastings* (4 vols., London, 1928–47), iv, p. 160.

4 *Cal. S.P. Ire., 1603–6*, p. 565; E.S. Shuckburgh, *Two biographies of William Bedell, bishop of Kilmore* (Cambridge, 1902), pp. 56–7.

5 For Clogh Oughter castle see Connleth Manning, 'Clough Oughter castle' in *Breifne*, viii, no. 1 (1990) pp. 20–61.

6 Simington, *Civil survey*, x, pp. 75–6.

7 For the pattern of settlement *c.*1630, Philip Robinson, *The plantation of Ulster* (Dublin, 1984), p. 94.

8 H.M.C., *Hastings MSS*, iv, p. 165.

9 TCD, MS 833, ff 223–4; Gerard Boate, *Ireland's naturall history* (London, 1652), pp. 56, 70–1, 121–2, 124–30, 144.

10 Philip O'Connell, *The diocese of Kilmore* (Dublin, 1937), p. 11; Eileen McCracken, *The Irish woods since Tudor times* (Newton Abbot, 1971) pp. 53–4, 165.

11 B.L., Add MSS 4756, f. 100.

12 R.J. Hunter, 'The Ulster plantation in the counties of Armagh and Cavan, 1603–41' unpublished M. Litt thesis, TCD, 1969, pp. 57–63, 164–5, 390–3. The Old English held 13.7 per cent of the land of the county in 1610 and 21.4 per cent in 1641, Hunter, 'Ulster plantation', p. 577.

13 *Cal. S.P. Ire., 1599–1600*, p. 328; *Cal. S.P. Ire., 1608–10*, p. 55; H.M.C., *Hastings MSS*, iv, p. 163; J.B. Cunningham, *The history of Castle Caldwell and its families* (Enniskillen, 1980), p. 26.

14 James Carney (ed.), *A genealogical history of the O'Reillys* (Cavan, 1959), p. 81.

15 Carney, *Genealogical history*, p. 111.

16 M. Hickson (ed.) *Ireland in the seventeenth century* (2 vols., London, 1884) ii, p. 392.

17 Printed in John Richardson, *The great folly, superstition and idolatry of pilgrimage* (Dublin, 1727), p. 60.

18 Canice Mooney (ed.), 'Topographical fragments from the Franciscan library' in *Celtica* i (1946–50), pp. 65–7.

19 Mooney 'Topographical fragments', pp. 65–7.

20 Bodleian Library, Oxford, Rawlinson MS A237, ff 85, 85v, 86v.

21 James Carney, *Poems on the O'Reillys* (Dublin, 1950), pp. 24, 48.

22 TCD, MS 832, f. 56v.

23 N.A., RC5/25, ff 133–133v.

24 For this see Raymond Gillespie, 'Destabilising Ulster, 1641–2' in Brian Mac Cuarta (ed.), *Ulster 1641: aspects of the rising* (Belfast, 1993), p. 116.

25 TCD, MS 832, f. 81.

26 TCD, MS 832, ff 79v, 142.

27 For Teate's experiences see Raymond Gillespie, 'The murder of Arthur Champion and the 1614 rising in Fermanagh' in *Clogher Record*, xiv, no. 3 (1993), pp. 61–2.

28 Shuckburgh, *Bedell*, p. 58.

29 Hence the government in London examined the genealogy of the O'Reilly's carefully, *Cal. S.P. Ire., 1608–10*, p. 419.

30 Carney, *Genealogical history*, pp. 18–20; for an edition of one of these, Paul Walsh, *Irish chiefs and leaders* (Dublin, 1960), pp. 141–5.

31 Carney, *Genealogical history*, p. 81.

32 For the O'Neill demands, Myles Dillon (ed.), 'Ceart Uí Néill' in *Studia Celtica*, i (1966), p. 5. The document claims to be fifteenth century but the Breifne entry cannot be earlier than the middle of the sixteenth century to judge from the reference to 'salfas' or debased coinage. The fact that the tribute is entirely in cash, apart from one billeting requirement also suggests a late date.

33 Carney, *Genealogical history*, p. 81; *A.F.M.*, 1591; Carney, *Poems on the O'Reillys*, pp. 81, 99, 100.

34 Shuckburgh, *Bedell*, p. 29.

35 Carney, *Genealogical history*, p. 88.

36 *Cal. S.P. Ire., 1608–10*, p. 54.

37 H.M.C., *Report on the manuscripts of the earl of Egmont* (2 vols, London, 1905–9), i, p. 16; N.A., RC9 /1 ,p. 221; Hunter, 'Ulster plantation', pp. 79–80.

38 John Mc Cavitt, ' "Good planets in their several spheares"—the establishment of the assize circuits in early seventeenth century Ireland' in *Irish Jurist* n.s. xxiv (1989), pp. 248–78; H.M.C., *Egmont MSS*, i, p. 39.

39 *Cal. S.P. Ire., 1647–60*, p. 383; *Cal. S.P. Ire., 1666–9*, pp. 144, 253, 274. For the argument that toryism represents a relic feature of an older social order, albeit reorganised in the 1660s see Raymond Gillespie, 'The transformation of the borderlands, 1600–1700' in Raymond Gillespie and Harold O'Sullivan (eds), *The borderlands: essays on the history of the Ulster-Leinster border* (Belfast, 1989), pp. 84–7.

40 For example Walsh, *Irish chiefs and leaders*, pp. 157–69.

41 Gillespie, 'Destabilising Ulster', pp. 113–14. Much of the Cavan evidence is conveniently gathered together in Thomas Fitzpatrick, 'The Ulster civil war, 1641: "the kings commission" in county Cavan' in *Ulster Journal of Archaeology*, 2nd ser., xiv (1908), pp. 168–77, xv (1909), pp. 61–4.

42 J.T. Gilbert (ed.), *A contemporary history of affairs in Ireland* (3 vols., Dublin, 1879), i, pp. 364–5.

43 O.F. Traynor, 'More Kilmore clergy lists' in *Breifne*, iv, no. 14 (1971), pp. 202–7.

44 John Hagan (ed.), 'Miscellanea Vaticano Hibernica' in *Arch. Hib.*, v (1916), p. 81.

45 TCD, MS 1383, pp. 110, 121. This manuscript also contains more traditional devotional matter such as litanies and poems suggesting the presence to both traditonal ond Tridentine ideas.

46 *Cal. S.P. Ire., 1633–47*, p. 206.
47 Hagan, 'Miscellanea Vaticano Hibernica', p. 81.
48 TCD, MS 832, ff 84v, 105, 120.
49 John Hanly (ed.) *The letters of Saint Oliver Plunkett* (Dublin, 1979), pp. 343, 346; Carney, *Genealogical history*, p. 111.
50 P.F. Moran (ed.), *Spicilegium Ossoriense* (3 vols, Dublin, 1847–9), iii, p. 113.
51 Shuckburgh, *Bedell*, p. 101.
52 Carney, *Genealogical history*, p. 105.
53 Hagan, 'Miscellanea Vaticano Hibernicae', p. 81; Moran, *Spicilegium Ossoriense*, iii, pp. 111–12.
54 Hunter, 'Ulster plantation', p. 337.
55 Carney, *Genealogical history*, p. 77.
56 Pynnar's survey is printed in George Hill, *An historical account of the plantation of Ulster* (Belfast, 1877), pp. 451–74.
57 For the terms on one estate, R.J. Hunter, 'The English undertakers in the plantation of Ulster' in *Breifne*, vi, no. 16 (1973–5), pp. 492–3.
58 N.A., RC5/25, ff 138v–42.
59 For markets and fairs W.H. Crawford, 'Markets and fairs in county Cavan' in *Heart of Breifne* (1994), pp. 55–65; for the 1685 estimate Patrick Bourke, *Hibernius Merlinus* (Dublin, 1685).
60 Geariod Mac Niocaill (ed.), 'Cairt Ó Mhaolmhordha O Raighilligh, 1558' in *Breifne*, i, no. 2 (1959), pp. 134–6.
61 Shuckburgh, *Bedell*, pp. 125–6; *Cal. S.P. Ire., 1625–32*, p. 468.
62 Hunter, 'Ulster plantation', pp. 325–6, 577.
63 *Cal. S.P. Ire., 1608–10*, p. 306.
64 Grainnne Henry, *The Irish military community in Spanish Flanders* (Dublin, 1992), pp. 51, 107–8, 111. In fact some Cavan men had served in Flanders since 1589, Henry, *the Irish military community*, p. 60.
65 Brendan Jennings (ed.), *Louvain papers*, (Dublin, 1968), pp. 55, 72 n., 100–1; M.J. O'Doherty (ed.), 'Students of the Irish college, Salamanca' in *Arch. Hib.* ii (1913), p. 21.
66 *Cal. S.P. Ire., 1663–5*, p. 519; *Cal. S.P. Ire., 1647–60*, p. 159; Bodleian Library, Oxford, Carte MS 34, f. 466 names of a number of Cavan men as tories in 1665 who had been serving in the regiment of Col. Philip O'Reilly in Flanders five years earlier, Brendan Jennings (ed.), *Wild geese in Spanish Flanders* (Dublin, 1964), p. 18.
67 Hunter, 'Ulster plantation', pp. 407–8.
68 Robinson, *Ulster plantation*, p. 215.
69 TCD, MS 833, ff 64, 144.
70 TCD, MS 833, f.189; Hunter, 'Ulster plantation' pp. 407.
71 Shuckburgh, *Bedell*, p. 57.

THE FORMATION OF THE MODERN CATHOLIC CHURCH IN THE DIOCESE OF KILMORE *James Kelly*

1 Philip O'Connell, 'The parishes of Crosserlough and Kildrumfertan' in *B.A.S. Jnl.*, iii (1927), p. 73; Philip O'Connell, 'The parishes of Munterconnaught and Castlerahan' in *B.A.S. Jnl.*, ii (1923–6), pp. 291–302; Philip O'Connell, 'Moybolg and its ancient church' in *B.A.S. Jnl.*, ii (1923–6), p. 203.
2 Philip O'Connell, *The diocese of Kilmore: its history and antiquities* (Dublin, 1937), pp. 386–92; Canice Mooney, 'Some Cavan Franciscans of the past' in *Breifne*, i, no. 1 (1958), pp. 19–20; C.P. Meehan, *The rise and fall of the Irish Franciscan monasteries* (5th ed., Dublin, n.d.), pp. 40–7; 'Papers relating to the nine years war' in *Arch.*

Hib. ii (1913), p. 301; H.M.C., *Report on the Franciscan manuscripts, Dublin* (Dublin, 1906), p. 94.

3 O'Connell, *Kilmore*, pp. 394–6; 'Students of the Irish College, Salamanca' in *Arch. Hib.*, ii (1913), p. 21; Canice Mooney, 'Some Leitrim Franciscans of the past' in *Breifne*, i, no. 4 (1961), p. 330; Brendan Jennings (ed.), 'Brussels MS 3947' in *Analecta Hibernica*, no. 6 (1934), pp. 49–50.

4 O'Connell, *Kilmore*, pp. 396–404; E.S. Shuckburgh (ed.), *Two biographies of William Bedell, bishop of Kilmore* (Cambridge, 1902).

5 Philip O'Connell, 'The ecclesiastical history of the parish of Lurgan' in *B.A.S. Jnl.*, ii (1923), pp. 34–7; P.J. Corish, *The Catholic community in the seventeenth and eighteenth centuries* (Dublin, 1981), p. 28.

6 D.F. Cregan, 'The social and cultural background of the counter–reformation episcopate, 1618–60' in Donal McCartney and Art Cosgrove (eds), *Studies in Irish history* (Dublin, 1979), p. 85.

7 S.P. O'Mordha, 'Bishop Hugh O'Reilly (1581–1653): a reforming primate' in *Breifne*, iv, no. 13 (1970), pp. 4–5, 16–23, 25; O'Connell, *Kilmore*, pp. 405–9; H.M.C., *Franciscan Mss*, pp. 96–7; Meehan, *Franciscan monasteries*, pp. 170–2; Corish, *Catholic community*, p. 36.

8 P.F. Moran, (ed.), *Spicilegium Ossoriense* (3 vols, Dublin, 1874–84), i, pp. 171–2; Benignus Millett, 'Calendar of Scritture originali riferite' in *Coll. Hib.*, no. 10 (1967), p. 37; O'Mordha, 'Hugh O'Reilly', pp. 21, 39; O'Connell, *Kilmore*, pp. 424.

9 O'Connell, *Kilmore*, pp. 425–7; Brendan Jennings (ed.), *Wadding Papers, 1614–38* (Dublin, 1953), pp. viii–x, 312–14, 419–20, 442–3, 556, 581; H.M.C., *Franciscan Mss*, pp. 30, 48–9, 51; Millett, 'Scritture originali', pp. 37, 57; Benignus Millett, 'Catalogue of … Scritture originali riferite' in *Coll. Hib.*, no. 13 (1970), p. 36; Moran, *Spicilegium Ossoriense*, i, pp. 192, 208–10, 241–3; Brendan Jennings (ed.), 'Acta Sacrae Congregationis de Propaganda Fide' in *Arch. Hib.*, xxii (1959), pp. 83, 102.

10 O'Connell, *Kilmore*, pp. 424–9; Millett, 'Scritture originali', pp. 11–12, 15, 26–7, 36–7, 57; Millett, 'Catalogue of Scritture originali' in *Coll. Hib.* no. 12 (1969), p. 34; Moran, *Spicilegium Ossoriense*, i, pp. 208–10, 241–3; W.H. Grattan Flood, 'Episcopal succession in the diocese of Kilmore 1590–1910' in *B.A.S. Jnl.* iii (1927–33), p. 90.

11 O'Connell, *Kilmore*, pp. 410–13; Seamas O'Mordha, 'Hugh O'Reilly, part 2' in *Breifne*, iv, no. 15 (1972), pp. 346–52, 357–8; John Hagan (ed.), 'Miscellana Vaticano-Hibernica' in *Arch. Hib.*, vi (1917), pp. 116–17, 153.

12 O'Connell, *Kilmore*, pp. 410–15; Anselm Faulkner, 'Philip O'Reilly, O.F.M.' in *Breifne*, v, no. 19 (1979), p. 321; Dean Monahan, *Records relating to the diocese of Ardagh and Clonmacnoise* (Dublin, 1886), pp. 140–7.

13 O'Connell, *Kilmore*, pp. 417–18; Moran, *Spicilegium Ossoriense*, ii, pp. 93–6; E. Clancy and P.J. Forde, *Ballinagleara parish* (privately published, Dublin, 1980), p. 12.

14 Corish, *Catholic community*, p. 48.

15 MacSweeney to Cardinal Protector, 1657 in Benignius Millet, 'Calendar of vol 14 of Fondo di Vienna' in *Coll. Hib.*, no. 33 (1991), p. 59.

16 O'Connell, *Kilmore*, pp. 432–3; Clancy and Forde, *Ballinagleara*, p. 12; Benignus Millett, *The Irish Franciscans, 1661–65* (Rome, 1964), pp. 299, 338.

17 'Commonwealth records' in *Arch. Hib.*, vi (1917), p. 179; vii (1918–22), pp. 20, 25–6; Mooney, 'Some Leitrim Franciscans', p. 333.

18 Benignus Millett, 'Calendar of vol 13 of Fondo di Vienna' in *Coll. Hib.*, no. 25 (1983), p. 56; Benignus Millett, 'Calendar of vol 14 of Fondo di Vienna' in *Coll. Hib.*, no. 33 (1991), pp. 59–60; Millett, *The Irish Franciscans*, pp. 333, 335 n. 114.

19 Millett, 'Calendar of vol 13 of Fondo di Vienna' in *Coll. Hib.*, no. 25 (1983), p. 58; Monahan, *Records relating to Ardagh*, pp. 27–31; 'Synod of Clonelly' in *Journal of the Ardagh and Clonmacnoise Antiquarian Society*, i, no. 6 (1937), pp. 84–6.

20 W.P. Burke, *Irish priests in the penal times* (Waterford, 1914), pp. 2–4; Mooney, 'Some Cavan Franciscans', p. 24.

21 Millett, *The Franciscans*, p. 317; Corish, *The Catholic community*, p. 49.

22 Millett, 'Calendar of vol 14 of Fondo di Vienna' in *Coll. Hib.*, no. 33 (1991), pp. 70–1; Millett, *The Irish Franciscans*, p. 521.

23 Monahan, *Records of Ardagh*, p. 31; K.S. Bottigheimer, *English money and Irish land* (Oxford, 1971), p. 215.

24 Benignus Millett (ed.), 'Archbishop Edmund O'Reilly's report on the state of the Church of Ireland, 1662' in *Coll. Hib.*, no. 2 (1959), p. 108.

25 Benignus Millett, 'Calendar of Irish material in Fondo di Vienna' in *Coll. Hib.*, no. 24 (1982), pp. 67, 76; Millett, 'Calendar of vol 13 of Fondo di Vienna', in *Coll. Hib.*, no. 25 (1983), p. 38; Millett, 'Calendar of vol 13 of Fondo di Vienna' in *Coll. Hib.*, no. 26 (1984), pp. 23–4, 25, 29, 32, 35, 39; Millett, 'Calendar of vol 14 of Fondo di Vienna' in *Coll. Hib.*, no. 33 (1991), p. 88; Millett, 'Calendar of Scritture riferite' in *Coll. Hib.*, nos 6 & 7 (1963–4), pp. 105–6, 128–9, 131, 134; Cathaldus Giblin, 'Calendar of material of Irish interest in the collection Nunziatura di Fiandra, part 2' in *Coll. Hib.*, no. 3 (1960), p. 11.

26 Millett, 'Calendar of vol 14 of Fondo di Vienna' in *Coll. Hib.*, no. 29 (1987), pp. 41, 54; Benignus Millett, 'Calendar of vol 13 of Fondo di Vienna' in *Coll. Hib.*, no. 26 (1984), pp. 23–4, 25, 29, 35, 39; Millett, 'Calendar of vol 14 of Fondo di Vienna' in *Coll. Hib.*, no. 33 (1991), p. 88; Millett, 'Calendar of scritture riferite' in *Coll. Hib.*, nos. 6 & 7 (1963–4), pp. 106, 134; Millett, *The Franciscans*, p. 233.

27 Millett, 'Calendar of vol 13 of Fondo di Vienna' in *Coll. Hib.*, no. 25 (1983), p. 38; Giblin, 'Nunziatura di Fiandra, part 2', p. 11; O'Connell, *Kilmore*, p. 434.

28 Millett, 'Calendar of Scritture riferite' in *Coll. Hib.*, nos 6 & 7 (1963–4), pp. 72, 75, 78, 99–100, 110–11; Millett, 'Calendar of vol 13 of Fondo di Vienna' in *Coll. Hib.*, no. 26 (1984), pp. 42–3; Benignus Millett, 'Calendar of vol 2 of Scritture riferite' in *Coll. Hib.*, no. 16 (1973), pp. 12, 20, 23; O'Connell, *Kilmore*, p. 435; John Hanly (ed.), *The letters of Saint Oliver Plunkett* (Dublin, 1979), pp. 22–3, 481–2.

29 Hanly, *Letters of Oliver Plunkett*, p. 410; O'Connell, *Kilmore*, p. 451.

30 Hanly, *Letters of Oliver Plunkett*, pp. 98, 100, 111, 153, 175, 184, 248, 311–12, 346, 442; see also, Millett, 'Calendar of scritture riferite' in *Coll. Hib.*, nos. 6 & 7 (1963–4), p. 37; Cathaldus Giblin (ed.), 'A congregatio particularis on Ireland and propaganda fide, May 1671' in *Coll. Hib.*, nos. 18 & 19 (1976–7), p. 28

31 Hanly, *Letters of Oliver Plunkett*, pp. 255, 272, 326–7; Brendan Jennings, 'Miscellaneous papers' in *Arch.Hib.*, xvi (1951), pp. 64–5.

32 Hanly, *Letters of Oliver Plunkett*, pp. 133–4, 137–8.

33 Millett, 'Calendar of scritture riferite' in *Coll. Hib.*, nos 6 & 7 (1963–4), pp. 30–1.

34 Hanly, *Letters of Oliver Plunkett*, p. 442. There were also two Franciscan convents.

35 John Brady, 'Some Kilmore clergy of the seventeenth and eighteenth centuries' in *Breifne*, i, no. 3 (1960), pp. 215–20; O'Connell, *Kilmore*, p. 445.

36 Hanly, *Letters of Oliver Plunkett*, pp. 461, 478, 481–2; Grattan Flood, 'Episcopal succession', pp. 92–3; O'Connell, *Kilmore*, p. 446–7.

37 Hanly, *Letters of Oliver Plunkett*, pp. 481–2, 484–6; Patrick Power (ed.), *A bishop of the penal times* (Cork, 1932), pp. 15, 54–6. Tyrell, who was cited as a possible future bishop of the diocese in 1673, had petitioned the pope that he should be awarded its administration for financial reasons, Millett, 'Calendar of scritture riferite' in *Coll. Hib.*, nos 6 & 7 (1963–4), p. 38; *Coll. Hib.*, nos 21 & 22 (1979–80), pp. 24–5; O'Connell, *Kilmore*, pp. 447–9.

38 Brendan Jennings (ed.), 'Miscellaneous documents iii' in *Arch. Hib.*, xv (1950), pp. 65–6; Benignus Millett, `Calendar of scritture riferite' in *Coll. Hib.*, nos. 6 & 7 (1963–4), p. 43.
39 Hanly, *Letters of Oliver Plunkett*, pp. 483–4, 508, 537–8, 546.
40 W.J. Walsh, 'An act for registering the popish clergy' in *Irish Ecclesiastical Record*, xii (1896), pp. 308–11, 392–3, 440–3.
41 Hanly, *Letters of Oliver Plunkett*, pp. 516–23.
42 Burke, *Irish priests in penal times*, pp. 77–80, 454; O'Connell, *Kilmore*, pp. 452–3; Grattan Flood, 'Episcopal succession', pp. 93–4.
43 Moran, *Spicilegium Ossoriense*, ii, 109–15; Desmond Keenan, *The Catholic church in nineteenth century Ireland* (Dublin, 1983), pp. 46–7.
44 Brendan Jennings, 'Irish preachers and confessors in archdiocese of Malines, 1607–1794' in *Arch. Hib.*, xxiii (1960), p. 156; O'Connell, *Kilmore*, pp. 464–73; Walsh, 'An act for registering the popish clergy', pp. 308–11, 392–3, 440–3; Anselm Faulkner, 'Thomas Magauran O.F.M. (1640–1715)' in *Breifne*, iv, no. 13 (1970), pp. 90–1.
45 *Portrait of a parish: Mullagh, county Cavan* (Mullagh, 1988), pp. 37–8; John Brady, 'Remedies proposed for the Church of Ireland, 1695' in *Arch. Hib.*, xxii (1959), pp. 163–5.
46 Walsh, 'An act for registering the popish clergy', pp. 308–11, 392–3, 440–3; Mooney, 'Some Cavan Franciscans', p. 24; Cathaldus Giblin, 'Nunziatura di Fiandra, part 9' in *Coll. Hib.*, no. 13 (1970), pp. 75–6.
47 Burke, *Irish priests*, p. 439.
48 Burke, *Irish priests*, pp. 285–7, 443–4; O'Connell, *Kilmore*, pp. 474–80; N.A., 'Calendar of presentments 1698–1813', f. 22.
49 Walsh, 'An act for registering the popish clergy', pp. 308–11, 392–3, 440–3.
50 Moran, *Spicilegium Ossoriense*, ii, 481–2; O.F. Traynor, 'More Kilmore clergy lists' in *Breifne*, iv, no. 14 (1971), pp. 201–7; O.F. Traynor, 'Kilmore clergy list of 1723' in *Breifne*, iii, no. 12 (1969), pp. 481–91.
51 Liam Swords, 'Calendar of papers of Irish College, Paris' in *Arch. Hib.*, xxxv (1980), pp. 36, 63, 128; Micheline Walsh, 'The diocese of Kilmore, the Irish College in Paris and Alexander MaCabe' in *Breifne*, v, no. 19 (1979), p. 336; T.P. Cunningham, 'The will and foundation of Rev Eugene Brady, 1767', in *Breifne*, ii, no. 8 (1966), pp. 460–6.
52 'Irish Catholics licensed to keep arms' in *Arch. Hib.* iv (1915), pp. 59–65.
53 O'Connell, 'Parochial history of Killinkere', *B.A.S. Jnl.*, iii (1929–30), pp. 319–20; O'Connell, 'Lurgan', p. 39; *Mullagh*, pp. 114–15; Mooney, 'Some Leitrim Franciscans', pp. 333–5; Clancy and Forde, *Ballinagleara*, pp. 8–9, 12–13, 31–5.
54 Traynor, 'Kilmore clergy list of 1723', pp. 481, 485; Moran, *Spicilegium Ossoriense*, ii, pp. 481–2.
55 O'Connell, *Kilmore*, pp. 454–5; Traynor, 'More Kilmore clergy lists', p. 200.
56 Traynor, 'More Kilmore clergy lists', p. 201.
57 Grattan Flood, 'Episcopal succession, pp. 94–6; O'Connell, *Kilmore*, pp. 455–61; Hugh Fenning (ed), *The Fottrell papers* (Belfast, 1980), p. 77; F.J. McKiernan, *Diocese of Kilmore: bishops and priests 1136–1988* (Cavan, 1989), passim.
58 Hugh Fenning, *The undoing of the friars of Ireland* (Louvain, 1972), p. 157, n. 1; Fenning, *Fottrell papers*, pp. 123–7; Hugh Fenning, 'Michael MacDonagh, O.P., bishop of Kilmore, 1728–46' in *Irish Ecclesiastical Record*, cvi (1966), pp. 139–41.
59 *An abstract of the number of Protestant and Popish families in the several counties and provinces of Ireland* (Dublin, 1736); H.M.C., *Reports on various collections, Eyre Matcham Mss*, p. 60.
60 Fenning, 'Michael MacDonagh', pp. 142, 147–8; Fenning, *Fottrell papers*, pp. xv–xvi.

61 Fenning, *The undoing of the friars*, pp. 47, 135, 140–2; Hugh Fenning, 'John Kent's report on the state of the Irish missions, 1742' in *Arch. Hib.*, xxviii (1966), pp. 59–63, 74–6, 96; Fenning, 'Michael MacDonagh', pp. 147–50; Cathaldus Giblin, 'Nunziatura di Fiandra part 6' in *Coll. Hib.*, no. 10 (1967), pp. 88–91; 'Report of Bishop MacDonagh, 1741' in *Breifne*, ii, no. 8 (1966), pp. 438–40.

62 Hugh Fenning, 'Some problems of the Irish mission' in *Coll. Hib.*, no. 8 (1965), p. 77.

63 Fenning, 'Michael MacDonagh', pp. 139–40, 151–2; Burke, *Irish priests*, pp. 287, 289, 291, 444; O'Connell, *Kilmore*, pp. 484–5; Giblin, 'Nunziatura di Fiandra, pt 6', pp. 103–4.

64 Fenning, 'Michael MacDonagh', p. 152; O'Connell, *Kilmore*, pp. 488–9; Giblin, 'Nunziatura di Fiandra, pt. 6', pp. 105–06; Giblin, 'Nunziatura di Fiandra, pt. 10' in *Coll. Hib.*, no. 14 (1971), p. 76.

65 O'Connell, *Kilmore*, pp. 495–7.

66 O'Connell, *Kilmore*, pp. 497–9.

67 O'Connell, *Kilmore*, p. 495.

68 Hugh Fenning, 'Laurence Richardson, O.P., bishop of Kilmore' in *Irish Ecclesiastical Record*, cix (1968), passim; Fenning, *The undoing of the friars*, pp. 156–8, 178–9, 211–12, 218; Hugh Fenning, 'Letters from a Jesuit in Dublin, 1747–8' in *Arch. Hib.*, xxix (1970), p. 147; Cathaldus Giblin (ed.), 'Ten documents relating to Irish diocesan affairs, 1740–84' in *Coll. Hib.*, no. 20 (1978), p. 76; O'Connell, *Kilmore*, pp. 494–9.

69 Corish, *The Catholic community*, pp. 97–8; Fenning, 'Laurence Richardson', pp. 146–7; Brian Mitchell, *A guide to Irish parish registers* (Baltimore, 1988), p. 10.

70 Fenning, 'Letters from a Jesuit in Dublin, 1747–8', p. 147.

71 O'Connell, *Kilmore*, pp. 497–9; Fenning, 'Laurence Richardson', p. 149.

72 O'Connell, *Kilmore*, pp. 502–8.

73 O'Connell, *Kilmore*, pp. 509–10; Grattan Flood, 'Episcopal succession', p. 98; Mitchell, *Irish parish registers*, p. 10; O'Connell, 'Lurgan', pp. 36, 40.

74 T.P.Cunningham, 'The 1766 religious census: Kilmore and Ardagh' in *Breifne*, i, no. 4 (1960–61), pp. 358–9.

75 Traynor, 'More Kilmore clergy lists', pp. 210–11, 213; O'Connell, 'Killinkere', pp. 323–4.

76 O'Connell, 'Munterconnacht and Castlerahan', p. 305.

77 O'Connell, *Kilmore*, pp. 515–17.

78 O'Connell, *Kilmore*, pp. 518–19.

79 *Mullagh*, p. 115.

80 Brian Ó Mordha, 'Ordnance survey statistical reports on parishes' in *Breifne*, i, no. 1 (1958), p. 54; P. O Gallachair, 'A forgotten penal day church in Kinlough' in *Breifne*, i, no. 1 (1958), pp. 28–9. O'Connell, 'Killinkere', pp. 320–23; O'Connell, 'Moybolg', pp. 222–3; O'Connell, 'Munterconnacht and Castlerahan', p. 302; O'Connell, 'Crosserlough and Kildrumfertan', p. 79; O'Connell, 'Lurgan', p. 43.

81 Archives Propaganda Fide, Rome [hereafter A.P.F.], Fondo di Vienna, vol. 28, ff 188–9. I wish to thank Dr Patrick O'Donoghue for this and other references from this collection.

82 O'Connell, 'Lurgan', p. 32; Moran, *Spicilegium Ossoriense*, iii, p. 393.

83 Brady, ' Some Kilmore clergy', pp. 220–2; A.P.F., Fondo di Vienna, vol. 28, ff 188–9.

84 Grattan Flood, 'Episcopal succession', p. 99; A.P.F., Fondo di Vienna, vol. 28, f 81.

85 Fenning, *The undoing of the friars*, pp. 52–3.

86 A.P.F., Fondo di Vienna, vol. 28, f. 81; Kevin O'Neill, *Family and farm in pre-famine Ireland* (Wisconsin, 1984), p. 38; *Mullagh*, pp. 38–9.

87 Monahan, *Records of Ardagh*, pp. 151–7; Daire Keogh, 'The Catholic church and radicalism in Ireland in the 1790s', unpublished Ph. D. thesis, TCD, 1993, p. 187.

88 *Mullagh*, pp. 39–41; Marquess of Londonderry (ed.), *Memoirs and correspondence of Viscount Castlereagh* (4 vols, London, 1848), iv, pp. 118–20.

89 Raymond McGovern, 'Father Tom Maguire' in *Breifne*, iv, no. 14 (1971), p. 278 note; Terence Small, 'Churches and priests of Knockninny' in *Breifne*, i, no. 2 (1959), pp. 148–9.

90 O'Connell, *Kilmore*, pp. 529–39; Grattan Flood, 'Episcopal succession', pp. 99–101.

91 F.J. McKiernan, 'Kilmore priests' in *Breifne*, vi, no. 24 (1986), pp. 311–12.

92 McKiernan, 'Kilmore priests', pp. 309–10. The parishes that acquired a curate permanently were Ballaghameehan (1829), Castletara (1820), Cloonclare (1823), Crosserlough (1801), Drung (1801), Inismagrath (1827), Kindallan (1829), Kilasnett (1817), Killinagh (1815), Killinkere (1825), Kilmainham Wood (1826), Kilmore (1824), Kilsherdany (1827), Kinawley (1829), Knockninny (1824), Lurgan (1815), Templeport (1825) (McKiernan, *Diocese of Kilmore*, passim).

93 S.J. Connolly, 'Catholicism in Ulster 1800–50' in Peter Roebuck (ed.), *Plantation to partition* (Belfast, 1982), pp. 159–60.

94 McKiernan, 'Kilmore priests', p. 315.

95 Donal Kerr, 'James Browne, bishop of Kilmore 1829–65' in *Breifne*, vi, no. 22 (1983–4), pp. 118, 121, 129–30; S. Ó Dufaigh, 'Notes relating to Patrick Maguire, coadjutor bishop of Kilmore 1819–26' in *Breifne*, iv, no. 13 (1970), pp. 94–5; McGowan, 'Father Tom Maguire', pp. 278–80.

96 Cathaldus Giblin (ed), 'Papers of Richard Hayes' in *Coll. Hib.*, no. 33 (1991), pp. 126–7, 174–5; John Forsythe, 'Clogher diocesan papers: 2' in *Arch. Hib.*, xliv (1989), pp. 18–20; Kerr, 'James Browne', pp. 119–20.

97 Kerr, 'James Browne', pp. 114–7; McGovern, 'Fr Tom Maguire', p. 280; O'Neill, *Family and farm in pre-Famine Ireland*, pp. 38–9.

98 T.P. Cunningham, 'Catholic rent list from Kilmore' in *Breifne*, ii, no. 6 (1962–3), pp. 210–11, 213–14, 216–19; T.P. Cunningham, 'The 1826 general election in county Cavan' in *Breifne*, ii, no. 5 (1962–3), pp. 9, 20–1, 26–7, 31; Fergus O'Ferrall, *Catholic emancipation: Daniel O'Connell and the birth of Irish democracy* (Dublin, 1985), p. 141.

99 This account of Bishop Browne's episcopacy draws heavily on Donal Kerr's important article in *Breifne*, vi, no. 22 (1983–4).

100 As well as Kerr, 'James Browne', pp. 118–21, 129–33, see Connolly, 'Catholicism in Ulster', pp. 159–60; Donal Kerr, *Peel, priests and politics* (Oxford, 1982), p. 33; Keenan, *The Roman Catholic church*, p. 140; Mitchell, *Irish parish registers*, pp. 10–11, 69.

101 *Mullagh*, pp. 115, 116–17; O'Connell, 'Killinkere', pp. 320–23; O'Connell, 'Moybolg', pp. 222–3; O'Connell, 'Munterconnacht and Castlerahan', pp. 302–4; O'Connell, 'Crosserlough and Kildrumfertan', p. 79; O'Connell, 'Lurgan', pp. 36, 43; Clancy and Forde, *Ballinagleara*, pp. 10, 72; Small, 'Knockninny', pp. 150–1; McGowan, 'Fr Tom Maguire', p. 282, 284 n.

102 Mitchell, *Irish parish registers*, pp. 10–11, 45–6, 69; McGowan, Fr Tom Maguire', pp. 282, 284n.

103 Kerr, 'James Browne', pp. 126–7, 134–6; James Kelly, 'The Catholic church in the diocese of Ardagh 1650–1870' in Raymond Gillespie and Gerard Moran (eds), *Longford: essays in county history* (Dublin, 1991), pp. 79–81.

104 T.P. Cunningham (ed.), 'Cavan town in 1838, part 1' in *Breifne*, iv, no. 12 (1969), pp. 548–9; Patrick Gaffney (ed.), *The book of Kilmore cathedral* (Cavan, 1947), p. 19; Peter Galloway, *The cathedrals of Ireland* (Belfast, 1992), pp. 40–1.

105 T.P. Cunningham, 'The Great Famine in County Cavan', *Breifne*, ii, no. 8 (1966), p. 437; Joel Mokyr, *Why Ireland starved: a qauantative and analytical history of the*

Irish economy, 1800–1850 (London, 1983), p. 267; Mary Purcell, 'Murray papers' in *Arch. Hib.*, xxxvii (1982), p. 94; Mary Purcell, 'Murray papers' in *Arch. Hib.*, xl (1985), p. 58; Mary Purcell, 'Murray papers' in *Arch.Hib.*, xli (1986), p. 16; Kerr, *Peel, priests and politics*, pp. 11, 60–1, 84, 176, 320–1, 327–30, 334; Kerr, 'James Browne', pp. 136–44; Mark Tierney, 'Catalogue of letters relating to Queen's Colleges ... in Slattery papers' in *Coll. Hib.*, no. 9 (1966), p. 85.

106 Cunningham, 'Great Famine', p. 427; Kerr, 'James Browne', pp. 145–6; Purcell, 'Murray papers', p. 70.

107 David Miller, 'Irish catholicism and the Great Famine' in *Journal of Social History*, ix (1975–6), p. 86; Forsythe, 'Clogher diocesan papers, part 2', p. 36; *Mullagh*, pp. 104–05; *The Church establishment in Ireland* (Dublin, 1868), p. 156.

108 Emmett Larkin, *The making of the Roman Catholic church in Ireland 1850–60* (Chapel Hill, 1980), pp. 30–1, 150–1, 477; P.J. Corish (ed.), 'The Kirby papers' in *Arch. Hib.*, xxx (1972), p. 33.

109 Kerr, 'James Browne', pp. 149–50.

110 Kerr, 'James Browne', pp. 150–2; Emmett Larkin, *The consolidation of the Roman Catholic church, 1860–70* (Dublin, 1987), pp. 211–13.

111 Gabriel Kelly, 'Nicholas Conaty, bishop of Kilmore 1865–1886' in *Breifne*, vii no. 25 (1987), pp. 421–31; Corish, 'Kirby papers', p. 35; A.H. Leaden, 'The sisters of Mercy in Kilmore 1868–1968' in *Breifne*, iii, no. 12 (1969), pp. 562–81.

112 K.J. Mitchell, 'Students of All Hallows College, Dublin from the diocese of Kilmore, 1842–1895' in *Breifne*, ii, no. 8 (1966), pp. 467–84; McKiernan, 'Kilmore priests', p. 310.

POVERTY AND THE FAMINE IN COUNTY CAVAN *Margaret Crawford*

1 I wish to thank the staff of Cavan County Library and the staff of the database of Irish historical statistics at Queen's University of Belfast who gave me access to valuable material for the preparation of this essay.

2 Charles Coote, *Statistical survey of the county of Cavan with observations on the means of improvement drawn up in the year 1801 for the consideration and under the direction of the Dublin Society* (Dublin, 1802).

3 *Ordnance survey memoirs of Ireland* [hereafter *OSM*]. The county Cavan Ordnance Survey memoirs have been edited by Angelique Day *et al.* and deposited in the Library of Queen's University of Belfast, 1989.

4 *Report of the commissioners appointed to take the census of Ireland of the years 1841* [hereafter *Census Ire.*], H.C. 1844 [504] xxiv; and *The census of Ireland for the year 1851*, part vi, H.C. 1856 [2134] xxxi.

5 *Report of her Majesty's commissioners of inquiry into the state of the law and practice in relation to the occupation of land in Ireland*, H.C. 1845, xix–xxii.

6 *Report of commissioners for inquiring into the condition of the poorer classes in Ireland* [hereafter *Poor Inquiry (Ireland)*] , H.C. 1836, xxx–xxxii.

7 Ruth–Ann Harris, *The nearest place that wasn't Ireland: early nineteenth-century Irish labor migration* (Iowa, 1994), p. 86.

8 *Census Ire., 1851*, part vi, H.C. 1856 [2134] xxiv, p. 654; *Census Ire., 1861*, part v, H.C. 1864 [3204–iv] lvi, p. 554.

9 Several of the baronies of Cavan have a variety of spellings Clankee may also be spelt Clonkee, Clanmahon as Clonmahon, Tullaghagh as Tullyhaw, Tullaghgarvey as Tullygarvey and Tulloghonoho as Tullyhunco.

10 See L.A. Clarkson, 'Population change and urbanisation 1821–1911' in Liam Kennedy and Philip Ollerenshaw (eds), *An economic history of Ulster 1820–1939* (Manchester 1985), pp. 138–9.

11 Clarkson, 'Population change and urbanisation 1821–1911', pp. 139–40.
12 *OSM parish of Drung, county Cavan*, p. 8.
13 *OSM parish of Drumlonnon, county Cavan*, p. 9.
14 *Poor Inquiry (Ireland)*, appendix E, p. 294. Although the report states that Pierce
    Morton's information comes from the parish of Kildrumferton it was later called
    Crosserlough in the census of 1841 and that of 1851.
15 *OSM parish of Drumlommon, county Cavan*, (Lieu. Andrew Beatty, Nov, 1835)
16 *Poor Inquiry (Ireland)*, appendix E, p. 297.
17 *Poor Inquiry (Ireland)*, appendix E, p. 293.
18 *Poor Inquiry (Ireland)*, appendix E, p. 295.
19 Kevin O'Neill, *Family and farm in pre-Famine Ireland*, (Wisconsin, 1984), p. 86.
20 L.A. Clarkson and Margaret Crawford, 'Dietary directions: a topographical survey
    of Irish diet', in Rosalind Mitchison and Peter Roebuck, (eds), *Economy and society
    in Scotland and Ireland 1500–1939* (Edinburgh, 1988), p. 178; Margaret Crawford,
    'Dietary considerations in pre-Famine Louth and its environs' in Raymond Gillespie
    and Harold O'Sullivan, (eds), *The borderlands: essays on the history of the Ulster-
    Leinster border* (Belfast, 1989), pp. 111–13.
21 Clarkson and Crawford, 'Dietary directions', p. 178.
22 *Poor Inquiry (Ireland)*, appendix E, p. 33.
23 Crawford, 'Dietary considerations in pre-Famine Louth and its environs', p. 125.
24 Stanley Davidson, Reginald Passmore, J.F. Brock and A.S. Truswell, *Human nutri-
    tion and dietetics* (7th ed., Edinburgh, 1979), pp. 153–4; Michael Gibney, *Nutrition,
    diet and health* (Cambridge, 1986), p. 12.
25 T.W. Freeman, *Pre-Famine Ireland: a study in historical geography* (Manchester,
    1957), p. 271.
26 *OSM parish of Drumdoon*, (Lieu. P. Taylor, 1835), p. 16.
27 Coote, *Statistical survey of the county of Cavan*, p. 73.
28 *OSM parish of Drumdoon*, (Lieu. P Taylor, 1835), p. 16.
29 Cited in Joan Thirsk, 'Industries in the countryside', in F.J. Fisher (ed.), *Essays in
    the economic and social history of Tudor and Stuart England* (Cambridge, 1961), as
    P.R.O., E134, 10–11 Chas. I, Hil. 22.
30 Freeman, *Pre-Famine Ireland*, p. 272.
31 O'Neill, *Family and farm in pre-Famine Ireland*, p. 100.
32 Harris, *The nearest place that wasn't Ireland*, pp. 46–8. Although the wage rates are
    labelled weekly the data are in fact daily rates.
33 Patrick Lynch and John Vaisey, *Guinness's brewery in the Irish economy 1759–1876*
    (Cambridge, 1960), pp. 9–17.
34 *Poor Enquiry (Ireland)*, appendix D, q. 11.
35 Joel Mokyr, *Why Ireland starved: a quantative and analytical history of the Irish
    economy, 1800–1850* (London, 1983), p. 20.
36 Mokyr, *Why Ireland starved*, p. 23.
37 See Crawford 'Dietary considerations in pre-Famine Louth and its environs', pp.
    117–18.
38 Kennedy and Ollerenshaw, *An economic history of Ulster*, p. 34.
39 The network was extended to 163 towards the end of the Famine crisis.
40 Although the lion's share of Cootehill and Bailieborough unions were in county
    Cavan small parcels of land were in adjacent counties.
41 Bawnboy Union was not formed until 1849.
42 In 1840 and 1841 legislation was passed (3 & 4 Victoria, c. 29) making poor law
    boards responsible for arranging with local doctors a vaccination service. All paupers
    entering the workhouses were checked for vaccination and given it if necessary.
43 Cavan County Library, Cavan, Minute book of the Cootehill poor law board of
    guardians, 12 Jan. 1849.

44 Gerard O'Brien,'Workhouse management in pre-Famine Ireland' in *R.I.A. Procs.*, lxxxvi, sect. C (1986), p. 115.

45 George Nicholls, *A history of the Irish poor law* (London, 1856, reprinted New York, 1967), p. 171.

46 O'Brien, 'Workhouse management', p. 132.

47 Helen Burke, *The people and the poor law in nineteenth century Ireland* (Littlehampton, 1987), p. 125.

48 Initially the Irish poor law was administered from London, with an office in Dublin. In August 1847 the link was severed and a new commission was established in Dublin.

49 Cavan County Library, Minute book of the Cavan poor law board of guardians, 11 Nov. 1845.

50 Public Record Office of Northern Ireland, Belfast, BG1/A/1, Minute book of the Antrim Poor Law Union, 1845.

51 Cavan County Library, Minute book of the Cavan poor law board of guardians, 26 May 1846.

52 Cavan County Library, Minute book of the Cavan poor law board of guardians, 28 July 1846.

53 Cavan County Library, Minute book of the Cootehill poor law board of guardians, 5 Aug. 1848.

54 Cavan County Library, Minute book of the Cootehill poor law board of guardians, 11 June 1847.

55 *Correspondence relating to the state of Union workhouses in Ireland*, First Series, H.C. 1847 (766) lv, p. 26.

56 T.P. Cunningham, 'The Great Famine in county Cavan' in *Breifne*, ii, no. 8 (1966), p. 416.

57 *Correspondence relating to the measures adopted for the relief of distress in Ireland (Board of Works Series), First part*, H.C. 1847 (797) lii, p. 151. Correspondence between Mr Forsyth and Mr Mulvany written from Belturbet 16 Feb. 1847.

58 See Cunningham, 'The Great Famine in county Cavan', p. 421.

59 'Report of the recent epidemic fever in Ireland' in *Dublin Quarterly Journal Medical Science*, vii (1849), p. 107.

60 Cunningham, 'The Great Famine in county Cavan', p. 427; Peter Froggatt, 'The response of the medical profession to the Great Famine' in Margaret Crawford (ed.), *Famine: the Irish experience 900–1900* (Edinburgh, 1989), pp. 134–56.

61 *Census of Ire., 1851, table of deaths, vol. i*, H.C. 1856 [2087–I] xxix, p. 247.

62 *Census of Ire., 1851.*

63 *Report of the commissioners of health (Ireland), on the epidemics of 1846 to 1850*, H.C. 1852–3 [1562] xli p. 7.

64 *Census of Ire., 1851*, p. 329; W.P. MacArthur, 'Medical history of the Famine', in R.D. Edwards and T.D. Williams (eds), *The Great Famine: studies in Irish history 1845–52* (Dublin, 1956), pp. 279–80.

65 'Report of the recent epidemic fever in Ireland', p. 107

66 Michael Scott, (ed.), *Hall's Ireland: Mr and Mrs Hall's tour of 1840* (London, 1841), p. 319.

THE EMERGENCE AND CONSOLIDATION OF THE HOME RULE
MOVEMENT IN COUNTY CAVAN, 1870–86 *Gerard Moran*

1 D. George Boyce, *Nineteenth century Ireland: the search for stability* (Dublin, 1990), pp. 129–31.

2 For an account of how the Farnhams treated their tenantry between 1823 and 1868 see Eileen McCourt, 'The management of the Farnham estate during the nineteenth century' in *Breifne*, iv, no. 16 (1975), pp. 531–60. On their political significance see K. Theodore Hoppen, *Elections, politics and society in Ireland, 1832–1885* (London, 1984), pp. 153, 156.

3 For violence at Irish elections see Hoppen, *Elections, politics and society*, pp. 388–408; J.H. Whyte, *The Irish Independent party, 1850–1859* (London, 1958), pp. 68–75.

4 The polling stations were now situated at Arva, Bailieborough, Ballina, Ballyconnell, Ballyjamesduff, Bawnboy, Belturbet, Cavan, Cootehill, Killashandra, Kilnaleck, Kingscourt, Mountnugent, Virginia, Chercock, Swanlinbar and Virginia.

5 W.E. Vaughan and A.J. Fitzpatrick, (eds), *Irish historical statistics: population, 1821–1971* (Dublin, 1978), pp. 54–9.

6 B.M. Walker, 'The Irish electorate, 1868–1915' in *Irish Historical Studies*, xviii, no. 71 (March, 1973), pp. 381, 397–8; B.M. Walker, 'The land question and elections in Ulster, 1868–1886' in Samuel Clark and James S. Donnelly, Jr. (eds), *Irish peasants: violence and political unrest, 1780–1914* (Madison and Manchester, 1983), p. 238.

7 Donal Kerr, 'James Browne, bishop of Kilmore, 1825–65' in *Breifne*, vi, no. 22 (1983–4), p. 17.

8 For the problems of the Catholic church in Cavan in this period see Kerr, 'James Browne', pp. 125–38 and James Kelly's essay above.

9 Kerr, 'James Browne', pp. 121–2.

10 Gabriel Kelly, 'Nicholas Conaty, bishop of Kilmore (1865–86)' in *Breifne*, vii, no. 25, (1987), pp. 434–5; for Saunderson see B.M. Walker, *Ulster politics: the formative years, 1868–86* (Belfast, 1989), p. 56.

11 David Thornley, *Isaac Butt and home rule* (London, 1964), p. 39.

12 *Nation*, 2 Jan, 1869, p. 309; *Irishman*, 2 Jan, 1869, p. 430; Emmet Larkin, *The consolidation of the Roman Catholic church in Ireland, 1860–70* (Chapel Hill, 1987), p. 461. He was following the example of John MacHale of Tuam and William Keane of Cloyne.

13 For an account of fenian activities in Cavan see Seán Ó Luing, 'A contribution to the study of fenianism in Breifne' in *Breifne*, iii, no. 10 (1967), pp. 155–74. The only expression of concern about fenianism in Cavan that I have come across is from Archibald Godfrey of Killegan, Belturbet, who in March 1867 urged that martial law be proclaimed: Archibald Godfrey to chief secretary, 11 March 1867 (N.A., S.P.O., Fenian papers, F/4212). For the state of fenianism in Cavan in 1869 see Fasscett to Dublin Castle, 31 Nov. 1869, (N.A., S.P.O., Fenian papers 5129 R). Support for the incarcerated prisoners existed in Ballyjamesduff and Crosserlough, but it was low compared to other counties. Cavan nationalists attended the Dundalk amnesty meeting on 12 September and 1000 people from the county signed a petition calling for the release of the prisoners, *Nation*, 3 April 1869, p. 524; 1 May 1869, p. 589; *Irishman*, 18 Sept. 1869, p. 188; *Anglo–Celt*, 23 Jan. 1869, p. 2; 30 Jan. 1869, p. 2. Cavan nationalists were also involved in the 1869 Longford by-election when they supported the nationalist candidate, John Martin. Many travelled into north Longford on the days before the contest and intimidated and threatened the Liberal candidate's supporters, Gerard Moran, 'Politics and electioneering in county Longford, 1868–1880' in Raymond Gillespie and Gerard Moran (eds), *Longford: essays in county history* (Dublin, 1991), pp. 178–9.

14 *Anglo–Celt*, 10 Dec. 1870, p. 3.

15 *Nation*, 6 Nov. 1879, p. 181. On the issue of symbolism and Irish nationalism see Gary Owens, 'Constructing the repeal spectacle: monster meetings and people power in pre-Famine Ireland' in Maurice O'Connell (ed.), *People power* (Dublin, 1993).

16 See R.W. Kirkpatrick, 'Origins and development of the land war in mid-Ulster, 1879–85' in F.S.L. Lyons and Richard Hawkins (eds), *Ireland under the union: varieties of tension, essays in honour of T.W. Moody* (Oxford, 1980), pp. 204–13; Walker, 'Land question and elections in Ulster', pp. 237–8.

17 *Anglo–Celt*, 28 Jan. 1871, p. 2; 12 Oct. 1872, p. 2.

18 For an overall view of the farmers clubs in Ireland in the 1860s and 1870s see Samuel Clark, *Social origins of the Irish land war* (Princeton, 1979), pp. 214–21.

19 *Nation*, 20 Aug. 1870, p. 4; N.L.I., MS 8620 (10), Isaac Butt papers, Nicholas Conaty to Butt, 9 Sept. 1870. At the same time Conaty's support for the Liberals was evident when he wrote to Cardinal Cullen asking him to seek the support of Earl Spencer for Mr O'Reilly Dease as lord lieutenant for Cavan. Dease was a former Liberal MP and had unsuccessfully contested Cavan for the Liberals in 1859, see Dublin Diocesan Archives, Cullen papers (Bishops, 1870), Conaty to Cullen, 12 Dec. 1870.

20 *Anglo–Celt*, 14 Jan. 1871, p. 2.

21 *Anglo–Celt*, 27 Jan. 1872, p. 3.

22 *Anglo–Celt*, 27 Jan. 1872, p. 3. The only influential member of the farmers' club to join the Cavan Home Rule Association was Edward Fitzpatrick of Greeaghcrotter.

23 Kelly, 'Nicholas Conaty', p. 446.

24 C.C. O'Brien, *Parnell and his party, 1880–90* (Oxford, 1974), p. 125

25 For a more comprehensive account of the 1872 Galway by-election see Gerard Moran, 'The clergy and the 1872 Galway by-election' in *Journal of the Galway archaeological and historical society* (forthcoming).

26 *Anglo–Celt*, 15 June 1872 p. 2; 22 June 1872, pp. 2–3; 6 July 1872, p. 3; 3 Aug. 1872, p. 3.

27 *Anglo–Celt*, 24 Aug. 1872.

28 *Anglo–Celt*, 5 Oct. 1872, p. 3. Callan in his speech called for legislation to benefit Irish education, land reform and an Irish parliament.

29 The farmers club wanted the Liberals to take over many of the political functions that it carried out such as the registration of voters and the selection of parliamentary candidates, issues which divided its membership, *Anglo–Celt*, 1 Feb. 1873, p. 3.

30 *Anglo–Celt*, 22 Feb. 1873, p. 3; 15 March 1873, p. 3.

31 *Anglo–Celt*, 13 April 1873, p. 3.

32 On the failure of the central body of the Home Rule League to help in the 1874 election, see O'Brien, *Parnell and his party*, p. 124. In Longford the clergy selected the candidates and their service to the church rather than their support for nationalist principles was the main criterion. In Louth the local independent club was the major influence in the selection and support for tenant right and nationalism were the important issues. In Mayo the fenians played a role in the selection of candidates. See Gerard Moran, 'Politics and electioneering in county Longford' pp. 187–9; Gerard Moran, 'Philip Callan: the rise and fall of an Irish nationalist MP, 1868–1886' in *Journal of the Louth archaeological and historical society*, xxii, no. 4 (1992), pp. 399–400; Gerard Moran, 'The changing course of Mayo politics, 1868–74' in Raymond Gillespie and Gerard Moran (eds), *'A various country': essays in Mayo history, 1500–1900* (Westport, 1987), pp. 147–52.

33 For accounts of the Monghan and Derry city by-elections see Walker, *Ulster politics*, pp. 79–83; Thornley, *Isaac Butt*, pp. 119–20; 133–5; Gerard Moran, 'The advance on the north: the difficulties of the home rule movement in south-east Ulster, 1870–1883' in Raymond Gillespie and Harold O'Sullivan (eds), *The borderlands: essays on the history of the Ulster–Leinster border* (Belfast, 1989), pp. 132–4.

34 Saunderson's position was undermined by his remarks at the Church of Ireland general synod in April 1873, when he attacked the Catholic mass and condemned 'the real presence' at the consecration, see *Anglo–Celt*, 26 April 1873, p. 2; 3 May 1873, p. 2; Kelly, 'Nicholas Conaty', p. 449. For a good overview of Saunderson's career, Alvin Jackson, *Colonel Edward Saunderson: land and loyalty in Victorian Ireland* (Oxford, 1994).

35 *Nation*, 7 Feb. 1874, p. 2.

36 Walker, *Ulster politics*, pp. 94–105.

37 *Freeman's Journal*, 29 Jan. 1874, p. 2; *Ulster Examiner*, 30 Jan. 1874, p. 3; *Nation*, 31 Jan. 1874, p. 4.

38 *Daily Express* [Dublin] 6 Feb. 1874, p. 2. This was the view of the Presbyterian minister in Shercock, Revd R.M. Collum. During the 1852 election the Presbyterians in Ulster and Cavan failed to support the Tenant League candidates, Hoppen, *Elections, politics and society*, p. 266; Whyte, *Irish Independent party*, pp. 84–6; Terence P. Cunningham, 'The 1852 general election in county Cavan' in *Breifne*, iii, no. 9 (1966), p. 121.

39 *Freeman's Journal*, 26 Jan. 1874, p. 2; *Ulster Examiner*, 27 Jan. 1874, p. 3. Conaty realised the difficulties that could arise in the popular ranks having witnessed the split that occured in 1852, see Cunningham, 'The 1852 general election in county Cavan', pp. 124–6.

40 *Irish Times*, 31 Jan. 1874, p. 2; *Nation*, 7 Feb. 1874, p. 2.

41 See Moran, 'Politics and electioneering in Longford', pp. 187–9.

42 N.A., C.S.O., 1875/4403, Letters from constabulary to Dublin, 4 Jan. 1879; 5 Jan. and 5 July 1875. For problems of ribbonism see W.E. Vaughan, *Landlords and tenants in mid-Victorian Ireland* (Oxford, 1994), pp. 180–1, 193.

43 *Nation*, 7 Feb. 1874, pp. 2–3

44 *Freeman's Journal*, 9 Feb. 1874, p. 3. This contrasts with Tipperary, often regarded as one of the most nationalist counties in nineteenth century Ireland, where the clergy did not nominate any of the six home rule candidates, Gerard Moran, 'The fenian involvement in Tipperary politics, 1868–1880' in *Tipperary historical journal*, (1994), pp. 80–1.

45 At Ballyjamesduff Fr D. McBreen chaired the proceedings, while in Belturbet on 5 Feb. Revd P. O'Reilly was in the chair, see *Freeman's Journal*, 6 Feb. 1874, p. 3; *Ulster Examiner*, 7 Feb. 1874, p. 4.

46 *Nation*, 7 Feb. 1874, p. 5; *Ulster Examiner*, 9 March 1874, p. 4. This was no doubt done to show that the constituency would never again accept representatives like Saunderson and Annesley.

47 *Ulster Examiner*, 10 Feb. 1874, p. 2. See also L.J. McCaffrey, 'Home rule and the general election of 1874' in *Irish Historical Studies*, ix, no. 34 (Sept. 1954), p. 196. This also occurred in those constituencies where there were no home rule candidates, but not in Cavan or Monaghan.

48 *Daily Express* [Dublin], 19 Feb. 1874, p. 3. For Conaty's lenten pastoral see *Ulster Examiner*, 16 Feb. 1874, p. 3.

49 *Nation*, 28 Feb. 1874, p. 4.

50 Belfast nationalists, for example, now maintained that with proper organisation and motivation further successes could be achieved in the province. For details of rejoicing in Belfast after Biggar's victory see *Ulster Examiner*, 18 Feb. 1874, p. 3.

51 See Thornley, *Isaac Butt*, pp. 180–1; Moran 'Advance on the north', pp. 139–40.

52 See T.M. Healy, *Letters and leaders of my day* (2 vols., London, 1928), i, pp. 190–2; Jack Magee 'The Monaghan election of 1883 and the invasion of Ulster' in *Clogher record*, viii (1974), pp. 147–66. One recent writer has pointed out that Healy's success in Monaghan in 1883 prompted an all-out attempt to win support for the party in Ulster, but the long term effect was to give rise to the growth of the Orange

Order, see Pauric Travers, 'Parnell and the Ulster Question' in Donal McCartney (ed.), *Parnell, the politics of power* (Dublin, 1991), pp. 64–5. As late as 1880 some Ulster Catholics were bemoaning the poor political state of Catholic organisations in the province, *Ulster Examiner*, 15 March 1880, p. 3. This dispondency was first noted in 1872 when it was stated that the home rule movement was doing nothing to aid the movement in Ulster, N.L.I., MS 8694 (8), John Ferguson to Isaac Butt, 14 Aug. 1873.

53 *Nation*, 7 March 1874, p. 2.

54 *Ulster Examiner*, 20 April 1874, p. 2.

55 See *Nation*, 19 Dec. 1874, p. 3. Power was also on the supreme council of the Irish Republican Brotherhood at this time. Biggar joined the fenian movement after being elected for Cavan and eventually became a member of the supreme council.

56 *Nation*, 8 April 1874, p. 2; 5 Sept. 1874, p. 2; *Ulster Examiner*, 2 Sept. 1874. The process of the representatives addressing their constituencies was taken up in other counties, see Moran, 'Changing course of Mayo politics', pp. 152–3. The Belturbet meeting was also significant in that a riot occurred when a crowd from Cavan attacked a group from Fermanagh as they were returning home. The cause of the dispute was a white flag which the Fermanagh group carried and was reputed to represent ribbonism, which had been condemned by the local parish priest, Fr O'Reilly, see N.A., C.S.O., R.P., 1875/4901.

57 *Nation*, 18 July 1874, p.2; 8 Aug. 1874, p. 3.

58 By 1886 the revision courts lasted only eight days in Cavan, while it took 176 days in county Tyrone, a constituency where the electoral support of the parties was very evenly balanced and each vote counted, see B.M. Walker, 'Party organisation in Ulster, 1865–92; registration agents and their activities' in Peter Roebuck (ed.), *Plantation to partition* (Belfast 1982), pp. 195–7. One elector in 1880 blamed the defeat of the Conservative candidate, Maxwell, on the failure of the Cavan gentry to involve themselves in the registration of voters. He stated that if the gentry had employed solicitors in 1879, the Conservatives would have taken one of the Cavan seats, *Daily Express* [Dublin], 13 April 1880, p. 3.

59 B.M. Walker, *Parliamentary election results in Ireland, 1801–1922* (Dublin, 1978), pp. 115–23. In Monaghan during the early 1870s the Protestant electorate had a majority of 400–500 over the Catholic voters, N.L.I., MS 8693 (5), L.J. O'Neill to Butt, 2 July 1871.

60 *Ulster Examiner*, 19 and 20 March 1874; Moran, 'Advance on the north', p. 137. As early as Sept. 1871 Revd Joseph Galbraith of the Home Rule Central Council was urging Butt that the way forward was for local clubs to be established throughout the country, N.L.I., MS 8693 (6), Joseph Galbraith to Butt, 28 Sept. 1871.

61 An example of this is the ordered assembly that met in Mountnugent churchyard before the Kilnaleck demonstration, *Nation*, 26 April 1879, p. 12. At least seven bands attended the Cavan demonstration on April 1876 and fourteen priests were present, *Nation*, 29 April 1876, p. 5.

62 Clark, *Social origins of Irish land war*, p. 219.

63 *Nation*, 14 Oct. 1876, p. 4. Other constituencies, such as Roscommon, held meetings where they condemned their parliamentary representatives, see Gerard Moran, 'James Daly and the land question, 1876–9' in *Retrospect* (1980) pp. 33–40.

64 Nine priests were on the platform at the Bailieborough meeting on 19 Sept. 1878 and fifteen at the Kilnaleck meeting on 14 April 1879, *Nation*, 28 Sept. 1878, p. 2; 19 April 1879, p. 2.

65 *Nation*, 27 Nov. 1875, p. 6; for the way in which Ulster constituencies upheld the land question at the 1880 election see Hoppen, *Elections, politics and society*, p. 328; Francis Thompson, 'Attitudes to reform: political parties in Ulster and the Irish land bill of 1881' in *Irish Historical Studies*, xxiv, no. 95 (May 1985), pp. 333–6.

66 *Nation*, 14 Oct. 1876, p. 5.
67 *Nation*, 28 Aug. 1875, p. 3; 5 Aug. 1876, p. 12.
68 Biggar and others were critical of the Home Rule League and its failure to promote local associations throughout the country, see his speech at Bailieborough meeting on 19 Sept. 1878, *Nation*, 28 Sept. 1878, p. 2.
69 *Nation*, 19 April 1879, p. 2. A good account of Parnell's speech at Kilnaleck and its importance for the land and political movements in 1879–82 can be found in Robert Kee, *The laurel and the ivy: the story of Charles Stewart Parnell and Irish nationalism* (London, 1993), pp. 177–8.
70 *Nation*, 1 Sept. 1877, p. 5.
71 See letter of Fr John Boylan, P.P. Crosserlough, *Nation*, 27 Oct. 1877, p. 2. See also letter of Fr P. Briody, C.C. Mountnugent, who was totally disillusioned with Butt's policy, *Nation*, 2 Nov. 1878, p. 7.
72 For the problems of the home rule movement in this period, see Thornley, *Isaac Butt*, pp. 286–99.
73 *Nation*, 29 June 1878, p.3; 13 July 1878, p. 6.
74 For poverty in Cavan see Kirkpatrick, 'Origins and development of the land war in mid-Ulster', pp. 214, 220–1. The failure of the Land League to make progress in Cavan in the early stages was partly due to Conaty's opposition and the small number of actual evictions since the level of rent abatements was quite substantial. Its advancement after October 1880 coincides with Conaty deciding to support it, Kelly, 'Nicholas Conaty', pp. 453–6. According to Robert Kee the first major Land League meeting in Ulster was held at Belleek, county Fermanagh on 9 Nov. 1880, see Kee, *The laurel and the ivy*, p. 290. However the first meeting under the National Land League auspices took place in Bailieborough on 20 Oct. 1880 at which Biggar, Fay and Thomas Sexton addressed a large assembly, *Nation*, 30 Oct. 1880, p. 3; 20 Nov. 1880, p. 4; 4 Dec. 1880, p. 2; *Irishman*, 30 Oct. 1880, p. 279. The Ballyconnell Independent Home Rule Tenant Right and Denominational Educational Club was established on 5 June 1880, combining all the major Catholic grievances of the period. However, it catered largely for the wealthier tenant farmers and was controlled by the clergy, *Nation*, 19 June 1880, p. 4.
75 *Nation*, 20 March 1874, p. 4; see also *Irishman*, 20 March 1874, p. 597.
76 *Irish Times*, 5 April 1880, p. 5. The first candidate mentioned as a possible Conservative candidate was Richard Nugent, J.P., *Ulster Examiner*, 26 March 1880, p. 3; *Daily Express* [Dublin], 15 March 1880, p. 5.
77 *Irish Times*, 26 March 1880, p. 6; *Ulster Examiner*, 31 March 1880, p. 3; 1 April 1880, p. 4.
78 Fitzpatrick said that he and his brother priests would not stand on the same platform as Biggar if the reported remarks made by him in Cork were true, *Ulster Examiner*, 1 April 1880, p. 4. For an account of the problems in Leitrim at the 1880 election see Kelly, 'Nicholas Conaty', pp. 451–2. Biggar spoke at a home rule demonstration in Carrick on Shannon on 18 March, at which he recommended the candidature of Nelson, *Ulster Examiner*, 19 March 1880, p. 3.
79 *Freeman's Journal*, 30 Mar, p. 6; 31 March 1880, p. 7.; 10 April 1880, p. 7.
80 R.V. Comerford, *The fenians in context, 1848–82* (Dublin and New Jersey, 1985) p. 232
81 *Irishman*, 3 April 1880, p. 631; *Nation*, 3 April 1880, p. 7.
82 Fay was described by one elector as being like P.J. Smyth, the discredited home rule MP for Tipperary, who was then being condemned by his constituents. Some electors were calling for the convening of a county meeting which would force Fay to resign, see *United Ireland*, 10 June 1882, p. 1. To Parnellites like Biggar, Fay was 'merely a gold-medalist' who used the movement for his own purposes, See Healy, *Letters and leaders*, i, p. 94.

83 For the importance of newspapers to the careers of nationalist politicians see James Loughlin 'Constructing the political spectacle: Parnell the press and national leadership, 1879–1886' in D. George Boyce and Alan O'Day (eds), *Parnell in perspective* (London and New York, 1991), pp. 224–7.

84 *Nation*, 29 Jan. 1881, pp. 7, 12; 12 Feb. 1881, p. 3.

85 *Nation*, 5 Feb. 1881, p. 12. By July the split was final as can be noted from Fay's speech in the house of commons when he criticised his fellow Irish members for their attack on the Irish chief secretary, Forster, *Nation*, 16 July 1881, p. 12.

86 O'Brien, *Parnell and his party*, p. 26.

87 *Nation*, 24 Oct. 1885, p. 2.

88 See Walker, 'Elections and land question in Ulster', p. 218.

89 O'Brien, *Parnell and his party*, pp. 126–32.

90 Walker, *Ulster politics*, p. 158. *Nation*, 25 Nov, 1882, p. 2. Nevertheless there were nationalists who were disappointed with the League's progress in the county. See letters of James Cooke of Bailieborough in *United Ireland*, 28 July 1883, p. 1 and 'Breffny' in *Nation*, 29 March 1884, p. 11.

91 Kelly, 'Nicholas Conaty', pp. 459–60. The branch in Kingscourt was founded on 3 December after mass, *Nation*, 9 Dec. 1882, p. 7. One of the first Cavan clerics to become actively involved in the new organisation was Revd P. Briody, C.C., who at a meeting at the hill of Ross on 19 November called on his fellow priests to give it their wholehearted support, see *Nation*, 25 Nov. 182, p. 3; *United Ireland*, 23 Nov. 1882, p. 3.

92 *Nation*, 24 Oct. 1885, p. 2. Under an agreement between the bishops and Parnell the county clergy were to be represented at the county conventions which selected the candidates. However, the main event was the private meeting before the public convention which largely ensured that the nominee which Dublin central office wanted was selected, C.J. Woods, 'Parnell and the Catholic church' in Boyce and O'Day, *Parnell in perspective*, pp. 22–4.

93 *Return showing the religious denominations of the population, according to the census of 1881, in each constituency form in the Ulster by the redistribution of seats act, 1885,* H.C. 1884–5 (335) lxii, p. 2.

94 This was the perceptive view of Michael Davitt, see T.W. Moody, *Davitt and Irish revolution, 1846–82* (Oxford, 1981), p. 513.

CAVAN IN THE ERA OF THE GREAT WAR   *Eileen Reilly*

1 For recent work on Ireland and the First World War see Terence Denman, *Ireland's unknown soldiers; the 16th (Irish) Division in the Great War* (Dublin, 1992); Tom Johnstone, *Orange, green and khaki; the story of the Irish regiments in the Great War 1914–18* (Dublin, 1992); David Fitzpatrick (ed.), *Ireland and the First World War* (Trinity history workshop, Dublin, 1986); Keith Jeffery, 'The Great War in modern Irish memory' in T.G. Fraser and Keith Jeffery (eds), *Men, Women and War* (Dublin, 1993), pp. 136–57; D. George Boyce, *The sure confusing drum: Ireland and the First World War* (Swansea, 1993).

2 David Fitzpatrick, *Politics and Irish life 1913–21; provincial experience of war and Revolution* (Dublin, 1977), p. 85.

3 Patrick Buckland, *Irish unionism: Ulster unionism and the origins of Northern Ireland 1886–1922* (Dublin, 1973), pp. 2–3.

4 *Anglo–Celt*, 6 Jan. 1912.

5 Fitzpatrick, *Politics and Irish life*, pp. 85–7.

6 Fitzpatrick, *Politics and Irish life*, p. 97

7 *Anglo–Celt*, 12 Jan. 1912

8 *Anglo–Celt*, 12 Jan. 1912

9 *Anglo–Celt*, 3, 17, 24 Feb. 1912.

10 *Anglo–Celt*, 6 April 1912.

11 *Anglo–Celt*, 20 April 1912.

12 *Anglo–Celt*, 27 April 1912.

13 *Anglo–Celt*, 6 July 1912.

14 *Anglo–Celt*, 20 July 1912.

15 *Anglo–Celt*, 3, 10, 24 Aug. 1912.

16 *Anglo–Celt*, 31 Aug. 1912.

17 *Anglo–Celt*, 21 Sept. 1912. John Dillon MP was the speaker.

18 *Anglo–Celt*, 21 Sept. 1912.

19 *Anglo–Celt*, 12 Oct. 1912.

20 *Anglo–Celt*, 12 Oct., 12 Nov. 1912.

21 *Anglo–Celt*, 22 Feb., 1 March 1913.

22 *Anglo–Celt*, 7 June 1913.

23 *Anglo–Celt*, 21 June 1913.

24 *Anglo–Celt*, 19 July 1913.

25 Brendan MacGiolla Choille (ed.), *Intelligence notes 1913–16* (Dublin, 1966), pp. 19–20, 27.

26 MacGiolla Choille, *Intelligence notes*, pp. 33–4.

27 *Anglo–Celt*, 8 Nov. 1913.

28 *Anglo–Celt*, 13, 27 Dec. 1913.

29 *Irish Post*, 17 Jan. 1914.

30 P.R.O., CO 904/92, County Inspector's confidential monthly report, Jan. 1914.

31 P.R.O., CO 904/92, County Inspector's confidential monthly report, Feb. Mar. 1914.

32 *Anglo–Celt*, 14 March 1914.

33 MacGiolla Choille, *Intelligence notes*, p. 75.

34 P.R.O., CO 904/93, County Inspector's confidential monthly report, May 1914.

35 P.R.O., CO 904/93, County Inspector's confidential monthly report, July 1914.

36 MacGiolla Choille, *Intelligence notes*, p. 75.

37 *Anglo–Celt*, 8 Aug. 1914.

38 *Anglo–Celt*, 8 Aug. 1914.

39 *Anglo–Celt*, 15 Aug. 1914.

40 P.R.O., CO 904/94, County inspector's confidential monthly report, Aug. 1914.

41 Sir Bernard Burke, *A genealogical and heraldic dictionary of the landed gentry of Ireland* (London, 1912); *A genealogical and heraldic dictionary of the peerage, baronetage, and knightage of Great Britain*, (104th edn. London, 1967).

42 MacGiolla Choille, *Intelligence notes*, p. 101.

43 P.R.O., CO 904/94, County Inspector's confidential monthly report, Sept. 1914.

44 *Anglo–Celt*, 22 Aug., 1914; N.L.I., MS 18616.

45 *Anglo–Celt*, 29 Aug., 19 Sept., 3, 10 Oct., 7 Nov. 1914.

46 *Anglo–Celt*, 17 Oct. 1914.

47 *Anglo–Celt*, 29 Aug. 1914.

48 *Anglo–Celt*, 5 Sept. 1914.

49 MacGiolla Choille, *Intelligence notes*, p. 102.

50 *Anglo–Celt*, 12 Sept. 1914.

51 P.R.O., CO 904/95, County Inspector's confidential monthly report, Sept., Oct. 1914.

52 P.R.O., CO 904/95, County Inspector's confidential monthly report, Oct. 1914.

53 *Anglo–Celt*, 3 Oct. 1914.

54 P.R.O., CO 904/95, County Inspector's confidential monthly report, Nov. 1914.

55 P.R.O., CO 904/95, County Inspector's confidential monthly report, Nov. 1914.

56 *Anglo–Celt*, 12 Sept. 1914.

57 *Anglo–Celt*, 10 Oct. 1914.
58 *Anglo–Celt*, 10 Oct. 1914.
59 *Anglo–Celt*, 10, 17 Oct. 1914.
60 *Anglo–Celt*, 31 Oct. 1914.
61 *Anglo–Celt*, 3 Oct. 1914.
62 *Anglo–Celt*, 21, 28 Nov. 1914.
63 Margaret Sheridan, 'Political Life in Cavan, 1913–21', unpublished M.Ed. thesis, University College Galway, 1985, pp. 3, 22.
64 P.R.O., CO 904/96, County Inspector's confidential monthly report, Feb–May 1915.
65 MacGiolla Choille, *Intelligence notes*, p. 112.
66 R.F. Foster, *Modern Ireland 1600–1972* (London, 1988), p. 474.
67 *Anglo–Celt*, 12 Feb. 1915.
68 *Anglo–Celt*, May–June 1915.
69 *Anglo–Celt*, July 1915.
70 *Irish Post*, 26 June 1915.
71 P.R.O., CO 904/96, County Inspector's confidential monthly report, Aug. 1915.
72 *Anglo–Celt*, 7 Aug. 1915; MacGiolla Choille, *Intelligence notes*, pp. 181–2.
73 P.R.O., CO 904/98, County Inspector's confidential monthly report, Sept. 1915.
74 Sheridan, 'Political life in Cavan', p. 26.
75 P.R.O., CO 904/98, County Inspector's confidential monthly report, Nov. 1915.
76 *Anglo–Celt*, 24 Dec. 1915, 12 June 1916.
77 *Anglo–Celt*, 1 Jan. 1916.
78 *Anglo–Celt*, 1 Jan. 1916.
79 *Anglo–Celt*, 8 Jan. 1916.
80 P.R.O., CO 904/99, County Inspector's confidential monthly report, Jan.–Mar. 1916.
81 P.R.O., CO 904/99, County Inspector's confidential monthly report, April 1916.
82 *Anglo–Celt*, 29 April 1916.
83 *Anglo–Celt*, 6 May 1916.
84 *Anglo–Celt*, 6, 13, 27 May, 1916.
85 MacGiolla Choille, *Intelligence notes*, pp. 216, 269–70.
86 Henry Harris, *The Royal Irish Fusiliers* (London, 1972), pp. 84–7; M. Cunliffe, *The Royal Irish Fusiliers, 1793–1950* (London, 1952), pp. 279–81.
87 P.R.O., CO 907/100, County Inspector's confidential monthly report, June 1916.
88 P.R.O., CO 907/100, 101, County Inspector's confidential monthly reports, May–Sept. 1916.
89 Public Record Office of Northern Ireland, Belfast, D989/A/9/7.
90 *Statement giving particulars regarding men of military age in Ireland* (London, 1916).
91 P.R.O., CO 904/101, County Inspector's confidential monthly report, Sept., Oct., 1916.
92 P.R.O., CO 904/101 County Inspector's confidential monthly report, Nov. 1916.
93 Buckland, *Irish unionism: Ulster unionism*, pp. 103–4.
94 *Anglo–Celt*, 3 Feb. 1917.
95 P.R.O., CO 903/19, Intelligence notes, 1917.
96 *Anglo–Celt*, 7, 21, July 1917.
97 *Anglo–Celt*, 21 July, 18 August 1917.
98 *Anglo–Celt*, 3 Nov. 1917.
99 *Anglo–Celt*, 20 April 1918.
100 *Anglo–Celt*, 4 May 1918.
101 P.R.O., CO 903/19, Intelligence notes, 1918.
102 N.L.I., MS 10575.
103 Cunliffe, *The Royal Irish Fusiliers*, p. 361.

Index

Adams, Benjamin 26
Aghanure 102
Airghialla 17, 18, 43
Aldrich, William, 97
Ancient Order of Hibernians (AOH) 178, 179, 180, 191, 192, 193
Andrews, William 96
Anglo-Celt 13, 162, 163, 165, 178, 179, 180, 181, 182, 184, 185, 186, 187, 188, 189, 191, 192
Annagelliff parish 81, *see also* Urney and Annagelliff parish
Annagh parish 29
Annals of the Four Masters 53, 54, 71
Annesley MP, Lord 165, 167
Annesley family 25, 26, 159
Ardagh diocese 74, 80, 81
Ardee 57
Ardee Poor Law Union 156
Ardpatrick, 1678 synod 123
Armagh, county 18, 195; diocese 74, 79; ecclesiastical province, 74; Poor Law Union 156
Armstrong, Gloster 188
Artina 162, 172
Arva 166, 184, 187
Ashe, Sir Thomas 22

Bailieborough 20, 32, 164, 167, 170, 186, 187, 193; fever hospital 157; Home Rule and Tenant Right Association 171; Home Rule Club 163, 166, 171; Land League branch 171; parish 29, 161; Poor Law Union 148, 150, 151, 155, 156; Ulster Volunteer Force (UVF) 181; workhouse 150, 152
Ballaghanea castle 19
Ballinagh 186, 190, 192
Ballinamore 161; ironworks 101
Ballintemple 190
Ballyconnell 111, 163, 164, 166; Home Rule Club 166
Ballygawley 169
Ballyhaise 82, 104, 185
Ballyjamesduff 164, 186
Ballymachugh 175
Ballymagauran 55
Barnewall, Isabella 57
Barnewall, Patrick, Lord Trimleston 67

Barrett, Walter 96
Bathe, William 67
Bawnboy parish 170
Baxter, Martin 98
Bayly, William 91–2, 98
Bearchan, St 103
Beatty, Lieutenant 143
Bedell, William, bishop of Kilmore 18, 75, 84, 88–96, 97, 98, 100, 105, 109, 112, 113, 116
Bedell, William, son of bishop 83, 84, 86, 97, 104
Belfast 174, 189, 190
Belturbet 11, 25, 39, 82, 102, 104, 113, 158, 162, 182, 186, 189, 193
Benburb, battle of 99
Benedict XIV, Pope 127
Berenger, Gabriel 20–1
Beresford family 23, 24, 26
Bernard, Nicholas 97
Betagh family 65; daughter of William 49
Betagh, James 68
Betagh, Sinead 57
Biggar, Joseph 166, 167, 168, 169, 170, 171, 172, 174, 175
Biggot, Mary 104
Bingley, Sir John 86
Birr 99
Black death 50
Blacklion 187
Boate, Gerard 101
Bolston, William 97
Bostock, John 96
Bottigheimer, Karl 75
Boylan, John 161
Boyle, Maxwell 26
Brady family 78, 115; *see also* MacBrady
Brady, Bernard 122, 123, 126
Brady, Charles 77
Brady, Ciaran 60
Brady, Hugh 86
Brady, Patrick 94
Brady, Philip 124, 125
Brady, Richard, bishop of Kilmore 116
Brady, Thomas 22
Brady, Thomas 97
Brady, Thomas of Lisboduff 162
Brady, Revd Thomas 83

231

O'Reilly, Giolla Iosa Ruadh, 40, 41, 42–4
O'Reilly, Goffraidh 38
O'Reilly, Captain Hugh 71
O'Reilly, Hugh, bishop of Kilmore, archbishop
 of Armagh 108, 110, 116–17, 118, 138
O'Reilly, Sir Hugh *see* O'Reilly, Aodh
 Conallach
O'Reilly, Captain John 71
O'Reilly, John, prior of Kells 49
O'Reilly, Revd John 161
O'Reilly, Sir John *see* O'Reilly Seaán ruadh
O'Reilly, MacFarrell 65
O'Reilly, Maelsheachlainn 42, 46
O'Reilly, Maghnus 42, 44
O'Reilly, MaolMordha 106
O'Reilly, MaolMordha mac Prior 71
O'Reilly, MaolMordha son of Aodh 52, 69–70,
 71
O'Reilly, MaolMordha son of Cú Chonnacht 44,
 45
O'Reilly, MaolMordha son of Seaan 49, 52, 54,
 55, 57, 58, 64
O'Reilly, Mathghamhain 43, 46, 55
O'Reilly, Michael 126, 128, 133
O'Reilly, Mulmory 22
O'Reilly, Myles 112
O'Reilly, Niall an Chaoch 48
O'Reilly, Patrick 174
O'Reilly, Revd Patrick, 161, 167, 170
O'Reilly, Philip 100, 104
O'Reilly, Philip son of Philip 111
O'Reilly, Pilib 54
O'Reilly, Pilib, abbot of Kells 49
O'Reilly, Pilib son of Giolla Iosa 42, 44,
O'Reilly, Pilib an Prior 57
O'Reilly, Pilib dubh 52, 63, 66, 68, 69–71
O'Reilly, Prior balbh 102, 105
O'Reilly, Risteard 41, 48, 50
O'Reilly, Risteard og 48
O'Reilly, Risteard, bishop 42
O'Reilly, Risteard, 45
O'Reilly, Roolbh 41
O'Reilly, Seaán ruadh (Sir John) 52, 56, 63, 64,
 65, 66, 69, 71
O'Reilly, Seán son of Pilib 42, 44, 47,
O'Reilly, Seán an Einigh 46, 48, 52
O'Reilly, Seán son of Cathal, 53, 54
O'Reilly, Seán son of Toirdhealbhach 52, 53
O;Reilly, Seán son of Tomas 48
O'Reilly, Sefraidh 41
O'Reilly, Shane 112
O'Reilly, Teaboid 41
O'Reilly, Toirdhealbhach 47, 48
O'Reilly, Toirdhealbhach son of Sean 52, 55
O'Reilly, Tomás 43

O'Reilly, Tomás og 43
O'Reilly, Turlough 104
O'Reilly, Revd Dr 171
Ormond, earl of *see* Butler
O'Rourke family 17, 37, 39, 40, 41, 42, 48, 50,
 51, 65, 71, 76
O'Rourke, Brian na Murtha 69, 105
O'Rourke, Conchobair 40
O'Rourke, Domhnall 47
O'Rourke, (O Ruairc), Tighernan, 38, 39
Osborne 184
O'Sheridan, Cornelius (Cohonaght) 90
O'Sheridan, Owen 90, 97
O'Siredok, Patrick 97
Oughteragh parish 125
Oxford 12

Paine, Thomas 131
Pale, The 10, 17, 22–3, 51, 57, 58, 59, 68, 72,
 111; *see also* Dublin, Meath, Louth,
 Leinster, etc
Paris, Irish college 125
Parker 26
Parker, Francis 83
Parnell, Charles Stewart 170, 171, 173
Parsons, Richard 94, 97
Patrick, John 96
Patrick, St 103, 108
Perrott, Sir John 59, 76, 105
Pettit, Ralph 41
Phelim, St 103
Plunkett (Plunket) family 17, 58, 65
Plunkett, Gerald 68
Plunket, Luke, earl of Fingal 101, 102
Plunkett, Mary 58
Plunkett, Mr 17
Plunkett, Oliver, archbishop of Armagh 109,
 121, 122
Plunkett, Patrick, bishop of Meath 121
Plunkett, Robert, baron Dunsany 58
Poor Clare Sisters 138
Port na Holla 71
Portugal 127
Pratt, Colonel 26
Price, Thomas 98
Pynnar, Sir Nicholas 110, 111

Queeley, Malachy, archbishop of Tuam 117
Queen's Colleges, 137, 138

Radcliffe, Thomas, earl of Sussex, lord deputy
 17
Raphoe diocese 74, 79
Rathkerry 182
Raven, Thomas 21